ARMAND VAN DORMAEL

THE
SILICON
REVOLUTION

Cover by Pierre Van Dormael

Contents

Prologue

Several eminent historians have drawn attention to the gaps they detected in the history of computing. Michael Mahoney notes:

> It should be easy to do the history of computing. The major problem is that we have lots of answers but very few questions, lots of stories but no history, lots of things to do but no sense of how to do them or in what order. Simply put, we don't yet know what the history of computing is really about. A glance at the literature makes that clear. We still know more about the calculating devices that preceded the electronic digital computer - however tenuously related to it - than we do about the machines that shaped the industry. We have barely begun to determine how the industry got started and how it developed. [1]

> History helps us to know where we might be going by establishing where we are and how we got there... It is especially important to bear that in mind with respect to computers and computing because they have always been surrounded by hype... and hype hides history. [2]

Alfred D. Chandler has observed that the evolution of the computer industry is a largely untold story and presents opportunities for business historians of the twenty-first century for further investigation. Current literature focuses almost exclusively on the history of the American computer industry. And he concludes:

> I hope that this review of the opportunities for writing the history of electronic-based businesses and industries... will encourage economic historians trained as historians to return to the history of business enterprises and their industries. If they do, they will be able to open a new field of historical investigation... Moreover, because so few enterprises were involved in commercializing the products of the new electronic devices, historians will be able to analyze the competitive successes and failures not only of companies but of major industries—successes and failures that led to worldwide domination or the near death of crucial national industries. [3]

Both have an honored place in the pantheon of great teachers. They did not identify any specific gaps, leaving to future historians the task of exploring aspects of events that have been overlooked or cast aside. History celebrates the winners and discards the losers. Thousands of books and research papers have been published covering every phase and aspect of the computer industry as it developed in the United States. The history of the American computer industry is part and parcel of a broader retrospective; but the United States - the economic and academic superpower - has established the generally accepted contours of the evolution of computer technology, leaving out large areas that have not been adequately researched. Implicitly, research in the history of science presupposes a world-view with the purpose of building a global picture from fragmented pieces of research, with the right pieces in the right order.

The program-controlled electromechanical computer, the programmable electronic computer, the general-purpose computer, the commercial computer, the transistor, the transistor radio, the microcomputer and the www originated in the Old World. Initially conceived for military use, the first commercialization of the computer was successfully taken up in Britain. The technology was perfected by several large U.S. companies that soon dominated the global computer industry. In Europe, the legacy of the scientific innovators went under-exploited, largely because of industrial and commercial mis-management and political and bureaucratic meddling.

During the years following World War II, a technologi-cal gap developed between the United States and Europe. Governments observed with mounting concern their plants and offices operating with American computers, their air-lines flying American planes, their people cured by American drugs. Was the gap really technological or something quite different? On the one side, there was within the United States an apparently irresistible force of invention and application of invention, creating new demand for goods and services. Using their superior financial, technological and organiza-tional capacity, huge and growing corporations could afford the costs of basic research and development and the risks of innovation. Young entrepreneurs were establishing small enterprises for the development and exploitation of advanced technologies. Europe had no such tradition of broad-based industrial entrepreneurship. The European capital market was not organized to provide the initial financing needed by small, innovative enterprises. Venture capital for exploit-ing new ideas was practically inexistent. All this, combined with rigid social structures, hampered the formation of new businesses based on new technologies. Governments and business leaders were increasingly worried, without knowing quite what to do about it.

In December 1941, when he pushed the button to start the Z3, his experimental automatic calculating machine, Konrad Zuse heralded the computer age. In 1949, he established the Zuse KG and developed a line of computers that soon became popular with scientists and engineers. Since he did not have the financial resources to develop large machines, his production focused on minicomputers. The Graphomat was the first computer-controlled automatic drawing board. Unable to compete with the large companies, he was forced him to sell his company. It was finally taken over by Siemens. Zuse must be credited with several fundamental inventions: the use of the binary system for numbers and circuits; the use of floating point numbers, along with the algorithms for the translation between binary and decimal - and vice-versa; the look-ahead which allows to read a program two instructions in advance and test it to see whether memory instructions can be performed ahead of time; the mechanical binary cells that make up the memory, etc.

In 1951, LEO (Lyons Electronic Office) became the world's first business computer. By the late 1950's, the American computer giants such as IBM and UNIVAC entered the British market. LEO Computers did not have the resources to compete in the long term. In 1963, the firm was sold to English Electric Computers and in 1967 it became part of ICL, the Wilson government's attempt to create a flagship computer company able to compete with the Americans.

In January 1973, a French government agency, the INRA, took possession of the world's first microcomputer, the Micral. It had been designed and built by François Gernelle and a small team of engineers who developed a microprocessor-based operating system for Intel's 8008. Production was limited and delivered mainly to government departments and large companies. In 1974, the Micral was demonstrated without success at the National Computer Conference in Chicago. The editor of *Popular Electronics* picked up all the technical information he could lay his hand on. He gave it to Ed Roberts, the owner of a small hardware store, who put together a computer kit that had the looks of the Micral. They called it the Altair. Paul Allen and Bill Gates added the software.

For more than five years, the owner of the small French company had within his grasp a world monopoly. His clumsy and erratic management and poor marketing led to bankruptcy. He sold the majority of the shares to Machines Bull. The microcomputer was a disruptive technology and Bull was not ready to give up its traditional production. For several years, the machines were marketed separately under the name Bull-Micral. Gernelle was dissatisfied with Bull's policy. In 1983, he set up his own company, but was unable to compete with the U.S. and Japanese companies. The Micral faded away.

The computer age began in 1953, when IBM switched from punched cards to vacuum tubes for its data-processing machines. IBM set up production in Europe, followed by several competitors. By 1970, American manufacturers supplied 80 percent of the mainframes, while the European office-machine industry produced the remainder, mostly under license. Alarmed by the technology gap, in the early 1980s the European commission took responsibility for computer technology and decided on a strategy to take on IBM and the other American giants. The commission's leadership had not noticed that the U.S. computer industry was in the throes of a shake-up and that a new breed of entrepreneurs was beginning to eclipse the vertically-integrated companies by developing an open system and that Silicon Valley had invented an entirely new way of doing business.

In an effort to catch up by emulating American and Japanese companies, the policy-makers set out on the wrong track. Although Apple, Commodore, Compaq and other microcomputers had made their appearance in Europe, the commission's technology planners were unaware of the fact that the microcomputer was reshaping the industry.

Technology policy and the promotion of the information society became the European commission's big project. Big projects meant big money. The European commission distributed mind boggling amounts of subsidies. Instead of spurring innovation, they cosseted a vast number of research laboratories and the industry with tax money. By the mid-1990s, they had been driven out of the computer business.

For years, European computer companies were kept alive with massive public subsidies, to be eventually undone by the onslaught of American and Japanese manufacturers. Europe is a high-tech disaster area entirely dependent on American technology and Asian productive skills. The extinction of the computer industry is due to a mixture of political and industrial bungling. It covers a multitude of sins and reflects the lack of managerial expertise, the high cost of employing labor, the regulatory burden, the counterproductive bureaucratic and legislative interference in the economy and the anti-entre preneurial climate. For decades, Europe's best and brightest scientific minds left in droves. Silicon Valley would be a very different place without Jean Hoerni who built the bridge between the transistor and the integrated circuit, Federico Faggin who designed the microprocessor, and Intel's Andy Grove.

Personal computers and access to the web have immensely enriched our lives and profoundly changed the way we work, learn and communicate. Cyberspace makes unlimited knowledge and information available at our fingertips. Yet despite its pervasive use, computing has not established a significant presence in the history of science and technology.

The historical community stands before the daunting complexity of an arcane science and of an industrial technology that has grown exponentially in size and prowess. Moreover, it is confronted with the difficulties of understanding a technical language and basic concepts that lie largely outside its customary domain.

Many books and a huge number of papers provide an abundantly documented exposé of the early years of electronic computation. But the story breaks off at the point where computing becomes a significant factor in society. Historians know almost everything about the devices that link the abacus to the ENIAC, but surprisingly little serious scholarship has been devoted to the origin of the transistor and of the personal computer.

The nuts and bolts of the history of computing do not rivet. There are several blank spots and discrepancies that must be dealt with. Fundamental inconsistencies and contradictions must be resolved. Three chapters are in need of renewed attention: the failure of European technology policy, the place of origin of the transistor and of the personal computer.

The dominance of American scholarship and literature has made English the lingua franca of the history of science. A major portion of the literature stems from the people involved, either through seminal papers or reminiscences and retrospectives. Much of it represents insider history.

Hardly anything is known about the preliminary research by German scientists on the electron-conducting properties of semiconductors that led to the invention of the transistor. History is shaped by the information that is accessible at the time and in the place it is written. Evidence available in some countries remains unknown elsewhere. The language barrier narrows the horizon, the scope of research and the historian's perspective.

Practically inexistent in Europe, science history captivates a vast readership in the United States. News reports are the first stage of historiography. Journalists describe what they witnessed or heard about. On February 24, 2003, John Markoff made history by publishing an article in *The New York Times* revealing that, in June 1948, an unknown German scientist, Herbert Mataré, had produced functional solid state amplifiers for account of the French government about the time Bell Labs announced the invention of the transistor.

As the computing revolution enters its sixth decade, little is known about the origin of the transistor. Considered the most important invention of the twentieth century, it has attracted the attention of journalists, but the academic community has conspicuously and cautiously stayed aloof. Transistor history and semiconductor technology have become the playground of amateur historians and science hobbyists who clutter the web with their ruminations.

The history of computing has deviated from the right track. The United States is the academic superpower that establishes the paradigms of the history of science and technology. Paraphrased and translated, American literature becomes world history. In the history of computing, each technological advance is celebrated as an emblem of national ingenuity and a source of national pride.

The debâcle of the European computer industry has consigned to oblivion the pioneers whose groundbreaking work is at the origin of the silicon revolution. European companies were eventually undone by the onslaught of American and Japanese manufacturers. Europe is a high-tech disaster area largely dependent on American technology and Asian productive skills.

Many people in many countries have contributed to the genesis and the development of the computer. Over the centuries, the cumulative learning of mathematicians, philosophers, physicists, chemists and engineers - overwhelmingly German - laid the foundations of the theoretical and practical knowledge that contributed to the automation of arithmetical processes. In the early 20th century, a stay in Germany was *de rigueur* for any aspiring young physicist. It took a long time to gain insight into the material structures involved in all of these theoretical constructions. Solid-state physics was a domain in which there was only a very modest scientific competence outside Germany, where the term *Festkörperphysik* was commonly used among specialized physicists.

World War II had been a contest of science. At war's end, Russian, American, British and French intelligence teams roamed occupied Germany in search of military, industrial and scientific booty. Among their most precious "spoils" were the scientists and engineers. They were captured, interrogated and recruited, which allowed the victors to acquire quickly, easily and cheaply an immense amount of advanced scientific and technological know-how.

For several decades, Germany lost its memory. Ever since the end of the war, German historians and publicists have chosen to close the Nazi page of history and have kept a politically-correct low profile about the extraordinary scientific achievements during the 1930's and 1940's, such as the invention of the computer, the jet engine, radar technology that would lead to the transistor, nuclear fission, long range missiles, synthetic fuel, synthetic rubber, the tape recorder and many other technical innovations that would later benefit mankind. Because of the break between nationalist Germany and the internationalist Nobel institution, followed by the law prohibiting German scientists from accepting the Prize, the names of many of the inventors are hardly known outside Germany.

Microelectronics gradually came to the forefront of engineering science. Solid-state physics progressed immensely before and during the war. But the names of major scientists such as Clemens Winkler, Karl Ferdinand Braun, Walter Schottky, Karl Bädeker, Oskar Heil, Robert Pohl and Rudolf Hilsch are hardly ever or never mentioned in English literature. The first functional semiconductor amplifiers were produced in France in June 1948, by two German scientists. It was the result of advanced scientific research in the field of solid state physics, financed by the French government intent on acquiring radar technology. The government agencies that had subsidized the research were not interested in transistors. They presented the "transistron" as *a brilliant realization of French research*, and laid it aside. For more than five decades, the memory of the transistron was buried in oblivion - and occasionally suppressed - until *The New York Times* brought it to public attention.

The personal computer was also invented in France, but because the owner of the small company that produced it was unable to commercialize it successfully, the PC became part of the American Heritage. Taken at face value and routinely translated into many languages, the history of their origin has been codified from an American vantage point, unaware of the fact that these new technologies had spawned a fledgling industry in France and Germany, several years before production runs started in the United States.

Computer vocabulary is not easy reading for historians. The subject is arcane and esoteric and has given rise to improbable legends. A book claiming that computer technology was brought to earth by extraterrestrials whose spaceship crashed in the New Mexico desert was a popular bestseller. The invention of the transistor has dogma status. An amateur engineer who had never worked with computers is credited with the invention of the microcomputer. A fast-talking Frenchman, friend of the owner of the company that developed the Micral, but who never met with the engineers who built it, was able to convince American audiences and historians that he wrote the software. "*A beau mentir qui vient de loin.*"

History as an inspiring tale of national prowess can become emotionally charged. Being "first" engenders collective pride. Pride and prejudice distort perception and analysis. According to German historians, the inventor of the vacuum tube is Robert von Lieben. In English literature, the inventor is Lee de Forest. There are quite a few similar cases.

Truth is the first victim of war. To the victor belong the spoils of war history, the patent and technology booty and the moral high ground. Truth and credibility become his appanage. In the long run and in many cases, history is self-correcting thanks to detached and unprejudiced research. Rooting out historical misrepresentation in a sensible way should be a primary responsibility for historians.

Commercial interests distort and squash the facts, thus leading to the misrepresentation of history. For more than a century, Alexander Graham Bell has been credited with inventing the telephone. In October 2003, the curator of the London Science Museum discovered "confidential" archives documenting that Bell had simply copied and adapted an apparatus and patented the invention. The report had been covered up for almost five decades. Tests conducted in 1947 by Standard Telephones and Cables (STC) of Britain prove that a telephone "reproducing speech of good quality but of low efficiency" was built by a German teacher, Philipp Reis, 13 years before Graham Bell created a somewhat similar device. The tests occurred while STC was bidding for a contract with AT&T. Fearing that any public reference to the fact that Bell was not the inventor might jeopardize the negotiations, the chairman of STC ordered that the tests be kept secret.

As a result of a conspiracy of silence between the STC and the then-museum's curator, Philipp Reis was written off by history. No German historian has been motivated to devote a book to his work. The names and the accomplishments of several scientists, whose inventions changed the world and determine the architecture of the digital computer as we know it, are practically unknown.

The documentary heritage is very scant. The interaction between invention, technological innovation and the applications that fueled industrial take-up of information technology has been insufficiently explored.

The impact of government technology policies in the United States, Europe and Asia has hardly been probed. Documents that have been laid aside and overlooked for decades occasionally turn up, bringing a new historical perspective and shedding new light on unexplored episodes and half-forgotten names.

It took time, perseverance and a certain amount of luck to discover that transistors were developed and produced in June 1948, by Herbert Mataré and Heinrich Welker, two German scientists employed by a small company under contract with the French government. The microcomputer was invented by François Gernelle in 1972. Both accomplishments represented quantum leaps in human knowledge. Although they are at the origin of the digital age, Herbert Mataré and François Gernelle have been passed over by history.

Precursors and innovators, it was their misfortune to work under unfavorable circumstances. Nobody remembers the losers. The visionary entrepreneurs who changed the world by commercializing their inventions accumulated enormous wealth and legendary fame, while the pioneering scientists came out empty-handed and ignored even in their homelands. The journey was worth taking. It has allowed me to recuperate a piece of history that had fallen by the wayside.

The idea of a personal computer was unquestionably thought up by François Gernelle. He had studied physics, chemistry and electronics and held a doctorate in applied physics. Starting in January 1973, the Micral computer went into serial production. It served as a model for the Altair, a computer kit oriented towards hobbyists that spawned Apple

and all the rest. The owner of the French company that produced the first personal computers had for several years a world
monopoly. His clumsy management forced him to sell out.

A. Van Dormael; J. M. Ackermann; J. Lacombe; F. Gernelle; J. C. Beckmann.

The personal computer has given rise to one of the most
unfounded stories of the Information Age. It proves that despite
the Internet and instantaneous global communication networks,
information does not travel well. Historiography should be a
cooperative and cosmopolitan exercise that thrives on inquisitive
curiousness, open interaction and on the exchange of ideas,
information and materials. It should gradually transcend
national boundaries and tend to universality and a world-history
standard. By lessening the national focus we would gain a more
reliable and trustworthy picture of the whole.

Who invented the transistor? This simple question has a simple
answer that requires a very complex explanation. In June 1948,
Herbert Mataré and Heinrich Welker, after more than two years
of experimentation in the laboratory of a small French company,

Compagnie des Freins et Signaux Westinghouse located near Paris, succeeded in synthetizing germanium crystals of sufficient purity to bring about transconductance and thus the transistor effect. Both held a doctorate in semiconductor physics. The company was under contract with the French Post and Telegraph Ministry. They installed these solid-state devices in experimental telephone lines and in radio and television sets. The French authorities showed no interest. Only after Bell Labs announced the invention of the transistor did a few government officials visit the laboratory. In 1952, Mataré set up a company in Düsseldorf and supplied transistors to the nascent German electronics industry.

Dr. Mataré holds more than 80 patents. He has published several books and a vast number of scientific articles. In one of them, he describes how the development of radar technology during WW2 brought him upon the idea of a solid state amplifier. The transistor effect based on minority carrier injection was achieved in June 1948, when crystal of higher quality could be obtained.

Herbert Mataré; Mrs. Van Dormael; Mrs. Mataré; Armand Van Dormael

The "transistron" had a long prehistory. It was an extraordinary technological breakthrough and the most complex man-made creation in history. It was made possible by the knowledge gained in solid state physics, a new materials science which was had been developed in Germany. Between 1930 and 1945, interdisciplinary research had contributed immensely to the understanding of semiconductors. Until 1938, solid-state research remained essentially academic. It was conducted to advance fundamental knowledge with no thought of practical use, until it seemed to have a military and industrial potential as a substitute for the vacuum tube.

In 1957, the "pocket radio" catapulted Sony at the cutting edge of semiconductor technology. In 1953, the company had paid $25,000 to Western Electric for a license to produce transistors. The management of Western Electric had made it clear that the transistor could only be used in hearing aids. Solid state technology was unknown at Sony. It took three years for a team of 40 electronics engineers to familiarize themselves with the arcana of solid state technology and to learn how to apply it. In 1955, Sony produced its first transistor radio, followed in 1957 by the TR-63 which took the world by storm and established Sony as a world leader in consumer electronics. For this they had to re-invent the transistor almost from scratch. Sony's chief engineer, Leo Esaki, would later receive the Nobel Prize.

Scholars should be critical and permanently acknowledge the limitations of historiography. When necessary, they should deconstruct master narratives and reconstruct events in the light of new information. Historians must ask questions which they see their way to answering. Questions are the engines of the mind which convert curiosity to controlled inquiry. There can be no questioning without hypothesizing, and no systematic testing of hypotheses without the construction of hypothetical models which can be put to the test. Some questions will yield empirical answers and others will not. In the case of transistors and microcomputers, the yield exceeds my initial expectations.

Documents recently brought to light contradict accepted wisdom and established truth. They should be thought-provoking and raise new issues and insights, a challenge to the historical profession as a whole. This should stimulate solid-state scientists and historians to take a searching look behind the conventional accounts and recast, wherever necessary, our understanding of the evolution of computing. It will not be an easy exercise.

For a variety of reasons, there will always remain a grey zone. Much of what happened will never be documented and remain a behind-the-scenes saga. Many sources of information have been lost or destroyed. Mataré's wartime laboratory notes were destroyed by Soviet bombs. It seems fair to predict that an exhaustive history of the transistor - the story behind the story of the most important invention of the twentieth century - will never be written.

The following chapters cover a comparative description and an analysis of the origin of the solid state amplifier and of the personal computer, both in the United States and in Europe. A critical review should open up opportunities for historians to renew their investigations from a broader perspective. This should ultimately lead to a better understanding of the evolution of the technology and of the chronology, to a documented and coherent historiography and a curriculum that reflects a world view of history.

The computer has catapulted electronics to the status of a dominant global industry. Silicon memory has brought about a revolution by the availability of inexpensive information acquisition and distribution. No device in history has come close to achieving this sort of ubiquity. The real significance of the transistor, far beyond its original application, is not that it replaced the vacuum tube, but that it can do things the vacuum tube could not do.

The computer is the brainchild of a small number of scientists whose creative imagination, sparked by a stroke of genius, allowed them to push forward the frontier of technology. Some have their place in Hall of Fame; many of them toiled intensively for practically no reward. Their technical innovations, dispersed by accident, were picked up and appropriated by whiz-kid entrepreneurs who made a fortune from marketing their ideas. Commercially successful players have come to dominate historical accounts, while leaving many true innovators and pioneers on the sidelines. A full and accurate representation of the emergence of the digital computer is missing in the history books.

Historiography is selective; it has focused mainly on the United States. This is quite normal, since American entrepreneurialism has played the dominant role in computer development. However important, it conveys a fragmented image. Some of the scientists who built the first transistor and the first microcomputers are alive and well. It is still possible to gather information firsthand and put on record their personal recollections. Future historians, not blessed by access to the pioneers, will construct their own histories, their own way.

The material condensed in this book has been immensely enriched by information, documents and feedback received from the scientists who are at the origin of the digital age. Their reminiscences provided ample documentation about their contribution to the computer revolution.

They did what nobody had done before. Their inventions spread to never-thought-of applications. They did not live in the limelight. For decades, their pioneering work remained unknown and unrecognized. Their accomplishments represent a quantum leap in human knowledge and in technological advance. They may still witness how the world restores them to their proper place in history.

The evolution of computing shows how cultural and political values influence the development of technology. Both success and failure of new ideas and new products usually have more to do with local conditions and marketing skills than with scientific and technological capabilities of individual scientists. The following chapters provide in broad strokes a historical perspective and an overview of the computer industry in the United States, Europe and Asia, and an explanation of what made the difference between success and failure. It is an account of the process of creative destruction that led to worldwide domination by a few giants and to the ultimate liquidation of huge segments of European industry.

The world has become a single market operating by a process of natural selection. The technological and institutional infrastructure of the computer industry was determined in the crucible of international competition. Approaching the issues from a comparative perspective defines more precisely the dynamics of the technology-policy process than a single case study would. It also addresses more sharply the issues involving the interaction of government and industry in the development of new technologies.

The silicon revolution, like any industrial development, emerged from the chance combination of three elements: scientists with their inventions, entrepreneurs to market them and investors willing to risk their money. The evolution of the American, European and Asian micro-electronics industries bears the stamp of the dominant values that make individuals and communities think and act within established patterns.

Most of the technological breakthroughs in the automation of arithmetical processes and in computing technology were conceived by British, German or French scientists: But transforming novel ideas and technology into industrial success demands different skills and environments. American and Japanese entrepreneurs have an astounding track record of turning scientific inventions - both home-grown and borrowed - into new and useful products. Today, largely because of its excellence in microelectronics, the United States, driven by the inventiveness, the marketing and management skills, the brainpower and the relentless drive of its high-powered entrepreneurs, is on the cutting edge of computer technology. American companies compete one against another; Japan's, for national honor, compete against the world.

In the United States, embryonic technological advances draw streams of funding from venture capitalists and "business angels" eager to finance start-ups, not on asset value, but on their ability to generate cash in future. According to the Center for Venture Research, in 2005 there were 225.000 such active investors.

Entrepreneurs relentlessly develop new products and set up new enterprises that provide massive new employment and wealth. They create new markets with products hitherto unknown. America's social contract is based on self-determination. By and large, Americans consider themselves autonomous individuals, quite capable of taking care of their lives and eager to do so without much government interference. The country's favorite heroes are the young entrepreneurs who made something big out of nothing.

An industry that exploded 20 years ago has generated a winner-takes-all economy. Global competition has changed in its nature and its extent. It is impossible to comprehend the essence of the electronics industry without forming an overall view of how it works globally. The United States holds a commanding lead in most areas that are crucial to the information society. Successful and innovative start-ups have the skills to create proprietary standards that allow them to capture monopoly or semi-monopoly profits. Understanding the direction of technological change is the key to success in the computing industry. This means: identifying the hardware and software standards around which mass markets and business are coalescing; funding and developing the technology, and marketing it on a global scale.

In the global IT industry the winner sets the *de facto* market standards while taking care of protecting his intellectual property rights. Companies able to control proprietary architectural standards are in a privileged position to further develop products that maximize their position and hold competitors at bay. Their comparative advantage rests on their ability to constantly upgrade their products.

Silicon has become the "nerve cell" that drives the world. Transistors were commercialized in Germany and personal computers were produced in France several years before they appeared in the United States. But the initial advantage provided by the head start of the   pioneers failed to materialize.

The computer age began in 1953, when IBM switched from punched cards to vacuum tubes for its data-processing machines. IBM soon dominated the American market with its multi-million-dollar mainframes. The company set up production in Europe, followed by General Electric and several other competitors. By 1970, American manufacturers supplied 80 percent of the mainframes, while the European office-machine industry made the remainder, mostly under license.

European governments became alarmed by the technology gap. Dependence on external sources of supply in innovative technologies threatened to render large segments of European industry uncompetitive and prevent the training of scientists, engineers and technicians. Moreover, the new computer industry would create a very substantial number of well-paid new jobs.

In the early 1980s, the European commission took responsibility for computer technology policy. The commission's experts had not noticed that the American computer industry was in the throes of a shake-up and that a new breed of entrepreneurs had eclipsed the vertically-integrated computer giants by developing an open system and an entirely novel way of doing business. A few companies led by Microsoft, Intel and Apple, gained proprietary control over specific segments of the technology. Each of them concentrated on core activities: components, assembly, marketing and services. In the early stages, most computer start-ups simply put the parts together without doing much scientific research. The pace of change was rapid, and so was the ferocity of competition. To succeed, firms needed stamina and the ability to constantly reinvent themselves. The industry was not only growing, but changing rapidly. This, in turn, changed the rules of the game.

From the beginning, the European research environment was bureaucratized; it lacked accountability and peer review. The power to distribute huge amounts of money without any personal liability resulted in promiscuous decision-making. Those who held the public purse had no knowledge of the technology, of the market, of competition and of the state of the art. They were not qualified to evaluate the validity of the projects submitted to them by the industry's representatives and by the research institutions. Because the money they distributed was taxpayers' money, they were not accountable for the consequences of their decisions. Their mistakes were ignored and hushed up. Instead of mounting an effective challenge to US and Japanese dominance, their policy founded on misconceived assumptions, proved to be futile and costly.

Politicians and bureaucrats have no innate ability to pick among competing technologies. If they did, they'd be entrepreneurs. New technologies have been the products of capitalism and entrepreneurship, not of central planning and government R&D. The government does a poor job of picking winners. Analyzing business risks and opportunities is better left to the private sector. Subsidies foster corruption and generate an unhealthy relationship between business and bureaucracy. While "market entrepreneurs" have to work to create new businesses, subsidies create "political entrepreneurs" who spend their energies seeking handouts. Companies receiving subsidies usually become weaker and less efficient, not stronger.

Poor management was another handicap. ICL, Bull, Siemens and Philips suffered shortcomings in management flair and in the ability to expand on a global basis. They supplied the home market where contracts were guaranteed and failed to develop a global marketing strategy. Global markets are important because economies of scale enable successful companies to draw enough revenues to sustain the demand for high levels of research funds.

America's victory in the computer wars of the 1980s is due to young electronics addicts whose success owed nothing to government attention. The key of their success was the control over a segment of the system. A few companies emerged by establishing the codes and standards of their products as industry norms. This gave them an edge in the race to constantly upgrade. The market was created by visionary and intensely competitive youngsters, whiz-kids endowed with flair, ego and drive. They stepped straight out of school or laboratory into fame and fortune. They had a bright idea, a "can do" mentality and the passion and energy to make their dream reality.

Very few of them drew on fundamental research and hardly anyone had a PhD. Some picked up existing generic technology, plodded an incremental improvement and put it into the marketplace. The x factor that distinguished them as juggernauts in this game of one-upmanship was their IQ and their guts, their business acumen, ruthless efficiency and some luck. Connections provided the spark, venture capital the fuel, marketing clout the prize. They spawned new businesses in their apartment or in their garage and created a new global industry. Driven by passion and by the energy of genius, they turned their hobby into a hugely profitable business. They were impatient to show what is possible, determined to get there first and to carve a niche in the hall of fame.

The computer industry has been the major source of newfound wealth. Companies that did not exist a few years ago have a market value superior to that of old industrial giants. The market showered money on those with the skills to manufacture the hardware, to draw up a program or to put them together. Some became billionaires almost overnight. They personify the qualities of entrepreneurship, vision and business excellence upon which economic and social progress depends.

They are inspiring examples and role models for young entrepreneurs, and in many ways exemplars of humanity at its best. But the essence of entrepreneurial activity is risk; like any revolution, the high-tech revolution devours its children. In a world addicted to stress and tension, "only the paranoid survive." In today's global IT industry, the major players are few, and can easily be arranged on a small scorecard.

The uniqueness of the computer resides in the interaction between hardware and software. The hardware is an assembly of disks, disk drives, display screens, keyboards, printers, boards and chips. The software represents the brains of the machine. It has no substance, but it programs intelligence into inanimate structures. Without it, the hardware would be an inert and useless object, an unexpressed potentiality frozen in the abstract pattern of its informational bits. In the human brain there is no distinction between hardware and software. The relationship, however, is similar. The biological neural networks of the brain are a special kind of intelligent hardware that is not fixed at birth but evolves and modifies with time, experience and patterns of use.

Microelectronics is fundamental to the industries of the future. The computer industry has become the world's second-largest, and keeps growing. No business in history has come close to achieving this sort of ubiquity and instant wealth creation. It is the culmination of the interaction between entrepreneurial tinkers and pragmatic dreamers, a combination of scientific research and business instinct, a mix of brilliant insights and borrowed ideas, of science-fiction coming true. It is a saga of huge successes and devastating failures, of bitter rivalries and enduring partnerships, of genius, hubris and staggering wealth. It is also a case study showing what creative research and entrepreneurial thinking, in combination with hard work and determination can accomplish, and why businesses and industries grow or fail.

The history of the computer is tied up with larger questions of socio-economic engineering, genetic code and geopsychology.

The links are, in fact, inseparable. The evolution of the American, European and Asian micro-electronics industries bears the stamp of the dominant values, sustained by the myths, the mental barriers and ingrained prejudices, and by the socio-political priorities that make people and their policymakers think and act within established patterns according to their past experience and peculiar outlook on life. It mirrors their relative successes and failures as well as their moral underpinnings.

America has an astounding track record of applying inventions -borrowed and home-grown - in an economically useful fashion. The American psyche embraces the capitalist system, in which nothing is preordained. Opportunity and insecurity coexist, alternatively rewarding and punishing. In American practice, the market decides about industrial fortunes. On a daily basis, American businesses cut product lines, close facilities and lay off workers. But they also launch new strategies, fund new ventures, and hire. "Creative destruction" can extend to the very top of management. Laggards succumb, freeing brains and capital for newcomers.

The market-based economic order has, to varying extents, become the worldwide norm. The entrepreneur and the private sector have a prominent role and visible status. The business hero is admired for his ability to create wealth and as a source of inspiration for ambitious youngsters. When kids admire successful role models like Bill Gates or Michael Dell; they tend to emulate them.

Public assistance is widely regarded as full of waste, fraud and inefficiency. Working hard and hitting it big is the American Dream. A youngster who thinks up a business plan knows he can start from scratch, possibly fail, start again, and get rewarded if he succeeds. He will confront rivals and countless obstacles that must be surmounted, by-passed or hammered flat. The burning desire to get ahead spurs economic creativity and destruction. Brought up in an environment that worships free enterprise, fierce competition, glamour companies, self-determination, innovation, meritocracy, creative insecurity, marketing skill, high-risk financing and minimal government intervention, a vast number of whizz kids grow up as youngsters eager to try their luck in business. Their purpose is not to create jobs, but they are the ones who create the new enterprises that provide massive new employment and wealth.

Asian companies tend to be paternalistic, family-oriented, consensual, authoritarian and clientelistic. Quiescent, people respect hierarchy and emphasize duty, the value of work, social cohesion. Governments refrain from intervening actively in the economy, and let the entrepreneurs run the show. They only see to it that the infrastructures, the educational system and minimal corporation taxes give the country the greatest possible comparative advantage. Consensus and the need for escaping destitution makes workers identify with their company rather than their class. In case of need, the family, not the government, is the safety net.

Japanese companies excelled at perfecting technologies that were not fully developed or had been abandoned by their originators. They incorporated these innovations into products that consumers wanted to purchase. Master copycats and disciplined workers, efficient at improving whatever they imitated, they adjusted smoothly to changing circumstances by constantly upgrading their industrial capabilities. Conservative governments stood aside while a dynamic business-cum-civil-service machine regenerated the country from wartime destruction into an advanced industrial power. The integrated keiretsu combinations did not lead to a cartelization of the industry. Competition between the leading manufacturers is fierce.

Visionary and highly motivated Japanese entrepreneurs operating in small and medium-sized firms took on projects when there was still much research and development work remaining to be done. For the technologies they licensed, some paid sizable sums. They also took rough technology initiated by the Americans and worked with it until it was suitable for the market.

The tacit decision by the government to embrace capitalism has released the extraordinary vitality of the Chinese people, after a long oppression by Communism. The Asian industrialized nations have joined the United States in the capitalist front line by manufacturing gadgets dreamed up in California and increasingly in Asia. This turning point has the potential to change the competitive balance throughout the world. The Asian genie is out of the bottle, and there's no way of putting it back. China's unique combination of a first-world infrastructure and third-world labor costs is a solid foundation for continued progress. China has seen two decades of blistering economic growth, which has led to wealth creation on an unprecedented scale. Its entrepreneurs and disciplined workers can out-compete anyone in the world. The economy is developing in ways very similar to the most developed markets, but doing it much quicker.

The historical achievement of European social democracy was the "domestication" of capitalism by striking a balance between labor and capital, between the state and the market, between competition and solidarity. The cultural bias against entrepreneurial activity significantly prohibits the emergence of new firms. There is no sympathy for "start-ups" when they fail.

Over the last few decades the worldwide "borderless" economy has significantly eroded the ability of governments to plan economic policy. Globalization has stitched the world's labor markets together, leaving rich-country workers unsure about where they stand. A process of international economic integration has unhinged the balance in favor of the market, of competition and of capital investment. Governments have become spectators of forces over which they have no control. The technological and institutional infrastructure of any large industry is determined in the crucible of international competition. Once manufacturing goes offshore, is it just a matter of time before product design and development jobs follow.

The European egalitarian social contract is in danger. Destabilized by threatening forces it cannot control, the political establishment puts its hopes in a European Union that will be powerful enough to negotiate a social and environmental regulatory framework that would protect the European model from further falling back in industrial productivity. By joining the West with the East into a political union, Europe would again become a global power to be reckoned with. The idea of a free market Europe was hijacked by proponents of an interventionist federal super-state.

The conflict between national competitiveness and the ideals of social justice has not been perceived by European policymakers. All over Europe, factories large and small are closing down, with no hint of new investments on the horizon. Millions of people have lost their job during the last three decades, victims of the awesome productive capacity of innovation and production inherent in American and Asian capitalism.

Much of what goes on in American and Asian industry is inconceivable and incompatible with the values and principles professed by the European social model: the hiring and firing, restrictions imposed on trade unions, the 12-hour shift for production workers, the 60-hour-plus work-week, poverty amidst fabulous wealth, tax exemptions for manufacturing and venture capital industry, and much more.

The electronics industry is the most striking example. For three decades, Europe's political leaders warned that dependence on the import of high-technology products would subject the economy to decisions made elsewhere, and would expose it to unforeseeable risks. A combination of government policies and commercial realities rapidly led to the industry's demise.

Public financing was not supplied to companies or institutions with the brightest ideas, but to those with the best connections and the most effective lobbyists. In 1978, the European Community more or less broke even on trade in computers, telecommunications, and other information technology. By 1991, despite a variety of interventionist policies,

Europe had sunk to an information technology trade deficit of $40 billion a year. Though Europe accounted for roughly one-third of the world economy, its consumption of semiconductors had fallen to about one-sixth of the world total. Philips, Olivetti, Bull and Thomson were all mired in losses, with no recovery in sight.

When the "champions" faded away, it attracted little public attention. Now that the demise of the European computer industry is a *fait accompli* and a lost cause, the issue is no more the order of the day. Political rhetoric has shifted from "national champion" policy to an "information society" strategy, from *manufacturing* to *dissemination* and *use* of technologies. The technology policy pursued by the commission has hardly been called in question or cast a shadow over the image of the European establishment.

The commission conducted an investigation into the causes of the inability of Europe's electronics industry to turn research and development into globally competitive products. A *Green Paper* identified the discrepancy as the "European Paradox". The mistakes of the past were exorcized by the announcement of a renewed technology policy. Conceding that past concepts and ideologies might need rethinking is a difficult exercise. Europe has nevertheless reached a milestone which demands urgent self-assessment.

A sense of insecurity haunts the global electronics industry, spurring to continuous effort and creativity to stay ahead of the game. The euphoria generated by the prospects of European integration permeates the political talking shops and masks the industrial decline and scientific retro-gradation, while propagating complacency about a bright and dynamic future.

The European ambitions were grandiloquently announced in March 2000, at the Lisbon Summit. The assembled heads of state set themselves the goal of giving Europe within ten years "the most competitive and dynamic knowledge-based economy in the world, capable of sustained economic growth with more and better jobs and greater social cohesion." António Guterres, prime minister of Portugal, said that the European

Union "faces a true revolution in the way it works... and that its new attitude represents the triumph of prioritizing the social-political over the economic-financial."

Such oracular predictions may comfort the political visionaries, but they are farcically out of touch with reality. No credible program was put forward about how this was to be accomplished and no progress has been made since. The incantations delivered on such occasions make a mockery of reality. The strategies for dealing with the major chronic problems have failed. The real big challenge will be to attack the legacy costs of the European social model. Unable to tackle the issue of unemployment, politicians focus on dubious Concorde- and Airbus-type projects of prestige.

The most important source of growth and employment is the advance of scientific knowledge and its massive application in industry. Microelectronics is the highest of high-tech. Semiconductors and computers are the most crucial technologies of the 21st century. They are the foundation of the information age. They enable and underlie virtually every system involved in the manipulation and movement of information, from laptop computers to satellite-based global communications networks. Semiconductors have become as vital to economic growth as were the materials and tools that generated the industrial revolution. Ever since its inception, the semiconductor industry has been a protean generator of new companies, technologies, and market niches. While most industries have long since reached staid maturity, the semiconductor industry consists not only of a few giants. Innumerable device designers keep adding new features.

High-technology industry is disruptive and global in outlook. Even the largest computer firms buy components such as microprocessors, disk drives, printed circuit boards and software in the open market and assemble them to make them functional.

The history of the computer industry provides a case study in the implementation of public intervention in the marketplace. European governments squandered huge subsidies among inefficient manufacturers. Science-based industries require an ever-increasing number of ever-more experienced engineers. But most high-school students chose the social and humanistic disciplines leading to secure bureaucratic careers, rather than the arduous mathematics and natural sciences.

The quality of math and science education in the European secondary schools - from kindergarten to college - does not prepare the students to fend for themselves in the coming IT world. Social democracy - the egalitarian thrust of the "third way", an amalgamation of social ideals and economic imperatives - delivers generous living standards on many measures, both social, economic and welfare. But the extension of social benefits for all "from the cradle to the grave" also generates disincentives and protects freeloaders from the vagaries of modern life. Standing aloof from the sweep of the global capitalistic economy, it has failed on the most important measure of all: the stimulation of the entrepreneurial spirit that creates new manufacturing jobs and new activities. Pragmatic economists suggest that the security of guaranteed incomes provided by welfare state has led to lethargy and needs reforming.

Science and technology are widely seen as sources of power and prosperity. High-tech will continue to be a determining factor of industrial strength. As with nuclear power, chain reactions of innovation require a critical mass. Countries having the technological capacity are obviously best placed to innovate further. Ever since the Industrial Revolution, Europe and the United States provided the expertise and the capital that produced manufactured goods for world markets. During the past two decades, a new technology ideally adapted to the international division of labor, has shifted the geography of production and capabilities. It has fundamentally reshaped the world economy, and reordered the hierarchy of technological excellence, comparative advantage and productive power.

The global economy is now dominated by three geo-economic centers: the United States, Europe and Asia. But the industrial epicenter of high technology and of the knowledge economy has shifted from the Atlantic to the Pacific. China's growing domination of global manufacturing and India's booming IT services sector have led to a shift of skilled jobs from the west to the east. In China a revolution is waiting to happen - or perhaps two. One is a bourgeois revolution led by the emerging property-owning middle class; the other, more violent, by poor farmers expelled from their homes.

The United States and Asia are setting the standards of industrial efficiency. America provides the technical innovations and the marketing; South East Asia supplies the brawn, but increasingly also the brains. Combined, they have become the foremost technology regions in the world. Both are interdependent and intimately complementary, but also highly competitive. American manufacturers contract out the production of components and the final assembly. Most of the computers sold in Europe under American labels are assembled from components produced in Asia. Japan, Taiwan and South Korea and China have developed their own computer industry. The international division of labor has made production and distribution increasingly transnational. We are witnessing a fundamental realignment of global economic structures.

The strongest force propelling material progress has been the swift advance and wide diffusion of technology. Competitive manufacturing is the foundation of a dynamic, robust and resilient industrial economy, of long-term growth and a rising standard of living. Competitiveness depends on the commercial application of leading-edge scientific knowledge, on the ability of a firm, an industry or a nation to produce on a profitable basis goods and services that consumers choose over competing alternatives. The Asian governments and business leaders, obsessed with the long-term growth of their electronics industries, have realized that their competitive advantage can only be sustained by constantly moving up to the next level of higher value-added, higher design content products.

High technology is the most ruthless of markets and is not concerned with social issues. Its heroes respect only cold calculation and market power. It is characterized by near-monopoly, steep entry barriers, and overwhelming advantages for those who are first to capture the field. Firms or nations that establish front position and leadership can enjoy those advantages long enough for the economic benefits to accrue globally.

Since the mid-1990s, the Internet puts the world at our fingertips and in the palm of our hand. It has become a unique corpus of knowledge and the largest source of learning and information on earth. Much of humankind's memory has been capsuled and committed to an automated reference library. Internet is the land of knowledge, and the exploration of that land empowers every person to pursue a course of study in his or her own way. Millions of virtual travelers throng cyberspace's invisible highways; their e-messages are bounced off the stratosphere by commercial satellites. They can establish instantaneous communication practically free of charge with correspondents across the world. Cyberspatial "warehouses" accumulate data, knowledge and information at an explosive rate. We can collect material on practically any subject and search out for instant answers to about any query that may come to our mind.

The computer revolution didn't just happen. For decades, a succession of trailblazing scientists invested in the fundamental research that provided the insights into the nature of matter, allowing physicists to turn silicon wafers into the brains of the computer and create the silicon revolution. Today, the specialization of economic activity is firmly apportioned between America and South East Asia. This synergy of scientific supremacy, managerial know-how, high-powered marketing and low production costs has generated product leadership and an impregnable comparative advantage.

Driven by Moore's law, computer technology is constantly upgrading. The companies in control of the market have unlimited funds to spend on research and development, and to explore technical trails that no European manufacturer dares peer down. Their ultimate goal is to stay in the forefront of the world's most competitive and profitable industry. Barring a miracle, a truly European computer industry is unthinkable for quite some time to come. Once evicted, there is no way of vaulting back. What does this imply for the future?

Adam Smith ascribed economic growth and the resulting wealth of nations to the division of labor and to the ratio between productive and unproductive labor. Europe enters the 21st century with the highest living standards in history but also the highest production costs, ageing populations, the adverse social impact of changing family structures and of the declining work effort, regulation-induced unemployment levels that have become an intractable problem and an acute shortage of technical expertise.

Governments give and governments take. They cast their beneficence widely across the electorate, and people like it. But the resources consumed by governments, social security benefits, state-supported pension schemes, minimum wage and employment protection legislation raise employment costs.

The world has become a single-market economy. The main beneficiaries are the consumers who enjoy a multitude of low-priced products, while the internationally exposed part of each national economy is increasingly vulnerable. Information technology is the archetype of a globalized sector. While the American and Asian IT industries have become closely integrated, large segments of European industry have become obsolete and extinct. The jobs have moved elsewhere. In the face of globalization, the future character of the social partnership will need a new balance in order to meet the requirements for competitiveness.

The European economy is at a crossroads mainly because its industry has failed to meet the world challenge and has fallen into "second division." Whether we like it or not, our societies have been organized for more than a century around manufacturing. Well-established industries have disappeared and have not been replaced by firms exploiting new technologies. Old-fashioned, low-level jobs are protected by law to preserve and enhance the "European social model", while sophisticated high-tech mass production has moved to Asia. Prices are set on the global market, but production costs are determined locally.

The future is unknown territory, but there are trends, clues and forecasts pointing to the challenge. The threat must be faced collectively in an orderly and rational manner by the political class and by the "social partners", using common sense and understanding of the long-term problems.

In Europe, industrial production has historically involved class conflict. The fundamental causes of the problem must be recognized and attributed. The market disposes but the market is not uppermost in the minds of some trade union bosses. By refusing to understand that by inciting their members to strike and by featherbedding them, they simply put many of them out of their jobs. EU employment laws are a disincentive to recruiting. Dealing with the complexities of employment legislation and complying with its rigidities is a hindrance to business expansion. Europe is littered with barriers to risk-taking and innovation, from an archaic education system that fosters rote learning to bureaucratic impediments set against start-ups. The social policy of the European Union flies in the face of elementary economics. The regulatory interference by the commission has strangled entrepreneurial spirit and brought economic growth to a halt. The investment climate has dangerously deteriorated. Energy costs, wage- and taxation levels are by far the highest in the world, and the entrepreneurial ecosystem is extremely low. Inhibited by red tape, by rules and regulations, the aspiring entrepreneur will take refuge in a more secure salaried job.

The economic clock cannot be turned back. When the dust settles on the silicon revolution, a very different prosperity hierarchy will emerge among the nations of the industrialized world. How will this affect the long-run sustainability of the European socio-economic model? A historical, comparative and analytical perspective should shed some light and provide elements of an answer.

Technology affects societal structures, attitudes, and mores. But because it is so rapidly and completely assimilated, the profound interplay of technology and other social endeavors in modern history is hard to recognize. A steep learning-curve lies ahead. All one can do is analyze the past and the present, rationalize the lessons of history, come out with an open-eyed perspective and construct a few possible scenarios for a plausible future, knowing that there will be surprises. The evolution of the computer industry during the past three decades inaugurates a new era full of unforeseeable consequences.

In a globalizing economy, the sustenance of the welfare state depends substantially on attitudes towards work and on increased industrial productivity. Manufacturing industries are the lifeline of any developed economy. Europe's economies face increased competition from a growing range of nations able to produce cheap, well-made, labor-intensive manufactures as well as high-tech electronics.

In the course of history, nations unable to apprehend the technical and economic forces that drive industry and thus rise to a higher value level, have entered into a period of low growth and decline. In a technology-based economy, nations falling behind are soon outclassed in the kind of businesses that require the most sophisticated engineering and marketing capabilities. If Europe is unable to overcome the drag of backwardness, catch up with tomorrow, create new innovative products and withstand the shock of inevitable cyclical downturns, when the pendulum swings to a major global deceleration, more job losses are to be expected.

Information technology has triggered a historical dislocation of the old economy. It has changed the rules and redefined our futures. In the creation of new wealth, manufacturing industries have given way to knowledge and service industries. A few individuals dominate the scene: they are the visionary aces, catalysts of the technology economy that must constantly anticipate and act. They develop new products, provide new services, and market them in competition with everyone else. There are driven by ego and money, engaged in a global conquest game; they build - and lose - their accidental empires constructed around proprietary knowledge or wizard marketing. They provide jobs for the innumerable army of footmen - and women - beavering away to churn out the components, assemble and sell them.

American realpolitik is based on practical and material factors and political realities, as distinguished from the ideological, ethical and moralistic objectives prevalent in Europe. Americans focus on finding the world-beating winners that keep them ahead of the game. The European political establishment continues to pride itself in the superior merits of the welfare state and persistently refuses to understand the awkward truths, or even to acknowledge them.

Flawed as it is at times, the free enterprise system has demonstrated a unique ability to generate new technology. Industrialized capitalist economies have increased their productivity more in the last two centuries than in all the millennia of previous human history. The basis for this advance is the pursuit of profits, which forces companies to innovate. This incentive depends fundamentally on the commitment to free enterprise by the institutions that determine and administer ownership of the fruits of industrial progress.

Nothing in economic history has ever moved as fast as, or had a greater impact than the Silicon Revolution. The dynamics of economic growth have shifted to totally new industries that emerged after the invention of the transistor. Much is happening and will happen that no one foresaw. It has already brought about fundamental changes in the economic foundation of nations, impacting on the social and political environment. The new economy is creating and dislocating industrial structures, jobs and labor markets. It has spawned an economic order in which the entrepreneurial drive, combined with cutting-edge knowledge, and the venture capitalist with the means and the mentality to finance the unexpected and unproved, are the key resources. Investment finance is abundantly available in the US for novel ideas and technologies. In Europe it is available for established technologies, but not new ones.

Throughout history, technology has been handmaiden of innovation, investment and higher living standards, and - when things get rough - of clout and strategic power. Technological progress creates and feeds new consumer demands in unforeseen markets. Nations failing to cope with disruptive technological advances in a competitive environment inevitably fall behind in high value-added products and technology-intensive industries, thus running the risk of being relegated into an industrial backwater. Competition knows no boundaries. Millions of industrial jobs have gone elsewhere, and for good. The Silicon Revolution has destroyed much of the competitive advantage Europe managed to acquire during the past two centuries and undermined the economic foundations of the welfare state.

The cumulative impact of arrested development, grim demographics, the destructive misuse of trade-union power and mutual mistrust between left and right, the failure of the much trumpeted "common economic and employment policy", the costs of "social overstretch" forced onto business' and workers' incomes, the high levels of persistent unemployment, restructurations and bankruptcies, ageing populations undermining the future of pensions and health care programs, a growing demand for social services, the dependency on high-technology imports, is coalescing a critical mass and a mortgage that augurs a somewhat precarious tomorrow. The attractiveness of Western Europe as a location for industry is in constant decline as industry wanders to other areas.

A heavy state, heavy taxation, high unemployment, slow growth, unsustainable entitlements, social tensions, unresponsive governments, a huge bureaucracy - both national and international - weighing on trammeled markets, is no ideal wellspring of economic renaissance. The European social model inhibits economic growth, rather than boosting it. Youth unemployment is a social disaster. It will take many years to repair the damage done by the Social Chapter to the European economy. As a result of the legislation imposed on industry not enough people work, those who do fail to work enough, and industrial wages are globally uncompetitive. Too many people are filling in too much paper, enforcing too many rules.

Margaret Thatcher opted out of the Social Chapter and initiated a series of microeconomic reforms: privatization, deregulation and the neutralization of trade unions. Sensing that the euro would not deliver what was being promised by the supporters of monetary union, the Labour government opted out. These moves transformed the British economy from one of the worst in the rich countries to one of the best performing.

When the euro was launched, optimism was in the air. No region in the world had higher hopes for economic growth than Europe. Unable to analyze and deal successfully with the ever-changing business environment of the twenty-first century, the political class can only administer the decline. Dealing with the future of a delusion will not be an easy enterprise. The welfare state will have to dismantle itself to save itself. If past is prologue, the burden is unlikely to become lighter with the passage of time. The urgent task is to counteract the decline and turn an increasingly globalized menace into an opportunity. Success can be achieved by taking the time to learn how it's done elsewhere. There is no golden rule for sustainable economic growth; but a high economic participation rate, good labor-management relationships and technological advancement largely determine the degree of economic expansion. Conflicting relations between management and the workforce are apt to increase production costs more rapidly than any other factor. In today's competitive world, management, workforce and shareholders prosper or fail together.

Scientific knowledge and technology are the foundation of economic prosperity and an improved standard of living. Innovation flourishes when knowledge, skills, energy and experience are allowed to interact. The future of Europe depends on the contribution its innovative entrepreneurs can make to address the challenges of the Global Age and not on the ambitions, the grand designs and the history-making decisions of its political opinion-makers. Traditionally, prosperity and economic power go hand in hand with technological excellence. The global economy is in the middle of a fundamental transformation. The input by the European industry is shrinking. European governments do not seem to have taken measure of the forces at work and of the emergence of a new world order. Radical global power shifts have been common throughout history. Globalization and technology speed up these shifts and accomplish in a few years what used to transpire over centuries.

For several decades, the citizens of Western Europe have enjoyed the best of both worlds: the capitalist and the socialist. They will have to adapt successfully to the forces of globalization, adjust to changes which are beyond their control and re-invent themselves to make globalization a positive development. But it will be very hard to change a culture that has evolved for a long time in a particular environment. And it is obvious that those in authority do not have the knowledge and the will to decide what should and could be done.

Globalization has created a common labor market about which national politics are powerless. We are witnessing a seismic shift in the world economy. Europe is being squeezed between two formidable business models: the United States with its cutting-edge technologies and East Asia whose unbeatable production costs and entrepreneurial spirit make it the fastest growing economy in the world. The long-term consequences are unforeseeable. The European model of balancing competitiveness with social justice is in the long run unviable in a ruthless and fiercely competitive free-trade world. It will require severe economic pain followed by a mix of radical changes to put it back on course. There are no magic answers and no miracle cures.

Much of Europe is teetering on the brink of stagnation and recession. It doesn't take an academic economist to see that several major countries keep falling further and further behind in virtually every meaningful economic indicator: income levels, job creation, unemployment rates, research and development, capital formation. There is no way of guessing when and where the downward spiral will end. Sooner or later the governments will have to come to grips with the realities of globalization and with the eviction of the European industry from the information technology. The European high-tech industry has suffered a number of indignities from which it will not recover. It seems inevitable that the countries of Western Europe will increasingly face the harsh reality of global industry and continue their slide down the international scale. Looking far and wide, no growth impulses are to be seen on the horizon. The cost of resurrecting and breeding fresh life into a European computer industry is beyond reach. There is no indication that history will give Europe a second chance. Re-entry would demand an insuperable range of scientific, technical and marketing skills, as well as immense financial resources and organizational ability. The failure of Europe to take an active part in the furtherance of the Silicon Revolution will doom the continent to playing a marginal role in the future of the global high-tech economy. That is the price to pay for misguided policies.

1

FROM ABACUS TO INTEGRATED CIRCUIT

The prehistory of the computer extends to very olden times and includes the numerous disciplines that contribute to the body of knowledge eventually leading to what we call Information Technology. Electronic computers are the legacy and the crowning of a secular chain of discoveries, each major breakthrough opening up new lines of exploration and further innovations. Most were the brainchild of a brilliant mind driven by the urge to know: mathematicians, physicists, chemists, scientific philosophers, engineers. They explored abstruse realms for which there exists no easy language. Many of their findings remained theoretical until industrial technology made it possible to build the instruments materializing their ideas. Some of the most creative inventors were ignored or derided during their lifetime.

The computer is a compound of tangible hardware and intangible software. Its dual nature is reflected in its diverse origins: the electronic calculator belongs to the history of mechanical technology and engineering; the defect-electron conduction to the history of mathematics and physics. Between mathematics that makes the device theoretically possible and solid-state physics that makes it practically feasible lays the programming that makes it usable. Both combine to make a computer work properly. They remain separate but they must be compatible.

Over the centuries, gifted inventors, imaginative crafts-men and artisan/engineers who were often far ahead of their time, added bits and pieces, each making a contribution to the advancing frontier of scientific knowledge and to the automa-tization of arithmetical processes. Most innovations resulted from a synthesis of existing principles or a reallocation of known concepts. Their story has been told many times in sub-stantial detail. This brief résumé is intended as a preamble highlighting the major innovations that culminated in today's computer. An account of the creation and development of the computer is an adventure story about remarkable people and the legendary companies they built. It is a tale of bitter rivalries and steadfast partnerships, of huge successes and shattering failures, of genius, vision, ambition and fabulous wealth.

The technology evolved from pure and applied research in the field of mechanization, which had its beginnings in the Industrial Revolution. The predecessors include the slide rule, typewriters, adding machines, calculators, accounting machines and punched-card systems.

Computer science is an arcane domain combining math-ematics, physics, chemistry and electrical engineering. Mathematics provides the concept that all information can be represented as sequences of 0's and 1's. Physics, chemistry and electrical engineering provide the hardware. Software is the programming language. The binary digit - the bit - is the basic unit of data storage and transmission of the computer system. It is the smallest unit of information a computer can hold.

Ever since people used their ten fingers to show "how many", it was possible to accumulate larger numbers in groups of ten by holding up both hands. Ten became thus the basis of the modern number system and of digital technology. One of the first counting devices invented to express numbers was the abacus whose origin is lost in the dust of time. The abacus was widely used in China, and spread from there to many countries.

It allows users to make calculations by sliding beads arranged on a rack. In some places it is still the preferred calculating device. A skilled operator can total the cost of a large number of purchases on an abacus much faster than most people could enter them into a calculator. It is utilized today by shopkeepers in Asia and in American Chinatowns. Asian schoolchildren are taught how to work it.

The process of transforming calculation into a mechanical operation has a very long history. Computer science can be traced back to the earliest stages of Greek philosophic speculation. Euclid taught a method for the determination of the greatest common divisor of two numbers, the algorithm. Archimedes' *Method of Mechanical Theorems* outlined fundamental discoveries in the fields of mechanics, hydrostatics, geometry and the integral calculus, thus anticipating modern mathematical physics. Hero of Alexandria studied mathematics and pneumatics and described several devices operated by water, steam, and compressed air.

The decimal system using the zero was well developed in India by the sixth century, and later used extensively by Arab mathematicians. The algorism, the system of Arabic numerals which allows calculating by means of 9 figures and 0, was methodized in the 9th century by the Arab mathematician Al-Khowarizmi. The Moslems brought the Arabic numerals to Europe, introducing the concepts of zero, tens, hundreds, thousands and multiples, which replaced Roman numerals and simplified mathematical calculations.

A Scottish clergyman, philosopher and mathematician, John Napier (1550-1617) improved on the abacus by inventing the logarithm, which transformed multiplication and division into addition and subtraction. He is remembered for a small instrument nicknamed "'Napier's Bones", a mechanical device for multiplying, dividing and taking square roots and cube roots. The "bones" were strips of ivory or horn, with numbers written on them. Each rod contained the multiples of a number. By moving the rods around and reading rows of numbers, the user could quickly and easily find the result of a multiplication operation. Logarithms are considered one of the great computational breakthroughs of all times.

In 1630, William Oughtred used Napier's logarithms to create a circular slide rule that became the primary calculator used by engineers. Made up of two identical logarithmic scales fastened together, it was adjusted by hand. His claim of priority of the circular rule was contested by one of his former students, the philosopher René Descartes.

THE MECHANICAL CALCULATOR. Leonardo da Vinci's notebooks contain drawings of a mechanical calculator. The idea of using an apparatus to solve mathematical problems can be traced to the early 17th century, when the first adding machines were built by philosophers who also practiced mathematics and felt an aversion for endless calculations with pencil and paper. In

1623, Wilhelm Schickard designed an automatic adder with a geared mechanism, capable of multiplying large numbers. The prototype he built was lost in a fire, but the drawings of his device resurfaced after more than three centuries and allowed the construction of a working model.

Blaise Pascal (1623-1662) was requested by his father, a French tax collector, to add and subtract endless rows of figures. He loathed the time-consuming drudgery and built a machine comprising a series of toothed clockwork gears and levers, which allowed him to add sums up to eight figures. It used movable dials manipulated by a stylus. He called it Pascaline. Addition was easy; subtraction required a somewhat tedious procedure; multiplication was possible, but very complicated. The numbers 0 through 9 were printed on the edges of a row of wheels. When a wheel made a complete turn from 1 through 9, a small notch caused the next wheel to the left to move up one number. Gear cutting was not accurate, and the mechanisms were forever out of order; only Pascal and one of his workmen could fix them. Improved versions of the Pascaline were used for the next three centuries. About the same time, Samuel Morland built a mechanical calculator that would add and subtract.

Gottfried Wilhelm von Leibniz (1646-1716) holds a special place in the annals of computation. He is remembered as mathematician, philosopher and logician who deliberately ignored the boundaries between disciplines. He invented the differential and integral calculus. His lifelong interest was the idea that the principles of reasoning could be reduced to a formal symbolic system, an algebra of thought. He designed a machine whose mechanism had a stepped cylindrical drum and a variable number of teeth that could be set by slipping a keyway concentrically with it. The machine allowed him to add, subtract, multiply, divide, and calculate square roots.

Leibniz's interest in mathematics was aroused during a visit to Paris, where the Dutch mathematician Huygens introduced him to the theory of curves. He immersed himself for several years in the study of mathematics, investigating relationships among the summing and differencing of finite and infinite sequences of numbers. In *Nova Methodus pro Maximis et Minimis* he developed his concept of integral and differential calculus. To mark his election to the Paris Academy, he published a theory of the binary system which underlies modern technology of electronic digital computers.

While exploring binary arithmetic, he envisioned a digital counting machine controlled by punched cards. Binary numbers were represented by spherical pellets. A container provided with holes opened at places corresponding to a 1 and remained closed at those that corresponded to a 0. Through the opened gates small marbles were to fall into tracks, while the other gates remained shut.

Leibniz studied the written symbols used in China and observed they were the key to resolving language problems. The multitude of Chinese tongues were mutually unintelligible in the spoken form, but each written symbol represented a similar notion regardless of the sounds involved, thus allowing people from different regions to communicate. He corresponded with a French missionary, Joachim Bouvet, who was conducting research on the languages used in China. Bouvet sent him a copy of the I Ching, the binary system that had been in use for millennia. Leibniz became increasingly convinced that the I Ching was the divine prototype for his own binary system. In one of his last writings, *Discourse on the Natural Theology of the Chinese*, he repeated the principle that binary arithmetic and logic were in some sense indistinguishable: 0's and 1's could be made to represent positive and negative, or true and false.

In *De Arte Combinatoria* Leibniz described a method of discovering truths by combining concepts into judgments in exhaustive ways and then methodically assessing their truth. He later developed what he called a "universally characteristic language." Concepts were represented by means of icons, graphs or pictures in a way that could be understood by readers, no matter what their native tongue. *De Arte Combinatoria* is the theoretical ancestor of the modern computer: all reasoning, verbal or not, is reducible to an ordered combination of elements, such as numbers, words, sounds, or colors.[1]

Leibniz liberated the term "algorithm" from its limitation to figures and numbers, and expanded it to a game with objects of any given meaning, a game based on specified and fixed rules. The notion of "algorithm" in this general sense defines what has come to be known as data processing or information processing. Leibniz also worked on hydraulic presses, windmills, lamps, clocks, and a wide variety of mechanical devices. He opened mathematics to semiotics, and semiotics to infinite translation. He garnered a compendium of knowledge probably unequalled in history. He dreamed of mechanizing reason and mathematics, but did not have the wherewithal. His discoveries were premature and laid aside by the scientific community.[2]

It took about three centuries for his fundamental concept of the binary yes-no/on-off to be rediscovered. In the 1930s, while studying at the Technische Hochschule Berlin-Charlottenburg, Konrad Zuse familiarized himself thoroughly with Leibniz's binary arithmetic and put together the world's first operational electromechanical program-controlled calculator. A copy is on display at the Deutsches Museum, in Munich.

By the end of the 17th century, the intellectual foundations and the scientific preconditions for a technological revolution were in place: mathematics and mechanics had come together. Understanding and application had converged. Galileo, Leibniz, Newton, Huygens, Hooke and others were technological innovators as well as scientists. Galileo, a pioneer of mathematics and astronomy, made telescopes and other instruments; Huygens invented the pendulum clock and conceived an internal-combustion engine; Newton improved the marine sextant and invented the reflecting telescope.

The third Earl of Stanhope invented a multiplying calculator. Several philosopher-mathematicians such as Gottfried Ploucquet, Jean-Henri Lambert and Léonard Euler contributed to the development of formal logic, although none went far beyond Leibniz and none influenced subsequent developments.

At the 1801 Paris Exhibition, Joseph-Marie Jacquard showed a programmable weaving loom that was to revolutionize the textile industry. It was controlled by punched cards connected in an endless belt. Each card had a "program" of punched and un-punched holes (a binary system) to automatically control the pattern woven into the material. The concept of punched cards - the stored program or instruction sequence - would later contribute in a major way to the development of the computer. An instant success, the machine became known as the Jacquard loom. Still used today, it is now controlled by direct connection to a computer.

In 1820, Charles Xavier Thomas, known as Charles de Colmar, started producing mechanical calculators in commercial quantity. His Arithmometer won a gold medal at the International Exhibition in London. The machine could add, subtract, multiply, divide and calculate square roots. Over the next century, many people improved the calculating machines and by 1900 they were widely used in government and commerce.

The first character code for processing textual data was invented by Samuel Morse. It used a single wire and an electromagnet that attracted a small armature for transmitting signals. Like the binary system, it was based on simple patterns of "dots" and "dashes". The duration of a "dash" was three times the duration of a "dot". The incoming signals could be recorded on a moving strip of paper. By 1900, the introduction of tape-reader machines allowed traffic to speed up to 400 words per minute.

George Boole (1815-1864) schematized a mathematical system of symbolic logic that would later become the basis for modern computer design. Boole's father was a shoemaker who had a passion for science, literature and the classics. The family was too poor to pay grammar school fees. A child prodigy, George borrowed books to study mathematics, Greek, French, German and Italian, which enabled him to read scientific publications before they appeared in English. He expanded on Leibniz's ideas about the correlation between logic and calculation, but argued that logic was primarily a discipline of mathematics rather than philosophy.

Appointed professor of mathematics at Queen's College in Cork, Ireland, he published about 50 papers and was among the first to investigate the basic properties of numbers. In *An Investigation into the Laws of Thought, on Which Are Founded the Mathematical Theories of Logic and Probabilities,* he brilliantly combined algebra with logic, transforming logic from a philosophical into a mathematical discipline. In *The Mathematical Analysis of Logic,* he analyzed the possibilities for applying algebra to the solution of logical problems. He studied the uses of combined algebra and calculus to process infinitely small and large figures and perceived the potentiality of applying algebra to the solution of logical problems.

The mathematical system of symbolic logic he conceived was to become the basis for modern computer design. Computers function on Boole's logic system: microchips contain myriads of tiny electronic switches arranged into logical "gates" that produce predictable and reliable conclusions. The basic logic gates allow the computer to execute its operations by using binary language. Each gate assesses information consisting of high or low voltages, in accordance with predetermined rules, and produces a single high or low voltage logical conclusion. The voltage itself represents the binary yes-no, true-false, 0-1 concept. Boole is considered the seminal originator of computer science and artificial intelligence research.

Charles Babbage (1791-1871) is generally considered the "grandfather" of computing. His calculating engines are among the most celebrated icons in the prehistory of information technology. The son of a wealthy London banker, he taught himself mathematics, and particularly algebra. He was elected a Fellow of the Royal Society in 1816 and played a prominent part in the foundation of the Astronomical Society. While studying the astronomical tables used by sailors for navigational purposes, and by astronomers for locating star positions, he observed mathematical errors and miscopy by printers.

Such tables had to be calculated manually. Frustrated by these inaccuracies, he decided to build a calculating-printing machine and developed an interest in mechanics that became his consuming passion for the remainder of his life. In semi-seclusion, with an initial government grant, he started building a machine which he called the Difference Engine. In 1822, Babbage proposed that the government provide substantial funds for his project.

He believed he could build the machine in three years, but he kept adding improvements and underestimated the financial and technical resources he would need. Over the years, the government provided £17.470 while Babbage claimed to have put in the same amount. Never satisfied with his work, he kept rebuilding and refining the same parts over and over again. When the expenses got out of hand, the government decided to stop funding. He continued working for about a decade, and by 1832, he completed a prototype which proved the feasibility of the concept. The Difference Engine was the first successful automatic calculator and remains one of the finest examples of precision engineering of the time. But it was too small for table-making and had no printing unit.

After failing to complete a workable Difference Engine, Babbage fell out of favor with his mathematical peers, and with government. Between 1834 and 1846, without any outside support, he designed the Analytical Engine. He devoted most of his time and his fortune towards its construction, but never succeeded in completing any of his designs. For this engine, he borrowed a concept from the weaving industry: punch cards. Mathematical functions can be punched on cards, so that if a mathematician creates the right card, anybody could operate the machine.

Conceived as a general symbol manipulator, it included many of the elements associated with a modern electronic computer. It contained a "mill" where the operations of addition, subtraction, multiplication and division could be performed. A control unit allowed processing instructions in any sequence, while output devices produced printed results. The Analytical Engine anticipated virtually every aspect of subsequent computer architecture. The sheer scale of the machine rendered its construction impossible without government finance. Ten years after the project had begun he had no tangible results to show.

Babbage covered thousands of manuscript pages, but the government considered the machine worthless, and refused any financial support. By 1846 he had gone as far as he was able with his work on the Analytical Engine. He produced designs for what he called the Difference Engine Number 2, but did not build it. Babbage learned about manufacturing while visiting factories in various countries in search of components and processes for his Difference Engine. He published a book titled *Economy of Manufactures and Machinery*. In his last years, he lived in isolation, filling notebooks with impenetrable scribbles. The failure to construct his calculating machines, and in particular the failure of the government to support his work left him in his declining years a disappointed and embittered man.

Considered an eccentric by his contemporaries, Babbage was a visionary genius and a prophet whose ideas were far in advance of his time. His insights into the process of computation,

the representation of computable problems and the fundamental characteristics of the computer were remarkable. He
invented the computer in an age of mechanical gears. It took
100 years for the full significance of his work to be appreciated.
Babbage considered himself a failure. His son, Henry, assembled pieces of his machines. In 1991, a Difference Engine was
constructed at the Science Museum, in London.

A Swedish printer, Georg Scheutz, learned about Babbage
and spent 20 years building a Tabulating Machine based on the
designs for the Difference Engine. The Scheutz engine had to
be frequently adjusted and was not very reliable; but it could
process 15-digit numbers, calculate fourth-order differences
and print out mathematical, astronomical and actuarial tables
with unprecedented accuracy, making it the first printing calculator in history.

In 1867, Christopher Latham Sholes patented what was
to be the first useful typewriter. He licensed his patent to
Remington & Sons, a noted American gun maker. In 1874,
the Remington Model 1, the first mechanical word processor, was placed on the market. Remington remained a leading
manufacturer of typewriters until well into the twentieth century. Based on Sholes' mechanical typewriter, the first electric
typewriter was built by Thomas Alva Edison in 1872. Some of
the standards developed for the typewriter are still in use on
today's computer keyboards.

In 1888, a young bank clerk, W. S. Burroughs, became convinced that banks needed a machine that would add figures
accurately and print them. He built and patented an adder/
printer. By 1926, Burroughs Corporation had sold over one
million machines.

The next milestone in the history of computing was the
Tabulating Machine invented by Herman Hollerith. He developed a punch-card system that revolutionized statistical computation. He began working on the tabulating system while
teaching mechanical engineering at MIT and filed for the first
patent in 1884. He developed a hand-fed "press" that sensed
the holes in punched cards; a wire would pass through the

holes into a cup of mercury beneath the card closing the electrical circuit. This process triggered mechanical counters and sorter bins and tabulated the appropriate data. Hollerith's system - including punch, tabulator, and sorter - allowed the official 1890 population count to be tallied in six months. Within another two years all the census data was completed and defined. The cost was $5 million below the forecasts and saved more than two years' time. His later machines mechanized the card-feeding process, added numbers, and sorted cards, in addition to merely counting data. In 1896 Hollerith founded the Tabulating Machine Company.[3]

In 1911, financier Charles R. Flint engineered the merger of Hollerith's company with Computing Scale Co. of America and International Time Recording Co. to form Computing-Tabulating-Recording Co. The new firm manufactured and sold machinery ranging from commercial scales and industrial time recorders to meat and cheese slicers, tabulators and punch cards. When the diversified businesses of CTR proved difficult to manage, Flint turned for help to an experienced manager.

Thomas J. Watson had started out as a $6 a week bookkeeper. He went to work for the National Cash Register Co. as a salesman and stayed there for 18 years, rising to general sales manager. When he was named president of CTR, he found a debt-ridden, disorganized and amorphous outfit. Within a few years he transformed it into a prosperous enterprise and renamed it International Business Machines (IBM). He created a new corporate culture: employees were encouraged to be enthusiastic, loyal and cooperative team players Watson demanded strict and professional conduct in exchange of a commitment to lifetime employment. In doing so, he largely reshaped the American business landscape.

Tom Watson built IBM into the world's largest manufacturer of data-processing equipment. Backing an aggressive research-and-development program, he assembled a highly motivated, well-trained and well-paid staff. He used to give pep talks, enforced a strict dress code and a set of core values, and had "THINK" signs posted in company offices. IBM achieved spectacular success with its tabulating machines and its punch cards and developed a huge customer base.

When the Depression struck, Watson estimated it would be momentary. He kept IBM's workforce intact, trained more engineers and substantially increased spending on research and development. The company kept building machines and parts and stockpiled them in its warehouses. To outsiders Watson's logic looked like an insane wager. His gamble seemed disastrous. Revenue from 1929 to 1934 stalled and IBM edged toward insolvency. In 1932, its stock price fell to 1921 levels. When he brought the company close to insolvency, the board of directors discussed ousting him, but put it off.

Watson had his back against the wall when President Roosevelt signed the Social Security Act. This created a gigantic national bookkeeping problem. To make the system work, every business had to track every employee's wages and the amount to be paid to social security. Overnight, demand for accounting machines soared. Businesses and government offices needed them by the boatload. Only IBM could meet the demand. It delivered better, faster and more reliable machines than any other company. IBM won the contracts to do all of the New Deal's accounting. Revenue jumped from $19 million in 1934 to $31 million in 1937. In the 1930s and '40s operations expanded worldwide. IBM dominated the market and climbed unabated for the next 45 years.

Thomas J. Watson epitomized the American Dream. After ruling as the firm's benevolent dictator for several decades, in 1956 he relinquished his executive position. Shortly afterwards he suffered a fatal heart attack. His son succeeded him as president and later as chairman. Until the early 1980s, IBM would dominate the data processing industry. Whereas Watson Sr. stands for IBM's success as a punched card company, Watson Jr. stands for its success in computer technology.[4]

THE ELECTRONICS AGE. Electronics refers to devices and systems that operate on the information content rather than the power transmitted by an electrical signal. The electronics industry was built largely on the invention, in 1907, of the three-element vacuum tube by Robert von Lieben in Germany and by Lee De Forest in the United States. While working on wireless telegraph equipment, they developed the amplifying vacuum tube, based on the light bulb. By adding a third electrode into the two-electrode electron tube, they created the triode which could amplify radio signals and generate oscillations. The triode was essential to the development of radios, telephones, television sets and computers.

The milestones on the way to cyberculture are marked by the names of a few extraordinary people. In 1931, Vannevar Bush completed work on the Differential Analyzer, a precursor to the modern computer. It used electrical motors to drive shafts and gears that represented terms in complex equations and significantly reduced the time required to carry out calculations. As such it was highly valuable to scientists and engineers in ballistics, acoustics, and physics.

In an article of *The Atlantic Monthly* titled, "As We May Think", he proposed a mechanical machine that would master the glut of information coming out of academia and the government offices, and improve the storage and the communication of information.

Claude Shannon paved the way for the digital transmission of data. In 1948, the publication of *A Mathematical Theory of Communication* produced a major conceptual breakthrough. He combined mathematical theories with engineering principles and set the stage for the development of the digital computer and the modern digital communication revolution.

Shannon described how information could be manipulated in a precise, mathematical way. He laid the foundations of the theory that ``bits" could carry information in a digital form. He created the mathematical foundations for efficiently packaging and transmitting data information. He visualized the binary digit as the fundamental element of electronic communication and formulated a theory describing an ideal communications system in which all information sources - voices, computer keyboards, video cameras - have a "source rate" measured in bits per second.

Shannon's information theory gave engineers the mathematical tools needed to figure out channel capacity. He invented the source-encoder-channel-decoder-destination model. The channel through which the source's data travels has a capacity measured in bits per second. Information can only be transmitted if the source rate does not exceed the channel's maximum capacity, now known as the Shannon limit.

George Stibitz, a Bell Labs researcher, had a similar thought. Realizing that Boolean logic could be used for the circuitry of electromechanical telephone relays, he gathered together a conglomeration of old relays, batteries, flashlight bulbs, wires and tin strips and built a prototype binary adder circuit - an electromechanical circuit that controlled binary addition. He devised a machine that could calculate all four basic mathematical functions with complex numbers. The Model I Complex Number Calculator was the first demonstration of a large-scale digital machine for complex calculation. Technically, it was not a computer because it was not controlled by a program. Rather, it was operated directly through a teletype. Although it lacked the speed of the electronic computers that were to appear a few years later, its relays were far less liable to failure than vacuum tubes.

John Vincent Atanasoff and Clifford Berry conceived a machine that used binary numbers instead of the traditional base-10 numbers. It was a mechanical, semi-automatic device which they set out to adapt because it was not capable of executing the operations they had in mind. The Model 1 Complex Calculator was the first electronic digital machine to use vacuum tubes and capacitors. The capacitors were located in a rotating drum that held the electrical charge for the memory. The desk weighed 700 pounds, contained about 300 vacuum tubes and a mile of wire. It could solve 29 simultaneous equations with 29 unknowns, and calculate an operation every 15 seconds. It was not programmable. Atanasoff tried to interest Remington Rand in his invention, but was turned down. He left the patent application in the hands of the university's attorneys who did not grasp the value of his work and failed to take any action. Atanasoff never made any money from his invention. The Atanasoff-Berry computer was finally dismantled.

At the outset of World War II, the US and the UK governments allocated substantial financial and human resources to the development of computers. The military desperately needed accurate ballistics tables for artillerymen to compute bomb trajectories. Conventional means were too slow, and the idea that an automatic calculator would speed up the operation prompted the Ballistic Research Laboratories to contact John Mauchly at the University of Pennsylvania's Moore School of Electrical Engineering. He had created several electric calculating machines and had drafted a memo outlining a large-scale digital electronic computer. The US Army commissioned an electronic calculator and provided a substantial grant.

A team of scientists headed by John Mauchly and J. Presper Eckert built a 30-ton machine, almost 100 feet long and 10 feet high. It contained 17.468 vacuum tubes, about 70.000 resistors, 10.000 capacitors and five million hand-soldered joints. An IBM card reader and card punch were used for input and output. It could calculate a gun trajectory in 30 seconds. Since it broke down very often, it required numerous attendants. The ENIAC was a monster, but embodied almost all the components and concepts of today's high- speed, electronic digital computers.

By the time it was completed in the fall of 1945, the war was over. For several years, it was used extensively on a variety of projects including wind tunnel design and the H bomb. It was never duplicated, but the machine's importance lay in the concept rather than its usage. The ideas generated from the work done by Mauchly and Eckert led to a controversy with the University over the patent rights. Unable to reach an agreement, they decided to leave their jobs and to set up their own company.

Since they had no personal resources, they approached the Census Bureau, and signed a contract for the development of a stored-program computer. Known as UNIVAC, it was the first computer using magnetic tape. Capable of storing one million bytes of information, it showed the results on an electric printer. But the development costs soon exceeded the funds available and Eckert and Mauchly faced insolvency.

They approached the Northrop Aircraft Company which funded the development of a slightly different computer, named BINAC. Northrop took delivery, but was unable to make it run properly. They contacted IBM, but Thomas Watson turned them down. In 1950, Remington Rand absorbed the company owned by Eckert and Mauchly, while retaining their services. Remington Rand built 46 UNIVAC computers for both government and business uses. This established the company as the world's first large-scale American manufacturer of commercial computers and a direct competitor of IBM. In 1955, Sperry Corporation bought Remington Rand and formed Sperry-Rand. Eckert remained with the company as an executive. Although UNIVAC was a technical success, Sperry-Rand could not compete with IBM's imaginative marketing initiatives and sophisticated sales forces.

Eckert and Mauchly belatedly realized that their ideas had commercial value. They had filed for a patent in 1947; it was granted in 1964. Sperry-Rand notified all computer companies that they were violating its patent rights and offered to license competitors for a fee. IBM was excluded as it had previously reached a settlement. Sperry sued Honeywell and Control Data Corporation. Honeywell countersued, accusing Sperry of trying to enforce a fraudulent patent. The trial lasted 135 days. The judge declared that the patent was invalid because it had been filed more than a year after the ENIAC was in public use. He also concluded that Eckert and Mauchly did not invent the automatic electronic digital computer, but instead derived that subject matter from Atanasoff. Mauchly died almost penniless while Eckert got not credit for the creation of the modern computer.[5]

John von Neumann, who was present as a consultant while the ENIAC was under construction, had written a report which became known as the von Neumann architecture. Although he had not actively contributed, he was the first to spell out the requirements for a general purpose electronic computer, presenting it as his idea. In fact, the first computer having an arithmetic logic unit, a control unit, a memory and input-output devices was the Manchester Mark I, designed and built at Manchester University.

Born in Budapest in 1903, von Neumann was a child prodigy. After studying chemistry and mathematics, he moved to the United States and was appointed professor at Princeton University. He developed a formal description of a system that could support self-reproducing machines able to withstand some types of mutation and pass these mutations on to their offspring. He was convinced that computers could be made to execute any kind of computation effectively by means of a programmed control. His expertise in hydrodynamics, ballistics, meteorology, game theory and statistics led him to consider the use of mechanical devices for computation. His two main contributions were his concept of the implosion method for bringing nuclear fuel to explosion and his participation in the development of the hydrogen bomb. His computer design, which came to be referred to as the stored-program technique, became the foundation upon which future generations of computers were built.

After the War, he focused his attention on the cognitive processes of the brain, and on computers. This led him to the conclusion that data could be stored in a single location and in identical form within the computer's memory. Von Neumann identified five functional units in a computing machine: central control, central arithmetic, input, output, and memory. The memory unit would hold both a program's instructions and the numerical data on which it operated. It should be able to store not only its data and the intermediate results of computation, but also the instructions that effectuated the computation. The instructions must be as changeable as the numbers they act upon, by encoding them into numeric form and storing them and the data in the same memory. He then defined the control organ as that which would automatically execute the coded instructions stored in memory. All computers since that time have been stored-program computers.[6]

Another sequence of machines was produced at Harvard University. Howard H. Aiken, a Harvard engineer was able to convince IBM to build a large-scale automatic digital computer based on standard electromechanical parts. Started in 1939, his all-electronic calculator was operational by 1944, and was used to create ballistic charts for the US Navy. The Harvard-IBM Automatic Sequence Controlled Calculator, called Mark I was eight feet high and 55 feet long; it weighed about five tons; it contained more than 750.000 components and about 500 miles of wiring. It performed simple computations: addition, subtraction, multiplication and division. It also had built-in programs to handle logarithms and trigonometric functions. It was fully automatic and could complete long computations without human intervention.

The Mark I, was the first electronic relay computer, using electromagnetic signals to move mechanical parts. The machine was slow and inflexible, but it could perform basic arithmetic as well as more complex equations. At the request of the Navy, Aiken constructed the Mark II which was much faster. It required 125 milliseconds for an addition and 750 milliseconds for a multiplication. Aiken built two more machines, and spent his last years teaching at Harvard and organizing university computer centers.

Developments in the United States closely paralleled those in Britain. In both countries the various groups developed their own individual approaches to programming methodology. It wasn't a race between contestants; it was more like a mutual run toward achieving technological breakthroughs.

British scientists made substantial contributions to electronics. Alan Turing applied the concept of the algorithm to digital computers. His research into the relationship between machines and nature generated the field of artificial intelligence. He conceived machines that would emulate the processes of the human brain and pioneered the concept of the digital computer.

The universal mathematical machine he imagined would read a series of 1s and 0s from a tape. This described the steps that needed to be done to solve a particular problem or perform any programmed task. The binary system would be fed, via punched tape or some other medium, into a mechanical device.

The Turing Machine embodies the essential principles of the programmable computer: a single machine which can be turned to any well-defined task by being supplied with a stored program. The Turing Machine would read each of the steps and perform them in sequence, resulting in the proper answer.

At the outbreak of the war, the government had established an ultra-secret Code and Cypher School at Bletchley Park, between Oxford and Cambridge. Its mission was to find ways to break the German military codes. Some of the country's most brilliant minds, both mathematicians and engineers, were recruited to help. One of them was a 26-year-old Cambridge mathematical genius named Alan Turing. In 1936, while a graduate student, he had written a ground-breaking paper *"On Computable Numbers, with an Application to the Entscheidungsproblem."* One of the premises of the paper was that some classes of mathematical problems do not lend themselves to algorithmic representations and are not amenable to solution by automatic calculators.

The paper anticipated many computer-related concepts, like input, output, memory, coded programs and algorithms. The theoretical model became known as the Turing Machine. It was an abstract concept, a hypothetical general-purpose computing device. However, it was a buildable machine. It could store programs as well as data, and instantaneously switch to perform tasks as diverse as arithmetic, data processing and chess playing. A theoretical automaton, it could recognize and process symbols according to a programmed "table of behavior."

Turing was assigned to participate in the design and creation of machinery that would allow the decryption of secret German messages. Since the 1920s, the German army used an encryption machine, called the Enigma, for secret transmission of messages via radio or telephone lines. To encode a message, the operator set small wheels on a panel; at the destination, the message could only be decoded by an operator using an Enigma with rotors set in the same positions. The settings were regularly modified, so that if an enemy captured a machine, without knowing the current settings, messages could not be decoded. In 1928, Polish secret agents had been able to lay their hands on an Enigma and had built their own electro-mechanical model. When Poland fell to the Germans in 1939, some of the staff of the Polish decryption service escaped to England. The information they gave allowed the engineers at Bletchley to build machines that were very successful in decoding German messages. Enigma codebooks were rescued from a U-boat that was forced to surface and had been captured. The Intelligence Service picked up enemy signals via its world-wide network of intercept stations and forwarded them to Bletchley. The code breakers also had a lucky break in August 1941, when a German operator sent a long message that had been keyed in, and the operator at the receiving end confirmed it in clear text.

Then a more sophisticated machine, the *Geheimschreiber*, was captured in North Africa. Its permutations were almost unlimited and could not be dealt with. Turing and his engineers, realizing that a different approach was needed, designed and constructed a huge electronic computer which they dubbed Colossus. It comprised 1.800 vacuum tubes and became operational in 1944. Colossus was not a fully-fledged computer. It was rather a revved-up calculator but it could factor logical problems and was programmable. It demonstrated that machines could do more than handle purely numerical problems. Colossus read teleprinter characters from a paper tape at

5,000 characters per second, giving the Allies access to German strategic secrets. It reduced the time to break the German messages from weeks to hours. It was crucial for the deciphering the binary-based messages of the Enigma code, which gave vital information prior to D-Day and during the breakout from the Normandy beachhead.

Colossus II went into operation on June 1, 1944, just in time to intercept a coded message which confirmed that the German high command had fallen for an Allied ruse suggesting that the long expected cross-channel invasion was aimed at the Calais area, rather than the Normandy beaches. This allowed Eisenhower to finalize his plans for Operation Overlord. Ten Colossus were built in all. Immediately after the war, they were dismantled. In 1960, all the drawings were destroyed; its very existence was kept secret until the 1970s.

At the end of the war Britain had a vast concentration of electronic computing devices and a significant number of engineers with practical skills in building complex electronics. Military programs were wound down and research expertise was taken over by civilian institutions.

Colossus had relatively little direct impact on the evolution of computing. It was a top secret operation. Its key contribution was that people closely involved, as they moved into civilian occupations, would have both a vision of future possibilities and useful practical experience. In fact, several enterprising scientists started investigating whether it would be possible to build a small but powerful computer by using a digital memory in which both data and program would be stored.

Three groups undertook the construction of electronic computers while testing out new ideas: one under Professor F. C. Williams at Manchester University; one under the direction of Maurice Wilkes at Cambridge University, and a third at the Mathematics Division of the National Physical Laboratory.

The key problem was the memory technology. Research concentrated on the development of a reliable memory in which a program and data could be stored. Williams had discovered the "anticipation pulse" effect which made charge- regeneration, and hence long-term storage, a relatively simple matter. In particular, the timing of the anticipation pulse gave an early warning that the scanning electron beam was about to arrive at an area of charged phosphor, and the shape of the pulse determined whether this area was currently storing a binary 1 or binary 0. Appropriate regeneration could then be arranged in time. Williams cathode ray tube stores became a widely used form of electrostatic storage.

During the war Maurice Wilkes had worked in radar and operational research. Appointed Director of the University of Cambridge Mathematical Library, he decided to build a computer as quickly as possible. During a visit to the United States he had the opportunity to familiarize himself with the technology of the EDVAC under construction by Eckert and Mauchly. Their fundamental idea, which was also a major breakthrough, was that a program should be stored in memory.

A practical man, Wilkes did not spend much time on research in electronics. He wanted a working machine as quickly as possible and preferred to use the available technology: mercury delay memory and von Neumann architecture. He decided to build a machine of modest capabilities from stock parts, or as near to stock as he could get.

Helped by a limited staff, he built a general-purpose computer along the lines of the EDVAC and called it EDSAC – Electronic Delay Storage Automatic Calculator. He used mercury delay lines for memory and derated vacuum tubes for logic. EDSAC had 3,000 vacuum valves. A sequence of holes punched into a paper tape fed a program into the machine. The EDSAC was the first fully operational and productive stored-program computer. It could store a list of instructions, and perform the required calculation. Programming involved writing out in tortuous detail the sequence of steps required to perform a calculation, using a set of instructions provided by the computer's designers As soon as it was constructed, it immediately began serving the University's research needs. The first successful program was run in May, 1949. It ran reliably until 1958, although much time was required by maintenance.

In 1951, Wilkes developed the concept of microprogramming from the realization that the central processing unit of a computer could be controlled by a miniature program in high-speed <u>ROM</u>. This concept was implemented in EDSAC 2, which also used multiple identical "bit slices" to simplify design. Similar but faster, it was based around the ferrite core memory, widely used until the 1970s. Interchangeable and replaceable tube assemblies were used for each bit of the processor. EDSAC 2 was the first micro-programmed computer.

EDSAC 2 was followed by the Titan, a joint venture with Ferranti which inaugurated the mainframes era. It eventually supported a time-sharing system and provided wider access to computing resources. Wilkes is also credited with the idea of symbolic labels, macros and subroutine libraries. These are fundamental developments that paved the way for high-level programming languages.[7]

Max Newman who had organized the use of the Colossus, became professor of mathematics at Manchester University. He recruited Freddie Williams who brought in Tom Kilburn. Within a few months they developed a memory device called the Williams-Kilburn tube, able to store binary information as electric charges on the face of a cathode ray tube. The Williams tube memory was to come into widespread use in computers, both in Britain and in the United States, until the core memory was perfected.

The next step was to build a small computer around a cathode ray tube memory. They nicknamed it: the Manchester "Baby". It had a minimal amount of storage and an abbreviated instruction, but it was capable of running simple programs. It included the stored-program concept so that the random access memory was used not only to hold numbers involved in calculations but also the program instructions. This meant that instructions could be read successively at electronic speed and that running a different program only involved resetting part of the memory by using a simple keyboard rather than reconfiguring the electronic circuitry. The "Baby" ran its first successful program on June 21, 1948. It was the first operational computer to have random access memory and the stored-program principle. By using what we now call "software", the "Baby" became the model for the modern-day computer.

The "Baby" demonstrated the feasibility and potential of a stored-program computer. It was decided to develop a full-fledged computer based on the same principles. By October 1949, the team had built the full-sized <u>Manchester Mark 1</u>, the first computer with a fast random access two-level store (i.e. with a magnetic drum "backing" store, the ancestor of the hard disc). The Williams tube memory had a big advantage over delay line memory in that it allowed fast random access: any memory location could be addressed and read directly.

The Manchester Mark I was the first to store both its programs and data in RAM, as modern computers do. Development of the machine finished at the end of 1949, and it ceased operation in the summer of 1950. It was replaced by the <u>Ferranti Mark 1</u>, which had a number of improvements/enhancements. This was the world's first commercially available computer.

Computation has a long history; but these were the first computers as we understand them today. Those who invented the computing machines, those who learned how to program them, those who defined the theoretical foundations, those who established the industry and made it work, had different backgrounds when they became involved in computing. They had to draw from past experience. Having no precedents for their work, they had to create their own precedents.

By 1950, Britain was in the forefront of computer technology, with the first working computers in the world. From an "invention" to one-off laboratory prototypes, the computer now became an industrial product. With its leading position in the innovation of computer technology and the prompt involvement of a commercial firm in the manufacture of a product to order, Britain appeared well placed in the development of the early computer industry. The Manchester machine was commercialized by Ferranti Ltd., the EDSAC by Leo Computers, Ltd., and the Pilot Ace by English Electric, Ltd. But by the

1960's the American manufacturers had captured most of the market. Their machines were better engineered, more reliable and less expensive.

Developments in the United States closely paralleled those in Britain. In both countries, the work of the pioneers led to commercial developments. The machines in Manchester and Cambridge both began to perform calculations at about the same time in the summer of 1949. The first American computer to run was the SEAC at the National Bureau of Standards in Washington DC, which was running in 1950. It was followed shortly afterwards by the SWAC, built in Los Angeles also for the National Bureau of Standards.

The Eckert Mauchly Computer Corporation built the BINIAC for the Northrop Aircraft Corporation. It was tested and ran successfully for 44 hours in April 1949. It was then dismantled and delivered to Northrop in California were it was never successfully rebuilt. At Princeton, von Neumann was struggling with the Selectron and switched to the Williams-Kilburn tube soon after the Manchester team announced the Baby.

The war had sparked the initial development of computer technology, but the vast amounts of capital and manpower needed to innovate and produce them fell to the commercial sector. IBM and Remington Rand took the lead. For decades, IBM had been building and marketing electromechanical punch card machines for processing large volumes of data. Until the introduction of the UNIVAC, the IBM management was reluctant to replace the punch card machines with an electronic computer, but circumstances forced them to change their policy. Launched in the 1950s by IBM, Remington Rand, Burroughs, National Cash Register, Control Data, Honeywell, General Electric, and RCA, the computer industry became a fast-growing market. The first computer produced by IBM, the 701 was delivered to the government in 1953, followed by the IBM 650. In 1956 IBM sold 76 computers and overtook Remington Rand. IBM's involvement in computer development set the trend for the design philosophy and engineering standards.

Computers were huge, fragile and unreliable metal boxes using thousands of vacuum tubes. One big disadvantage was that they only worked correctly for a few hours consecutively. The hundreds - or thousands - of vacuum tubes generated a tremendous amount of heat. When a number of them burned out, the computer would not function properly anymore. Slow and expensive, the machines failed frequently and required highly trained personnel. The main disadvantages of vacuum tubes concerned their cathode heaters. They consumed huge amounts of electrical power and were wasteful of energy. The heat they produced was not put to good use in providing electrons inside the valve, and surplus radiated heat had to be disposed of by forced-air cooling. Furthermore, the heating elements deteriorated with time, especially if the equipment was turned on and off periodically rather than left running.

The logical solution was to develop a device that performed the same role but without the disadvantages. However, the dominant electronics firms were heavily engaged in the production of vacuum tubes, and wary of undermining their existing businesses.

THE TRANSISTOR was going to dramatically change the innards of the computer. On June 30, 1948, Bell Labs' research director Ralph Bown announced at a press conference in New York that the company had made a crucial breakthrough. He showed a contraption made of a slab of germanium, a thin plastic wedge and a shiny strip of gold foil. "We have called it transistor" he said, "because it is a resistor or semiconductor device which can amplify electrical signals as they are transferred through it." He told the few reporters who were present that the transistor accomplished the same functions as the vacuum tube, but could do them much better, while using less power. The press paid little attention and for several years hardly anything was announced about the invention.

Since the late 1930s, as the telephone system expanded, AT&T faced the urgent need to find a substitute for the cumbersome, inefficient and unreliable vacuum tube. The telecommunications systems were hampered by the slow speed of the electro-mechanical relays, the high power dissipation and poor reliability of vacuum tube amplifiers. Bell Labs was the research arm of AT&T. Mervin Kelly who headed the laboratory, was convinced that the company needed a better device to amplify the signals of its telephone lines.

In 1945, the Bell Telephone company reorganized its laboratories. The administrative head of the project was Jack Morton. Bill Shockley was the team leader and overseer responsible for providing ideas and vision. He assembled an eclectic mix of chemists, engineers and physicists. Among them, Walter H. Brattain and John Bardeen had the highest credentials. John Bardeen had been awarded a PhD at Princeton University. He was interested in pure rather than in applied science. He was the theoretician who suggested experiments and interpreted the results. Walter Brattain was awarded a PhD by the University of Minnesota. He liked to play with laboratory equipment and ran the tests.

Shockley suspected that a varying electric field applied to germanium would induce a varying current, thus making germanium an amplifying device. But the experiments did not confirm his theory. He assigned Bardeen and Brattain to the task of finding out why. For two years, both worked unsupervised, while Shockley spent most of his time all by himself, filling notebooks with theoretical analysis.

After many unsuccessful attempts with silicon, Bardeen suggested to Brattain that he try germanium. Then, during what came to be known as the "Miracle Month", they came up with one wonder-working idea after another, building several devices, each one a little better than the precedent. One day, an unexpected breakthrough made a hit. Brattain had built a silicon contraption to study the behavior of electrons at the surface of a semiconductor, hoping to discover what was causing electrons to block amplification; condensation, however, kept accumulating on the silicon and messed up the experiment.

On November 17, to get rid of condensation, he dumped the device into a thermos of water and witnessed the largest amplification he had ever seen. Stunned, he began fiddling with different knobs and buttons: by turning on a positive voltage the amplification increased; a negative voltage reduced it to nothing. It seemed that the amplification had somehow been canceled out by the water. The major obstacle to building an amplifier had been overcome. He knew they were on the right track.

Bardeen then suggested that he push a metal point into the silicon surrounded by distilled water. The water would eliminate the electron problem just under the point as it had in the thermos. The problem was that the contact point must only touch the silicon, and not be in contact with water. But Brattain was a laboratory genius. He could do anything. Using different materials, different techniques and different electrolytes in place of water he tried to get an even bigger increase in current. On December 8, Bardeen suggested that he replace the silicon with germanium. The amplification increased some 330 times but in the exact opposite direction they had expected.

Unfortunately, the amplification was insufficient for a telephone line, which had to cope with the complex frequencies of the human voice. Now the problem was to get it to work at all kinds of frequencies. On December 12, Brattain inserted the point contacts into a slab of germanium. Nothing happened. He realized that there was no oxide layer, since he had washed it off by accident. Furious with himself, he decided to fiddle with the point contact anyway. To his surprise, he got some voltage amplification at all frequencies. The gold contact put holes into the germanium and these holes canceled out the effect of the electrons at the surface, the same way the water had.

Within four weeks, the two scientists had managed to produce a large amplification at some frequencies and a small amplification for all frequencies. The problem was to combine the two. The key components were a slab of germanium and two gold point contacts just fractions of a millimeter apart. Brattain put a ribbon of gold foil around a plastic triangle^ and sliced it through at one of the points. By putting the point of the triangle gently down on the germanium, they saw a signal come in through one gold contact and increase as it raced out the other.

For a week, they kept things secret. Then, Shockley asked Bardeen and Brattain to show their invention at a group meeting of the lab personnel and top management. On December 23, after conducting a few tests, it was official: this tiny bit of germanium, plastic and gold was a solid-state amplifier. They called the device a point-contact transistor since the wires were directly embedded into the semiconductor material. It was a crude looking collection of wires, insulators, and germanium, but represented a crucial breakthrough: they had invented a new kind of valve to let electricity flow, or not flow, and amplify it.

Instead of being elated, Shockley was upset and frustrated at being upstaged. Determined to make his imprint on the discovery, he decided to improve on the design. In a burst of creativity and anger, he developed a different type of amplifier. Working with paper and pencil at home and in a Chicago hotel room, he described in great detail how a strip of semiconductor material - silicon or germanium - with three wires attached, one at each end and one in the middle, would improve upon the point-contact transistor. It would be easier to mass-produce and more reliable.

Then, in a remarkable series of insights made over a few weeks, he greatly extended the understanding of semiconductor materials and developed the underlying theory of another, much more robust amplifying device, a sandwich made of a crystal with varying impurities added, which came to be known as the junction transistor.

Bell Labs coined the word transistor, a concatenation of transfer and resistor. The transistor was solid, but had the electrical properties of the vacuum tube. The problem of whose names should be on the patent, and who should be featured in publicity photographs was hotly debated. Shockley felt that the person who had the original idea was the inventor. The original idea had been his own; never mind it didn't work. Several patents were filed by the summer of 1948, just before Bell announced the invention to the press. Bardeen and Brattain got a patent for their point contact transistor, while Shockley got a patent for the junction transistor.

It would take several years for Bell scientists to perfect the techniques needed to grow germanium crystals with the right characteristics to amplify electrical signals and for transistors be produced. By 1951, sufficient progress had been made to overcome the limitations of this type of transistor, and production began at the Western Electric plant in Allentown, Pennsylvania. The manufacturing was highly complex and tooling costs expensive. The whole process was done by hand, under sterile conditions. Rows of women, hunched over worktables, squinting through microscopes, cut layers of germanium; they then picked up small rectangular pieces and attached them to wires. Depending on how well the germanium had been cooked and doped, anywhere from 50 to 90 percent of the transistors would turn out to be defective.

In September 1951, Western Electric began licensing the right to manufacture transistors for a $25,000 fee. Companies were allowed to send a delegation of two or three people for a two weeks teach-in at Murray Hill and Allentown. More than 100 companies, both American and foreign, responded and were shown how to manufacture point-contact and junction transistors. Western Electric made available two volumes entitled *Transistor Technology*. Shockley's magnum opus, *Electrons and Holes in Semiconductors* became known as "Ma Bell's cookbook."

For six years, numerous companies tried to develop transistors without ever achieving a useful level of functionality. For several years, the transistor was perceived as an expensive laboratory curiosity when a small company, Texas Instruments, one of the early companies to pay for a license to manufacture transistors, began producing them commercially.

In 1950, Gordon Teal resigned from Bell Labs and joined Texas Instruments. He was put in charge of the laboratory, and in 1954 the company produced the first US-made commercial silicon transistors. The transistor was a turning point in Texas Instrument's history. Sales rose almost vertically and the company was suddenly in the big leagues.

Since transistors did not fit into the vacuum tube connections of existing machines, acceptance was not immediate. The military requirements of the cold war hastened their use in all areas of electronics. As production increased, the price dropped. Then a small Japanese company, called Sony, started selling portable transistor radios. Transistors gradually gained recognition and became widely used in radios, telephones, hearing aids, and other equipment. The first large-scale machines using transistors were the supercomputers: Stretch by IBM and LARC by Sperry Rand. Both were developed for atomic energy laboratories. They could handle an enormous amount of data, a capability much in demand by atomic scientists.

When the first stored-program computers went into operation in the 1950s, American corporations began to explore how computers could be sold as office equipment. Computers operated in air-conditioned rooms isolated from people. IBM was the leader in the effort to make commercial machines available. In 1964, IBM's System 360 revolutionized office computing because it combined miniaturization with large-scale integration to engineer a minicomputer. Thus a new data-processing industry emerged. Computer hardware enabled companies to manage their accounting procedures with punch cards that could be processed.

By 1970, two distinct types of computers were available. IBM, Control Data Corporation, Honeywell and a few smaller companies built room-sized mainframe computers. These machines were often custom-built one at a time; they cost hundreds of thousands of dollars and their design required a vast number of engineers. The minicomputers built by companies such as Digital Equipment Corp. (DEC) and Hewlett-Packard (HP) were relatively inexpensive and compact. Built in larger quantities than the mainframes, they sold primarily to scientific laboratories and businesses. The size of a refrigerator, minicomputers incorporated semiconductor devices, which reduced the volume of the machine. Time-shared computers could support many terminals connected via the telephone line to the host.

Only four of the top 10 vacuum tube manufacturers - General Electric, Sylvania, RCA and Westinghouse - achieved the technical transition to the transistor. New companies, set up as transistor manufacturers without ever having made vacuum tubes. A decade later, in 1965, when the chip market was exploding, Sylvania, Hughes, Westinghouse and Clevite were elbowed out of the top 10 semiconductor manufacturers by pushy newcomers. As usual, only the companies that could correctly catch the technological drift and had the rare skills to get new technologies to work were successful.

THE INTEGRATED CIRCUIT was destined to be invented. Ten years after the advent of the transistor, the idea of connecting a vast number of them within a single piece of semiconductor material was in the air. The transistor had caused a snowball effect in the electronics industry and given rise to faster computers with ever more complex electronic equipment and an increasing number of components. These components had to be hand-soldered to form electronic circuits, which was expensive, time-consuming and unreliable. Every soldered joint was a potential source of trouble. The obvious challenge was to create a monolithic device by combining transistors, diodes, resistors and capacitors on a single piece of semiconductor material and join them without using wires. The semiconductor material would obviously have to be carved, etched, coated, and otherwise fabricated. There were many missing pieces to the puzzle and several technological barriers had to be overcome. Throughout the 1950s, researchers of various disciplines sought to unravel the essence of the behavior of silicon crystals and to learn the art of semiconductor production, while refining their trial-and-error methods. When they ran into a problem, they tried to figure ways around it.

When the Soviet Union launched the Sputnik and set off the space race, the government needed small computers that could be installed in rockets and provide automatic onboard guidance. In 1957, eight engineers defected from Shockley Semiconductor Laboratories. With financing obtained from Sherman Fairchild, they set up Fairchild Semiconductor in an idyllic spot that was to become Silicon Valley.

The "traitorous eight" set in motion one of the most amazing chains of events in American business history, sparking an entrepreneurial behavior pattern that became the trademark of the Valley. They started out with silicon transistors wired together by hand and selling at $150 apiece. It was a cumbersome, laborious process. Robert Noyce, director of research and development, came up with a plausible theory based on the idea of combining transistors in a solid block of silicon.

Fairchild concentrated on exploratory work. One of its pioneering products was known as the 'mesa' transistor. It was the first silicon transistor built by the batch process and the first device that used photolithography to produce the structures. The transistor works by controlling the flow of electrons through a structure embedded in silicon. This structure is composed of adjoining regions of silicon with different concentrations of impurities. These impurities are atoms of elements like boron, phosphorous, and arsenic. By putting all these elements together, several transistors can be combined to create a simple functional circuit. Noyce used a new chemical etching method, not only to print transistors on silicon wafers, but also to lay down tracks between them. This eliminated expensive wiring. Fairchild was the first company to successfully manufacture a micro-sized device capable of integrating large numbers of electrical "on-off switching functions, stored in simple memory cells, all etched onto a silicon chip.

Their research focused on making the connections between the transistors and various components an integral part of the manufacturing process itself. In 1958, at a time when the Fairchild founders were completely stalled in their research, one of them, Jean Hoerni provided the breakthrough when he developed the planar process. Swiss-born Hoerni had completed doctorates in physics in Cambridge and Geneva, before emigrating to the United States. Hoerni's approach yielded transistors that were buried beneath a layer of silicon dioxide. To create an integrated circuit, one must embed large numbers of transistors on a single miniature component. The planar process was a means of fusing an insulating layer of silicon dioxide onto the chip before the application of the conducting metal circuitry.

The planar process, which uses oxidation and heat diffusion to form a smooth insulating layer on the surface of a silicon chip, allowed the embedding of insulated layers of transistors and other elements in the silicon. Each layer could be isolated electrically, which eliminated the need to cut apart the layers and wire them back together as had been necessary in the past. Hoerni showed his planar transistor to Bob Noyce, who came upon the idea of making one planar transistor on a bar of silicon, interconnect transistors and other circuit elements through holes etched in an insulating layer by using thin-film interconnections over the top of the silicon oxide, and of using extra junctions in order to isolate one transistor from another. These two associated ideas turned the planar transistor into an integrated circuit. The solid-state transistor had undergone a miraculous metamorphosis, more profound in its implications than the transistor itself. Integration was the ability to print dozens, later thousands, today millions of connected transistors on to a single piece of silicon.

The integrated circuit was a minuscule chip of silicon, the size of a fingernail, on which connected transistors had been printed. It combined the functions of hundreds of transistors, resistors, diodes and other components that, made up the conventional printed circuit It put all the functions on a single panel, making it possible to create miniature computers, and opening up' every field of engineering imaginable, from robots to voyages to the moon.

The integrated circuit set off the silicon revolution. The exponential increase in the number of transistors incorporated onto a single piece of silicon, while continuously increasing capability and performance, led to the replacement of large, expensive and complex systems by small, high performance and inexpensive computers.

The development of integrated circuits revolutionized the fields of communications, information handling and computing. Integrated circuits reduced the size of devices and lowered manufacturing and system costs, while at the same time providing high speed and increased reliability.

Sherman Fairchild had agreed to invest $1.5 million, with the proviso that the new company could be taken over for twice that price whenever he decided to do so. In 1959 he exercised the option to buy Fairchild Semiconductor for $3 million. The next day Noyce, Moore, Hoerni, and the other five former Shockley defectors woke up much richer than they had ever dreamed of being. Each received $2.5 million worth of Fairchild stock.

The first practical integrated circuit was fabricated in 1959, the year when Noyce was named vice president and general manager. Commercial manufacture started in 1961. Although the smallest company in electronics business, Fairchild attracted much public attention when IBM bought 100 mesa silicon transistors.

In 1961, Fairchild started selling commercial planar integrated circuits comprising simple logic functions marking the beginning of the mass production of integrated circuits. The company had the right technology and, as a result, it became the most productive in the business. The demand was terrific and prices were high. In 1967, Fairchild introduced a device called the Micromosaic, which contained a few hundred transistors. The key feature of the Micromosaic was that the transistors were not initially connected to each other. A designer used a computer program to specify the function the device was required to perform, and the program determined the necessary transistor interconnections and constructed the photo-masks required to complete the device. The Micromosaic is credited as the forerunner of the modern application-specific integrated circuit, and also as the first real application of computer aided design.

In 1967, a young Italian scientist, Federico Faggin joined their team. He had worked briefly at SGS-Fairchild and was sent to the United States to work for Fairchild Semiconductor. There he developed the MOS silicon gate process, and designed the world's first commercial integrated circuit to use that technology.

Unaware of Robert Noyce's work, another engineer had developed integrated circuits using the same technology. At Texas Instruments, Jack Kilby after spending months wrestling with the same problem had filed a patent based on a technology called the integrated circuit. Kilby had earned a masters degree in electrical engineering, and had developed a background in die design of ceramic-base silk screen circuit boards and transistorized hearing aids. Assigned to work on miniaturization, he started pursuing the idea that resistors, capacitors and transistors could be combined in one block of semiconductor material. After several months, he had a working model half the size of a paper clip.

Kilby's invention had a serious drawback. His prototype was a thin piece of germanium containing five separate components linked together by wires. It used transistors that protruded above the plane. This required interconnections above the surface with lengths of gold wire. The technique would hardly have been suitable for mass production. In February 1959 Texas Instruments filed for a patent and publicly unveiled Kilby's discovery, calling it the integrated circuit. Fairchild Semiconductor filed a patent for a semiconductor integrated circuit based on the planar process in July. The patent for the miniaturized electronic circuit was issued to Jack Kilby and Texas Instruments; the patent for the silicon based integrated circuit was granted to Robert Noyce.

This set off a decade-long legal battle between the two companies. Eventually, the US Court of Customs and Patent Appeals upheld Noyce's claims on interconnection techniques but gave Kilby and Texas Instruments credit for building the first working integrated circuit. After spending huge amounts of money in the courts, the two rivals decided to regard themselves as co-inventors, and agreed to acknowledge one another's contribution. They decided to cross-license their technologies. Noyce's silicon device turned out to be more efficient to produce than Kilby's, and set the standard. The semiconductor industry ended up paying licensing fees to both: Texas Instruments for the basic integrated circuit structure and Fairchild for the manufacturing process and interconnection techniques. The Japanese patent office refused to recognize the patent. For 30 years, the Japanese manufacturers did not pay any fees until 1989 when Japan gave in. Jack S. Kilby and Robert Noyce are both considered as the inventors of the integrated circuit, which became the building block of the electronics industry.

By 1968, Fairchild Semiconductor had become a large company with many divisions. NASA had chosen its integrated circuits for the computers the astronauts were to use on board of its spacecrafts. Year after year, Fairchild's profits and personnel continued to rise.

But Bob Noyce and George Moore wanted to transform the silicon transistor into a memory device. They were frustrated when management refused to let them go ahead. They left Fairchild Semiconductor and founded Intel Corporation. Soon Fairchild's glory days began to fade. Its employees defected en masse. They carried with them not only cutting-edge of semiconductor technology, but also the company's distinct culture. It was the "Fairchildren" who turned Santa Clara valley into Silicon Valley. More than fifty companies were set up in the area within a short period of time. Among them were Raytheon Semiconductor, Signetics, General Microelectronics, Intersil, Advanced Micro Devices and Qualidyne.

Kilby went on to pioneer military, industrial and commercial applications of microchip technology. He co-invented both the pocket calculator and the thermal printer mat was used in portable data terminals. He explored, among other subjects, the use of silicon technology for generating electrical power from sunlight. In October 2000, the Royal Swedish Academy of Sciences awarded Jack Kilby the Nobel Prize for "for basic work on information and communication technology."

Robert Noyce died in 1990 and the Academy does not award prizes posthumously. Together with Gordon Moore, he had founded Intel, a company that made its mark in 1971 when it announced a major breakthrough: the computer-on-a-chip, *alias* the microprocessor.

2

THE "FRENCH" TRANSISTOR

On May 18, 1949, Monsieur Eugène Thomas, Secrétaire d'Etat aux Postes, Télégraphes et Téléphones, presented to the press two *"brillantes réalisations de la recherche française"*: the transistron and synthetic quartz. The reaction was overwhelming. Two German scientists, Herbert Mataré and Heinrich Welker, were hailed as 'the fathers of the transistron."[1]

The newspapers reported that the transistron was an extraordinary achievement of French ingenuity. *Combat* carried a picture of Mr. Thomas holding in his hand a vacuum tube and a tiny ceramic device. The article read: "The transistron, an invention of the engineers of the Service des Télécommunications makes it possible to replace vacuum tubes in radio sets. The active principle of the "transistron" is a mineral - germanium - comparable to galena, but whose amplifying power is as good as the best vacuum tubes. Our picture shows the hand of the minister holding a vacuum tube and a much smaller "transistron". Besides, it consumes less current and lasts longer."[2] The *Figaro* predicted that the "transistron" would be installed in radio and television transmitters and receivers, and in telephone lines.

MONSIEUR EUGÈNE THOMAS
SECRÉTAIRE d'ÉTAT aux POSTES, TÉLÉGRAPHES et TÉLÉPHONES

prie M. *D͞r H. WELKER*
de lui faire l'honneur d'assister le
Mercredi 18 Mai 1949, à 16 heures,
dans les Laboratoires de l'Administration,
24, rue Bertrand (VII*), à la présentation du

T R A N S I S T R O N

et du

QUARTZ DE SYNTHÈSE

brillantes réalisations de la recherche française

R.S.V.P. à l'Inspecteur Général, Directeur du S.R.C.T. (Tél SÉG. 44-20)

For about three years, Mataré and Welker had conducted experiments in the laboratory of the *Compagnie des Freins et Signaux (CFS) Westinghouse,* a small government-owned company, no relation to the American Westinghouse) located in the neighborhood of Paris. In 1946, the company had signed a contract with the Ministry of Post, Telegraph and Telephone.

The government wanted to set up production of semiconductor diodes for use as rectifiers in radar. Radar technology was unknown in France, but German detectors had proven very precise and effective during the war. French officers interrogated a number of scientists who had worked on the radar program and invited Herbert Mataré and Heinrich Welker to Paris.

Welker was even given permission to board the Orient-Express to Paris. Welker was a solid-state physicist; Mataré focused on electronic transport problems and did the testing and the measuring. Both were personally interested in developing semiconductor amplifiers. Their wartime research on ultra-high-frequency rectifiers had led them to the idea of a solid-state amplifier, but production pressure to deliver duo-diodes for radar had prevented them from pursuing their experiments.

Their combined experience, separately acquired during previous research, enabled them to interconnect the existing knowledge of semiconductor structure and to produce germanium crystals of sufficient purity to bring about defect-electron conduction, and thus the transistor effect.

The transistron and the synthetic quartz climaxed the theoretical and practical research by generations of scientists - mainly German - each of them making an original contribution that paved the way for the next breakthrough. They followed the noble tradition of physicists who used to freely exchange knowledge and ideas, without caring about making money out of them.

The semiconductor amplifier culminated in the most spectacular advancement in the discipline of solid-state physics. The advent of the transistor illustrates that a basic understanding of materials properties is essential for scientific progress and that advances in one field can pave the way for progress in another.[3]

Once the basic principles are understood and the conceptual framework set in place, they must be corroborated by laboratory tests and verifications. Technical innovation requires a certain period of gestation. Breakthroughs occur when research is driven by an urgent need - in this case the demand for radar receivers in the ultra-high-frequency range.

Radar technology had changed the nature of warfare by making it possible to "see" faraway objects, even at night. Radar technology had been developed in Germany in the early 1930s and in Britain somewhat later. It worked by sending out a radio wave and analyzing the reflected wave after it bounced off any objects in the air or under water. The rectifier translated the reflected signal into the direct current necessary for visualization on the screen. The transistor was a legacy of the microwave technology developed by the military which needed crystal rectifiers operating at the gigahertz frequencies required for radar receivers.

The frantic efforts that were undertaken on both sides of the Atlantic propelled semiconductors into the mainstream of research to improve the signal-to-noise ratio and frequency response of radar receivers. The constant drive toward higher operating frequencies, with a move from discrete devices to resonant cavities and hollow tubes, demanded ever smaller detectors. Wartime research on the ultrahigh-frequency rectifier had led to the idea of a solid-state amplifier. Germanium and silicon proved to be the most suitable semiconductor materials.[4]

F&S Westinghouse put at their disposal a small building in Aulnay-sous-Bois, near Paris. They were given complete freedom for the installation of the laboratory, the acquisition of materials and equipment and for the layout. While setting up the laboratory, Mataré had amplification in mind.

In the basement Welker installed an HF-generator. It served to heat the quartz tube in which was mounted the graphite holder with the germanium ingot. There was also some test equipment to measure resistivity with a four-point probe and Hall constants test for carrier mobility. Since he had no equipment to outgas the graphite after every crystallization, Welker tried to clean the graphite run by heating the empty boat under hydrogen. The problem was that the so-called "pure" hydrogen contained varying amounts of water. The generator was not working properly and Mataré had to redesign the coupling coil.

Welker used a Bridgman-type furnace to cast pencil-like germanium rods which were cut into small segments with a precision diamond saw, and installed in the detector holders. The material was impure and reverse voltage of the detectors was too small. Mataré asked Welker to increase the diameter of the boules, which helped to obtain larger reverse voltages.

On the first floor Mataré installed the equipment needed for the production of diodes and the test equipment for the measurement of diode properties, namely the I-V characteristics, the base resistance, the breakdown voltage and the frequency response. New equipment was built and patented to precisely measure the detector capacity, the noise figure at 10 cm wavelength, the frequency response and, in the case of duodiodes, the equalization of characteristics. A crystal saw for dicing was later replaced by a band saw. Much equipment was not purchasable and had to be made in-house. Two technicians helped by several mechanics familiar with jewelers' lathes built microwave test equipment like test emitter, dosimeter, contact pulse formation set, test recovery time by pulse injection. Some of the equipment was shown at the Paris Radio Show in 1948, which prompted several engineers from the *Ecole Normale d'Electricité* to apply for a job. A microwave generator was purchased from a US company.

The transistron was not "one" innovation; it had a long prehistory. It was the culmination of decades of theoretical speculation, seminal ideas, false starts, precursor devices, and many related and directed innovations. The solid-state amplifier was an extraordinary technological breakthrough and one of the most complex man-made creations in history. It was made possible by the knowledge gained in the confluence of chemistry, physics and metallurgy. Its historical roots reach back to a few outstanding scientists whose names are rarely cited in the literature dealing with solid-state history. None of them could have foreseen that crystal physics would one day transform the way we conduct our daily lives.[5] On the other hand, a few people gained fortune or fame - or both - by stealth.

Semiconductors are the perfect example of how scientists analyze the properties of various materials out of pure curiosity and without any interest in their practical use. Some of their discoveries are picked up by entrepreneurs who create new industries and revolutionize the way we live.

The ancestor of <u>semiconductor</u> devices was the crystal detector, used in early wireless radios. This device was made of a single metal wire - called a "cat's whisker" - touching against a <u>semiconductor</u> crystal. The result was a "rectifying <u>diode</u>" (so called because it has two terminals), which lets <u>current</u> through easily one way, but hinders flow the other way. By 1930, vacuum-tube <u>diodes</u> had all but replaced the smaller but much quirkier crystal detector. The development of radar during World War II did much to revive the fortunes of crystal detectors and of <u>semiconductors</u>.

Lavoisier's (1743-1794) quantitative experiments had inaugurated modern chemistry by exposing the fallacy of the

age-old popular belief that matter is composed of four basic elements: earth, water, air and fire. His contributions to chemistry are multitudinous. He demonstrated that many ordinary substances familiar to the chemists and the alchemists of the day consisted of a multitude of primary materials. He created a method of chemical nomenclature. But he was also a financier, a *fermier général* who had purchased the right to levy taxes. The French Revolutionaries cut off his head.

Mineralogy evolved towards a rigorous science when **<u>René-Just Haüy (1743-1822)</u>** formulated his theory on the structure of crystals. He laid the foundations of crystallography, describing

crystals by using geometrical measurements of dihedral angles between faces of crystals, as measured with a goniometer. He discovered that crystals of the same composition possessed the same internal nucleus, even though their external forms differed. He also established the law of symmetry and was able to show that the forms of crystal are perfectly definite and based on fixed laws. During the <u>Revolution</u> he was imprisoned. Released, he was appointed professor of mineralogy at the Ecole Normale. Napoleon held him in admiration and made him one of the first members of the Legion of Honor. After the Restoration he was deprived of his professorship and spent his last days in poverty. His *Traité de Minéralogie* and *Traité de Crystallographie* make him the founder and the precursor of modern crystallography.

A vast number of scientists pursued and broadened his vision. **Friedrich Wöhler (1800-1882)** is considered the founder of organic chemistry which requires predictive abilities and

manipulative techniques. He established the principles upon which modern science is founded. While studying medicine, he became interested in chemistry and went to Stockholm to work with Jakob Berzelius who had discovered silicon in 1823. Berzelius had isolated several new elements, which made him the most famous and influential chemist of the day. After teaching in Berlin and Kassel, Wöhler was appointed professor of chemistry at the University of Göttingen where he lectured and experimented for 44 years. His masterly analytical skill and his ability to formulate chemical theory made him supreme among the chemists of Europe and his teaching attracted many foreign students.

In 1828, while heating ammonium cyanate, an inorganic molecule, he accidentally synthesized urea, an organic compound produced by living organisms. This discovery is considered one of the most important contributions to scientific knowledge. It contradicted the traditional belief that organic chemicals could only be formed in living organisms. It shattered the vitalism theory claiming that a transcendent "spark of life" was needed for producing organic compounds. Wöhler proved that such a compound could be produced in a laboratory from inanimate matter. The discovery set off theological debates across Europe. He also demonstrated that organic molecules within a living organism obeyed the physical and chemical laws of nature. This opened up an entirely new domain of scientific investigation.

While Wöhler was working on cyanic acid, Justus von Liebig investigated the metallic compounds of fulminic acid. The result of their investigations showed that the explosive fulminic acid and the innocuous cyanic acid were of identical composition. The idea of substances composed of the same elements united in the same proportion while possessing essentially different properties was new to science. Jointly with Liebig, he published a fundamental and seminal contribution to physics, chemistry and mineralogy. Based on study of related compounds, they introduced the idea of compound radicals in organic chemistry.

Wöhler was a very versatile scientist. He devised a new method for isolating aluminum, boron, titanium, beryllium, selenium, phosphorus and yttrium. He discovered that silicon could be obtained in crystals. He also discovered silicon nitride, silicon tetrahydride, and calcium carbide.

He participated in the discovery of the crystalline form of boron and of the hydrogen compounds of silicon. He developed a process for obtaining nickel and established a factory for the production of the metal. In electrochemistry he constructed galvanic elements for batteries.

Wöhler was an honorary member of various academies of science and scientific societies around the world, and he received numerous scientific honors. Wöhler's discoveries and his contributions to scientific journals had an immense impact on the theory of chemistry.[6]

Faraday had been the first to discover semiconductor material when, in 1833, he observed that the electric conductivity of silver sulphide increases as its temperature rises. From thereon, groundbreaking insights by generations of scientists resulted in the theoretical construct and ultimately in the production of semiconductor material and from there to the transistor. Transistors are made up of bands of electron-rich and electron-poor areas sitting next to each other. The flow of electric current can be controlled by manipulating the quantum transitions between bands. It was mostly German physicists who fashioned a revolutionary explanation of matter: Albert Einstein, Max Planck, Wolfgang Pauli and Erwin Schrödinger were among the most prominent. Werner Heisenberg made the breakthrough to quantum mechanics.

Karl Ferdinand Braun (1850-1918) studied physics at the University of Berlin and received his doctorate in 1872 with a

paper on the oscillations of elastic strings. After appointments at Würzburg, Leipzig, Marburg, Karlsruhe and Tübingen, he became director of the Physical Institute and professor of physics at the University of Strassburg. His interest in the electrical conductivity of metal salts led to his study of metal sulfide crystals and other crystalline solids.

At the age of 24, he discovered asymmetric conduction in metal sulfide crystals. He used the rectifying properties of the galena crystal, a semiconductor material composed of lead sulfide, to create the cat's whisker diode. Named after the object it most resembles, a cat's whisker is merely a thin, sharply pointed wire. In fact, he discovered the point-contact rectifier effect. Thus was born the first semiconductor device. The result was a "rectifying diode" which lets current through one way but hinders flow the other way. Braun's groundbreaking discovery opened the field of semiconductor microelectronics, marking the beginning of the electronics age. But the potential and the practical importance of his experiments were not understood.

In 1897, he built the first cathode ray oscilloscope - the Braun tube - a display device used today in computers, automated teller machines, video game machines, video cameras, monitors, oscilloscopes and radar displays. It was known that if high voltage was applied between two electrodes in a low pressure glass tube, electrons were emitted from the cathode and traveled to the anode. It also was known that certain materials would luminesce when struck by the electrons. Using this information Braun built the cathode ray tube. He succeeded in producing a narrow stream of electrons guided by means of a magnetic field and alternating voltage that could trace patterns on a fluorescent screen. This invention also became an important laboratory research instrument. He never patented his invention, but published a detailed description.

In 1898, he became interested in wireless telegraphy. Marconi had patented a system of wireless telegraphy, but the signals could be sent only over short distances. Braun solved the problem by producing a sparkless antenna circuit - patented in 1899 - that linked transmitter power to the antenna circuit inductively. This invention greatly increased the range of a transmitter and has since been applied to radar, radio, and television. Braun's contributions to the development of wireless telegraphy are overshadowed by Marconi who actively sought publicity while Braun saw his work in terms of contributing to the advancement of science. In 1909, he shared the Nobel Prize in Physics with Marconi for achievements in wireless telegraphy.

Ferdinand Braun was not only a scientist; he was also a pioneer in the field of technology transfer. He co-founded a company named Telebraun, which after several mergers became Telefunken. In 1915, he sailed to New York to testify in a radio-related patent case. When the United States entered the war, he was unable to return to Germany and died in New York in 1918.[7]

A century ago, Max Planck formulated the notion of the quantum. The advent of quantum mechanics provided the first real understanding of how atoms were bonded together into solid crystals. Technologies such as the transistor, the laser and the light-emitting diode, exploit the wave-like nature of the electron. Einstein concluded that the fact that a light beam could knock electrons out of metal can only be explained if the light comes in discrete lumps, called photons. As it evolved, quantum theory held that, under some conditions, at the subatomic level, matter behaves like a particle, but under others like a wave.

In 1879, the Russian chemist Mendeleev created the periodic table of the elements, giving each known element a position. He also identified gaps that would be filled with as yet undiscovered elements.

Clemens Alexander Winkler (1838-1904) was born in Freiberg, Saxony, the son of a chemist who operated smalt works. As a boy,

he was fascinated by minerals. When he entered the Freiberg Bergakademie, he knew more about analytical chemistry than his teachers. He made an electrochemical analysis of gases and, at the age of 25, he published *Lehrbuch der technischen Gasanalyse*. He built new laboratory equipment and invented novel procedures. In 1873, he was appointed professor of chemistry at the Bergakademie Freiberg.

In 1885, a silver ore of unusual appearance was extracted from a mine nearby. It was a metallic-looking greyish ore that consisted mainly of silver and sulphur, with small quantities of mercury and iron oxide, plus traces of arsenic.

After making a quantitative analysis, he observed that the sum of all the ingredients did not add up to the original quantity. When the analysis consistently came out 7 percent low, he spent four months finding a sulfide that was soluble in water and dilute acids but quite insoluble in concentrated acids. At first he attributed this to some substance that escaped in the vapor produced while the ore which was being heated with chlorine ions in an acid solution. He tried to locate the missing substance and experimented with several formulas until he eventually succeeded in isolating it.

He investigated the material and after careful analysis he concluded that 6 to 7 percent could not be identified. After several weeks of painstaking search, he came to the conclusion that argyrodite contained an unknown element.

He could not identify it but discovered that it fitted the description of the hypothetical mineral whose existence Dmitri Mendeleev had predicted and for which he had left a space in his *Periodic Law of the Chemical Elements*. He had called it eka-silicon. Winkler decided to rename it germanium, in tribute to his homeland.

A rare element, never found pure in nature, germanium has a metallic appearance. It is not a metal but a metalloid, intermediate in properties between the metals and the non-metals. It conducts electricity, but not as well as true metals. Therefore it is called a semiconductor. Ultra-pure germanium, doped with arsenic, gallium or other elements is used in a vast number of electronic applications.[8]

Julius Edgar Lilienfeld, (1882-1963) studied physics, chemistry and philosophy at the University of Berlin with

special emphasis on experimental physics. In 1905, he obtained his Ph.D. with a dissertation on the use of light spectra for quantitative analysis of gas mixtures.

In 1910, he became a physics professor at the University of Leipzig where he undertook research on various electrical discharge phenomena. His interests focused on cryogenics, the branch of physics that relates to the production and effects of very low temperatures. In 1911, he filed a US patent for separating gas mixtures. From 1914 through the early 1920s, he made important contributions to x-ray tube design, and received six US patents.

In the 1920s, Lilienfeld operated the first large scale hydrogen liquidation facility in Germany. The product was used to fill Zeppelin airships and for cryogenic research. He continued his work on electrical discharges, extended his investigations to field emission of electrons, and applied this to the development of cold-cathode high-vacuum X-ray tubes.

In 1921, he visited the US to lecture and to attempt recuperation of the rights to his US patents which had been seized during the war by the Alien Property Custodian. In 1926, he emigrated to the US and held a series of temporary appointments, including one at New York University.

In 1926, he applied for the first of three patents that described solid-state amplifying devices. The invention related to a "method of controlling the flow of an electric current in an electrically conducting medium of minute thickness, which comprises subjecting the same to an electrostatic influence to impede the flow of said current by maintaining at an intermediate point in proximity thereto a potential in excess of the particular potential prevailing at that point."

In his patent application of December 8, 1928 he claimed: "An amplifier for electric currents, comprising two outer layers and an intermediate layer in intimate contact therewith, the layers being of material such that asymmetric couples are formed by the respective outer layers with the opposite faces of the intermediate layers and being interconnected in part thereby, means to apply potentials of same sign to the outer layers, and means to apply a potential of the opposite sign to the intermediate layer."

The patents correctly outlined the field-effect principle. The concept was that an electric field applied through the surface of a semiconductor could modify the density of charge in the body of the material and, thereby, change its conductivity. All attempts to make such a device had to that point been unsuccessful.

In 1928, he took a research and development position with Amrad, Inc., a manufacturer of radios and radio parts. There he began work on the electrochemistry of anodic aluminum oxide films and their application in the manufacture of electrolytic capacitors. An eclectic scientist, Lilienfeld obtained 15 German patents and 60 US patents on a wide variety of devices: a loudspeaker, a spark plug, vacuum tube seals, a pupillograph for eye examinations, a motion picture camera for industrial use, elastic fabrics and garments, and improvements in electrolytic capacitor construction, electrolytes, foil anodizing methods, and assembly techniques.[10]

Robert von Lieben (1878-1913) attended lectures at the University of Vienna without ever passing an examination. He

spent one year as assistant to Professor Walter Nernst in Göttingen, after which he created his own laboratory in Vienna to perform physical and chemical experiments. Ever since high school he had been interested in physics and chemistry. He even worked as an unsalaried employee at Siemens, in Nuremberg. His parents were very wealthy. In 1904, he bought a company manufacturing telephones and decided to expand it.

He systematically improved the electronic components of the system. Being financially independent, he was able to switch from one project to another. Together with a team of highly competent scientists, he concentrated on whatever topic he was momentarily interested in.

Robert von Lieben became fascinated with the problem of amplifying voice signals and wanted to build an effective amplifier. In 1905, he built a cathode-ray tube, its electron beam being steered towards or away from a target electrode by magnetic coils. A patent was granted in 1906. This made him the inventor of the amplifying valve, although it would be quite some time before it was perfected.

He was the first to discover that the anode current can be controlled by means of a perforated metal plate - a grid. In 1910, he patented the cathode ray tube with grid control. Both were essential for the development of radio and television technology. This was another path-breaking advance in the developmental level of electronic valves.

The two patents dated 1910 show the different constructions, especially the introduction of the grid which can be understood as a simplification of the former arrangement of the electrodes - thus making the valve more reliable. Nevertheless, there were still problems as regards the dependence on temperature and the stability of the pressure of the mercury vapor.Von Lieben wanted to find out if his ideas could be commercialized. He negotiated with several German companies who set up a consortium to commercialize his ideas. For the patent rights von Lieben obtained the huge sum of 100,000 German marks; plus a license fee for each valve. The Lieben Konsortium - AEG, Siemens, Telefunken and Felten & Guilleaume - was made up of companies engaged in fierce competition for control of the German telephony market. Each tried to improve on the von Lieben valve. Several scientists, including Schottky invested much research to make it work. Due to the instability of the valves, the industry soon switched from gas-filled tubes to vacuum tubes. In 1913, von Lieben volunteered for the military service; he accidentally fell from a horse and was heavily injured. He never completely recovered and his accident was probably the reason for his early death. The Lieben valve never became a central element in electronics, but it paved the way for the transistor and the information age.[11]

Walter Schottky (1886-1976) was awarded a doctorate at the Humboldt University for his thesis on the Special Theory of Relativity. His tutor was Max Planck. For several years he

alternated between an academic career and industrial research in vacuum electronics and semiconductor electronics.

In 1913, he formulated the basic law relating current in a valve to the applied voltage, or what is known as the "three-halves law". Between 1915 and 1919, at Siemens' industrial research laboratories in Berlin, he pursued his investigations in electronic valves resulting in the invention of the screen-grid the tetrode, the first tube and multigrid vacuum tube.

In 1918, in his classic paper on noise in valve amplifiers, he reached the conclusion that there are two sources of noise. The first occurs in the input circuit and results from the random motion of charge caused by the thermal motion of the molecules in the conductors. The second source of noise is caused by the randomness of the emission from the cathode and the randomness of the velocity of the emitted electrons. His findings led to better valves and benefited the next phase of his career, semiconductor research.

His work with semiconductors is considered the most important part of his career. Throughout the 1920s, he gathered material which he used for his book *Thermodynamik* in which he formulated the thermodynamic theory of purified solids and revealed the existence of electron "holes" in the valence-band structure of semiconductors. The material had become pure enough for controlled applications. In 1935, he noticed that a vacancy in a crystal lattice results when an ion from that site is displaced to the crystal's surface, a type of lattice vacancy now known as the Schottky defect.

In 1938, he formulated a theory explaining the rectifying behavior of a metal-semiconductor contact as dependent on a barrier layer at the surface of contact between the two materials. The metal semiconductor diodes later built on the basis of this theory are called <u>Schottky barrier diodes</u>. The Schottky diode is electrically similar to a p-n junction, though the current flow in the diode is due primarily to majority carriers having an inherently fast response. It is used extensively for high-frequency, low-noise mixer and switching circuits.

He also discovered that the current emitted from the metal cathode into the vacuum depends on the metal's work function, and that this function was lowered from its normal value by the presence of image forces and by the electric field at the cathode. This effect became known as the Schottky effect.

Schottky worked at Siemens until his retirement in 1958. He prefigured developments and made inventions that revolutionized the field of electronics. In today's electrical engineering community the word "Schottky" has been transformed from a name into a technical term associated with the construction of a wide range of electronic components. [12]

Oskar Heil (1908-1994) was a many-sided and versatile scientist. He studied physics, chemistry, mathematics and music at the

Universities of Heidelberg, Berlin and Munich. In Göttingen he graduated in molecular spectroscopy.

In 1934, he developed the theory of the field-effect semiconductor and applied for a German patent for the *"Anordnung zur Steuerung von Strömen."* When the excessive thoroughness and meticulousness of the German patent office delayed the examination, he translated the application and filed for a patent in Britain claiming the invention of *"An electrical amplifier or other control arrangement or device wherein one or more thin layers of semi-conductor traversed by current is or are varied in resistance in accordance with control voltage applied to one or more control electrodes arranged close to and insulated from said semi-conductor layer or layers so as to be in electrostatic association therewith. "*

The patent was issued within nine months. It refers to the p-n junction principle. Both ends of a thin semiconductor chip are covered with a metal strip and serve as source and drain contacts. A third electrode serves to regulate the conductibility of the semiconductor material. He suggested tellurium or vanadium pentoxide. There is no evidence that Heil actually tried to build a functioning device based on this concept. Practical implementation was impossible because the materials required did not yet exist. But it constitutes the theoretical invention of the capacitive current control in field-effect transistors.

In 1935, together with his wife, Agnesa Arsenjeva, he published a groundbreaking theoretical article *"Über eine neue Methode zur Erzeugung kurzer ungedämpfter elektromagnetischer Wellen grosser Intensität. "* This is the first description of the fundamental principles behind high power linear beam microwave electron tubes. They described a transit-time tube in which the three characteristic features velocity modulation, phase focusing and energy transfer were designed to occur in three separate regions, an arrangement which is also characteristic of the klystron. Shortly after, a working model was built at Stanford University.

For several years he was absorbed by an intensive research program covering the human ear and the listening and vocal apparatus of animals able to produce very loud sounds despite their small size. This led to his discovery of the principle on which the Air Velocity Transformer is based. By applying this principle to the design of a loudspeaker diaphragm, he achieved a revolutionary breakthrough and solved the fundamental problems of diaphragm mass, inertia and self-resonance.

He spent some time in Britain working at Standard Telephone and Cables where he developed the Heil tube which is the forerunner of the klystron, the first vacuum tube able to overcome transit-time effects in triodes and tetrodes. Klystrons are the most efficient of linear beam microwave tubes and are capable of the highest peak and average powers.

Heil returned to Germany the day before Britain declared war. For several years he worked at Standard Elektrik Lorenz in Berlin. He was captured by the US Army before the end of the war and, since his name was on a list of important German scientists, he was hustled off to the US. He was sent to Dayton, Ohio where the Air Force had a vacuum tube research facility. After the war, this operation was transferred to Ohio State where Heil was involved as a consultant in projects that resulted from his original idea, but without recognition of his early work on the klystron. He felt some bitterness for not getting his just share of the fame and fortune. For several years, he taught at several universities, while being active in various research institutes. Like many German scientists, his contribution to the advancement of science was occulted by the outcome of the war. [13]

Robert Wichard Pohl (1884-1976) studied physics in Heidelberg and Berlin. In 1920, he was appointed professor at the

University of Göttingen where he taught experimental physics for 32 years. His methodical lectures and textbooks came to be widely known as the "System Pohl."

For several years, he investigated the electrical and optical properties of highly purified alkali halide crystals containing a stoichiometric excess of alkali metal atoms. He foresaw the possibility of controlling electric current in solid-state crystals through a grid. His first successful experiments in solid-state repeaters were conducted with the help of his assistant Rudolf Hilsch.

In 1933, in an address to the scientific community, Pohl made the visionary forecast that vacuum tubes would one day be replaced by semiconductors in radio sets, provided the movement of the electrons could be controlled. He had in fact forecast the transistor principle.

In 1938, Rudolf Hilsch and Robert Pohl published a paper called *"Versuche zur Steuerung von Elektronenströmen mit einem Dreielektronenkristall und Model einer Sperrschicht."* It was a description of a three-electrode crystal used as an amplifier. The rectification in a semiconductor boundary is analogous to that obtained in a vacuum tube diode. In the vacuum tube, current flows more easily in one direction than in the other when the cathode with the higher work function is made positive with respect to the other cathode. This is analogous to the n-type semi-conductor in contact with a metal which has a small work function. A p-type semi-conductor in contact with a high work function metal is analogous to a reversal in the sign of rectification. The charge carriers are now holes. This analogy stimulated a number of researchers to consider the insertion of a "grid" into the semiconductor, as in the vacuum tube triode, thus producing an amplifier. The unsolvable problem was the technique of placing this 'grid' at the proper position. Hilsch and Pohl succeeded in putting a grid in an alkali halide crystal, making, in principle, an active solid-state triode.

Unfortunately their device had a "high frequency cut-off" of about 1 Hz. It made the device unusable for practical purposes. However, this was the first solid state amplifier or three-electrode-crystal. The experiment foreshadowed the possibility of a new technology as a replacement of the vacuum tube and was an important milestone on the way to the transistor.

The device modeled the vacuum tube, but the materials properties were not well understood. This, however, was probably the first demonstration of a solid-state amplifier. All other tests on semiconductor layers to influence carrier flow by applied fields had been unsuccessful because of the negligible field influence (penetration) due to the shielding surface charges.[14]

These are the scientists who achieved the major revolutionary theoretical breakthroughs that led to the realization of a semiconductor able to control, amplify and generate electrical signals. They used semiconductor materials that have since been discarded, and did not succeed in developing the techniques required for purifying them. Each of them added new concepts and ideas that contributed to the advancing frontier of solid-state science. Without them, modern solid state physics is unthinkable.

Yet, their work has hardly been recognized. When national prestige is involved, historians tend to be parochial, neglectful and prejudiced. History is largely self-correcting, but it can take a long time. Written by the victors, postwar historiography has turned a blind eye to the achievements of the German scientists who formed the bedrock of computer science. Unlike William Shockley, Walter Brattain and John Bardeen who have their place of honor in the Hall of Fame, and pioneers such as Alan Turing, Charles Babbage and the code-breakers of Bletchley, who have their names on the cover of well published books, most of them are hardly known, even in their homeland. Despite decades of shared peace and prosperity, prejudice about Germany is still widespread. It seems this has somewhat afflicted German historians with a chronic fatigue syndrome which tends them to bow to what is politically correct.

The ultimate purpose of this fundamental research in the 1920s and 1930s was the steering of electric current. Germany has a long tradition of technical brilliance in engineering and in basic research. In 1939, Otto Hahn produced a nuclear reaction "in opposition to all the phenomena observed up to the present." The same year, an aircraft powered by a jet engine patented by Hans von Ohain made its first test flight. Between 1901 and 1940, 15 Nobel Prizes in chemistry were awarded to German scientists; six went to the UK and to France and three to the United States. After the war, hundreds of top scientists moved more or less voluntarily to the United States and to the Soviet Union, to work on military and civilian projects, initiating the most massive brain drain in history. In the field of semiconductor materials, the German scientific community has an historical record of research work and of patents that is unique.

The exchange of ideas between the laboratories and the universities led to a remarkably efficient style of scientific research, both co-operative and competitive, involving discussions, correspondence, advice, critical observations, occasional skepticism, disagreement and personality clashes. The interdisciplinary research, the co-operation between theoretical and experimental physicists, mathematical physicists and chemists contributed immensely to the growth of solid-state physics and semiconductor technology during the period 1930-1945. The term "solid-state physics" is a post-war expression. The term "*Festkörperphysik*" was commonly used before the war in German scientific literature. Until 1938, solid-state research remained essentially academic. It was conducted to advance fundamental knowledge with no thought of practical use until the scientific community began to realize that semiconductors might have a military and industrial potential as repeaters capable of replacing the vacuum tube.

The mechanism of semiconductors discovered by Walter Schottky and other physicists led to the invention of rectifiers and photovoltaic cells. Until then, germanium was used only for making point-contact rectifiers. In 1942, Heinrich Welker was granted a patent for a point-contact rectifier for high-frequency electromagnetic waves. Schottky had brought him upon the idea of trying semiconductor detectors. They discussed extensively the impact of impurities, both on the surface of semiconductors and inside. Welker experimented with germanium single crystals for the purpose of achieving ultra-pure quality. They were intended to be used for point-contact rectifiers and for the control of current in semiconductors. This allowed Siemens to manufacture a vast number of germanium crystal diodes during the war.

For the development of a functioning transistor, control of materials and technological execution are as important as the concept itself. An essential prerequisite for successful experiments was the availability of single crystals. During the 1920s, several unsuccessful attempts intended to control the current in solid-state diodes and convert them into triodes had been made. But the theory was ahead of available technology. It was achieved after the war, when high-purity silicon and germanium crystals for use in radar detectors led to a better theoretical understanding of the quantum mechanical states of carriers in semiconductors, and also to improvements in fabrication.

Wartime forced-march imperatives did wonders for the advancement of technology. Microelectronics came to the forefront of engineering science, creating a momentum that still goes on. Science and technology had become more effective weapons than masses of men. Electronic computers emerged out of the need of the military for superfast calculators that performed at lightning speed without human intervention. During World War II, Allied and German researchers had run a frantic race to achieve higher-frequency operations of airborne radar sets and had made substantial progress. Radar technology changed the nature of warfare by making it possible to "see" for hundreds of miles, even at night. Radar worked by sending out a radio wave and analyzing the reflected wave after it bounced off any objects in the air or under water. The rectifier translated the reflected signal into the direct current necessary for visualization on the screen.

The most advanced technology, based on decades of developing basic concepts and formulating theory had been put into practice and climaxed in applied research. Germany was far ahead in solid-state technology.

Every important technical advance requires gestation time. Basic research and applied research are necessary precursors to the development of any technology. Some theoretical work in the area of semiconductors had been conducted at university level but the results had not seeped through.

The processes applied in the fabrication of semiconductors are extraordinarily complex. Technology development normally involves theories that coalesce in conjunction with cumulative learning-by-doing. The transistor is made of a combination of materials and formulae whose composition requires a huge chemical and experimental warehouse. A functioning transistor requires crystals of a purity that was unobtainable at the time. There was neither the theoretical learning nor the practical expertise in purification technology.

Solid-state technology is complex, and was accessible only to very few scientists. To illustrate the problem: in 1942, Welker wanted to deliver a seminar about Schottky's barrier detector diode before an audience of scientists. Professor Thirring warned him:

Although the audience will consist exclusively of academics who have studied chemistry and physics, there is hardly anyone who is familiar with the junction field-effect concept, so that you may consider them at best as educated laymen. I leave it to you to decide whether such a subject can be made digestible in one talk. [15]

Scientists develop hypotheses, design and conduct experiments, collect and interpret data and write down the results. Technological innovation is a process resulting from intimate interaction between theory and experimentation. Adventurous hypotheses are followed by testing and speculative work. It requires the combination of new findings with the existing store of technical knowledge and scientific theory, plus an occasional analytical insight accruing from personal research. The study of solid-state matter is a multidisciplinary field that involves both experimentalists and theoreticians in physics, chemistry, chemical engineering, materials science and electrical engineering. The scientific process is a problem-solving method which follows a standard procedure in order to answer a question, based on facts and evidence. It is the systematic pursuit of accessible knowledge, and involves as necessary conditions the collection of data through observation and experiment, the formulation of hypotheses and the testing and confirmation of the hypotheses. Science advances slowly by answering one question at a time, which in turn opens the door for further research. Theories are construed as speculative and tentative conjectures or guesses in an attempt to overcome problems. Science moves by trial and error, by conjectures and refutations.

A true scientific test must be controlled and reproducible. One essential prerequisite for the functioning of a semiconductor is a high-purity material. The implementation of an idea or a theory requires the availability of qualitatively adequate materials, and an intimate understanding of the manufacturing process.

The research by German scientists was well documented; a vast number of articles and laboratory reports recorded the results of their experiments. These articles were published in scientific journals such as *Zeitschrift für Physik, Die Frequenz* and *Archiv der Elektrischen Übertragung.*

Heinrich Welker studied mathematics and physics at the University of Munich. For several years he was Assistant

Professor to Arnold Sommerfeld, one of the founders of modern theoretical physics. In 1940, he decided to shift from fundamental research to practical solid-state physics and joined the Flugfunkforschungsinstitut, a research institute dedicated to the application of microwave communications systems. There he experimented with ultra-high frequency radio waves.

In 1942, he returned to Munich University where he conducted experiments with germanium crystals for the purpose of achieving ultra-pure quality. He was granted a patent for a point-contact rectifier for high-frequency electromagnetic waves. He also studied the impact of impurities, both on the surface of semiconductors and inside. It was the beginning of a new materials science: solid-state physics and crystallography.

In 1945, shortly before the end of the war, he completed his research and applied for a patent relating to the use of electron currents germanium or silicon for control purposes. In the document he refers to Heil's and Schottky's concepts and to Pohl's and Hilsch's patents. He describes in detail the various experiments he conducted over a period of several years. The materials mentioned in the patent application are silicon and germanium. He mentions specifically that he considers these materials as semiconductors and not as metals. In the patent he formulated the theory of the field effect, but was unable to obtain transconductance in laboratory tests. After the war, until 1955, scientists were not allowed to pursue any advanced research in occupied Germany. That same year, Welker repeated his patent application. Because of high-powered pressures, it took until 1973 for the patent to be granted.

From 1946 to 1951, together with Herbert Mataré, he worked at the F&S Westinghouse laboratory, near Paris. The company had contracted with the French government for the production of germanium rectifiers with high reverse voltage. Germanium was chosen for the tests because it has a lower melting point than silicon. Welker concerned himself with the purification of crystals.

When the French government abandoned the semiconductor project, Welker joined the Siemens research laboratories in Erlangen, where he stayed until his retirement in 1977. There he identified the potential of intermetallic III-V compounds as semiconducting components, paving the way for microwave semiconductor elements as well as luminescent and laser diodes. The III-V compound semiconductors are now part of most cell-phone and optical TV channels and will be an essential part of the future high bandwidth fiber communications.

He also laid the scientific foundations for the development of the light-emitting diodes with his pioneering research into gallium arsenide. Some predict that if these tiny low-power luminaries can be commercially produced, the light bulb will face stiff competition. Welker did not live to see the results and witness the impact of his work. In 1976, Siemens set up the Heinrich Welker Memorial Medal for contributions to the field of III-V compound semiconductor development. [16]

Herbert Franz Mataré was born on September 12, 1912 in Aachen. His grandfather was managing director of a large

chemical company. His father was a portrait painter; his mother taught mathematics at school before her marriage. Since his early youth he enjoyed listening to classical music. At 11 eleven years old, he built a radio receiver with lead-sulfide crystals and cat's whiskers, tiny metal wires that are moved by hand around a crystal to pick up radio signals.

He became intrigued and fascinated by the fact that he could put together a detector receiver and thus capture several radio stations. At school he was mainly interested in mathematics. After finishing his secondary education, he went to Geneva to study mathematics, physics and chemistry. He returned to his home town and continued studies in mathematics, theoretical physics, chemistry, electrochemistry, physical chemistry, electrical machines and high voltage engineering at the Technical University Aachen. He also studied technical English and French.

In August 1939, with his diplomas in hand, he applied for a job at the Berlin research laboratory of Telefunken. Among solid state scientists, the basic chemical and physical properties of semiconductors were known. For several decades, research had been an academic pursuit. But scientists involved in radar technology began to realize that semiconductors might have a military and industrial potential as repeaters replacing the vacuum tube in radar.

On September 1, German troops invaded Poland. France and Britain declared war. Telefunken had set up a microwave department in 1933 to produce radar systems for the military. Originally, the company produced radar equipment working at about 50cm wavelength for ground-based antiaircraft batteries. The laboratory had started a program to refine microwave radar in order to achieve higher-frequency operation of airborne radar sets. The miniaturization of vacuum tubes had met a technical limit and a solid-state equivalent was urgently needed. Research on ultra-high-frequency rectifiers aimed at the development of an effective crystal mixer as a duodiode or three-electrode crystal.[17]

When Mataré joined the research team, it was obvious that a crash program was needed to overcome the difficulties with the miniature vacuum diodes, duodiodes and cm-wave generators (magnetrons, klystrons and other tube oscillators). Vacuum-duodiodes were in use to eliminate the oscillator noise in mixer stages of the heterodyne receivers. The director of the receiver laboratory asked Mataré to concentrate on receiver technology, the construction of mixer stages, the elimination of oscillator noise and the circuit construction of cm-wave concentric and hollow-tube resonant circuits the construction of test emitters for sensitivity measurements. As the available magnetrons for 10 cm wavelength were inefficient, Mataré started with a set-up for noise measurements at decreasing wavelengths, down to 10 cm.

Professor H. Rukop, a vacuum-tube specialist, suggested that he try point contact semiconductor diodes as mixers in heterodyne receivers. He used known compounds like silicon-carbide and lead sulfide, but obtained better reproducible results with germanium and silicon which had been developed by H. Welker at the University of Munich and by K. Seiler at the University of Breslau. In an extensive study of the signal/noise ratio, he compared the vacuum duodiodes with semiconductor detectors and tried to make crystal duodiodes to improve on the signal/noise ratio in push/pull microwave mixers. To this end he had to equalize the detector characteristics by projecting them on an oscilloscope and by trying to bring them into coincidence. This was difficult with compound crystals but feasible with germanium and silicon. In all cases, the whiskers had to be placed a fraction of a mm. apart, as the crystal material was very inhomogeneous.[18]

After a while, he was able to refine and focus his research on ultra-high-frequency rectifiers. But the crystal material then available was insufficiently homogeneous. Yet, he was able to measure the favorable noise values at the cm-wavelength as compared to vacuum diodes.

Highly doped silicon crystals were much better suited for diode mixers than highly purified germanium diodes. Rectification of such frequencies did not work with high barrier capacities. Germanium point-contact diodes had a higher capacity than silicon diodes, because of the larger space charge. Recovery time was much better with highly doped silicon detectors.[19]

In 1942, he published the results on noise measurements in crystal rectifiers. The following year, he applied for a patent on crystal diodes with electrolytic contacts.[20] In 1944, in Leubus, Silesia, while testing how to apply oscillator noise compensation with duodiodes made from crystal detectors, he found that a second whisker could influence the first barrier layer in certain crystals as proposed in the patents by Lilienfeld and Heil, who claimed a field influence. His research was not sufficiently advanced to decide whether it was a field effect or injection of minority charges.

In microwave detection, silicon had the advantage in terms of internal resistance as well as capacity. For space-charge injection, the higher purity of germanium resulted in a wider space-charge. He figured that if there was some way to control the flow of electrons from one barrier layer to the other, it might produce amplification. Germanium thus seemed a better candidate for amplification than silicon. Germanium was easier to purify because of its lower melting point. He did not have the time to concentrate on barrier layer interaction research, since he had to deliver mixer diodes for receivers and construct sensitivity test emitters.

The silicon layers supplied by K. Seiler were highly doped by evaporation of silicon on graphite and were excellent for the radar mixer circuit. Under pressure to deliver working prototypes, Mataré noted the possibility to influence one detector barrier by the other in the case of germanium but concentrated on the delivery of a mixer with silicon. In his notebook he mentioned this for later study of eventual use for amplification.[21]

Basis for evaluation of the barrier layer was Schottky's rectifier theory. Purified germanium crystals with whiskers of a contact area below 3×10^{-3} mm^2 had capacity values from less than $1/10$ pF at reverse bias but 2 to 3 pF at forward bias.

Schottky had used the term "defect electron". He found similar capacity values for Mg/Se and Bi/Se rectifiers. It became apparent that in the case of microwave detection, silicon had the advantage in terms of internal resistance (short recovery time) as well as small capacity. The wider space charge in germanium made this material a better candidate for eventual barrier-layer injection and amplification n three-electrode crystals.

When the Russian army closed in, the site was abandoned and most of its equipment was lost. The personnel were transferred to Thuringia and a new laboratory was set up. It was hardly in operation when American troops occupied the area and Mataré's research came to an end. He was given permission to join his family, and for several months he worked as a farmhand in the fields.

Fortunately, the US Army began organizing college level courses. He was appointed as an instructor and taught physics, mathematics and chemistry to students from Harvard and other schools. These courses were recognized by the US universities. At that time he received the patent for which he had applied while working at Telefunken in 1943, concerning a crystal detector with alloyed point contacts by electrolytic deposition of a metal like copper or silver through a thin insulator layer. It was claimed that by this method several contacts could be made to the crystal.[22]

When the military academies closed, he went to Aachen Technical University where he taught physics and electronics. On several occasions, British, French and US members of the Technical Field Information Agencies interrogated him about his research in semiconductors and radar. France had no scientists with any experience in radar technology or in solid state physics. The government wanted to catch up as quickly as possible. But solid state physics was a new and very abstruse science that had to be learned from scratch. Mataré was interviewed by French officers.

He spoke French very fluently and was invited to move to Paris and set up production of germanium diodes at F&S Westinghouse, a small company under contract with the French government. Heinrich Welker had been approached with a similar offer. At war's end he had settled down in Planegg, near Munich and tried to make a living as an engineering consultant. Since scientific research was strictly limited in Germany, he gladly accepted the invitation to work in France.[23]

Mataré and Welker met in the office of the director of F&S Westinghouse and were given the assignment of setting up production of germanium diodes for use in radar. They could thus use the considerable experience they had acquired in this field, but intended to actively pursue their research on crystal amplifiers.

Welker concerned himself with the growth of germanium crystals left over from the war years, while Mataré concentrated on the production of diodes and the testing of components. Their collaboration allowed them to fill in the loopholes and the blurred edges of the technology. It took quite some time to obtain satisfactory results. They had to equalize detector characteristics in an effort to make duodiodes - crystals with two whiskers - which had to yield equal characteristics.

Mataré had lost his laboratory notes and his reference books accumulated during the war, but the memory of his findings was clearly implanted in his mind. Together with Welker, he set up a production line of diodes. But he also wanted to pursue the research on duodetector mixers. Their wartime experience allowed them to refine their tests and to develop a better understanding of cause and effect. In 1946/47, the production of qualified detectors with sufficient reverse voltage proceeded until a monthly delivery of thousands of units was achieved.

Aside from Ge-diode production, Mataré was allowed to pursue his work on microwave tests and devices. Continuing his research on duodiodes and signal/noise ratios, barrier layer interference came up again. He resumed the research intended to eliminate the local oscillator noise in cm-wave mixer stages. In similar tests, he observed barrier-layer interference when duodiodes were tested for equal diode characteristics. He also noticed that in some cases he obtained injection and amplification when the crystal had been cut from a larger ingot.

The production of diodes required high-reverse voltage, which meant low impurity density of the crystal material. Progress was made when Welker obtained crystal material, which he tried to purify by re-melting in pure graphite. When testing duodiodes for balanced mixers, Mataré found again, as in 1944 that he could influence one detector side with the second whisker. But at that time his immediate project was noise reduction in mixer stages and building a test sender for sensitivity measurements.

When Welker was able to acquire germanium of better quality, Mataré obtained an amplifier effect. Amplification was entirely dependent on the purity of the germanium. Mataré used grain boundaries to space the emitter-collector whiskers farther apart, which cannot be done with monocrystalline surfaces. The fixation at sub-micron distances was very difficult and tended to produce a short circuit. These observations allowed Mataré to develop the theory of minority carrier injection.[24]

When testing duodiodes for oscillator noise compensation with germanium crystals, he was able to measure amplification. He found that the current of one side increased when the other side was biased positively. He discussed the amplification with Welker who interpreted the result as a field effect while Mataré was convinced it was due to a p-type zone in the crystal.

The fixation at sub-micron distances was very difficult and sensitive to a short circuit. He was able to keep point contact distances up to 100 microns. This was possible because he used a grain boundary (p-type core in n-type crystals) between the two whiskers to transport the emitter voltage to the junction on the other side. It was also proof that minority injection was involved.

As the high-reverse voltage meant low impurity density of the crystal material, results improved gradually due to repeated re-melting. With the development of crystal material from polycrystalline to monocrystalline germanium and silicon, diode production advanced to more stable and efficient rectifiers. When they were able to produce larger germanium crystals, they obtained a better mass/surface ratio. By improving the purity of the germanium, they obtained defect-electron conduction and thus the transistor effect with clear high-frequency amplification. As germanium was easier to purify than silicon, it was with germanium that minority-carrier injection was first realized.[25]

Mataré had designed the holders for the use of a binocular microscope which allowed a flexible adjustment of the whiskers, with a good base contact to the crystal. It also involved making a low resistivity base contact and holders or fixtures where he could adjust the distance of the whiskers (microns), while measuring the transconductance, base resistance and frequency behavior. Part of this was a pulse generator to fix the contacts by a thermal transit pulse. Such test stations had to be designed and built in-house.

The position of the whiskers had to be stabilized with epoxy. In addition, duodiodes for use in radar - which had no amplification action - had to be equalized on the oscilloscope and in a mixer circuit for cm-waves. This and the cm-wave mixing circuit had also to be built in-house. Mataré made the design which was executed by high-precision mechanics. Such test-stations had to be designed and built in-house, as none of these was on the market. Part of this was a pulse generator to fix the contacts by a thermal transit pulse.

Pursuing the research started in Silesia, Mataré constructed duodiodes which had to be equalized on the oscilloscope. With crystals of larger diameter and higher bulk/surface ratio some equalization of characteristics became feasible, but with higher resistivity Ge barrier layer interference (minority injection) became a problem. While these crystals were useless as mixer crystals, they became the first three electrode amplifiers. At tests on the oscilloscope, one side changed when the other was tested, especially when one side was biased in reverse and the other in the forward direction.[26]

This led Mataré to attach a high-frequency circuit on one side and to observe the signal strength on the other side. It became clear that this was due to carrier injection or p-type channeling. The work was delayed because there was disagreement about the actual carrier flow. Welker maintained that it was due to a local field change as described in his 1945 patent application. He had grown the crystals but did not participate in the tests and measurements and was not familiar with the mixer-diode problems of characteristics equalization. He was fully occupied with his research on the intermetallic III-V crystals and with the theory of superconductivity.

Mataré had done the testing and had observed a p-type zone in the crystal. In an article published in *l'Onde Electrique,* he detailed the form of the characteristics and the "interaction resistance" showing the right polarity or the bridge of positive charges which caused the reverse current of the second whisker to increase.[27]

Meanwhile, Welker was able to obtain germanium of better quality from Otavi Minen, a German company which had leftovers from its in South-West African operations, and from Vieille Montagne which mined it in Belgian Congo. The availability of purified germanium and the conversion to monocrystals resulted in the amplifier effect which broke open the whole field of epitaxial deposition of differently-doped semiconductor layers.

In micromanipulator tests on the oscilloscope barrier layer interference was definitely measured, but not recognized as injection of minorities. Early in 1948, he observed for the first time amplification with duodetectors. In May/June, he mounted the first three-electrode crystal (transistron) and showed it to the director of the company, Mr. Engel.

Working together, Mataré and Welker often discussed the theory of superconductivity and gradually improved comprehension and problem-solving skills. Welker stuck to the amphoteric conduction theory of superconductivity which he had developed as assistant to Arnold Sommerfeld in Munich.

Amplification was entirely dependent on purity of the germanium. The devices were relatively stable because Mataré used grain boundaries to space the emitter-collector whiskers farther apart, which cannot be done with monocrystalline surfaces. The fixation at sub-micron distances is very difficult and tends to produce a short circuit. He was able to keep distances up to 100 microns. The actual theory was developed later on, when he understood that the grain boundary was actually a nanostructure with high conductivity.[28]

The diode production began to work reproducibly at the end of 1947. But the crystals were still over-doped and Mataré asked Welker to change his boat design in order to obtain larger crystals. He found that the higher bulk-to-surface ratio improved the crystal structure and that there were more monocrystalline areas. This facilitated the search for equal characteristics of double diodes for microwave mixers. He also observed interference from one side (barrier) to the other, as he had seen already during previous tests in Leubus.

He discovered that crystals with grain boundaries offered barrier layer interference at much wider distances than was possible on monocrystalline areas. This was the beginning of the "grain boundary transistor", a precursor of the nanostructure devices. The diode and transistor-production was based on the ceramic holder design. Using grain boundaries as positive channels, he achieved amplification over 100 microns distant whiskers. Painstaking and meticulous testing with increasingly ultra-pure germanium and the conversion to monocrystals finally resulted in a more regular amplifier effect. In June 1948, satisfactory amplification was achieved.[29]

RÉPUBLIQUE FRANÇAISE

MINISTÈRE
DE L'INDUSTRIE ET DU COMMERCE

SERVICE
de la PROPRIÉTÉ INDUSTRIELLE

BREVET D'INVENTION

Gr. 12. — Cl. 6.

N° 1.010.427

Nouveau système cristallin à plusieurs électrodes réalisant des effets de relais électroniques.

Société anonyme dite : COMPAGNIE DES FREINS ET SIGNAUX WESTINGHOUSE résidant en France (Seine).

Demandé le 13 août 1948, à 15ʰ 44ᵐ, à Paris.
Délivré le 26 mars 1952. — Publié le 11 juin 1952.

(Brevet d'invention dont la délivrance a été ajournée en exécution de l'article 11, § 7, de la loi du 5 juillet 1844 modifiée par la loi du 7 avril 1902.)

On connaît déjà des systèmes cristallins permettant d'assurer la commande et/ou le contrôle de courants électriques à l'aide d'un semi-conducteur solide grâce à l'utilisation d'une ou plusieurs électrodes de commande, soit dans la couche d'arrêt ou de blocage dudit semi-conducteur (voir par exemple l'addition n° 38.744 du 3 juillet 1930 au brevet français n° 649.432 du 28 janvier 1928, le brevet français n° 866.372 du 5 octobre 1942), soit au voisinage immédiat des couches semi-conductrices avec un isolement approprié (voir le brevet français n° 786.454 du 1ᵉʳ mars 1935).
Mais les difficultés de réalisation industrielle de tels systèmes furent telles qu'ils durent être abandonnés ou que leur développement est resté pratiquement limité à de simples modèles expérimentaux ou à des curiosités de laboratoire. On pourra consulter, à l'appui de cette affirmation : Nachrichten von der Gesellschaft der Wissenschaften zu Göttingen, rapport annuel de R. W. Pohl 1933/34, p. 55; Schweizer Archives 1941, cahiers 1 et 3, Ueber Sperrschichten par W. Schottky; Zeitschrift f. Physik, volume 111, cahiers 5 et 6, 1938 (R. Hilsch et R. W. Pohl); Modern Theory of Solids, 1940 (F. Seitz); Crystal Rectifiers, 1948 (H. C. Torrey et C. A. Whitmer).
Pour réaliser pratiquement des systèmes comportant des semi-conducteurs solides agencés pour produire un ou des effets de relais électroniques similaires à ceux qu'on observe dans les lampes électroniques, il est nécessaire de résoudre deux difficultés. La première consiste dans le fait que le diamètre de la surface de contact entre l'aiguille métallique et le cristal doit être d'un ordre de grandeur correspondant à celui de l'épaisseur de la couche d'arrêt du cristal. La seconde consiste dans le fait que l'écartement entre les électrodes conductrices, au point de contact avec le semi-conducteur, doit être choisi de telle sorte que l'une des pointes d'électrode conductrice soit située dans la zone de la couche d'arrêt de l'autre pointe.
Avec les couches d'arrêt les plus épaisses qui ont pu être réalisées jusqu'ici, il aurait fallu prendre comme diamètre des surfaces de contact, d'une part, comme écartement des deux pointes, d'autre part, des valeurs inférieures à 5 μ. Si la première condition est réalisable, à condition de placer une aiguille sur un cristal sous une pression inférieure à 10 gr. par exemple, la seconde se heurte par contre à de très grandes difficultés mécaniques.
On a bien essayé de trouver des dispositions de semi-conducteurs à trois électrodes de dimensions macroscopiques. Mais, pour obtenir un effet de commande décelable, il faut choisir un cristal d'une concentration électronique ou à concentration de défaut électronique tellement faible que la résistance interne du dispositif, devient très élevée, ce qui rend les applications techniques absolument impraticables.
La présente invention due aux travaux des Docteurs Henri Welker et Herbert-Francois Mataré, permet de résoudre toutes ces difficultés et de porter sur le plan des réalisations industrielles de tels systèmes cristallins à plusieurs électrodes réalisant des effets de relais électroniques.
Ladite invention est essentiellement caractérisée par le fait qu'on associe dans un système à plusieurs électrodes au moins deux semi-conducteurs cristallins à caractères de conductibilité différents dont l'une des électrodes semi-conductrices constitue l'électrode de commande et comporte une couche d'arrêt ou de blocage superficielle.

On August 13, 1948, F&S applied for a French patent which was granted on 26 March 1954.

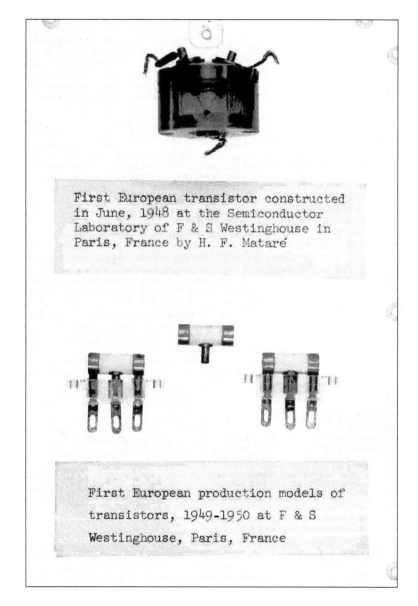

First European transistor constructed in June, 1948 at the Semiconductor Laboratory of F & S Westinghouse in Paris, France by H. F. Mataré

First European production models of transistors, 1949-1950 at F & S Westinghouse, Paris, France

Courtesy Deutsches Museum, Munich

On August 11, 1949, Mataré and Welker applied for a US patent. The application had to go through a lengthy claim adjustment procedure before the US patent was finally granted in 1954.

Patented Mar. 30, 1954

2,673,948

UNITED STATES PATENT OFFICE

2,673,948

CRYSTAL DEVICE FOR CONTROLLING ELEC-
TRIC CURRENTS BY MEANS OF A SOLID
SEMICONDUCTOR

Herbert François Mataré and Heinrich Welker,
Vaucresson, France, assignors to Societe Ano-
nyme dite: Compagnie des Freins et Signaux
Westinghouse, Paris, France

Application August 11, 1949, Serial No. 109,752

Claims priority, application France
August 13, 1948

3 Claims. (Cl. 317—235)

1

This invention relates to crystal devices for controlling electric currents by means of a solid semiconductor with the use of one or more control electrodes, either in a barrier layer of the semiconductor (see for example patent of addition No. 38,744 of July 5, 1930, to French Patent No. 649,432 of January 28, 1928, and French Patent No. 866,372 of October 5, 1942), or closely adjacent to semiconductive layers with a suitable insulator interposed therebetween (see French Patent No. 786,454 of March 1, 1935).

2

or n-type excess and p-type deficiency concentration, respectively, that the inner resistivity of the device becomes very high. Arrangements of this type cannot be used practically for technical purposes.

The present invention permits to eliminate the above-mentioned difficulties and to realize on a commercial scale multi-electrode crystal devices of this kind for producing electronic relay action.

A more specific object of this invention is a

What we claim is:
1. Multi-electrode crystal device for producing electronic relay action comprising a semi-conductor element having at least two zones of different conductivity characteristics, one of said zones being substantially of ring shape and the other zone comprising two substantially conically shaped portions extending axially from opposite directions along the axis and toward the center of the ring zone; said conical portions joining the ring zone in conical surfaces, said joining surfaces comprising at least one barrier layer, and said conical and ring shaped zones comprising individual metallic electrodes.

2. Device according to claim 1 wherein each of said conical portions has a separate electrode.

3. Device according to claim 1 wherein said conical portions meet with their tips at the center of the ring zone.

Fig. 1

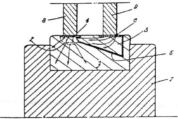

The volume of diodes produced for the PTT increased rapidly, requiring a growing number of girls to do the testing in a cramped room. The transistors were sold to the laboratory of the PTT and to the military. The engineers of the PTT or CNET (Centre National d'Etudes des Télécommunications)

mounted amplifiers and repeaters in experimental telephone lines and in radio and television receivers and transmitters. [23] Several sample shipments were also made to potential US customers.

The French authorities showed little interest. But when the invention of the transistor was announced by Bell Labs, the director of the PTT and the Secretary of State, Monsieur Thomas, came to visit the laboratory and alerted the press. [30]

For a brief period of time, the French government had a practical monopoly of functional transistors, but failed to recognize the potential of semiconductor technology. Nuclear physics had emerged as the dominant scientific discipline in the public mind and nuclear power was widely heralded as the wave of the future. France became enchanted with pursuing the nuclear genie, while ignorant of its promising transistron. It was a decision that changed the course of history.

Welker and Mataré had been working in tandem for almost three years. In 1951, realizing they had no future in France, they decided to return home. Welker joined Siemens where he continued his research on intermetallic III-V crystals. He was still convinced that the amplifiers produced at Aulnay-sous-Bois were based on the field effect which he had patented in 1945. He had often discussed the subject with Mataré and refused to accept the minority carrier concept. It seems he suspected Mataré was right after all, and decided to consign his experience in France to oblivion.

Through a French lawyer, Mataré came into contact with Jakob Michael, the owner of New England Industries, a company established in Wall Street. Before the war, Mr. Michael owned a very popular chain of department stores Defaka - Deutsches Familienkaufhaus. Being Jewish, he had migrated to the United States. After the war he recovered whatever was left of his property. Several stores had been reopened and profits were substantial. But exchange controls prevented him from converting his German marks into dollars. He thought up a scheme that would enable him to transfer his assets and was very much interested in buying German products he could sell in the United States. He supplied the funds which enabled Mataré to rent a building, buy machinery and equipment and hire the necessary personnel. It was understood that the company would produce germanium diodes and transistors, while the laboratory would continue research in silicon semiconductors which seemed to hold promise. Jacob Michael agreed to let the company grow for five years before cashing in any profits. His main purpose was to sell transistors to American customers.

Several French engineers came along and settled in Germany. Mataré was also able to attract physicists from Telefunken. Most of the machinery and equipment was supplied by Leybold. Three physicist-engineers took care of crystal growth and device operations. They were the first to apply vacuum-Czochralski-growth to silicon. Two physicists concentrated on research in III-V crystals and silicon. Three technicians built a line of test equipment and various measuring instruments, while three mechanics ran the machines. Twelve women controlled the transistors for transconductance, power amplification and frequency response. By the end of 1952, Intermetall was producing 2,000 diodes and 1,000 transistors a week. Transistors sold for the equivalent of about eight dollars; diodes four dollars. Transistor technology was breaking new ground and it was expected that the junction transistor would soon replace the point contact transistor. Silicon seemed more promising than germanium, but high quality silicon crystal was hard to produce.

The transistor presented Intermetall's team of scientists with challenges and opportunities hitherto unknown. They soon started dreaming up applications. One of them was a transistor radio. The transistor was a new technological marvel able to reduce the radio from a bulky lump of furniture to a hand-held, pocket-sized gadget. It required little power and did not burn out, thereby promising reliability and longevity.

In September 1953, at the Düsseldorf Radio Fair, a young lady wearing a black sweater and a multicolored flowery skirt demonstrated to the public a tiny battery-operated transistor radio. The housing was made of transparent Plexiglas; the sound was amplified by four transistors and transmitted through an earphone. It had been assembled by a French engineer, Georges Calon.

The press, the public, the industry and the radio technicians marveled at the size and the novelty. The magazine FUNK-TECHNIK noted:

It seems the transistor has transcended the stage of an electronic component with interesting physical properties, and has started to be put in good use in areas that were until now the exclusive domain of the vacuum tube. At the *Funkausstellung*, an impressive number of applications are on display. It may be interesting for radio technicians to learn something about how transistors are manufactured. [31]

At the fair Intermetall distributed advertising material which met with considerable interest. Graetz, one of the largest radio manufacturers, presented the world's first transistorized tabletop radio. Shortly after the end of the Radio Fair, the German government lifted the ban on foreign currency. Jacob Michael decided to sell the company. Several potential buyers showed interest; but it was Clevite Transistor of Waltham, Massachusetts, who closed the deal. Then, within a very short time, Clevite sold Intermetall to the International Telephone and Telegraph Company.

The transistors and diodes produced by Intermetall were technological marvels. The transistor radio remained a prototype. It was never produced and its ephemeral existence faded into oblivion. Since he was not allowed to conduct any scientific research in occupied Germany, Mataré decided to move with his family to the United States, hoping to resume his work in solid-state electronics.

Several years after the end of the war American intelligence officers were still looking for German scientists with advanced technical and scientific training. The Signal Corps was responsible for recruiting scientists, technicians and engineers who were ready to share their production and operational expertise in exchange for a job and eventual US citizenship.

As he was preparing to leave for the United States, Mataré received a letter from an officer of the Signal Corps inviting him to work at the Electronic Laboratory in Fort Monmouth. The US Army needed smaller and more robust equipment for its data transmission equipment and was very much interested in semiconductor amplifiers. Together with his family he sailed to New York on the US transport ship General R.E. Callan.

The employment negotiations were somewhat stand-offish and the salary was modest, but working conditions were pleasant. Mataré had long and frequent conversations with research director Harold Zahl who was very much interested in radar technology and solid-state physics and wanted him to work in semiconductor research and development. The fact that diodes and transistors had been produced at Intermetall proved that Mataré had solved problems that were still being debated in American laboratories.

Mataré's activities at the Signal Corps were limited to research in the field of crystal properties, especially lasting defects and dislocations as well as new methods for growing silicon monocrystals. The utilization of single crystals of germanium and silicon for the transistor was still controversial, even though the importance of high-purity material to achieve a high rectification current-voltage characteristic was understood. Many researchers were opposed to work on germanium single crystals because they thought that scientific research on transistors could be obtained from small specimens of polycrystalline masses of material.

Through the Signal Corps, he came into contact with Tung-Sol, a manufacturer of vacuum tubes located in Bloomfield, N.J. When Mataré was offered the job of setting up a production line of semiconductors and a research laboratory, he accepted and was pleased to get a well-paid job. He set up a laboratory for crystal growth and property measurements and ordered a Czochralski crystal puller from Leybold He put together a group of physicists and technicians and organized regular seminars on crystallography which were attended by scientists involved in semiconductor research, including W. T. Read of Bell Labs and Robert Noyce, who was then at Philco. The Signal Corps worked closely with Bell Labs on military research. He participated in several meetings of the American Physical Society and of the Electrochemical Society.[32]

Work at Tung-Sol-Lab progressed and Mataré was able to clarify essential properties of dislocations in semiconductor crystals. He had installed a first class x-ray goniometer laboratory and had started to produce installations for seed-crystal orientations. This facilitated the production of seed crystals for the Czochralski pulling method for single crystals and bicrystals. He succeeded in growing several defined grain boundaries into one boule. He also built equipment for the recrystallization of high purity silicon.

At Tung-Sol he was expected to be available any time for advice to the semiconductor production units. The high-frequency test equipment for diodes and transistors increased steadily. The laboratory was almost ready to start a test production of diodes and transistors when the director, J. Right was abruptly replaced by a Dr. Skellet who had no experience in solid-state physics and loudly claimed he had no confidence in the use of silicon. He cancelled the orders placed for machinery and equipment, including the Czochralski crystal puller.

Mataré saw no future at Tung-Sol and accepted an offer by Dr. Keck of Sylvania, to take over the semiconductor laboratory in Bayside, N.Y. Several of his colleagues went with him. Dr. Keck purchased the Czochralski equipment that had been cancelled by Tung-Sol. With his group of physicists Mataré studied cyclotron resonance on germanium monocrystals. The intent was to use this as a means to excite oscillations in the crystal as in masers.

But the lab director, Dr. Rudi Hutter and Dr. Esther Conwell who played an important role, scoffed at his experiments, saying: "Herb, one cannot bunch carriers in a semiconductor" Shortly thereafter, Charles Townes applied for a laser patent. Mataré had visited him at Columbia University a week before and had suggested that he try infrared bunching in crystals, which he rejected as impossible.

Monocrystallinity makes it possible to increase the wafer size while the microcircuit size can be decreased. Teal´s work was well known and Dr. Keck, lab director at Sylvania, had made the contribution of pulling silicon monocrystals in vacuo by a moving or floating zone. He had published this around 1952 in the Physical Review together with Dr.Golay. Walter Heywang, at Siemens, had also published an article about the "floating zone" method for silicon. When Sylvania was taken over by General Telephone and Electronics and the laboratory was transferred to Boston, Mataré decided to return to Germany.

At the TeKaDe laboratory, in Nuremberg, a group was working on new semiconductor devices such as mesa transistors, diodes and alloyed junction devices. There was also a chemist doing work on high purification of water needed in the chemical processes. His first task was to build a unit for the production of alloyed transistors. He tried to set up a special laboratory for these new devices but the management of the company did not have sufficient understanding of the detailed work needed. Director Ludendorff pressed for higher production numbers and claimed that the parameters did not meet the desired specifications. In addition, there were constant quarrels among the personnel.

When it became obvious that TeKaDe was not in a position to fulfill the demands of a modern semiconductor company, he decided to return to the United States. His expertise in solid state electronics was now well known.

Dr. Kock, the director of the laboratories of Bendix Corporation invited him to Southfield, Michigan. He was convinced that there was much potential in the field of semiconductors, especially in connection with the III-V-compounds and light generation in crystals. Mataré was put in charge of the laboratory for quantum electronics. Thanks to the company's excellent patent lawyers, he was able to apply for a number of patents and to publish about his work.[33]

The exceptional competence of his colleagues allowed him to make important measurements of the frequency-extension in photon absorption and emission at grain boundaries - the first nanometric devices. Many other topics were covered, such as the tunnel transistor about which he gave a keynote speech in the presence of the president of the American Physical Society, Dr. Goudsmith. He was also granted a patent for a light potentiometer where the resistance change was caused by a light beam, a very reliable device.

He had observed that a large number of new companies engaged in cutting-edge technology were operating in California and that the most important innovations originated from there. In 1962, when the management of Lear Siegler offered him to take over the direction of the laboratory, he moved to Santa Monica. The company was short of cash and unable to invest much in laboratory research. Management relied mainly on contract work. This allowed Mataré to establish good contacts with industry and with several government agencies in Washington.

While progress was very satisfactory, management decided to move the laboratory to the company headquarters in Grand Rapids, Michigan. Since he had just come from the area and did not want to return, he looked for another position in the neighborhood. At the Douglas Aircraft Company in Santa Monica, management wanted to set up a laboratory for electronics. He was appointed lab director heading a group of physicists and engineers with the task of installing working units for the most advanced topics in advanced electronics. He set up a group to study cyclotron resonance in semiconductors. He organized another group for optical heterodyne transmission combined with target-finding technologies. He also had started work on microwave modulation of laser beams, a project which, 40 years later, is still being discussed. But this field of research was foreign to a manufacturer of aviation hardware and rocket technology. Some of his colleagues resented having a "German" as their superior.

While he was teaching at the Fullerton California State University, he was approached by North American Aviation Inc. - later Rockwell Internat'l - to come to Anaheim. There, as laboratory advisor he was responsible for the supervision of the ongoing work, for giving advice to the engineers and presenting suggestions to the management. He advised one group to make measurements of the grain boundary barriers by electron beam injection current spectroscopy (EBIC) and by secondary electron injection current-method (SEBIC). He was first to publish about the effects of the dangling bonds.[34]

He accepted an offer to advise the Globe Union laboratory in El Monte, California. He had worked out the problem of GaAlAs/GaAs heteroepitaxy in view of the production of light emitters and solar cells for concentration. This was a melt-back process in a special oven with a programmed temperature profile. He drew up a detailed patent application for the construction of an epi-oven. This was new for Globe Union. He was put under pressure to change his consultancy contract into a full employee position with a very high salary. Globe Union filed the patent application and shortly afterwards terminated the employment contract. .It is inherent in the legal relationship of employer and employee that any product of the work which an employee is paid to do belongs to the employer. Mataré felt duped and went to court. A compromise was reached by which he was given the right to use the patent in connection with his own projects.[35]

In the course of further work in the field of epitaxy and light emitters (LED) Mataré obtained patents which served as a base for new light emitters used in TV transmissions at the companies Audio and Visual, International Rectifier Corp. and a French consultant group connected to ISSEC-France. They were also used in fiber-cable transmissions.

He left Rockwell Internat'l and set up ISSEC, a group of scientists, technical specialists, marketing specialists, financial experts and patent lawyers, who offered advice and practical assistance in technical projects concerned with electronic device design and production, as well as materials properties.

He also advised a group which was investigating the potential of producing ammonia by solar electricity and electrolysis. Cars driven by ammonia had been shown to the public and stock had been sold to investors. But the problems caused by the fact that hydrogen could be kept liquid only at low temperatures and that ammonia for cars results in dangerous nitrogen oxides had not been mentioned. Ample money was available to make tests in the desert in California. Mataré was able to start a production of heteroepitaxial GaAlAs/GaAs solar cells which at a concentration of 100 suns reached efficiencies in the 25 to 30 percent range.

Cells of about one sq-cm were placed on copper tubes with water cooling which were placed into the hollow-mirror concentrators. Another group of technicians led the generated electricity into electrolytic separator tanks for hydrogen production. Mataré had taken this task because he considered the technology as important for the future and because he had built this type of epitaxy before.

But he objected to the company's overblown advertisement campaign which tended to mislead potential investors. As it turned out, several investors felt duped by the unrealistic predictions and went to court. Mataré was asked to testify for the plaintiffs but pointed out that the technique as such was important and worthy of support, and that he could not conceive of a better method to solve the energy needs for the developing world.

The "energy crisis" of the 1970s convinced him of the need to end the over-reliance on finite coal and oil reserves or face severe economic distress. He became convinced that solar power is not only possible but eminently practical, not to mention more environmentally friendly. Having studied in detail all aspects of the energy problems, he had come to the conclusion that the industrialized countries would not be able to do away with the nuclear power stations, but that solar energy will play a decisive role in the developing countries. He discussed these conclusions in *Energy: Facts and Future* published in 1989.

Consultancy activity had become a full-time occupation and he decided to set up his own company. The contract with Globe Union allowed him to transfer some discarded equipment to the semiconductor laboratory of the University of California in Los Angeles, where he lectured. There he established the first hybrid microelectronic circuit laboratory. He also patented a new method of epitaxy on GaAs which later on was used for the construction of solar cells.

Research of crystalline imperfections has led Dr. Mataré to the study of the electronic properties of defects, especially dislocations and grain boundaries. Ten years of this work are condensed in *Defect Electronic in Semiconductors*. These results are also of importance in the present work of the effects of grain boundaries in high-temperature superconductors.

Dr. Mataré was involved with the original epitaxy work, particularly with silicon sapphire (SOS). He studied the interface defects and devised the gradient-growth method for semiconductors on insulators. Later, he concentrated on liquid phase epitaxy (LPE) for III-V compounds.

For many years, Dr. Mataré has worked on an application of modern epitaxial methods for the production of high-efficiency III-V-solar cells. He has studied differences between flat-plate solar arrays and concentrator systems. In cooperation with Pyron, a new system that has crystallized should be the ultimate power system for the underdeveloped world. With new III-V-QW solar cells of 40 percent efficiency, such systems should solve energy problems.

The application of a patented LPE process to GaAs-solar cells led Dr. Mataré to the derivation of the law of the super linear base current increase with concentration. From this effort III-V-PV-concentrator solar cells were produced. Dr. Mataré is also active in the area of highly efficient photovoltaic cells. He works in conjunction with several companies and has authored several papers in this field. He directs his work with solar concentrators toward electricity generation. Dr. Mataré holds 83 patents. He has published several books and numerous articles.

Aside from his scientific work, Dr. Mataré has abundantly philosophized about the future of humanity. In *Bioethics: The Ethics of Evolution and Genetic Interference,* he explores the evolutionary steps that have defined life on this planet. He describes the stages from cosmic to chemical and biological evolution and to the development of civilization and culture. From this scientific approach, he concludes that new rules of ethics are required in order to maintain and improve the civilization and culture of humanity.[36]

For more than fifty years, Mataré was the only person who knew what was understood and what was not understood in 1948 in the field of solid-state physics. He met with Shockley, Bardeen, Brattain, Gordon Teal, Lark-Horovitz and several people who had been involved in the development of the transistor. After emigrating to the United States, he never mentioned the work he and Welker had done in Paris, nor the production of transistors at Intermetall. The subject was ultra-sensitive and taboo. He quietly pursued his career.

One day, he discussed with Shockley their mutual patent procedures. Shockley remarked that Bell Labs had the advantage of strict organization. Anything that looked like a patentable or testable idea was immediately documented and signed by a group of colleagues as witness to the test result. In Germany, the practice was to apply for a test only after reduction to practice was assured.

On one occasion, did he hope to have the opportunity to inform the academic community about his work in Paris. In 1997, he proposed to contribute to the January 1998 issue celebrating the 50th anniversary of the invention of the transistor. At the request of the editor of *Proceedings of the IEEE, he* submitted a paper titled: *The lesser known history of the crystal amplifier.* After several months, not having received an answer, he phoned the editor and was told that the referees from AT&T refused to publish his article. He was even accused of having copied the Bell Labs transistor. Mataré agreed to change the wording, but the manuscript was rejected.

On February 24, 2003, John Markoff made history by publishing an article in *The New York Times* titled *Herbert F. Mataré: An Inventor of the Transistor Has His Moment.* He revealed that in June 1948, an unknown German scientist, Herbert Mataré, had produced functional solid state amplifiers for account of the French government about the time Bell Labs announced the invention of the transistor. It was the first time Mataré's name was ever mentioned in the press. The "French" transistor was rescued from oblivion. The journalist knew only half the story: the inventions were almost simultaneous, but Mataré's transistors had sufficient amplification power to be of practical use. Bell Labs' transistors did not work. The "French" transistor was rescued from oblivion. The genie was out of the bottle.

3

HISTORY REVISITED

The Voice of Bell Labs was like the Voice of God.
Akio Morita

On December 11, 1956, three scientists, William Shockley, John Bardeen and Walter Brattain shared the Nobel Prize in Physics "for their researches on semiconductors and their discovery of the transistor effect". A few weeks before, when Shockley received a phone call announcing that he had won the Nobel, he thought it was a Halloween prank. When he announced the news to his employees at Shockley Semiconductor Laboratory, they celebrated for two days.

Bardeen was at home when he heard his name pronounced on the radio. That night, his friends at the University of Illinois formed a candle-lit procession to his door, singing "For He's a Jolly Good Fellow." Walter Brattain wasn't taken by surprise. He was still employed at Bell Labs. He had heard about it through the grapevine and went to work as usual. The standing ovation he received. when he walked into the Bell Labs Auditorium brought tears to his eyes.

The Nobel Prize ceremony took place in Stockholm. The Swedish Academy of Sciences called their work "a supreme effort of foresight, ingenuity and perseverance" The three laureates received from the hands of King Gustav VI a <u>diploma</u>, a gold <u>medal</u> and a <u>certificate</u> representing an amount of money.

In their Nobel lectures they explained the concepts and experiments which had led to the discovery of the transistor effect. Each of them outlined from his own vantage point his ideas about electrical conduction in semiconductors. Bardeen was the first to speak. Recalling Bell Labs' program in solid-state research, he remarked:

> It is interesting to note that although Brattain and Pearson had considerable experience in the field prior to the war, none of us had worked on semiconductors during the war years. We were able to take advantage of the important advances made in that period in connection with the development of silicon and germanium detectors and at the same time have a fresh look at the problems. Considerable help was obtained from other groups in the Laboratories which were concerned more directly with wartime developments. Particular mention should be made of J. H. Scaff, H. C. Theuerer and R. S. Ohl. The general aim of the program was to obtain as complete an understanding as possible of semiconductor phenomena, not in empirical terms, but on the basis of atomic theory.[1]

He then gave a description of the research program involving the purification and control of the electrical properties of germanium and silicon. In fact, this procedure was unknown at Bell Labs in 1948.

Brattain's lecture was brief: "I would like to start out be emphasizing the importance of surfaces. It is at a surface where many of our most interesting and useful phenomena occur. We live for example on the surface of a planet. It is at a surface where the catalysis of chemical reactions occurs... In electronics, most if not all active circuit elements involve non-equilibrium phenomena occurring at surfaces." He was the only one still working at Bell Labs. But he was an experimentalist and had lost contact with the development of semiconductor technology. He was obviously unaware of the literature on solid state physics that had been published since the invention of the transistor.

Shockley read a long lecture about the characteristics and interactions of electrons, holes, donors and acceptors. As usual, he was brilliant and deft at expounding complex scientific concepts that are beyond the ken of a lay audience. He explained that because of their atomic makeup, germanium and silicon are poor carriers of electricity, but that they can become conductive when they are "doped" with impurities and voltage is applied to them. Free electrons that are not attracted to and paired with other charges, will wander toward or away from electrodes as the electrode charge is changed from positive to negative. This attraction-repulsion effect would allow a semiconductor to act as a switch that alternates between a conductive state and an insulating state.

At Bell Labs, he had designed what was then called a field-effect amplifier that did not work. When it was tested, it did not work. As Bardeen's and Brattain's supervisor, he had placed himself at the center of the research program. In 1955, he left Bell Labs to create the Shockley Semiconductor Laboratory. In 1960, he was compelled to sell the company without ever having produced a single transistor.

The term "transistor" had been coined at Bell Labs in 1948, but hardly anyone knew what it meant or had any idea of the applications the device might have. They had been tested by the military. Several companies had used them to amplify the sound waves in hearing aids. But nobody was able to predict what it would contribute to industry and to society. More than eight years had elapsed since Bell Labs had demonstrated the transistor to the press. Nothing of importance had happened since. In several laboratories, scientists were trying to improve the efficiency of the solid-state amplifier, but nobody was able to predict how well it would work. The Regency TR1, the first commercial transistor radio marketed in 1954, had been a commercial failure because the music transmission was unsatisfactory. It was a toy-like novelty priced at $49.95. So far, the transistor was only practicable in hearing aids.

Several patents had been granted in the past for the discovery of the transistor effect. In the 1920s, Julius Lilienfeld had patented a device which could be referred to as point-contact transistor. In 1934, Oskar Heil had been awarded a patent considered the theoretical invention of the field effect transistor. Their ideas and patents were of no practical value because they required semiconductor materials which were not available.

The fact that three unknown scientists were chosen in 1956 from among dozens of distinguished nominees is strange, unexplained and unique in the annals of the Nobel Prize. The transistor was still a laboratory device, of interest only to a small circle of semiconductor physicists. The Nobel Committee is no investigative body. Whatever its members knew about Shockley, Bardeen and Brattain, they learned from Bell Labs' management.

Mervin J. Kelly, Bell Labs' director of research, was a foreign member of the Swedish Academy of Sciences. He had been able to sway the voting members of the Academy in favor of his nominees. The Nobel Prize was above all a jewel in the crown of the American Telephone and Telegraph Company, a regulated monopoly and he world's largest corporation with over one million employees. Its research and development arm, Bell Labs, was the real laureate. The iconic status of the prize gave an immense boost to the image of the company.

Kelly was not interested in promoting the reputation of the laureates. They had fallen out and had nothing in common anymore. But he needed them. He had peremptorily excluded them from Bell Labs' semiconductor group. Shockley and Bardeen had left the company in anger; Brattain was still employed but had been alienated from the research department and relegated to a minor job. The members of the Academy did not know this.

After the ceremony the laureates adjourned for a great banquet organized in their honor. After dinner, Brattain, Bardeen, their families and friends sat around a table at their hotel and celebrated the event. Towards the end of the night, Shockley walked in and was invited to join the party. They had not met for several years and had nothing in common except their memories and shared secrets. But for one night they put their differences aside and sat together remembering the days when they worked at Bell Labs. For a while, it seemed that the hard feelings of the past had evaporated.

Each of the three laureates had played a different role in the discovery. John Bardeen was the resourceful theorist who thought up scientific concepts and formulated theories. Walter Brattain was the engineer with the magic hands who put together any contraption Bardeen suggested. William Shockley was the visionary who, long before anyone else predicted the advent of the solid state amplifier. Their personalities made them ill fit to work together. They had worked at Bell Labs on a common project, but the group had disbanded in a clash of egos, and they had gone their separate ways. Bell Labs management, however, consistently presented all three as a team.

Bardeen had left Bell Labs, venting his anger and frustration because Shockley had excluded him from the semiconductor group. He had joined the University of Illinois where he conducted research on superconductivity. Brattain remained at Bell Labs for several years, but was no more involved in solid-state research. After retiring, he became adjunct professor at Whitman College in Walla Walla, WA, teaching a physics course for non-science majors.

The choice of the Nobel Committee should have raised some questions. Alfred Nobel had bequeathed his fortune as an endowment to humanity. His last will and testament specified that the generated interest "shall be annually distributed in the form of prizes to those who, during the preceding year, shall have conferred the greatest benefit on mankind."

Ten years after its discovery, the transistor had hardly conferred any benefit to mankind. No one could have dreamed that it would one day be the heart of every modern appliance and spawn the world's largest industry. In the engineering and in the academic world, solid-state electronics was still a new discipline.

Over the years, "discovery of the transistor effect" was recast into "invention of the transistor." Shockley's name usually comes first in the hierarchy of the inventors. His greatest gift was self-promotion. He poached his way into history by borrowing theoretical concepts and formulas from scientific papers and patent literature. Knowing that nobody would care to verify his ideas, he proposed solutions to physical and mathematical problems, spinning off new concepts and publishing novel theories. He was awarded over ninety patents and made many contributions to the scientific literature, but never built a functional transistor. He made predictions and posed as a pioneering genius expanding the frontiers of scientific knowledge.

Shockley was also known for his quirks. At parties he showed off by performing magic tricks, pulling balls, coins or flowers out of people's noses or ears. He would announce that he knew how to stop inflation, take out a cigarette lighter and set fire to one-dollar bills. He was always a jump ahead of everybody and would not consider any theory he had not thought up himself. Convinced of his superiority, he insisted that his way of looking at things was better than anyone else's. It was Shockley who dubbed December 1947 "the miracle month."

Shockley left Bell Labs in 1955, returning to his boyhood home in California. He set up Shockley Semiconductor Laboratory in Palo Alto to manufacture silicon transistors. He proved such an abrasive manager that eight of his brightest engineers left in 1957 to form Fairchild Semiconductor, the mother company for scores of spin-offs in the area. In 1963, he was forced to sell out; the company was acquired by the Clevite Corporation. Shockley was appointed professor of engineering at Stanford University. The ultimate irony is that he never manufactured a salable transistor.

For purposes of gaining a historical perspective, it is necessary to backtrack in time. The Bell Labs transistor was the outgrowth of basic research programs financed by the military. The story illustrates the fact that a breakthrough in one area can pave the way for progress in a very different field.

In December 1941, the Japanese attack on Pearl Harbor catapulted radar as a primary weapon in air warfare. Radar technology had been developed in Germany and in Britain during the late 1930s. Initially the results of the British research had been kept secret. But the government needed American aid and decided to share its experience, thus bringing together .US and British radar scientists. The National Defense Research Council commissioned several universities and industrial laboratories to research ways and means to improve the radar system. In March 1942, with a grant from the Office of Scientific Research and Development, Purdue University undertook a research program with the purpose of developing crystal rectifier detectors.

In assessing the work at Purdue, it is necessary to appreciate the primitive nature of both the technology and understanding of semiconductors in 1942. In US scientific literature, silicon and germanium were hardly mentioned. Very little was known about semiconductors. There was even some question whether germanium was a semiconductor material.

These accomplishments appear even more astounding when it is realized how little was generally known at that time about semiconductors. There was even some question, at least in Lark-Horovitz's mind, whether germanium, the eventual target of Purdue's research, was a semiconducting material at all. At the time there was no such thing as a materials science, and no facilities for growing single crystals. The growth and doping of crystals to control semiconductor properties was hardly a science, and not even an art in those days, as evidenced by the fact that the initial polycrystalline, inhomogeneous germanium ingots grown at Purdue were doped with elements from a good portion of the periodic table in order to determine which would make the best diodes.[2]

In 1942, nobody at Purdue had any expertise in semi-conductors or radar. The contribution made by Purdue to the semiconductor project is due to Karl Lark-Horovitz who had earned his Ph.D. in physics at the University of Vienna before moving to the United States. Lark-Horovitz had established the Purdue Physics Department as a leader in innovative research and in undergraduate and graduate physics education. He organized an up-to-date library and set up an instrument shop to construct the necessary research equipment. He alone decided which research projects would be pursued and what curriculum would be followed. He translated and abstracted German patent literature and articles published in magazines such as *Zeitschrift für Physik, Die Frequenz* and *Archiv der Elektrischen Übertragung.*

In assessing the work at Purdue, it is necessary to appreciate the primitive nature of both the technology and the understanding of semiconductors in 1942... Although he did not actually contribute much to the analysis of specific problems, he did provide direction.... He began frequent group seminars with summaries of his extensive reading of the literature, and of what was happening in the world outside Purdue... In fact, a germanium crystal made at Purdue eventually was allegedly used for the first transistor built at Bell Laboratories.[3]

The Purdue Physics Department played an important role in nuclear physics research for which the university received nationwide recognition. Purdue was able to attract a host of distinguished physicists who organized seminars and explained theories which were gradually incorporated into the corpus of accepted knowledge. This gave Purdue a head start in the study of solid state physics.

Lark-Horovitz decided that it was necessary to begin by engaging in basic research into the properties of materials suitable to be used to produce rectifiers. He established several groups with different objectives: grow improved materials, evaluate them electrically and design, fabricate and test the crystal rectifiers. He organized and directed the project and assigned the problems to be studied. He continuously pressed his students to come up with results. In March 1942, he set up a group to explore the feasibility of doping germanium to develop crystal rectifiers. By doping semiconductors with different materials, they would learn which combinations produced the best results. The crystal rectifier project was the beginning of Purdue's pioneering involvement with semiconductor research.

Orchestrated by Lark-Horovitz, research at Purdue was a model of scientific organization. Although, as conceived and contracted for, the project was mainly of an applied nature, Lark-Horovitz insisted that it be supported by theoretical studies.

Much of the research focused on improving the properties of the so-called "rectifying interface," the tiny point of contact between a thin metal wire called a "cat's whisker" and a slab of semiconductor, either silicon or germanium. The oldest ancestor of the point-contact transistor was the crystal detector, used in early wireless sets. The device patented by Ferdinand Braun in 1899, was made of a single metal wire, touching against a semiconductor crystal. The result was a "rectifying diode", which lets current through easily one way, but hinders flow the other way.

A way to control the quality of semiconductor crystals was lacking. Solving that would turn out to be one of the greatest technological spin-offs of their research. The tasks were divided among three mutually supporting groups. Initially the most important was the group dealing with the purification of germanium. For this it was necessary to build a facility to grow crystals of relatively pure, high resistivity germanium crystals.

The electrical and galvanomagnetic properties of the doped germanium crystals were measured and analyzed. Such measurements were necessary to provide the feedback for improving the crystal growth techniques. The theoretical analysis of the results established the basic semiconducting properties of germanium: the width of the intrinsic energy gap and the activation energies of various impurities. From the temperature dependence of the mobility of electrons and holes, the relative contributions of lattice and impurity scattering could be determined. This work became the basis for making germanium the prototype semiconducting material.

The largest group was responsible for the fabrication, testing and evaluation of the crystal rectifiers. Seymour Benzer made a decisive contribution to the project. He discovered that a crystal of germanium could withstand higher voltage than any current rectifier. He tinkered with germanium until he realized that mixing in trace elements of tin produced rectifiers that were far more resistant than was standard. Germanium was thus established as a major element of semiconductor research. It was Benzer's discovery that led to the group's development of germanium crystal rectifiers capable of withstanding very high reverse voltages.

The crowning technological achievement of this group was the manufacture of high quality crystal diodes by a process which was patented by Purdue. This allowed the production of good germanium material, the development of successful surface chemical etching techniques and the discovery of the process of welding the tungsten "whiskers" unto the germanium chips.

Purdue became the leading authority on semiconductor theory in the United States, and was the first to recognize the benefits of using germanium. Thus, despite their initial lack of expertise and experience and despite the limited fiscal and physical resources available, the work of the Purdue group was remarkably successful. By the end of the war they obtained material that could be used for further tests. The first semiconducting germanium crystals ready for use were made at Purdue.[4]

The wartime research was carried out under strict secrecy. Results were communicated in secret reports only to those with appropriate clearance. But towards the end of 1945, all of the Purdue research on semiconductors was declassified.[5]

The story of the discovery of the transistor effect and its direct relationship to Purdue has been told by Ralph Bray. The initial attempts at Bell Labs to make a field effect transistor involved the use of silicon. When the experiment failed, Bardeen suggested that Brattain try germanium. He knew that Ralph Bray and Seymour Benzer had discovered some of the anomalous properties of germanium.

The genesis of the transistor is one of the great epics of modern physics and stands high in the history of human knowledge. The circumstances surrounding the invention are fragmentary. The literature on the subject keeps reproducing the same story. The extraordinary achievements of three scientists, whose figments of imagination led, over a period of a few weeks, to the century's greatest discovery, run counter to the laws of scientific research.

THE MIRACLE MONTH

In 1945, AT&T – the world's largest company with over one million employees - had a problem: consumer demand was overtaking transmission capacity. Telephone use continued to rise, requiring ever more long-distance operators. The company held a monopoly on national telephone service and needed an efficient switching system, a new means of routing calls. The vacuum tube made long-distance calling possible, but it consumed much power, created heat and burned out rapidly, requiring high maintenance. AT&T turned to its research laboratory to solve the problem.

Mervin J. Kelly, Bell Labs' director of research, felt that the progress in semiconductor technology achieved at Purdue might make it possible to replace the vacuum tubes and electromechanical relays in the system by solid-state amplifiers and switches. He set up a small multidisciplinary research group and appointed William Shockley as leader responsible for providing general guidance. Shockley had established a reputation in the scientific community by publishing a number of articles about complex scientific concepts no one else understood. A brilliant theorist, he seemed to be endowed with a phenomenal intuition. He was skilled at explaining his theories to anyone who would listen and enjoyed the full support of Bell Labs' management. He had acquired some information about electrical conduction in semiconductors and predicted that it should be possible to control the supply of movable electrons inside silicon and germanium by influencing them with an electric field imposed from the outside without actually contacting the material.

Bardeen was the theorist of the group. He had no experience in solid state physics before joining Bell Labs; but he read all the papers on rectification he could lay his hands on, and he familiarized himself with the vocabulary specific to semiconductor theory.

Brattain had been with Bell Labs for many years. He had magic hands and is regarded as the epitome of ingeniosity. He was a physicist who had a good understanding of theory, but his strength was in physically constructing experiments. He could build and fix just about anything and was able to force electricity to do seemingly impossible tricks.

The group was filled out with specialists in chemistry, physics, metallurgy and electronics. The work done at Purdue indicated that silicon and germanium were the most suitable semiconductor materials. Both were stable elements that readily assumed the crystalline state. It was decided to start out by trying to understand their properties and characteristics.

Just as Lee de Forest saw the potential of attaching a third electrode to Fleming's vacuum tube rectifier, they speculated that by adding a third electrode to a semiconductor detector, they would be able to control the amount of current flowing through. If the theory proved correct, the resulting device would amplify in the same way as the vacuum tube with much less power consumption and in a fraction of the space. They decided to pursue the ideas set forth in the field-effect theories which seemed to hold the most promise of leading to a working device.[6]

Shockley was the first to come up with the idea of a semi-conductor amplifier. He had sketched in his notebook a design for a silicon amplifier. An electric field was applied perpendicularly to a thin slab of silicon; the field was supposed to draw charges in the slab to its surface. Shockley expected that the field would cause a substantial change in the available charge carriers. In his design, the field would play the role of the grid in a vacuum tube. His idea was to attach a battery to a piece of semiconductor and place a metal plate just above it. Normally electricity won't flow through the semiconductor. But if an electric charge is applied to the plate, the resulting electric field should draw electrons out of the atoms, creating a path for the electricity. He called this the field effect.

The theory looked great on paper. Shockley was sure it would work. He asked Bardeen to double-check his mathematics. Bardeen reviewed the figures and could not find anything wrong. Shockley then assigned Bardeen and Brattain to test the idea. Bardeen was of the opinion that electrons were trapped on the surface of the silicon, creating a shield, so the electric field would not reach the electrons on the inside. They put the device together, tested it and found that the various attempts to observe the field effect did not materialize.

Shockley was surprised because had drawn on theories developed by Nevill F. Mott and Walter Schottky. He claimed that something was happening on the surface of the semiconductors that prevented the field effect from penetrating into the body of the material. Bardeen believed that the electrons were trapped on the surface of the silicon and created a shield, so the electric field could not reach the electrons on the inside. Additional research was necessary to understand the mystery of the surface barrier.

Bardeen concluded that the theory must be wrong or incomplete, and decided to find out why Shockley's field effect design had failed. He proposed a theory of surface state surface states: a double layer of charge - negative on the outside and positive just beneath - might be an intrinsic constituent of a semiconductor surface.

Brattain and Bardeen began tinkering with thin slices of silicon, searching for a better understanding of the surface barrier. They dipped the silicon into liquid nitrogen, figuring that this might neutralize the shield and allow the electric field to stimulate the flow of electrons. It worked only slightly, but enough to convince Bardeen that the theory might be correct.

Shockley decided to broaden the research and assigned specific tasks to several members of the group. Brattain studied surface properties such as contact potential; Gerald Pearson looked at bulk properties such a mobility of holes and electrons, while Robert Gibney contributed his knowledge of the physical chemistry of surfaces. Bardeen and Shockley supervised the work by suggesting new ideas and theoretical insights. By the end of 1946, they had done enough research on surface states to be confident that they existed.

The group spent several months carrying out experiments based on suggestions made by Shockley and Bardeen. They enjoyed working together in Brattain's lab, discussing and criticizing any idea that might come up. Bardeen liked to watch Brattain prepare his experiments. Sometimes he would offer him a hand in routine tasks, such as recording measurements or holding a piece of apparatus in place while Brattain soldered it. Bardeen probed Brattain for clarification on questions of technique or material. In pondering the data Bardeen often made interpretive suggestions. Their close co-operation gave them a sense of play and adventure. Shockley gradually distanced himself from the group to study new fields such as the magnetic properties of materials.

In the aftermath of World War II, officers of the Technical Field Information Agencies were equally active in France, and kept headquarters advised about their findings.

Bell Labs also became aware of the Mataré-Welker work and grew concerned that it might impede its efforts to obtain a patent on the transistor, according to Michael Riordan, a physicist and author of "Crystal Fire: The Invention of the Transistor and the Birth of the Information Age."

"There were ongoing worries about the Paris group at Bell Labs," Mr. Riordan said in an interview.

Dr. Mataré recalls that in 1950 one of the Bell Labs team, Dr. Shockley, visited his Paris lab, where he was able to demonstrate for the American an application of the technology by making a telephone call in which transistorized repeaters along the network carried the voice signal to Algiers.[7]

In the summer of 1947, after more than two years of experimenting, having made no progress and discouraged by the results of their tests, Shockley and Bardeen took a two-month-trip to Europe. They met with several scientists engaged in semiconductor research and visited a number of laboratories and universities. In Paris, they had a long conversation with Louis Néel, director of the laboratory of electrostatics and metal physics (Centre National de la Recherche Scientifique). A future Nobel laureate, he was closely associated with the Centre National d'Etudes des Télécommunications (CNET) which financed the research at the Compagnie des Freins et Signaux Westinghouse.

In the Netherlands, they called on Philips at Eindhoven. They also visited the University of Delft where Ralph Bray had been granted a fellowship, and the University of Leiden where Piet Keesom and Lex Gerritsen, two former Purdue students, were teaching physics. They picked up the vocabulary, the ideas and the formulas that allowed them to further study the principles of semiconductor physics and to write laboratory reports, without really understanding the basic electronic properties of the materials.

Upon their return, Shockley reported to his boss Ralph Bown that the scientists they visited had been surprised by the theories developed at Bell Labs. "Mott was much interested, asked many questions and took notes. It was evident that a number of ideas were new and that he understood them for the first time." And he added: "we are quite ahead of them on the theory of rectification."[8] Bardeen was somewhat more candid. He wrote his wife that they had "learned a lot during the trip, and picked up some ideas that may be useful to the Lab. Whether or not it's going to pay for the trip is hard to judge." In any case, it had been "very hard work - much harder than you can imagine without doing it – but it's also been a grand experience."[9]

Based on the new insights they gained during the trip, Brattain resumed his experiments under the watchful eye of Bardeen. He put together a curious-looking contraption. The key components were a slab of germanium and two point contacts, a few microns apart. He then placed a ribbon of gold foil around a plastic wedge kept in place by a modified paper clip.

One day, in the course of one of his experiments, Brattain encountered a problem. Droplets of water condensing on a device he had put together caused a spurious effect. He immersed the contraption in various types of liquid and was amazed to see that a layer of positive charge formed on one surface and a layer of negative charge on the other. It was the largest amplification he had ever observed. He called Bardeen who suddenly realized that this might enable them to build a field effect amplifier. Playing with various knobs and buttons, by turning on a positive voltage the effect increased; turning it to negative the effect disappeared. Whatever the electrons had been doing on the surface to block amplification had somehow been cancelled out by the water. The main obstacle to building an amplifier seemed to be overcome.

The discovery of amplification, however slight, encouraged them to pursue. Using different materials, different setups and different electrolytes in place of water they tried to increase the current. For several days, Bardeen and Brattain worked steadily on the problem. They changed only one or a small number of features at a time to keep track of their progress as they explored several variations of materials and geometry. They tried gold instead of tungsten for the electrodes; lacquer in place of wax for the insulation; and water, ammonium hydroxide, and a series of gels for the electrolytes.

Bardeen suggested they try germanium instead of silicon. He thought the germanium doped with tin developed at Purdue would improve the amplification significantly. Brattain had a piece in his laboratory and tried the experiment. They were startled to measure voltage amplification and power amplification, but not in the direction they expected. They began to realize that the holes were functioning as the grid.

On November 17, 1947, Brattain dunked his experiment under water. Suddenly, the device created the largest amplification he had ever seen. On December 8, Bardeen suggested he try germanium instead of silicon. The amplification increased substantially, but in the opposite direction they had expected. By mid-December, they achieved increasing power gain when they used high back-voltage germanium. They also obtained satisfactory frequency response by applying the gold contacts directly to the surface. They noted that a different phenomenon occurred at the interface between the gold spot and the germanium. The two surfaces seemed to make good electrical contact. This meant that they were not only contacting, but somehow introducing carriers into the layer. And these charge carriers were not electrons, but holes.

But most of the input power to the gold spot was being wasted, because most of the current flowing through the gold spot rushed through the germanium. They decided to place two point contacts on the surface sufficiently close together. Brattain asked his technician to cut a small plastic wedge and cement a strip of gold foil around one of its edges. He took a razor at the apex of the triangle and very carefully cut up a thin slit with the razor until the circuit opened. He then put the wedge on a spring and put it down on the germanium. The edges of the foil made contact with the surface but remained about 2 mils apart from each other. Both point contacts allowed the currents to pass when a positive voltage was applied but almost nothing to flow under a negative voltage.

When Bardeen returned home that evening, he parked his car in the garage and came in through the kitchen door. He found Jane there, peeling carrots at the sink. "We discovered something important today," he mumbled as he took off his coat. "That's great," she replied looking up for a moment.[10]

On December 16, Brattain hooked the device up to his batteries, and obtained a 30 percent power gain and a factor of 15 voltage gain. Soon he found a way boost the power gain tenfold while the voltage gain dropped. Almost exactly a month after Brattain and Gibney's breakthrough, they had amplified both power and voltage at audio frequencies. When the point of the triangle was placed onto the germanium, a signal came in through one gold contact and increased as it raced out the other. This meant their work had been crowned with success: they had created the first solid-state amplifier.

On December 23, the device was demonstrated to Bell Labs executives in a circuit that allowed them to hear amplified speech in earphones. Brattain spoke into a microphone while Bown and Fletcher listened on the headphones. They agreed that when the device was switched on, the result was a distinct gain in speech level with little change in quality.

The results obtained by Bardeen and Brattain galvanized Shockley into action and stimulated his inventiveness. He was frustrated because he had not played a direct role in the breakthrough. He soon developed a novel idea for a sandwich semiconductor that had current flowing laterally in the interior n-layer and two p-layers around it acting as control electrodes.

On New Year's Eve, Bill Shockley attended a conference in Chicago. Most of the time, he stayed in his hotel room, filling page after page with calculations and notes about how to build a stronger solid-state amplifier. He felt that the device conceived by Brattain and Bardeen would be fragile and difficult to manufacture and thought he had a better idea. Why not mimic the vacuum tube and create a three-layer sandwich? The two outer layers would be p-type germanium, a thin inside layer would be n-type. This way it would be possible to move the input around to the other side, just like in a vacuum tube. A small electrical signal in the grid would influence a larger electrical current flowing from the input to the output. The two p-n junctions at the interfaces would furnish holes to the inner layer on one side and extract them on the other. This structure avoided the unwieldy point contacts. It seemed like a compact and solid device.

Back at Bell Labs, Shockley remained silent about his new idea. One day, he called Bardeen and Brattain separately into his office and told them that he intended to write a patent based on the field effect. Both were terribly upset. The problem of whose names should be mentioned on the patent, and who should be featured in publicity photographs, exacerbated the rancor. Shockley claimed his name should be the only one on the patent, since the original idea was his and since he had instigated the research.

He went to see Bell's patent attorneys; since he was the head of the group, they were inclined to oblige. But they soon uncovered that Shockley's ideas bore suspiciously strong similarities to those of Julius E. Lilienfeld whose patents for a field-effect transistor had been registered in Germany in the 1920s. Although he had specified the use of copper sulfide as the semiconducting substance through which current had to travel, Lilienfeld seemed to have had the same fundamental idea as Shockley. The patent attorneys did not know whether Lilienfeld had actually built the artifact, but they realized that if they tried to file a claim based on the field effect principle, the application would most likely be rejected.

They decided to base instead the patent application on Bardeen's and Brattain's bipolar design, which was different and seemed original. The idea was new because holes - rather than electric fields - were functioning as the grid. The patent application titled "Three-electrode circuit element using semiconductive materials", dated June 17, 1948, Serial No. 33.466, claimed rights on 40 inventions.

Profoundly hurt in his pride and upset by the decision of the patent attorneys, Shockley went to see his own counselor, Rudolph Guenther, and gave him photostats of his notebook, with a summary of patentable ideas. Guenther wrote up a wide-ranging application, and despite the fact that there was very little experimental basis for the validity of the concepts, Bell's attorneys gave in, and filed four patents.

Shockley did manage to get a number of patents: one filed June 26, 1948 and issued September 25, 1951; another filed September 24, 1948, and issued April 4, 1950; and a third filed September 21, 1951, and issued December 23, 1952.

Bell Labs now wanted to announce the invention to the press. Since the technology had military applications, Kelly felt obliged to inform the Pentagon. The following day, Admiral Paul Lee, chief of Naval Research called Bell Labs, saying that the scientists at the Naval Research Laboratory had built a similar device based on the same technology. "We've got the same thing" he said, and the press conference should be a joint announcement.

Shockley flew to Washington, where he was shown a solid-state amplifier made of a commercially available copper-oxide rectifier, using techniques very similar to those invented at Bell Labs. Curves of the current versus voltage for this device indicated that it was behaving like a vacuum-tube amplifier. Shockley took a critical look at the crude gadget and the data, claiming it would obviously never produce any results. He asked some pointed technical questions, and after admitting that the device had never actually been tested, the Navy withdrew its demand for a joint press conference. After two wearisome days, Bell Labs had the stage all to itself.

A DEVICE CALLED A TRANSISTOR

On June 30, 1948, Bell Labs' research director Ralph Bown, demonstrated to the press the laboratory apparatus assembled by Brattain as "a fine example of teamwork, of brilliant individual contributions and of the value of basic research in an individual framework." Shockley was the star of the conference. An effective communicator, he brilliantly answered all questions.

> But the structure of the press conference, with Bown giving the delivery and Shockley taking questions, cast a shadow across the efforts of the two real inventors of the transistor. It made it seem as if their discovery had been planned and orchestrated from above.[11]

Bown acted as spokesman and master of ceremonies. He explained the individual contributions of Bardeen, Brattain and Shockley to the development of the transistor, but made it clear that Bardeen and Brattain were the inventors. Bardeen and Brattain, however, were not on the podium. He then began his demonstrations. He presented a receiver built without vacuum tubes but equipped with a new type of amplifier which was activated instantaneously and required no warm-up delay.

Each reporter had a headphone. As he spoke, Bown turned a switch on and off. When turned on, the reporters heard his voice amplified by a repeater circuit. He tuned in local radio stations and played their broadcasts through loudspeakers. In a measured and restrained tone, Bown described in detail the technical aspects of the solid-state amplifier. Bell Labs had called it a transistor because it was a resistor, or amplifier device which could amplify electrical signals as they were transferred through it from input to output terminals. It was the electrical equivalent of the vacuum tube, but was composed entirely of solid-state substances. It had no vacuum, no filament and no glass tube. It could do everything a vacuum tube could do, up to a power output of about 100 milliwatts and up to a frequency of about 10 megacycles. It was much more reliable than the vacuum tube whose lifetime was limited and had tendency to break down.

After the demonstration, Shockley took the reporters' questions. A brilliant orator, he was able to explain in elegant and understandable language the most abstruse technical concepts. The reaction of the newspapers was mixed. The reporters had no idea of the importance and the possibilities of the new device. Time was rather enthusiastic, but the article focused upon the well-known problems of the vacuum tube and how the transistor could solve the problem.

week. The supporting company will include Janet Waldo and John Brown. Harmon Alexander and Ben Perry will do the script. Frank Danzig will be the producer and Ben Elliott, the musical director.

Station WFUV, Fordham University's frequency modulation outlet, will observe the completion of its first year of operation today. Throughout the day there will be special programs to mark the occasion and a number of personages on local commercial stations will participate, including John Mc Caffrey, Eileen O'Connell, Pat Barnes, Mary Small, Alma Dettinger and Arlene Francis.

At 8:05 P. M. there will be a critical discussion of present-day radio, the members of the panel including the Rev. Robert I. Gannon, president of Fordham; Morris Novik, John Garrison and F. W. Carlington.

"On Your Mark," a new audience-participation item, will be added to WOR's schedule next Monday. It will be heard at 2:30 P. M. each weekday afternoon thereafter and will include prizes for questions which are correctly answered. Paul Luther will produce

"The Better Half," which is to go under commercial sponsorship on Sept. 16 over the Mutual network, will take to the air as a sustainer on Aug. 19.

A device called a transistor, which has several applications in radio where a vacuum tube ordinarily is employed, was demonstrated for the first time yesterday at Bell Telephone Laboratories, 463 West Street, where it was invented.

The device was demonstrated in a radio receiver, which contained none of the conventional tubes. It also was shown in a telephone system and in a television unit controlled by a receiver on a lower floor. In each case the transistor was employed as an amplifier, although it is claimed that it also can be used as an oscillator in that it will create and send radio waves.

In the shape of a small metal cylinder about a half-inch long, the transistor contains no vacuum, grid, plate or glass envelope to keep the air away. Its action is instantaneous, there being no warm-up delay since no heat is developed as in a vacuum tube.

The New York Times relegated the story to page 46.

Immediately after the conference, Shockley launched a media campaign. A Bell Labs' photo showed him seated at a workbench, in front of the transistor, with Bardeen and Brattain looking on. The caption stated that all three had invented the transistor. From then on, Bardeen and Brattain were practically excluded from the group. Shockley removed them from the project and kept it to himself, consulting them only when he ran into problems. When Shockley and his closest collaborators moved to a new building, they were relegated to another floor. They spent their time writing papers about the physics of the transistor and presenting talks about their invention. But they did not get involved in any further transistor research. Finding himself blocked, Bardeen considered leaving Bell Labs. He kept busy working with Brattain and others on projects of lesser importance, but eventually decided to drop semiconductor research.

The responsibility for creating a functional transistor fell increasingly upon Jack Morton. Two other members of the group, Gordon Teal and John Little had come up with an idea that seemed more promising. Without telling anybody, Gordon Teal had developed a process to fabricate ultra-pure single crystals. Gradually, he achieved greater uniformity by precise control of the crystal-growing. To purify their samples, they melted down crystals and used the resulting germanium to grow new ones. By repeating this cycle several times, they obtained very high purity. When doped with minute quantities of impurities, the crystals became semiconductors.

Shockley ridiculed the work of Morton's group. But when it became evident that he was not making any progress and that Teal's precisely controlled electrical characteristics of grown germanium produced vastly superior results, he was forced to admit that he had been wrong. Soon Bell Labs would have an entire group devoted to growing germanium crystals.

In 1950, Teal's and Little's crystal-growing technique began to pay dividends: they were able to produce amplifiers generating an output of about two watts. But progress was slow. That year, Shockley and Brattain attended a conference in London, and went from there to Paris to visit the F. & S. Westinghouse laboratory, under contract by the French Ministry of Post, Telegraph and Telephone. When Mr. Eugène Sueur, director of P.T.T., dialed Algiers and had a telephone conversation with one of his colleagues over a line in which the vacuum tubes had been replaced by semiconductors, Shockley showed surprise.[12]

For several years, hardly anything was heard about the invention of the transistor. Texas Instruments was the first company to develop successful production techniques and to manufacture silicon transistors in volume. In 1952, Gordon Teal had answered a want ad in the New York Times for a job at Texas Instruments. There he kept learning how to grow crystals of silicon and dope them with tiny impurities. In April 1954, he was able to produce the first production-worthy silicon transistors. This turned Texas Instruments from a start-up into a major producer.

In 1957, a small Japanese tape recorder manufacturer surprised the world by bringing out a radio powered by transistors. The "shirt pocket radio" catapulted Sony at the cutting edge of semiconductor technology. An achievement in miniaturization, it took the world by storm. It was a tremendous success and established Sony as the world leader in electronic consumer goods.

The company had been set up in a shack by two young engineers, Masaru Ibuka and Akio Morita. They called it Tokyo Tsushin Kogio. They had learned that Bell Labs had invented a device called "transistor" and that it was possible to buy a license for $25,000. They thought it might be worthwhile to find out if it could be used to replace the vacuum tube in radios. In 1953, they were able to convince the Ministry of Trade and Industry (MITI) to let them acquire a manufacturing license. It took six months to convince the MITI bureaucrats: exchange control was very rigid, the transistor was an unknown device and the company seemed too small to deal with a brand new technology. On a visit to the United States, Ibuka met with officials of Western Electric and signed a provisional patent licensing agreement. A year later, when Akio Morita signed the contract, he mentioned that he intended to use transistors in radio receivers but was told that the amplifying capacity was sufficient only for hearing aids.

l must make it clear that the transistor being made at that time wasn't something that we could license and produce and use right off the shelf. This miraculous device was a breakthrough in electronic technology, but it could only handle audio frequencies. In fact, when l finally signed the patent agreement a year later, the people at Western Electric told me that if we wanted to use the transistor in consumer items, the hearing aid was the only product we should expect to make with it. In those days there were no transistors made for use in radios. Of course, we were not interested in the hearing aid market, which is very limited. We wanted to make something that could be used by everybody, and we had plans to put our research scientists and technicians to work developing our own high-frequency transistor for use in radios.[13]

Solid state technology was something entirely new. Learning about it and deciding what could be done with it was quite a challenge. For three years, a group of about 30 engineers studied the properties of germanium and silicon. They upgraded the technology so that it enabled them to deliver sufficient high frequency to power a battery-operated radio. The name of the company was changed to Sony. In August 1955, their first pocket size transistor set - the TR-55 -.was produced in small quantities and only for internal consumption. The TR-63 was produced in March 1957.

It was very complicated work and our project team went through a long period of painstaking trial and error, using new, or at least different, materials to get the increased frequency we needed. They had to rebuild and virtually reinvent the transistor. The head of our research laboratories, Makoto Kikuchi, a leading expert in the semiconductor field, recalls that in those days the level of research and engineering in the United States was so high that 'the voice of Bell Labs was like the voice of God.[14]

A year later we surprised the Bell Labs people who had invented the transistor by reporting how we made transistors by phosphorous doping, something that had been tried and discarded, obviously prematurely, by them. And it was also during our transistor research and particularly the heavy use of phosphorous that our researcher, physicist Leo Esaki, and our staff discovered and described the diode tunneling effect, how subatomic particles can move in waves through a seemingly impenetrable barrier. Esaki was awarded the Nobel Prize for his work in 1973.[15]

Once Sony acquired the necessary new technology the company continued to learn by commercializing new products. From then on, the Japanese industry led by Sony and Matsushita conquered world markets. Sony became the world's foremost manufacturer of products integrating new technologies into consumer electronics. Matsushita became the industry's most successful company in product development, production and global sales. By the late 1980s, together with Sanyo and Sharp, they had driven both the US and European consumer electronic companies out of their own home markets.

Solid state physics was not an established academic disciplne in American universities at the time. Indeed, it was the eventual development of the transistor in 1948 that was to give a huge impetus to the subsequent expansion of this field in the university community. In the immediate post-war period, when Bell Labs launched its research program under Shockley's guidance, there were only a small handful of modestly-financed research programs in the university community. Jack Morton, who headed the fundamental development group that was formed at Bell Labs after the invention of the transistor, reported that it was impossible to hire people with a knowledge of solid-state physics in the late 1940s 'because solid state physics was not in the curriculum of the universities... US universities did, of course, undertake significant research on semiconductors, but the main thrust of such research came only <u>after</u> semiconductors had been developed by private industry.[16]

Transistor technology was not the eventual consequence of a prior buildup of resources devoted to solid-state physics.

Rather, it was the initial breakthrough of the transistor as a functioning piece of hardware that set into motion a vast subsequent commitment of financial support for scientific research... Moreover, Shockley also found it necessary to run a six day course at Bell Labs in June 1952 for professors from some thirty universities as part of his attempt to encourage the establishment of university courses in transistor physics.[17]

It was not until 1955 that semiconductor physics became a major discipline. But universities were slow to generate courses and books. Of the universities getting good starts in the 1950's, Stanford and Berkeley were leaders.

The progress in semiconductor research at Purdue played an essential role in the discovery of the transistor. The initial attempts at Bell Labs to make a so-called 'field-effect transistor' involved the use of silicon. This effort failed but promoted a program to overcome this failure. At a critical stage in his work, Bardeen suggested a switch from silicon to germanium. This suggestion was influenced by his knowledge of the properties of germanium as determined at Purdue. In fact, the experiment in which the point-contact transistor was discovered was made with a germanium sample supplied by Purdue.

Bardeen and Brattain were aware of the research going on at Purdue and its relation to the transistor. They were concerned that the Purdue group might also be interested in developing a solid state amplifier. The work at Bell Labs on the transistor was a tightly held secret until its public announcement in mid-1948.[18.]

Neil Armstrong was an engineering student at Purdue at the time when Professor Lark-Horovitz was involved in analyzing substances that were neither conductor nor insulator. Many years later, he recalled that scientific papers were circulated on 'electrical properties of germanium alloys.'

Based on the Lark-Horovitz work and others, M. J. Kelly, at Bell Labs, authorized research in semiconductors to be located in the then new Murray Hill Lab. There was a lot of skepticism and surprise that Bell would fund such a speculative project. But the group made rapid progress and developed a rather elegant theoretical analysis, which they called 'surface states.' The next year, based on the analysis, Walt Brattain built a device for the experiment of John Bardeen and William Shockley. Those developments led, in remarkably short order, to integrated circuits, solid state digital computers, and lightweight reliable navigation and communication equipment.[19]

In an article published in the *Bell Telephone Magazine,* Kelly explained how, in 1945, a group under Jack Morton decided to create new devices for the Bell System and for the military.

The thing itself was simple. Shockley's theory could predict the performance to be expected. The problem was to find ways to make it work... It has taken nearly five years for the transistor to reach a point of development and of general recognition commensurate with its initial promise.... The earliest transistors were made of germanium purified and allowed to solidify by conventional metallurgical and chemical techniques.... They showed erratic performance from one unit to the next. The problem was to get the germanium into one big perfect crystal... Research, invention, development, and application have grown at a hearty pace. But the field is still very new, and as the studies progress and understanding increases so also does the prospect.

Before the first announcement, five years ago, when the new physical phenomena were observed and radically new electronic devices invented, it was evident to us that we were seeing the beginnings of an era in electronics technology of significance not only to the telephone system but also to the military services and to industry and civilian use generally.[20]

Shockley, Bardeen and Brattain published a vast number of articles recapitulating their contribution to the invention. Their activities at Bell Labs had turned to a dead end. Each of them moved on in different directions. They had been at loggerheads for years, having nothing in common except their shared secrets. In 1956, they met briefly in Stockholm to share the Nobel Prize in Physics for "their researches in semiconductors and the discovery of the transistor effect."

The seminal impact of Purdue in the field of semiconductor research has been disregarded by historians. The Purdue research group was the first in the United States to recognize the benefits of using germanium as the material with which to work. Purdue researchers made the discovery of high-back-voltage rectifiers that opened up the possibility of using crystal rectifiers as detectors in radar and played an important role in the development of that wartime device.

The Bell Labs' people were aware of the ongoing research at Purdue. They were concerned that the Purdue group would be the first to announce the invention of a solid state amplifier and decided to file a patent application as rapidly as possible to get priority for the discovery. Whereas the Bell Lab group had been deliberately set up to develop a solid state amplifier, there was no such objective at Purdue where the significance of the anomalous properties of germanium, which might have suggested the possibility of making a triode amplifier, was not fully appreciated.

When the results of the research were declassified, the people at Bell Labs were fully informed about the semi conductor r work at Purdue through publications, reports and meetings between the two groups. But from then on, the work done at Bell Labs remained a tightly held secret until its public announcement in June 1948.

4

THE AMERICAN CHALLENGE

On December 5, 1941, when he pushed the button to start his experimental automatic calculating machine, Konrad Zuse heralded the computer age. It was the first functional program-controlled electromechanical digital calculator, using the binary numbering system as the basis for encoding information. While studying civil engineering at the Technische Hochschule in Berlin, he had learned how to find solutions to simultaneous linear equations. Such calculations were required to determine the stress on materials used in airplanes, bridges and other structures. The calculus was done by filling out forms on which formulas had been preprinted. The data had to be entered in the prescribed sequence.

After graduating, he worked as a mechanical stress analyst at the Henschel Aircraft Company, and soon became weary of the routine linear ciphering his job required. When doing large calculations with a slide rule or a mechanical adding machine, keeping track of the intermediate results and using them later in the operation was very cumbersome. Zuse wanted to overcome the difficulty. He started thinking about an automatic calculator that would do the repetitious number crunching faster and more accurately than hand-operated calculators.

A civil engineer, he had no formal training in electronics. This worked to his advantage since he had to rethink the whole problem of arithmetic computation and find original solutions. He decided to build a machine exploiting two basic ideas: it would function with binary numbers, and the computing and control unit would be separated from the storage.

He was familiar with Leibniz's writings on binary mathematics. The challenge was to turn these ideas into practical machinery. His research was initially aimed at pure number calculation, but soon led on to new concepts for dealing with data represented through 0/1 patterns. Numbers would be entered from an input unit and the results would be placed in an output device. Internally there would have to be a memory, an arithmetic unit and a control section. Arithmetic would be performed in floating point, with separate units for the exponent and fraction. Numbers and instructions would be represented in the binary number system, and bistable switching units would be used. Machine operations would be synchronized by a central clock. Computing operations would be carried out by relays operating according to the dual status principle. The machine would operate in many ways like the human brain.

In 1936, Zuse gave up his job. His parents were not wealthy, but they backed him financially; several friends helped cut the thousands of metallic plates needed for the apparatus as well as for preparing the other parts. Whereas traditional calculators had rotating mechanical components, Zuse used metallic plates that shifted position. He decided to base the memory device on the binary system and to divide the machine into cells able to hold data for a complete number. A small pin positioned right or left of a steel lug memorized the value 0 or I. Input and retrieval were arranged via a steel-plate construction, and the individual parts could be stacked in a system of layers. He had, in fact, rediscovered the basic computer architecture described by Charles Babbage a century before.

It took two years to build the Zl, the world's first program-controlled mechanical calculator. The Zl could be operated by hand or by an electric motor. It was a complicated labyrinth of circuits and relays; a board of light bulbs displayed the results. The Zl was operational in 1938. It was unreliable, and the mechanical design limited its potential. It could compute the four basic arithmetical operations, and the square root. The program was stored on used 35mm film and was read sequentially. Nobody except Zuse himself understood how the machine worked. He then decided to explore several groundbreaking technologies in calculator development: floating-point arithmetic, high-capacity memory and modules or relays operating on the yes/no principle.

The next step was a more sophisticated electro-mechanical version. The 22 had the same memory system but the mechanical arithmetic unit was replaced by electromechanical relays. This attracted the attention of the Aerodynamics Research Institute where he obtained financial support for further research. Construction of the machine was interrupted in 1939 when he was called up for military service. He was soon released and assigned to work at the Aerodynamics Research Institute. In his spare time and with the help of friends, he was able to complete the machine. By 1941, it was in operation. He demonstrated it and met with considerable interest.

The Z2 helped Zuse convince the German Airspace Research Office to partially finance the development of the 73. Made with recycled materials, it was the world's first properly functioning programmable computer. Computing and storage in the Z3 was done with ordinary telephone relays. The contacts were carefully adjusted so that their opening and closing times were all within a specific range. This was necessary to synchronize the running of the whole system. The programs and the data were stored on used movie film. The Z3's basic specifications were: a binary number system, floating point arithmetic, 22-bit word length and 2.400 relays.

The input was done manually by setting the memory content, it was automatic: once the machine was started, it did not require an operator, and could be left running unattended overnight. It could add, subtract, multiply, divide, take the square root and perform some ancillary functions. The time required for a multiplication was about three seconds. Up till then, only the human mind had been capable of this. Zuse then decided to study the chess game in order to find a way to formulate the rules of the game in terms of logical calculus. Chess offered a mass of data structures within a limited space. This led to his first confrontation with what is known today as artificial intelligence.

The Z3 was used by the German aircraft industry to solve systems of simultaneous equations and other mathematical systems caused by the problems of dealing with the vibration of airframes put under stress. Several components were used to build the control-automation elements that provided automatic onboard guidance for the V2 flying bombs. Destroyed during the war, the Z3 was rebuilt in 1960 and is now on display at the Deutsches Museum in Munich.[1]

While still employed at the Henschel factory. Zuse set up his own company, the Zuse Ingenieurbüro und Apparatebau with the purpose of building more powerful machines. Within a year he put together the Z4 which had a mechanical memory with a capacity of 1,024 words, and several card readers and punches to enable flexible programming. When the battle of Berlin threatened to destroy it, the German High Command ordered the one-ton machine out of the city. The Z4 was hidden in Hinterstein, a little village in the Allgäu Alps. It was the only computer to survive the war. Zuse gave himself up to American troops together with Wernher von Braun who was wkisked off to the United States. In 1948, he was taken to London to be interrogated, but it was decided that he had not done anything of importance.

After the war, severe restrictions were placed on scientific research. Prevented from pursuing his work, he took the Z4 to Switzerland, and installed it at the Technische Hochschule in Zurich, where he obtained 40,000 Swiss francs to restore the machine. The Z4 was eventually sold to the French Department of Defense where it remained in operation for several years.

In 1949, he established the ZUSE KG with five employees and developed a line of computers that soon became very popular with scientists and engineers.

Siemag Werke GmbH, a manufacturer of typewriters and mechanical accounting machines, took up production of the world's first minicomputer. Called Dataquick. It had a magnetic drum with 120 memory cells. A dozen machines were built and sold. Some were still running after more than ten years. [1]

Zuse registered some 50 patents and counted Zeiss Optics and Remington Rand as customers. In 1955, he started development work on commercial electronic computers with Siemens and Standard Elektrik Lorenz, an affiliate of the American firm ITT. Since he did not have the financial resources necessary to develop large machines, his production focused on minicomputers. The Graphomat was the first computer-controlled automatic drawing board. Gradually electronic components achieved a degree of reliability that warranted production in larger numbers.

At one point, Zuse's work attracted the attention of IBM, but discussions came to nothing. The success of the Z4 led Zuse to build another relay machine, the Z5, for the Leitz Optical Company in Wetzlar. Germany. This computer, delivered in 1953, was six times faster than the Z4. After producing the Z5, Zuse changed the name of the company to Zuse Kommandit Gesellschaft and began manufacturing computers on an assembly line basis. By 1962 the company had delivered 200 computers. Among these were forty-two Zll's with relays, fifty Z22's with electron tubes, and thirty-four transistorized Z23's.

The Z22, the first calculating machine equipped with vacuum tubes, was a relative success. It sold for approximately DM 200,000, a price much lower than a comparable machine by IBM. By 1965, Zuse produced more computers than Siemens, Telefunken or SEL. The company eventually employed about 1.000 people. Then, IBM, Sperry, Univac and other American manufacturers gradually took control of the market.

The dominance of the American computer industry, as well as the late adoption of a fully electronic design brought the Zuse KG into financial difficulties. Profits shrank, making it necessary to bring in new shareholders. When IBM started leasing computers instead of selling them, Zuse was forced to give up. The Zuse KG had built and delivered a total of 251 computers. In 1964, the company was sold to Rheinstahl, then to Brown Boveri and Co., to be finally taken over by Siemens. There, production of computers was stopped and the inventor of the computer became a consultant to Siemens, devoting most of his lime to purely scientific research until he left the company.

Zuse developed an algorithmic programming language called Plankalkül. A forerunner of today's programming languages, Plankalkül was an attempt to devise a notational and conceptual system for writing what today is termed a program. It incorporated features that are standard in today's programming languages. It was intended to cover the whole spectrum of general calculating; it featured binary data structure types and thus supported a loop-free programming style for logical or relational problems. Plankalkül is in some aspects equivalent and in others more powerful than the von Neumann model that came to dominate programming for a long time. It was not only the first high-level programming language but in some aspects conceptually ahead of the high-level languages that evolved a decade later.

Plankalkül was an "'algorithmic" language, conceived as a means to assist in establishing consistent laws of circuitry for floating point arithmetic, as well as in planning the sequence of instructions a computer would follow. The final version of Plankalkül was finished in 1946 and published in 1972. Plankalkül was the first high-level programming language for computers, but its impact was minimal.[2]

Zuse was a constant innovator. He wanted to create a small computer for business and scientific applications. He worked single-mindedly during many years to achieve this objective. His patent application of 1941 for the computing machine Z3 was rejected because it lacked inventiveness. His decision on the application was delayed because of wartime conditions and through obstructive tactics maneuvered by the computer industry.

Zuse's genius rested on a combination of pioneer inventiveness combined with wild imagination; this mind-set sparks non-logical jumps forward that are then proved to be right by working backward to known principles. Zuse must be credited with several fundamental inventions: the use of the binary system for numbers and circuits; the use of floating point numbers, along with the algorithms for the translation between binary and decimal and vice versa; the look-ahead which allows to read the program two instructions in advance and test it to see whether memory instructions can be performed ahead of time; the mechanical binary cells that make up the memory and several others.

Zuse's work had very little impact on the development of the computer industry. He was awarded an impressive number of honorary degrees and other distinctions by universities as well as private and public institutions. Until relatively recently, international fame and recognition largely eluded him. Zuse rightfully considered himself the inventor of the computer. In his memoirs he expressed disappointment: "the world long heard nothing about our work. Thus the impression arose that the computer is an American invention. Only step by step did the truth come out. Today it is hardly disputed that the Z3 manufactured in my Berlin workshop was the first satisfactorily working computer in the world.'" At the age of 77, he decided to rebuild a Z1 and once more put together 30,000 parts.

Looking back, he remarked: "I was guilty of trying to run before I could walk." In his later years, Zuse continued to tinker with electronics, but devoted most of his time to oil painting. His artistic talents equal his scientific inventiveness. His paintings would honor any museum of modern art. He drew a portrait of Bill Gates and handed it over to him at the Hannover Cebit Fair. Gates was amused and delighted when Zuse told him he never thought it would be possible to make money simply by selling software. His own customers used to tell that when they bought a washing machine, the operating instructions were given free; why should it be different for a calculator?

BRITAIN had a long history in the development of computer technology. Home of the Difference Engine and later the Analytical Engine, its scientists and engineers made essential contributions to the understanding of the guiding principles and fundamental procedures. During the war, the Colossus had been very effective in cracking the German secret codes. But computer technology was a closely guarded military secret. There existed a sharp divide between military and civil R&D.

Whereas Konrad Zuse dreamed up the computer as a calculating device, in Britain and in the US computers were the peace-time legacy of war-time radar. The pulse techniques developed in radar transmission were taken over by computer scientists. At the end of World War II, they competed with the Americans in the race to build electronic computers.

After the war, English universities constructed research computers and developed computer concepts that later found significant use in U.S. products. In 1946, three projects were started, one each at Cambridge and Manchester universities and another at the government-sponsored National Physical Laboratory. But because of the government blackout, scientists who had not participated in wartime research work had to re-invent and rediscover what had already been invented and discovered.

The EDSAC at Cambridge was the first working electronic stored-program computer. In 1947, J. Lyons & Company had given £3,000 to Cambridge University for the development of a computer in exchange of the right to use the experience for making their own. Professor Maurice Wilkes led the design team and David Wheeler wrote the program. The EDSAC (Electronic Delay Storage Automatic Calculator) improved upon the American Eniac in that it could be programmed for different tasks, and also upon Manchester University's 1948 Baby.

EDSAC was a huge contraption that took up a room in the university's Mathematical Laboratory. It had 3,000 vacuum valves arranged on 12 racks and tubes filled with mercury for memory. But despite its impressive size, EDSAC could carry out just 650 instructions per second. A program was fed into the machine via a sequence of holes punched into a paper tape. This generated pulses which the machine used to store the program and perform the desired calculation. From day one, it operated as a complete system. Unlike earlier machines, none of the wiring or switches had to be altered to perform a new calculation. It was a very well-engineered machine, designed to be a productive tool for mathematicians. Put in operation in May 1949, the first successful program was a computing a table of squares.

In 1951, Maurice Wilkes developed the concept of micro-programming from the realization that the central process-ing unit of a computer could be controlled by a miniature, highly specialized computer program in high-speed ROM. Microprogramming was first described at the Manchester University Computer Inaugural Conference in 1951. This concept was implemented in EDSAC 2, which also used mul-tiple identical "bit slices" to simplify design. Interchangeable and replaceable tube assemblies were used for each bit of the processor. The next computer for his laboratory was the Titan, a joint venture with Ferranti Ltd. It eventually sup-ported the UK's first time-sharing system and provided wider access to computing resources in the university, including time-shared graphics systems for mechanical computer aided design.

In 1948. at the University of Manchester, a team of engi-neers headed by Freddie Williams and Tom Kilburn designed a prototype computer, the Small-Scale Experimental Machine, known as SSEM, or the "Baby". The machine was built primar-ily to test out tubes as a storage device. The storage system became known as the Williams Tube, a type of altered cathode-ray tube. It had all the components now classically regarded as characteristic of the basic computer. It could store not only data, but a program in electronic memory could process it at electronic speed. Furthermore, the electronic memory was a true random access memory.

After the program ran correctly, the experimental machine was expanded upon, leading to the development of the Manchester Mark 1, which was completed by late 1949. Thanks to the integration of a high speed magnetic drum - the ancestor of today's disc - this machine had a fast electronic and magnetic two-level store. [4]

The government initiated a contract with Ferranti Ltd. to make a production version of the Manchester Mark 1. The main improvements - apart from improved engineering - were: magnetic drum stores, a much faster multiplier and an increased range of instructions. The magnetic drum store and the multiplier were substantially redesigned. The Ferranti Mark I had the same basic architecture as the Manchester Mark 1, but it was better engineered and included a number of enhancements that made it a significantly faster and more powerful machine. It was the world's first commercially available general-purpose computer. The machine off the production line was delivered to the University in February 1951. In all, nine machines were sold.

In 1949, die Labour government set up the National Research Development Corporation (NRDC) a publicly owned institution intended to insure that patents generated through publicly supported research were made available to private corporations for commercial exploitation. It was intended to stimulate the development of the British computer industry by establishing a link between the universities and industry, and to ensure that electronic computers would be available as quickly as possible. In 1953, the NRDC contracted with W. S. Elliott and Ferranti Ltd. for the development of the Pegasus. It took three years to complete the first Pegasus which proved to be a highly reliable general purpose serial computer. It was used to tackle scientific, industrial or commercial problems. Large enough to cope with a wide variety of calculations, it was much smaller much lower priced than previous machines. The Pegasus was one of the first low-cost medium sized, multi-purpose computers in wide use. Between 1956 and 1962, a total of 40 machines

were built and put to work in a variety of engineering companies, banks, universities and research establishments. One
of them was delivered to Vickers-Armstrong, where it was
used for the design of the Concorde. However, the business
world was divided on the desirability of introducing anything as esoteric as electronics into routine office work, and
was alienated by the massive nationalization program of the
Labour government.

J. Lyons & Company was the exception and became the
pioneer of the accounting revolution and office automation. With 230 teashops carrying a wide range of perishable
stocks and 33,000 employees, the company had problems
of daily scheduling production and delivery. The operations required routine accounting for a vast number of
small transactions. Management had the foresight to realize that great savings could be made in terms of manpower
and time if the payroll and various other clerical tasks were
automated.

Lyons decided to build a copy of EDSAC and contributed
£2,500 to the cost of the machine. In return, Wilkes agreed
to give Lyons whatever details of the design they might need
to build a machine for their own use. The company sent an
engineer to Cambridge to study the design of EDSAC and
its logic and circuit techniques. Upon his return, during the
next three years, a more or less experienced team designed
and gradually assembled piece by piece a re-engineered version of the EDSAC and called it the LEO, for Lyons Electronic
Office.

LEO occupied 2,500 sq. ft. of floor space. It was the first
business machine to operate on the "stored program" principle and the first office computer. On November 17, 1951,
it ran a program to evaluate the costs, prices and margins for
that week's output of bread, cakes and pies; it ran the same
program each week thereafter.

LEO calculated statistics in order to evaluate the requirements of the tea shops; it then summarized them by group and
printed out the best and the worst performers in each group.

LEO ran a 24-hour shift for almost 14 years. It was designed not just to automate clerical tasks, but also to provide management with a tool for analyzing near-real-time sales data. The time saving was remarkable: a job that took 50 hours now needed just eight hours of data preparation and 4.5 hours of computer time - which was reduced to 30 minutes as the full hardware facilities became available. In February 1951, LEO took on the weekly calculation of the company's payroll.

When several companies commissioned Lyons to undertake a range of tasks on their "calculating machine", it became obvious that there was a market for computers. In 1954, Lyons spun off a separate company, LEO Computers Ltd. to manufacture commercial computers. Within a few years, LEO computers were running payrolls for Ford Motor Company and working for British railroads, military services, and a variety of businesses. The company produced a series of machines, from LEO I to the LEO III, and installed them in many offices, both in Britain and abroad. The LEO III models were introduced around 1961; they were the first machines to use transistors, three years before IBM launched its landmark 360 series. Leo III allowed microprogramming and multiprogramming. The last operating machine was in service at the Post Office until 1981.

But Lyons was unable to invest enough in its off-shoot to face the growing competition from US companies. Its marketing techniques and engineering proved to be obsolete. In 1963, the company was merged into English Electric to form English Electric LEO. Subsequent mergers eventually found LEO incorporated into International Computers Ltd.

In 1968, English Electric LEO was compelled by the government to merge with International Computers and Tabulators and a number of smaller companies to form International Computers Limited (ICL). The software and the hardware of the various companies were incompatible, and the managements were reluctant to co- operate. LEO Computers thus vanished in a series of disastrous mergers. It was left to IBM's mainframes to easily dominate the British market. Some laid the blame at the door of the government; but the fledgling computer industry did not find in Britain the indispensable innovative entrepreneurs willing and able to invest in a technology of the future. Lack of entrepreneurship, ill-advised mergers imposed by successive governments and stop-go policies cost the U.K. leadership of the world IT industry. [5]

The Conservative government elected in 1951, ideologically committed to withdrawing from state interference in the economy, was more acceptable to industry. But by the time British industry began to realize the potential of the computer, the Americans had taken the lead.

During the 1950s and early 1960s several companies from the electric and the punched-card sectors had entered the computer market. Next to Ferranti, the most important were English Electric, Marconi, Elliott Brothers and EMI. Some developed their own design; others made computers under American license. These manufacturers had a solid technology and were supported by government procurement. But they failed to keep up with technological advance and were slow to develop new models. By the time their products came to the market, they were regularly obsoleted by more advanced American machines.

While British companies took their time, several American companies moved ahead. In 1959, IBM entered the British market in earnest with its range of its IBM 1401 transistorized mainframes, which marked the end of the punched-card machines and the onset of the electronic age in Europe. The IBM 1401 rendered the British tube-based mainframes obsolete. IBM had superior sales techniques and very effective strategies to tie in customers, ranging from compatibility criteria, leasing facilities and considerable discounts. IBM accumulated orders largely thanks to its targeted marketing. Within two years, about 100 units were installed. This prompted a shake-out of the British office machine companies which had half-heartedly established a small foothold in their own market.

In 1959, BTM and Powers-Samas merged to form International Computers and Tabulators (ICT), the largest data processing machine manufacturer in Europe with over 19,000 employees. ICT's 1900 range of computers released in 1964 was well received. Four months after its announcement, 124 machines had been sold. However, the company failed to foresee the huge increase in the demand for the software to be supplied with computers and fell behind.

In 1964, the Labour Party returned to power and decided on a strategy to take on IBM. The government instituted a "buy British" policy for its computer procurements, and granted a £5 million development loan to ICT to finance its research and development. Harold Wilson established a Ministry of Technology with wide ranging powers. The purpose was to stimulate a major national effort to provide British industry with state-of-the-art technology. He wanted Britain to be the 'pilot plant' of the world, exporting advanced-technology capital goods. The government would act as a proving ground for the development of new machines. The policy would generate a British culture in computing and ensure that a new generation of scientists and engineers be trained on British machines and in the use of British codes and operating systems. Centralization was also seen to be the key to solving, or at least reducing, the scale of problems related to software development, particularly in data processing.

When ICT ran into financial difficulties, the government granted another £5 million development loan. A larger loan was made to English Electric Computers. The National Computing Centre was established to strengthen diffusion of computing technology through training and software techniques. For a while, British computer manufacturers were fairly robust, partly protected behind a 15 per cent import surcharge. But they kept losing customers because of the unsatisfactory software support. The reputation of the machines was spoiled by programming errors, which gave them a reputation for sloppiness.

It seemed the only way to compete with IBM was to reduce duplication of effort and cost by consolidating. This resulted in the creation of two major British companies: ICT absorbed GEC, EMI and Ferranti; English Electric Computers was created by combining Leo Computers, English Electric, Marconi and Elliott Brothers.

The coalescence of these companies resulted in an amalgam of incompatible architectures and technologies, both in hardware and software. ICL in particular was burdened with an ill-assorted range of machines. Some had been developed in-house, while others had been made in collaboration with GEC or under license from Univac and RCA. The ICT management tried to rationalize the product line by eliminating the machines that were too high priced. The only mainframe with real merit was the Ferranti Packard 6000 which had been developed by Ferranti's Canadian subsidiary.

ICT had two options for its long-term program: either develop the Ferranti Packard 6000 from a single mid-range machine into a fully compatible range, or manufacture next-generation computers under license from RCA. The ICT planners were weighing the pros and cons of each route, when IBM announced its System/360.

RCA decided to produce an entirely new line that would be IBM-compatible while the ICT management wanted to challenge IBM with its own design based on the Ferranti Packard 6000. In 1964, ICT launched the 1900 series at a time when IBM was unable to satisfy the demand in the United States. This benefited ICT, although the machines were technically inferior. Acceptance of the 1900 machines exceeded all expectations.

Meanwhile, English Electric-Leo-Marconi was planning a new series, partly based on technology developed by RCA. In 1965, the company announced System 4, a range of four machines. The large 4-70 was a remarkable technical achievement. It had been designed in the expectation that the market would pay a higher price if real-time transaction processing and multi-access systems were offered. The government, the nationalized industries and the universities placed substantial orders. The 4-70 completely outclassed the ICT machines. This compelled ICT to also introduce integrated circuits. As a result, the two British companies were not so much competing against the Americans as nibbling at each other's share of the market.

In 1965, English Electric Corporation made an all-out bid to become the leading computer manufacturer in Britain and possibly in Europe, with a new range of computers whose innards were composed of micro-integrated circuits recently developed in the United States. This made them smaller, faster, more reliable and cheaper. The computers were very competitively priced, and the language was easy to learn.

Following the success of the 1900 series, ICT overshadowed its two British competitors. The position of English Electric-Leo-Marconi deteriorated as a result of high development costs and unsatisfactory sales. The third company, Elliott-Automation, was still in deeper trouble and was absorbed English Electric.

In 1967, a sudden recession culminated in the devaluation of the pound. Government spending was radically cut. In 1968, the Labour Government decided to create one large British computer manufacturer to respond to the American challenge. The Industrial Expansion Act was part of an industrial rationalization program intended to create an international presence in the computer market.

The formation of ICL was the culmination of a series of mergers and acquisitions during the late 1950s and 1960s. The merger brought together International ICT and English Electric Computers. Later, Standard Telephones and Cables (STC) became parent company. ICL was the largest computer manufacturer outside the US. The company employed over 34,000 people. For years, the government favored ICL with subsidies, loans and preferential access to procurement. In 1998, when ICL was acquired by Fujitsu, the last traces of LEO disappeared. LEO embodies the rise and fall of British computing. It was the first business computer in the world, but a combination of wrongheaded government policies and commercial realities led to its demise. [6]

GERMANY had reasonable prospects for taking its place in computer technology. Long ago, Leibniz had developed the conceptual framework that allowed Konrad Zuse to build the world's first electromechanical computer. German scientific and technological traditions embraced a long line of automatic calculating machines. In the immediate post-war period there was no possibility for German industry to become involved in high-technology research for two overriding reasons: economic devastation and restrictions imposed by the occupying powers. The Allies had planned to de-industrialize Germany, in order to eliminate forever its capacity to wage war. Four experimental computers had however been built: two at the Max Planck Institute in Göttingen, and one each at the Technical High Schools in Darmstadt and Munich.

IBM dominated the German market. In 1949, a German company called Dehomag was renamed IBM Deutschland GmbH, with head office in Böblingen. IBM, however, had competitors such as the UNIVAC made by the Battelle Institute in Frankfurt. In 1955, when the interdict on the development of commercial computers was lifted, four companies entered the field: Siemens, Standard Elektrik Lorenz (SEL), Telefunken and Zuse KG. They were not able to produce a saleable product until the late 1950s. SEL was the first to produce a commercial model in 1959, but was forced within four years to withdraw from production. Telefunken produced its first computer in 1961, but also found the costs of computer technology beyond its means. In 1964 it was rescued by the Allgemeine Elektrizitäts Gesellschaft (AEG), and became known as Telefunken-AEG.

In the 1960s and 1970s, several German companies entered the computer market producing proprietary minicomputers. In 1973 the German chemicals giant Hoechst announced it intended to become a force in the office equipment business in competition with IBM and Rank Xerox. The company announced a word processor at a very competitive price. But the lack of marketing power, the absence of close cooperation between the scientific community and the computer industry, plus American competition, all weakened the German industry from its birth.

In 1967, the German government decided that a national computer industry was needed and instituted a mandatory "buy German" policy. Siemens, Telefunken-AEG and several smaller companies were granted considerable subsidies. The government directed its support not only to the national champions, but also to small and medium enterprises. Germany also invested heavily in education and training in the use of information technology in order to ensure an adequate supply of skilled technicians.

Between 1967 and 1987, the German government spent DM 8 billion on research and development of information technology. Siemens and Nixdorf were the main beneficiaries, but medium and small companies, universities and laboratories also received substantial grants. These subsidies were pre-competitive, not intended to develop new products, but new concepts to meet long-term future demands.

During the 1960s and the 1970s Nixdorf, Konstanz, Triumph Adler, Kienzle, Dietz and Krantz produced proprietary mid-range systems, focusing on sector-specific applications and with specific software. These companies survived until the 1980s.

Nixdorf is the only outstanding success story in the German computer industry. Heinz Nixdorf founded his Labor für Impulstechnik in a cellar in 1952. Unencumbered by the electromechanical tradition of established office machine makers, he ventured into the field of electronics which was new at the time. He visualized the tremendous market potential for smaller office computers. He received a grant of 30,000 DM from RWE, Germany's largest power supplier, and developed a calculator for accounting and census taking. His minicomputers handled smaller processing loads than IBM's mainframes but cost considerably less. They were also known for engineering excellence.

By specializing in a restricted but largely uncontested market, Nixdorf expanded rapidly and by the early 1970s, his company had become the most successful European computer manufacturer, with an affiliate in the United States. Nixdorf grew into $3.5 billion Company with over 25,000 employees internationally. By 1974, the company had expanded into 16 countries.

In the mid-1970s, Nixdorf posted a serious challenge to the IBM 3600 with the launch of his 8864 bank terminal system which could support two different cash dispensers and a variety of workstations. The processor featured powerful mainframe-type TTL logical circuitry and MOS memory running at 125 nanoseconds. The meteoric rise of Heinz Nixdorf inaugurated a new era in the computer industry. The company kept growing by leaps and bounds and its reputation extended to Japan and other countries where its minicomputers competed favorably with IBM. In 1984, Nixdorf was Europe's second largest computer company after IBM.

Fortune Magazine named Heinz Nixdorf Europe's best manager. When the American and Japanese manufacturers started selling microcomputers with Intel chips and a Microsoft operating system, Nixdorf refused to admit that the era of proprietary technology had come to an end. The advent of the open standards systems reduced production costs for those who adopted it. Manufacturers who stuck to proprietary systems had to constantly upgrade their products, lest they fall behind. Nixdorf reacted too late to market changes. In 1988, sales volume dropped abruptly while production costs kept increasing. The refusal to pull away from the strategy based on proprietary software made his computers uncompetitive. The descent was swift. In 1989 the company lost DM 1 billion.

Nixdorf approached several companies outside Germany in view of a possible alliance, but the Deutsche Bank, a major shareholder, wanted a ,German solution', which limited the options to Siemens or Mannesmann, the engineering group which also owned the Kienzle minicomputer operation. A merger with any of these companies would have meant a subordinate role for Nixdorf's technology, and probably its management. This was fiercely resisted within the company.

In 1989 Nixdorf was bought by financial investors and renamed Wincor Nixdorf. In January 1990, Siemens announced that it would step in to rescue Nixdorf in order to avoid that foreign companies get a foothold in its home market. The arrangement was intended to create a strong company that would preserve Europe's technological independence. Nixdorf's minicomputers would dovetail with Siemens' mainframes, thereby complementing each other in foreign markets. The merger was delayed until October 1990, to give the management time to plan the synergy of two disparate companies. In anticipation of the merger, Nixdorf cut 4,000 jobs. After two decades during which Heinz Nixdorf was admired as the guiding star of the European computer industry, his company was confronted with catastrophe. Nixdorf died of a heart attack on a dance floor at the Hannover Trade Fair. [7]

FRANCE. After World War II, unlike the United States and Britain, the French scientific community had no experience in radar electronics. In higher education and research, pure mathematics was traditionally considered an autonomous discipline to be pursued by an intellectual aristocracy as a science dealing with the relationship and symbolism of numbers and magnitudes. Those who resorted to mathematics for practical or commercial purposes were merely "appliers of mathematics." Physics also was essentially a basic science. France did not have a differential analyzer until the mid-1950s, which prevented familiarization with the new electronics technology and culture.

When mainframe computers made their appearance in the United States, several French entrepreneurs set up computer production. They bought components from specialized producers and soldered them together. In 1952, the Compagnie des Machines Bull, France's largest manufacturer of punched-card equipment, entered the electronic calculator market. The Gamma 3 calculator was a success and the major factor in the spectacular expansion of the company during the following decade. Gamma 3 was an excellent machine. Development of mainframe computers required vast investments, but the growing cost of developing new models was beyond Bull's means. Besides, competition from IBM, Univac and other American companies was severe. In 1964, General Electric bought the company and renamed it Bull-General Electric. Shortly after the take-over, General Electric scrapped the development projects underway at Bull.

In 1955, the Société d'Electronique et d'Automatisme (SEA) was the first French manufacturer to produce digital computers. Very inventive, the company owned several patents in text processing, virtual memory, teleprocessing and electronic telephone switching. Its computer, the CAB 500 sold very well. But the company was unable to finance the development of new models and was absorbed by the Schneider group, which enabled a considerable investment and increased production. By 1967, the company had a staff of 850.

The Compagnie Européenne d'Automatisme Electronique (CAE) was a joint venture between the Californian company, Thompson-Ramo-Woolridge and CSF, a leading manufacturer of electronic hardware for the professional market, mainly for the military. CAE sold American calculators which included components made in France. The CAE machines were medium-sized calculators, relatively low-priced and destined mainly for scientific computation. Most were custom made for the army and for nuclear research.

In the early 1960s, about ten companies were making computers in France. The government decided something had to be undertaken to stop the domination of its market by IBM. General de Gaulle became alarmed over France's dependence on American technology. In 1963, he decided, to the annoyance of the US government, that France should become an atomic power. This required a supercomputer that only Control Data could supply. The threat by the American government to embargo delivery made the situation very irksome. The general initiated a technological program aimed at establishing a national computer industry able to guarantee France's independence. The project was called "Plan Calcul".

Plan Calcul was to federate and integrate the French manufacturers into a single company. This led, in 1966, to the creation of the CII, (Compagnie Industrielle pour l'Informatique) by the merger of SEA, CAE and a subsidiary of CITEC. The following year CSF Thomson became a shareholder of CII. Thought up by énarques and polytechniciens, no representative of the industry participated in the elaboration of the plan. The civil servants who conceived it had in mind the national independence rather than economic viability. The major strategic error of Plan Calcul was to challenge IBM in the top-of-the-range computers where it had a practical monopoly.

Bull was no longer considered "French" and the aim was to create a computer company that was authentically French and able to achieve technological independence. Its objectives were to develop a national computer industry in order for France 'to master its own destiny.' National resources were concentrated on CII. The company was to produce a French-designed mainframe computer, using French semiconductors. CII would have to cease all alliances with foreign companies for any components that could be produced by a French company. Plan des Composants was to help with the development of semiconductor devices, primarily for computer applications.

An inter-ministerial "Délégation à l'Informatique" reporting directly to the prime minister, included no computer scientist and no professional programmer. The government was to help the companies with grants and preferential purchases. The strategy turned out to be wrongheaded. The planned investment amounted to twice the amount of expected profits. At the end of 1968, CII's first computer, the Iris 50 was delivered. However, it was largely based on foreign technology inherited from CAE's agreement with a US company. Another computer, the Iris 80, soon followed but was largely incompatible with the first system.

The administrators of the Délégation à l'Informatique had taken control of both the company's strategy and its day-to-day operations. CII was effectively run by civil servants who saw no harm in the incompatibility between two computer ranges. They were convinced they were able to design a mainframe computer system to compete technically and commercially with IBM. The IRIS computers sold well, but the cost of production exceeded the selling price. CII grew rapidly, mainly because it was the only supplier of the public sector. Within four years the company employed 6,000 employees. [8]

The French government then thought up a "European" solution: co-operation with Siemens. A synergy between the technical excellence of IRIS and the financial power of Siemens would open the European market. Philips joined to form Unidata. The complexity of decision-making, the divergent technical systems and the permanent bickering soon put an end to the project.

By 1971, IBM had captured about half of the French private market. Honeywell-Bull came second. CII had hardly made a dent outside the public sector market. The government decided to initiate a second Plan Calcul, more than doubling its funding. In 1970, General Electric sold its computer division to Honeywell. Bull-General Electric was renamed Compagnie Honeywell-Bull (CHB) and, integrated into Honeywell. In 1975, the government pressed the owners of CII to merge with Compagnie Honeywell-Bull. The company was renamed CII-Honeywell-Bull. CII-Honeywell Bull was a French-American joint venture, the brainchild of President Giscard d'Estaing when he put an end to General de Gaulle's nationalistic policies. Originally the French government had a 20 percent stake.

French governments are fond of "plans" and "grands programmes" supposed to mobilize the energies and the resources of the nation to promote national grandeur. The plans are announced with fanfare, but are seldom preceded by a strategic analysis that integrates the imperatives of the market. Financial considerations are secondary since the costs will be covered by taxes. French ventures in the computer industry have been a combination of huge ambitions and deep disappointments, raison d'Etat and political impulses. Billions of old and new francs were engulfed in computer projects in the name of the national interest and independence. But with nearly three-quarters of R&D carried out in government-controlled institutions, the French electronics industry distanced itself from the market, thus stifling innovation and new ideas.

In 1971, Intel had set up a sales office in Paris, headed by Bernard Giroud. In the early 1980s, when the French government announced a plan for the development of a semiconductor industry, he was able to convince Bob Noyce to take a 20 percent interest in the new company. It was intended to create a "California à la française" in Nice or Toulouse. After lengthy negotiations, the project was abandoned, because the socialist.

Prime Minister, Pierre Mauroy, former mayor of Lille, wanted the plant to be set up in north of France or in Lorraine. In April 1972, Intel launched the 8008 microprocessor and placed an article in a specialized magazine. François Gernelle, a young engineer working in a small company located near Paris, was fascinated by the idea of a miniature electronic device that contained all the arithmetic, logic, and control circuitry necessary to perform the functions of a digital computer's central processing unit. By the end of December, with a small team of engineers, he produced the Micral, the world's first microcomputer for delivery to the Ministry of Agriculture.

ITALY was a latecomer in computing, but also produced the most spectacularly successful company. In the 1950s, four entrepreneurs briefly tried to manufacture mainframe computers: Giuseppe De Marco, Giovanni Mainetto, Serena Pisani and Pasquale Savino. They developed their own technology or built machines under license, but none of them lasted very long. IBM predominated while the other American companies took each a small share of the market. The industry and the government showed little interest in the new industry. In the early 1980s, with the appearance of the personal computer, the government and industry became conscious of their backwardness and of the need for schooling and training in data processing. In 1978, a report "Programma Finalizatto dell' Elettronica" issued by the Federation of Scientific and Technical Associations noted that Italy was the only industrialized nation without a policy to stimulate the computer industry. Several companies and universities started common projects, but due to the lack of funds, they were unable to show any results. In 1978, Carlo de Benedetti bought a stake in Olivetti and turned it for a few years into the most flamboyant and successful European computer company.

THE NETHERLANDS took an early start in the development of programmable electronic calculators. In 1946, the Amsterdam-based Mathematical Center set up a computer department. Several electrical engineers with experience in semiconductor technology and electronics developed an automatic calculator and by 1954 the machine was installed at Fokker. A manufacturing operation named Electrologica NV was set up in The Hague. Electrologica's ARRA computers were of excellent quality. But the company was too small to sustain competition when IBM upset the market by the introduction of its system 360. In 1967, Philips bought Electrologica in order to gain quick access to computer technology. Philips continued production, but was equally unable to sustain competition with IBM.

Philips had prospered during the war and benefited from the expropriation of German assets in the Netherlands. The company had developed expertise in the production of transistors and electronic calculators. With the profits earned from consumer electronics, plus substantial government subsidies, the company made a multibillion guilder investment in computer technology and became the Dutch national champion.

In the mid-1970s, Philips designed a range of medium and small office computers of excellent quality. Within a few years, the company had 18 percent of the European market.

Technically the machines were as good as any other, but Philips kept charging prices that gradually became uncompetitive and decided to give up.

THE AMERICAN CHALLENGE

In the early 1950s American mainframe computers made their appearance in Europe and immediately developed demand from banking, insurance and industry. Each computer was a one-of-a-kind hand-built machine IBM took the lion's share, leaving the rest to Honeywell, Remington Rand, Burroughs, National Cash Register, Control Data, General Electric and RCA. IBM defined the proprietary standards for computer technology and the trajectory of its development, earning oligopoly profits by dominating an industry that was lucrative, remarkably stable and growing fast. The company had approximately 85 percent of the US market.

IBM was the computer industry, a model of corporate profitability and performance. Its management cultivated the image of a business corporation eager to offer its services in the national interest, both to the government and to large corporations. IBM was an early pioneer of geographic dispersion. In 1949, in order to optimize its international operations, the company set up a transatlantic production network, the World Trade Corporation, a new model of international production. IBM was the first company to identify the advantages of integrating research and development, component production and systems assembly in different geographical locations, based on relative costs and the availability of specialized resources.

By the mid-1960s, the company had established a transatlantic production network where product development and manufacturing responsibilities were assigned to individual laboratories and production facilities; the labor-intensive assembly of components was shifted to low-cost offshore locations in Asia.

In 1961, IBM introduced time-sharing, which became the forerunner of technologies that would allow a high degree of interaction between the system and the end user. In 1964, IBM launched its 360 series, using interchangeable components, software and peripheral equipment. Instead of buying a whole new system whenever improvements came out, the customer could simply upgrade. The System/360 was intended to obsolete virtually all other existing computers. It secured domination of the mainframe market for three decades. In the first two years, the company was able to satisfy less than half of the 9,000 orders on its books. The computer mystique was reinforced every time new improvements became known. By 1965, the majority of large businesses routinely used computers to process financial operations. Banks began printing checks with magnetic ink so they could be processed automatically.

By the end of the 1960s, about 8,000 computers had been installed world-wide. The company maintained its position in the industry by giving each of its models a high rate of obsolescence. By the time Thomas Watson stepped down, as CEO in 1971, IBM was the unquestioned leader of the industry. Employees numbered more than 270,000 and gross income amounted to $8.3 billion.

IBM's lead in the United States was repeated in Europe, where several American companies invested $4 billion in manufacturing facilities. About 10 percent of the capital came from their own resources; the rest was supplied by European governments and Eurodollar loans. Production of computers was taken up in West Germany, Italy, France, Belgium, the Netherlands, Denmark, Norway, Sweden, Spain, Switzerland, Czechoslovakia, East Germany and the Soviet Union.

In 1964, General Electric took over Olivetti and Bull. Two small French computer companies, CAE and SEA, held about seven percent of the French market. Siemens accounted for about five percent of the German computer market. Only in Britain did local companies retain a reasonable market share.

In 1970, a recession hit the United States. IBM had forced the pace of technological development and the cost of research and development kept increasing. Several large manufacturers decided to give up production. General Electric pulled out in 1970 and RCA in 1971, with serious consequences for Bull and

Siemens. The remaining American companies set their sights on the European market, while IBM reduced its prices.

By 1970, nearly 20,000 mainframe computers had been installed in Western Europe; about 80 percent were built by American companies, and a significant share of the remaining 20 percent was manufactured under American license. Computers and electronics had emerged as a new industry and national computing capability symbolized technological competence and national prestige. European governments became convinced that computer would inaugurate a scientific-technical revolution and become an essential element of the industrial infrastructure. A series of reports by the OECD reinforced their fears and placed the computer industry at the center of their solicitudes.

The European governments watched American companies take control of their markets. Nowhere was "the American challenge" as evident as in computers. The microelectronics industry had come to symbolize technological competence and national prowess. The technology gap raised the specter of economic backwardness. It augured poorly for Europe's economy if it had no industry to rival American high- technology firms.

The French, British, Italian, West-German and Dutch governments intended to limit their technological dependence and started financing research, in order to build up their nascent computer industries. They prompted mergers in order to create national champions. The German, French and British governments established ministries for science and technology. The policy was based on the idea that economic growth was linked to national power and sovereignty and that it should be fostered through government intervention rather than market forces. Additional elements of the national champion policy included the creation of national technical standards to protect domestic manufacturers and national-source buying requirements for government and nationalized firms. Instead of bracing itself to compete globally, the computer industry soon became dependent on monopolistic advantages, on subsidies, tariffs and other defensive strategies.

Several governments decided to protect their industry by erecting tariff walls, by granting subsidies and soft loans and by giving effective monopoly rights on public contracts. Government departments were instructed to buy only the national products and pressure was put on private companies to do the same. The 1960s, and especially the 1970s, became the age of the state-sponsored national champions.

The recession of the 1970s increased unemployment and inflation, while diminishing the economic strength of the national champions, unable to adapt to changes in the world economy. The desire to keep national champions operating and to avoid additional unemployment led governments to channel considerable funds into uncompetitive manufacturers. They were slow to change their policies and remained committed to the national champion policy throughout the 1970s, and in the case of France into the mid 1980s.

The policy was to buy computers from national suppliers or from suppliers who built their computers locally - such as IBM - and only in third place from other European companies. The "buy national" policy, while it favoured the local companies, worked against other European suppliers and in favor of IBM. In fact, the "buy national" policy allowed American companies to penetrate all the European markets, whereas their European counterparts found it very difficult to get a foothold outside their national market.

The national champion model linked science and technology to economic growth, which was in turn linked to national power and sovereignty. Despite these strategies, the position of the European industry deteriorated year after year. When the Japanese came to challenge the Americans, they rapidly increased their share of the market. European firms, often badly organized and insensitive to market requirements, did very poorly. Government policy, if anything, made matters worse.

At the 1972 Paris Summit, Giscard d'Estaing and Helmut Schmidt decided to seek an alliance between Siemens and CII. Siemens had lost access to RCA technology, while CII faced increased competition in the French market through the merger of Honeywell and Bull. Both companies needed funds to invest in new technology. Negotiations proceeded swiftly and an agreement was signed to create a joint company. The aim was to produce a common range of computers, while each company would also sell and service the machines of its associate in its home market.

Philips, not wanting to be left out, announced it would join the alliance. After several months of negotiations, the three participants set up a management structure for a company called Unidata. The name was somewhat surprising, since there was already a Unidata computer company which, after some negotiations, was happy to accept a check for the rights to the name, and subsequently renamed itself Ventek.

Unidata was announced with great fanfare as a joint venture intended to become the largest European company. Maurice Allègre, head of the Délégation à l'Informatique claimed that it "marks the real beginning of the formation of a European computer industry which will be truly multinational... In a true multinational community, no decision-making body should have priority over another. On the contrary several decision-making bodies of different nationalities must cooperate, without one being subordinate to another."

Honeywell-Bull became concerned about increased competition from Unidata, and attempted to take over the German mainframe manufacturer, Telefunken-AEG, but this move was blocked by the German government. Siemens had insisted that the Unidata range of computers be IBM-compatible, whereas CII wanted an independent design. Siemens and Philips were giant companies, and the French feared they would be dominated. The decisions about CII were conducted by the Délégation à l'Informatique. The Prime Minister, the Minister of Industry, the Finance Minister and the French President had a voice in the decisions. The Minister of Industry increasingly pressed for a link with Honeywell-Bull, while the finance minister was concerned about the fact that French subsidies would indirectly help Siemens.

Philips was producing a computer that would be in direct competition with a new French minicomputer, Logabax. Philips also became increasingly disillusioned. When Unidata requested a substantial increase for development, Philips demanded that the three-way split in management be replaced by a single controlling body making decisions by majority voting. The other partners rejected the idea.

In mid-1973, they reviewed the structure and the technical strategy for the company. The program was scaled down to a single line of commercial computers. The idea of merging sales and distributing channels was abandoned. With three headquarters, three technical departments and three research centers, it would have been a very complex structure. Moreover, reaching decisions required unanimity which would have made the management of the company impossible.

After the take-over of CII by Honeywell-Bull in mid-1975, co-operation continued for about one year until the alliance was formally dissolved. The Unidata venture ended in May 1975 when the French government announced that its negotiations with CII and Honeywell-Bull had been successful and had taken a 51 percent stake in Honeywell-Bull, making it the new French national champion. The catch-up game was difficult in the fragmented European markets.

Policy-makers could only imitate the product mix and industrial structure they saw in the United States. Governments could only jump on the bandwagon, unable to play the entrepreneurial role of imagining and inventing new industrial futures. They reasoned from the structures they observed. Their policies pushed European firms directly into market segments dominated by the American giants. Firms were unable to develop their own distinctive technological niches, and consequently the possibility of innovative breakthroughs that could have permitted them to become leaders in limited sectors. The result was a deep and enduring technological dependence in virtually all segments of the industry. Policy of support for weak producers failed to regenerate industrial position in those sectors defined as critical.

Government intervention was lavish, but misfocused and self-defeating, as much a hindrance as an asset. Cooperation failed, because each company measured its success in relation to the others. Each government instituted "buy national" policies that secured the home market but undermined others' chances of developing an overseas market. Each government limited its interventions to its own national champion. Time had come for a serious attempt to create a European response to US domination of the computer industry. The major companies and the governments were increasingly in favor of joint action. The European Community encouraged alliances that could progressively develop closer links.

At the 1972 Paris Summit, a commitment was made for gradual implementation of a common European policy in scientific research and technological development. In 1973, the European commission created a specific Directorate-General for Research, Science and Education. A European policy was needed to develop a strong and competitive industry both in hardware and software. The most effective way would be the wide use of computers. Community funds would be made available to develop computer applications in pan-European projects such as air traffic control, meteorology and trade statistics. The Council of Ministers adopted the report, and the commission went on to produce a detailed program of action.

Among the key proposals were cooperative development projects as well as the standardization and the coordination of public procurement policies. The commission also proposed that the Council agree to the formation of a financing system intended to promote European-produced computers. In 1974, the commission also launched an investigation into IBM under the Treaty of Rome's competition rules.

Several attempts were made to develop European response to US domination. In 1973, the commission published a report stressing the need for a European industry in hardware and software, and recommended that Community funds be used for the development of pan-European projects. The report was adopted by the Council of Ministers.

Computer technology was overwhelmingly tied up in large firms. Each national champion had built up a customer base in its home market, but was insignificant elsewhere. In the markets outside the European Community, American and Japanese companies enjoyed an overwhelming competitive advantage. The national champions had been unable to cope with the rapid pace of change in the industry; they had failed to master the new technology and to adopt the adequate merchandizing techniques.

A broad consensus gradually developed that Europe must possess cutting-edge technologies and that their timely application was of critical importance to the development of the whole economy. Dependence on American technology would render large segments of European industry obsolete in the long term. The gap would have dramatic implications for other industries. Advanced computer industry has critical linking with other industries. The development of the microelectronics technology required a vast number of engineers and technicians, which in turn required increased spending on research and development.

The costs involved in the development of a new generation of computers and microprocessors were becoming too high for any single country to go it alone. By setting up alliances and sharing the burden and the risk, it was expected that the European electronics industry would meet the global challenge and maintain a global role. A European technological policy would produce economies of scale by pooling the scientific and engineering talent from several nations. Europe-wide research networks would increase the access of scholars to data and facilities across borders. Industry would also benefit from the Community's main asset: a market of 340 million people.

The idea of a European technology policy had its merits: the national champions were drawing easy pickings from a secure domestic market. Sustained by subsidies and content with easy profits, they had become used to a comfortable lifestyle. They had no interest in becoming involved in the strenuous and risky business of international competition. Their production runs, focused on their national markets, were too short and too costly to be globally competitive.

In 1967, the Council of Science Ministers asked the commission to propose a program of joint action to counter the US domination. The Aigrain Report recommended that six major companies, Siemens, Telefunken-AEG, ICL, Olivetti, CII and Philips develop a common computer range that would constitute the European standard. The industry turned down the idea. The governments refused to sacrifice their national champions on the altar of European integration.

The commission then launched a study in order to determine how to promote European cooperation. In 1970, the Colonna Report presented a project for a European technology policy. It proposed the creation of a single market for the electronics industry, combined with financial support and the granting of development contracts. The French government approved, but the German and Dutch governments who were funding their own computer industries, favored direct co-operation between companies.

The Treaty of Rome which set up the EEC, mentioned technology policy as a domain for common action capable of "strengthening the scientific and technological bases of the Community industry and encouraging it to become more competitive at the international level."

The tension between the advocates of free markets and those who wanted more state control through industrial policy is apparent in the compromises that determine the nature of the Treaty of Rome. The interventionists carried the day. Ever since, the history of the European Community is one of increased intervention in large sectors of the economy.

The accelerated decline of the European computer and microelectronics industries triggered a debate about the urgency of a European technology policy. The computer incarnated the information technology, and the chip was its heart. European champions were to become globally competitive through research and development and redistributive policies. Cross-border alliances and synergies would accelerate technological advances. Instead of competing against each other, which hurt the continent's position as a major technological power, integration would be a gigantic step forward. A common European response would overcome the fragmentation of national resources and create a network for European companies to co-operate and interact, thus upgrading their technological capabilities. By transferring responsibility and resources from the national to the supranational level, the scope and the scale of technology policy would be expanded.

In 1974, the Council of Ministers adopted a resolution authorizing the planning for a medium-term Community program to promote research, industrial development and the application of information technology. The European technology policy would be directly managed and administered by the commission.

The strategic justification for a European technology policy was clear: only by pooling capabilities could the European Community hope to achieve the economies of scale and the critical mass needed to compete in world markets and create high-value-added jobs. Governments bristled with projects of pan-European R&D programs. Instead of protective tariffs, subsidies would be granted to make European companies more competitive.

A consensus developed that there should be a European response to US domination of the global computer industry. This would require that several companies seek partners. On September 11, 1979, the Council of the European Communities invited the commission to examine the possibilities and methods of coordinating national projects in microelectronics technology and data processing.

5

EUROPEAN TECHNOLOGY POLICY

The national-champion strategy adopted during the formative years of the computer industry had not prevented American and Japanese manufacturers from increasing their market share by offering new and superior buyer value with upgraded products at lower prices. IBM was in a dominant position in every European country and had established a commercial and technological commanding position. The national-champion approach had a major drawback: each country's policies cancelled out the others, thereby weakening all. Each market required a national organization, a technical support staff and marketing managers; the sales achieved in each country could not support this sort of overhead. The problem was exacerbated by the fact that the four largest public sector markets, Britain, France, Germany and Italy, were in fact quasi-monopolies granted to the national champions.

The lack of industrial competitiveness and the accompanying losses in employment turned the problem into a public issue. Computer manufacturers, unable to hold their own in the marketplace, had for years beseeched the political class for financial help and protection from foreign competitors. Governments had featherbedded and cocooned their national champions with subsidies, defense and state contracts, in addition to shielding them from competition through tariffs, anti-dumping duties and "voluntary" export restraints. Instead of stemming the tide, these measures had induced American and Japanese firms to invest and produce in Europe. It became obvious that a new policy was needed to sustain the European computer industry.

The failure of the national-champion policies presented the commission with the opportunity to propose a forward-looking program and a radical reshaping of technology policy. This would substantially broaden its involvement in industrial affairs.

Information technology policy became an important responsibility and the co-ordination of industrial policies a flanking dimension of integration. A "European" industrial policy would be a gigantic step forward. In order to make researchers and industry think "European", the commission recommended programs of "pre-competitive" research that could be shared. The results of basic research would be spread between industry, private laboratories and universities. The Treaty of Rome forbids agreements likely to restrict competition, but pre-competitive research was exempted by the competition directorate.

The economic logic of collaboration seemed evident: research and development was becoming increasingly expensive. In the face of American scientific and technological superiority, only by sharing technological breakthroughs and pooling ideas could the European industry hope to achieve the economies of scale needed to compete in world markets.

So far, the bulk of public subsidies had been distributed to the most backward sectors of the economy. The commission had acquired notoriety as patron of farming, coal, steel and shipbuilding. The name "European Community" had become tarnished by association with the negative images of milk lakes and mountains of butter. A successful policy in the prestige field of electronics would be a dynamic factor in the revitalization of the European economy, and help recast the political and industrial bargain that underpinned the Community. It would be an antidote to the image of fraud that had damaged the common agricultural policy. Based on this rationale, the commission became the patron of a new technology policy which seemed a perfect catalyst for integration. The idea of making the European computer industry more competitive through increased support for industrial and academic research and development became the rallying cry of high-powered lobbies.

The year 1979 was pivotal in the implementation of the program. Commissioner for Industry, Etienne Davignon, had extensive discussions with the executives of the large computer companies and with government leaders. He invited a group of industrialists of the electronics industry to discuss the possibility of a European approach to the problem. Davignon conceived of EC research policy not as the regulation of a European space for science and technology, but as the distribution of research funds to flank the broader Single European Market project. He wanted to establish a network of synergies among industries, universities and research centers.

He recommended the reduction of subsidies to mature industries where Europe was no longer competitive, and to finance the R&D of new technologies that would provide jobs in replacement of those that had been shed. Europe would have to play a leading role in "sunrise" industries such as computing, telecommunications and microelectronics. He estimated that a well-conceived and bold industrial policy would secure 30 percent of the global market.

Davignon was confronted with an industry in which high-tech capabilities were tied up in 12 uncompetitive firms: ICL, GEC and Plessey from Britain; Siemens, AEG and Nixdorf from Germany; Thomson, Bull and CGE from France; Olivetti and STET from Italy; Philips from the Netherlands. He organized what came to be known as the Round Table of European industrialists, the Big Twelve.

On February 8, 1980, they had their first meeting. No details were given about the discussions, but it was learned that the creation of European standards, intensified research in microelectronics, plus the development and production of components were on the agenda. The most enthusiastic supporters of the European technology policy were the executives of the large companies who paid lip service to the "guidance" provided by the commission, while in a hurry to pocket the subsidies.

The Round Table marked the beginning of a new policy. It contributed to setting the principles, objectives and priorities for action. The future of the European computer industry was uncertain, but there was hope. In 1973, ICL was still competing successfully against IBM in Britain. In 1978, Carlo De Benedetti had taken control of Olivetti, a stumbling typewriter company and was on the verge of becoming Europe's champion, able to stand up to the Americans in their own market. He had even outsmarted the giant AT&T. In the European landscape, he was an unusual kind of businessman. A rare breed of entrepreneur, determined to shake the industry out of its dependency mentality, he took a dim view of government intervention in the economy. But the debate was short-lived: the dirigistes prevailed over the free-marketeer.

The commission decided that information technology could not be left to the mercy of market forces, but had instead to be coordinated by government policies. The purpose was to make the national champions "think as Europeans" and to pool their strategic resources in concernment with Brussels. The commission justified its role by its capacity to co-ordinate research and reduce duplication, to control and limit national subsidies, and by its mandate for foreign trade and competition policy. It was also intended to promote the development of a European consensus on standards and to make researchers feel they were part of a truly European scientific community.

It took two years of meetings for 400 people from the commission, industry and academia to work out proposals which they then submitted to the Council of Ministers for approval. Between 1980 and 1982, the commission drew up a program for research in microelectronics, computing, software technologies, office automation and integrated computer systems.

The commission set thematic focal points in research policy. The largest and most important focal area was information and communications technology. The vice-president of the commission, Karl-Heinz Narjes, claimed that information technology had a strategic role: it was impossible to devise a model for society, to secure European political and economic autonomy or to guarantee commercial competitiveness without complete mastery of the most sophisticated technologies. Furthermore, the Community was responsible for strengthening the scientific and technological basis of European industry, in addition to actively helping industry to become more responsive to the global competitive environment. [1]

The commission deliberately limited its selection to large companies, the industrial giants who were to be the backbone of the program. High technology seemed beyond the capabilities of small enterprises. From the beginning, two competing policy imperatives had to be considered: while technology policy sought to foster "European excellence", regardless of where that excellence was geographically located, cohesion between richer and poorer member states required that the allocation of subsidies be widely and fairly distributed.

Technology policy and the promotion of the information society became the European commission's big project. Big projects, of course, meant big money. Community funds would be used to foster technical co-operation between enterprises and to promote company mergers. A few large European firms would thus have the advantage of a huge integrated free-trade area, from where they would mount a resolute challenge for a global market share. The goal was to transform national champions into European champions by promoting economies of scale. Technology policy inevitably generated power politics. One of the side effects of the distributive policy was the spontaneous creation of clients and pressure groups: the EC's teams of "experts", lobbyists, academics, consultants, researchers, and the executives of the industry. They learned very quickly how to play the game.

Forward planning requires a thorough awareness of the industry and of the market. Unfortunately, the political and bureaucratic planners' perception of the world they were about to enter was an abstraction, far removed from reality. They had no privy information about the markets, the technology or the industry. They had no affinity with the products and were not in a position to learn about them, nor to evaluate their economic potential. They had no idea of the challenges ahead and were unqualified to participate intelligently in decisions on technology-based issues. But overweening self-confidence made them blind to their own shortcomings.

IBM had emerged as the world leader in mainframes,. In the 1970s the System 360 dominated the market. Two major US companies, RCA and GE, tried to build comparable mainframes, but suffered huge losses. In 1970, Gene Amdahl, the designer of the System 360, left IBM to start his own enterprise. Unable to raise the $40 million required, he turned to Japan's Fujitsu, which received him with elation and, in turn, made his plug-compatible equipment available to other Japanese computer makers. With the acquisition of Amdahl's technology, Japan's industry quickly captured its own rapidly growing domestic market for computers. Then in the early 1980s, the European computer producers turned to Fujitsu, Hitachi, and NEC to acquire plug-compatibles on an original equipment manufacturer basis, that is, to be sold as products of the European companies. The European computer makers were buying IBM technology from Japan. [2]

The Big Twelve had agreed on a concerted action: the best way to counterpoise American hegemony would be a policy emphasizing self-reliance and the development of a European standard for electronics components as a spearhead against IBM. They asked the commission to institute an "Open Systems Interconnect" (OSI) standard. Consequently no European government agency would be allowed to purchase equipment that did not bear the OSI stamp. Horst Nasko, board member of Nixdorf, declared that a European norm would free the industry and the consumers from being subjected to one single manufacturer. There was general agreement that a common European norm would take the edge off IBM's market power and improve the competitive position of European industry. IBM was unimpressed and welcomed the international harmonization of standards.

Having decided to catch up by emulating American and Japanese market leaders, the policy-makers set out on the wrong track. The national champions set their sights on trying to dislodge IBM by building "better" mainframe technology. They did not know that the computer industry was in turmoil and had no appreciation whatever of the revolutionary business model that was taking hold in the United States where a vast number of start-ups, such as Apple, Commodore and Osborne were producing microcomputers based on open standards.

Microcomputers increasingly undermined the mainframe-based networks, the foundation of IBM's power. As they grew, they pushed the price-performance curve steadily out of reach of the industry leaders, thus disrupting the established order. Their success had forced IBM to enter the personal computer market, using Intel microprocessors and software licensed from Bill Gates. Mainframes became a dead-end technology. The era of micro miniaturization had begun. By 1980, over one million personal computers had been sold in the United States. Some of the new companies soon went one step further: by shifting labor-intensive assembly to low-cost Asia, they learned the organizational technology of international production.

The computer had changed and so had the industry. Making a computer had been the exclusive province of a few very large vertically integrated companies. It required highly specialized expertise in an enormous range of disciplines. Now a vast number of high-quality commodized components were on the market at low cost. The personal computers did not arise from expensive, well-equipped laboratories. They were created outside the corporate and academic establishment, by amateur hobbyists and college dropouts.

The personal computers were assembled from standard components, using common architectural interface, determined largely by the world-beating breakthroughs of Intel and Microsoft. Building these machines did not require any research and development. Access to components, some engineering and assembly know-how were sufficient to set up production. The proprietary technology in these machines was buried in the components and the manufacturing processes used to produce them. Successful entrants to the industry pioneered new markets with new products tailored to those markets.

Mainframes are huge machines; the personal computer technology is entirely different. The people who eventually introduced the PC were rebels. Many had worked in some of the big companies. They retreated into their garages and started the silicon revolution. Intel had single-handedly beaten the giant Japanese semiconductor manufacturers. Gordon Moore had laid down his law: the number of transistors on a chip would double every 18 to 24 months. Bill Gates had outfoxed the IBM management by making them buy his Windows software while keeping it to himself. Intel and Microsoft were in the process of establishing global standards for the new horizontally-integrated computer architecture and cementing their quasi-monopoly position. The IBM PC introduced in 1981 was designed with an open architecture around Intel and Microsoft, enabling other computer manufacturers to create clones. The IBM PC had become the PC standard. But all this was terra incognita in the political world.

Although Apple, Commodore, Compaq and other microcomputers had made their appearance in Europe, the commission's technology planners were unaware of the fact that the microcomputer was revolutionizing and reshaping the industry and that Silicon Valley had invented an entirely new business model. While a continuing stream of innovation was changing the global computer industry, European policy focused upon an obsolescent technology.

In the United States, the "free market" ideology leaves the government without any officially recognized role for the technological advance of non-military sectors. The Reagan administration explained this position in its first "Science and Technology Report" to Congress in 1981: "the Administration is committed to the view that the collective judgment of innovators, entrepreneurs and consumers, made in a free market environment is generally superior to any form of centralized programming."

Military research has generated advances in technical knowledge for specific products that have been adopted by the commercial marketplace. But the US government is not used to designing national strategies for helping its industries compete with foreign companies. The firms involved in defense contracting are not the same as those who are at the spearhead of civilian consumer goods development. National security dominates the federal technology agenda. In semiconductors the military want unsurpassed performance under conditions of conflict, regardless of expense, while civilian industry needs reliability and low cost.

The "magic of the market" is the bedrock of American capitalism. The very concept of technology policy is anathema to most economists and legislators. The high-tech industry and the government have traditionally been at arm's length. Sematech was the short-lived exception. It was set up when the American microprocessor industry came close to being destroyed by Japanese competition. A medium-sized company, Intel, decided to take up the challenge without government help. After an epic battle in which "the difference between American and Japanese producers had depended on their relative capacity to endure pain", Intel developed the microprocessor technology. The American semiconductor industry never returned to the government for protection.

In 1983, a German and Dutch enquiry team, led by Siemens and Philips, went to Japan in order to find out how the Japanese industry had managed to be so successful. They came back with a story about massive government support and started a lobbying campaign for public funding. Their account completely distorted the facts. The Japanese government had guided and assisted the catch-up exercise of the electronics companies through tax breaks, low-interest loans and high tariffs; but the industry neither asked for nor received any substantial subsidies. In the 1970s, on several occasions the government provided funding, but insisted that it was up to the firms to be competitive by themselves in the global markets. The policy of MITI has always been to keep subsidies as low as possible. Private industry finances virtually all its own R&D. MITI had then seen to it that ruthless competition between the leading manufacturers kept the Japanese industry as a whole competitive with the Americans. [3]

The Japanese started out from a position far inferior to that of the European industry. But they were expert at acquiring American technology by any means, fair or foul, and then outdoing the original. They acknowledged the superiority of American technology and obtained trade secrets and manufacturing processes in order to overcome the disadvantage. In 1982, Hitachi was involved in a web of industrial espionage. It is well known that California is crawling with people ready to sell technical information, and that big money is available for an employee who will pass out company secrets. [4]

Fiercely competitive, each Japanese company chose its methods. The most common was an alliance with a leading American manufacturer. In mainframes, NEC had tied up with Honeywell, Hitachi with RCA, Toshiba with General Electric, Mitsubishi with TRW. They also resorted to acquisition of American companies: Fujitsu acquired a stake in Amdahl and American Telecom.

JACQUES DELORS TAKES OVER

In 1985, Jacques Delors became president of the commission. A visionary and persuasive proponent of ever-closer union, he decided that Europe needed a new institutional framework, a common and sophisticated approach to technology policy-making. He made his mark by vastly expanding the powers of the commission, unleashing a torrent of legislation, and proclaiming his belief in the political unity of Europe and the glories of a unique European social model.

Among the emblematic personalities who shaped public policy in post-war Europe, Jacques Delors personifies the most audacious political project of modern times: the plan to unite European countries under a single supranational government. His fulgurant career carried him within a few years from an obscure trade-union activist to the visionary founder of the European Union. His career offers an interesting insight into the accidental nature of political leadership.

His father was a courier at the Banque de France. While at school, the boy was active in the JOC (Jeunesse Ouvrière Chrétienne). At the age of 19, having obtained his baccalauréat, he entered the Banque de France. Amidst énarques and polytechniciens competing for advancement in the hierarchy of the Bank, Delors became a leading trade-union activist. Metaphysically inclined, he was an adept in personalist philosophy which advocated the forging of a middle way between neo-classical liberalism and communism. According to personalism, capitalism generates inequality and alienation and must be opposed through civic action in order to remedy economic and social injustice. He became involved in the class struggle, denouncing elitism as hostile to equality. A bustling autodidact and an avid reader, he believed that ideas can change the world. He was one of the founders of Citoyens 60, and edited its bulletin under the pseudonym Roger Jacques.

In 1969, Chaban-Delmas, destabilised by the student revolt
and the massive strikes, asked him to contribute in the preparation of the "New Society". He accepted, but recommended
that the government legislate on face-to-face management-
labour relations through collective bargaining. His proposals were badly received. Realising the difficulty of putting his
ideas into practice in the right-wing Gaullist Party, he joined
the Socialist Party where his economic and social theories were
highly appreciated.

After 30 years of trade union militancy, political ambition
pushed him to quit the shadows and seek public office. In
1975, at the mature age of 49, he published a book (with a
journalist co-author) titled *Changer*, in which he propounded
the basic principles and the fundamental tenets and commit-
ments that guided his political and social action, and which
he vowed he would never recant. He manifested his adhesion
to François Mitterrand's "Programme Commun", an alliance
with the Communist Party intended to give the left an absolute
majority in Parliament. He denounced the domination of capitalism, the prevalence of meritocracy and the authoritarian
and centralising tradition of French politics. He considered
the class struggle as the most effective engine of change and
cited Lenin's dictum: "Never be more than one step ahead of
the working class."

Excerpts from the book: Capitalism isn't dead yet; it may
even increase its potential and continue its existence. But
this can only be done at the expense of all those who have
nothing but their labour to assure their subsistence. (p.
136). This state of affairs can only be remedied by liberat-
ing the State from the subtle domination of private interests;
in other words, by reversing the balance of power between
the State and the dominating industrial forces, through
nationalisation, control of the banks and the Plan (p. 214).
In France, an agreement between the employers and the
trade unions is impossible, given the fact that their concepts of society are diametrically opposed (p. 204). There
is no difference between the multinationals and the large

French firms. They have too much power over society. Their power must be abolished, since it deviates economic activity from its real purpose, namely the personal fulfilment of the individual (p. 137). Time will come when workers will go on strike for no other reason than their determination to claim they are fed up, as they did in May 68 (p. 197). Their grievances are becoming ever more powerful. This is fortunate. Absenteeism is mounting; dissatisfied workers leave their job or simply sabotage their work by producing rejects, or by taking large-scale industrial action (p.175). Why work so hard and suffer all these constraints, merely to produce unnecessary goods and services that are simple gadgets, when there is no time to love, to dream, to communicate, and even to pray? (p. 172). Since there will always be dull chores, why not organise a compulsory national service to which every young Frenchman would be subject? (p. 178).

The book brought him to the attention of François Mitterrand who arranged to have him elected to the European Parliament, where he became chairman of the Economic and Monetary Committee. During the 1981 presidential campaign, he was Mitterrand's chief economic adviser. The fact that he had been employed at the Banque de France earned him the reputation of an experienced financial economist.

He formulated the Socialist program of jobs, growth, massive nationalisations and the redistribution of wealth. It announced a new era of creativity and fairness, a time of generosity and solidarity. The French voted overwhelmingly for change and wound up with François Mitterrand at the Elysée. As Minister of Economy and Finance in Mauroy's Socialist and Communist coalition government, Delors carried out Mitterrand's policy intended to break with capitalism. A very substantial share of French banking and industry was nationalised. Very soon, the strategy of 'dash for growth' through consumption generated a galloping inflation, which forced the government to freeze wages and prices, to devalue the franc and to adopt an austerity program aimed at preventing the erosion of the foreign-exchange reserves.

Social unrest increased as workers and farmers protested the austerity policies and the government plans to lay off thousands of workers in nationalised money-losing industries, such as steel and shipbuilding. Within four years, Mitterrand's popularity slid so badly in the polls that a new mandate was highly unlikely. Delors realised that the Programme Commun was a failure and decided to quit. He distanced himself from the government and publicly advocated a pause in social policies, a clear acceptance of the market economy and an alignment with European social democracy. He thus acquired the reputation of a moderate Socialist and an economic expert, which made him an acceptable candidate to the job of President of the European Commission. In January 1985, Delors arrived in Brussels with a ready-made plan for a new European society.

Technology policy seemed the perfect candidate for accelerated integration and for giving the commission a higher profile and stronger mandate, increased relevance and power. He advocated the creation of a unified European industrial and scientific space through intense collaboration between Community member states. He was convinced that the European research potential was comparable to American, but was less efficient because it was too fragmented. Consequently, Europe was in danger of falling into technological dependence. In order to meet the challenge of the technological revolution, close industrial and scientific co-operation was an essential step toward European construction.

Under Delors' presidency, policy-making at the European level increased spectacularly. The commission emerged as a branch of government in its own right, concerned with European integration and social cohesion at the national and supranational level. The EC had been conceptualized as a federation in the making, an intergovernmental bargaining club and a concordance administration. A process of gradual evolution gave the European institutions an ever-greater autonomy from the states that created them. Delors wanted to make sure that the institutions and policies of the European Union would be able to stand their ground against subsequent reassertions of national sovereignty. This creeping centralization resulted in a marble cake federalism of co-decision, with no rigid delineation of competence and authority.

Delors had been for years an active socialist trade unionist and was not a friend of big business; but he had forcibly come to terms with reality. Economically he had absorbed the lessons of Mitterrand's primitive anti-capitalism. As Mitterrand's Economics and Finance Minister, he had nationalized the French banks and the major national industries, including electronics. As president of the commission, he frequently met with the senior executives of the computer industry, and courted them as potential allies in the dynamics of European integration.

American and Japanese companies which had survived the initial shake-out were engaged in fierce competition to increase their share of the market. Delors was convinced that success would be achieved if the major European companies co-operated in research and development. The industrialists claimed they were a special case and deserved exemption from the rigors of a free-for-all market. Lured by the prospect of easy money and craving for subsidies and support, whatever they may have thought of doctrinaire Socialism or a federal Europe, they were on his side.

Delors participated in the meetings because he believed the corporate executives should contribute to the formulation of industrial policy. He listened even more attentively because of their implicit threat to withdraw their support for the integration process if their demands were not adequately accounted for. By providing them with subsidies, he expected to win them as important allies in the European integration process.

Delors was the architect of the Single European Act of 1986 and the Maastricht Treaty on European Union. Both translated his concept of research policy into specific rules and procedures. The Single European Act legalized research and technological development policy in support of international economic competitiveness and other Community policies. It legitimized the commission's central role in the formulation and implementation of research policy. Its core was to be a multi-annual framework program, setting out all activities of the Community that would establish the scientific and technological objectives to be achieved. The commission would determine the relevant priorities, indicate the broad lines of activities and fix the maximum overall amount and the detailed rules for financial participation. The treaties instituted a complex, time-consuming decision-making process requiring continual consultations and multiple votes.

The main political objective of the Single European Act was the completion of the internal market. It became the target of the Delors presidency, but it also included other procedural issues, such as reforms of decision-making procedures and the increasing role of the European parliament.

The Single European Act entrusted the European Union with the objective of strengthening the science and technology basis of European industry to make it more competitive at the international level. Only a few European countries had a high-technology industry and scientists familiar with microelectronics. Emphasis was placed on the fact that the less industrialized regions and those suffering from long-term industrial decline might be disadvantaged by the distribution of funds that did not take into consideration the vast disparities between the various member countries.

The policy would revitalize and enhance the competitiveness of their industry and their technological capacity, but also alleviate the notorious structural disparities. Technology-funded projects should offer a chance for scientists and engineers from countries which had no microelectronics industry to establish an initial presence, to learn how to build the necessary infrastructures and to conduct and manage advanced research. Therefore, a substantial share of the funds must be earmarked to help the less developed members of the Community establish the institutional and training facilities required to garner science and technology capabilities and to bring them up to par. Huge subsidies were allocated to universities located in countries which had no electronics industry.

THE FRAMEWORK PROGRAMMES

In 1984, the commission had launched the 'European Strategic Programme for Research and Development in Information Technology' - Esprit. Participation was open to business, research centers and universities. The Treaty of Rome contained the principle of non-interference by governments in market competition. Public money should not be used to favor certain firms over others. For this reason R&D was to be pre-competitive - at some distance from the market - and generic: results should be of widespread applicability. At least two companies or institutions from different member states had to collaborate on each project. The commission would provide a contribution of 50 percent to industrial participants and 100 percent to universities and research institutes. It was understood that each partner would be allowed to exploit any innovation generated by the research of any other partner. Within months, 227 projects involving 240 industrial participants and 180 universities and research institutes were granted subsidies.

The purpose of the European policy was to create a distinctly European cutting edge technology with enough scale and momentum to be competitive with the American and Japanese industries, and even surpass them in certain areas. The commission set out specific strategies to be pursued and determined which technologies and firms were to benefit most. The Framework Programme was intended to increase the global competitiveness of the European information technology industry. It was argued that Europe was not only losing market share, but also falling behind in both the development, production and use of new technologies, and consequently in the learning curve. Subsidies would help European companies keep up with future technological advances.

The Framework Programme required consultations with the European Parliament and a unanimous Council, resulting in a protracted time-consuming decision-making process of continual consultations between commission, parliament and council. Through the Framework Programme the European Union emerged as a source of funding alongside the national governments. From the beginning, the new technology policy was not a coherent set of actions, but rather an aggregation of initiatives taken by different - and often competing - directorates.

Grandiose mega-projects with uplifting names were discussed and drawn up. Plans were developed in consultation with abundantly staffed working groups and panels of researchers and evaluators. Some were "technical" experts responsible for the selection of the projects; others were "national" experts defending their national interests, and concerned mostly with ensuring a fair distribution of the funds. Technology policy was not only meant to be distributive, it was also to be redistributive.

Because they did not have a clear understanding of the industry, the decision-makers could not propose realistic aims and set market-conforming directions to their technology strategy. Personal computers were available but still rare in Europe, and except for the engineers of the Big Twelve, few of them had ever seen the innards. Unable to distinguish between science and high-in-the-clouds science fiction, they picked winners and losers, sifted the wheat from the chaff, spreading their bets, determined to make the European computer industry achieve through the political process what it had failed to stand up to in the market. The institutional norms, rules and practices set in place generated a huge bureaucratic apparatus too slow to respond to - let alone anticipate - new developments, causing an inherent inertia that impeded any possibility of efficient functioning. New projects took one year to call, select and negotiate a contract; then a further two years to complete. In a fast-changing industry, this created an obvious time-lag problem.

On several occasions, new inventions were announced with fanfare and abundantly subsidized before melting into thin air. Inmos, a small British company and subsidiary of SGS-Thomson, claimed that it had developed a high-performance chip - the transputer - and parallel computers that foreshadowed momentous changes in the established structure of the computer industry. The system integrated the transputer, hardware and software into a coherent set of high-performance products. The transputer was said to be more powerful and compact than the Intel Pentium. The invention would offer Britain and Europe an opportunity to build up an important presence in the world's microprocessor and computer industry. The company had been granted the 1990 Queens Award for Technological Achievement. The British Government had financed the creation of Inmos with an investment of £100 million, before selling the company to Thorn EMI. [5]

Jean-Marie Cadiou, director of the program, had predicted that this made Inmos a major supplier of 32-bit microprocessors and a world leader. He also stated that the microprocessor industry had increased its share of the European market from 35 percent in 1984 to 48 percent in 1987. His figures were widely published. Only a few commentators pointed out that these figures included sales by US and Japanese subsidiaries, and that the share of European manufacturers had actually fallen to 33 percent. [6]

Cadiou's outlook was widely shared. Speaking at the 1989 Esprit conference, Horst Nasko claimed: "European companies have acquired a new strength and credibility." He failed to mention that his own company, the German computer manufacturer Nixdorf, had just gone to the wall and was about to be rescued by Siemens.

The Framework Programmes set objectives, priorities and the financial package of support for a period of several years, usually five. The programs overlapped so as to maintain continuity. With the first Framework Programme (1984-87), the research and development activities were coordinated as part of a single structured framework. The programs became very popular with the industry and the research community.

The main objective was the development of a line of microprocessors. Over four years, the equivalent of $5.6 billion was earmarked for investment in the electronic and computer industries. Thomson received almost 20 percent. IBM was taking part in Esprit as an "honorary European", since the company sold more computers in Europe than any other firm. While the subsidies were intended to counter Japanese imports, its beneficiaries were furtively doing business with their competitors: Olivetti distributed Hitachi mainframes and developed laptops with a Japanese company; Siemens bought machines from Fujitsu, while Bull distributed NEC mainframes. [7]

The overwhelming majority of the contracts went to the large companies. Constantly confronted with the dilemma and the delicate exercise of balancing two competing imperatives, the commission had to take into consideration not only the adequate participation by small and medium-sized companies, but also the just return to the major contributors and the "adequate" participation of economically less-developed member states. Normally, in order to be effective, subsidies should be given to companies and institutions best placed to produce commercial results. But the subsidies were largely intended to reinforce cohesion between richer members whose high-tech production was developed and the poorer member countries which did not yet have an electronics industry.

The applicants had to fill in forms and then wait several months for an answer. The system of multilayered decision-making required different types of choices to be made at different levels each of them dominated by different participants. This led to collective, complicated and hermetic options, duplication and trivial tasks. The lobbyists of the large companies competed skilfully for public money, and the final decisions were largely based on guesswork and intuition rather than technical and market expertise. The evaluators did not have the necessary background to differentiate between proposals based on codified knowledge and made-up gimmicks. Each decision was the result of compromises and represented a bet in little-understood and fast-changing markets and technologies. The complex rules and regulations demanded a high level of administrative oversight and bureaucratic politics, absorbing time and energy.

Beneath the communautaire camouflage, competition for subsidies was a permanent contest. The great divide between north and south and the huge differences between the member states caused mutual suspicion, disagreements and jealousy. The commission's fonctionnaires reconciled, repaired, and saw to it that resources were fairly distributed. But despite occasional inconveniences and personal clashes, the beneficiaries and the administrators developed a joint stake and a vested interest in the program.

The Second Framework Programme (1987-91) also aimed at developing the technologies of the future, particularly in the area of information technology and electronics. It signalled an attempt to broaden technology policy by integrating environmental, social, industrial, agricultural and economic issues.

The Second Framework Programme was designed to coincide with the Single European Act, with its stress on research related to the needs of industry and the realization of the Single Market. About 60 percent of the funding was for industrial research, mainly information and communication technologies. Competitiveness in microelectronics and software was considered essential for market leadership. Information and telecommunications technologies were more than just another specific industrial sector; they enhanced the productivity of a vast number of other manufacturing and service activities. The program also introduced research intended to strengthen the Community's economic and social cohesion, as well as to the promotion of its harmonious and widespread development, while maintaining its consistency with the objective of technical and scientific quality.

The industrial orientation advocated by the association of big companies produced a reaction from scientific laboratories and academia. Disagreements arose between business leaders who wanted the research program to focus on projects able to come rapidly to commercial fruition, whereas the academic world claimed that basic research was essential for long-term future innovation.

The Third Framework Programme (1990-94) extended the life of Esprit into its tenth birthday. By now, the European computer industry was on the verge of extinction. The share of information and communication technologies was reduced, although it continued to receive more funding than any other single area. It focused on a number of priority themes such as multimedia, virtual reality, ultimate miniaturization, the dissemination of research findings, life sciences and technologies, training and mobility activities. It was not cheap: € 5.7 billion. Yet the research community let it be known that this was not enough. The European Parliament also estimated it was insufficient.

The Directorate General responsible for Esprit came under increasingly intensive criticism for being too interventionist and more interested in career building and cozy links with industrialists than in devising effective technology policies. It was said to be the home of dirigistes whose programs had failed to prevent the Community's deficit on high-technology trade from widening further.

In 1993, the commission published a White Paper on Growth, Competitiveness and Employment. Noting that the information society 'constitutes an upheaval but can also offer new job prospects', Delors recommended "a regulatory and political environment to stimulate investments and guarantee that they were used in the public interest." Globalization of the economy and the existence of unfair competitive practices constituted a serious handicap for European companies. The paper also recommended closer co-operation between European scientists and, surprisingly, a coherent plan for the development of the computer industry.

The paper passed over the fact that Esprit and the other programs had failed to stop the Community's deficit in high-technology trade from widening and had not prevented the decline of the computer and semiconductor industry. Philips was expected to scrap 40,000 jobs, and it was rumored that the loss-making electronics division would be sold. Olivetti had 5.5 percent of the market, and was still in the black; but profits were shrinking and layoffs had become a regular occurrence. Bull kept losing money and survived only with the help of regular cash hand-outs and layoffs. ICL would soon be taken over by Fujitsu. [8]

Despite the obvious failure of the program, in 1993, the Maastricht Treaty broadened the position of the commission in research, technology and innovation, by charging it with "strengthening the scientific and technological bases of Community industry and encouraging it to become more competitive at international level". The Maastricht Treaty also made it clear that the technology policy had to serve the objective of cohesion by narrowing the gap between the richer and the poorer regions.

As funding levels increased, a growing number of firms, public laboratories and universities submitted research projects. Between Framework Programme II and III the number of participants rose from 13,000 to more than 18,000. [9]

More and more organizations representing industrial, academic and government researchers cultivated contacts within the commission, banding together to create liaison offices in Brussels. In turn, the commission itself developed a growing stake in its continuity. The DG XII coordinated the numerous committees of scientific experts and national civil servants in charge of selection and oversight of research projects. The European Parliament consistently backed larger research budgets - not least because they required parliamentary approval. A broad partnership thus emerged in support of continued technology policy. Despite its obvious failure, nobody openly questioned the validity.

The Framework programs had generated funding streams and clienteles attached to the status quo; it became the milch cow of the research and development schemes in countries without any scientific or industrial infrastructure. These countries shared with the EU institutions the view that R&D policy was necessary for the promotion of ever-closer cohesion. The German, British and to a lesser extent, the French governments had gradually come to consider the prime purpose of research policy as a means to make their industry more competitive, while cohesion came second.

As the empirical record of the technology policy pointed to little visible commercial benefits, the Framework program met increasingly with disparaging criticism: over-bureaucratic administration; long decision times impeding the ability to adapt to changing circumstances; too much money spent on big projects; insufficient attention to the potential of SMEs. One critic put it bluntly:" 'Cohesion has been used to justify mediocrity." The Framework Programmes had been confined to basic and pre-competitive research, far away from the market. Since co-operative research between companies would deliver better results, the decision was made that future research should achieve a balance between competition and co-operation.

Within the commission it gradually came to be recognized that the interventionist policies had not succeeded in enhancing competitiveness. A row developed between Filippo Pandolfi, the research commissioner, and Leon Brittan, the competition commissioner. Pandolfi wanted the commission to finance the development of a series of pan-European projects that would link together the computer systems for social security, health service, VAT collection, education networks and so on. He also wanted pan-European networks linking industry and the national civil services to the commission's computer systems. Brittan was the most outspoken commissioner in favor of free-market policies. He denounced the unfair advantages state-owned companies held over private competitors. He wanted a thorough review of the technology policy as it had been conceived and a substantial curtailment of the subsidies. [10]

The interventionists argued that state support for the information technology industry was substantial in the United States and in Japan. If Europe did not sustain new technologies, the whole industry would become vulnerable to the pricing demands and even political demands of foreign powers. The companies participating in the funding also expressed the need for continuance of the programs.

In 1992, Martin Bangemann became commissioner for industry, responsible for EU information and telecommunication policies. He announced a radical change: the role of public authorities was to be a catalyst and pathbreaker for innovation, but the main responsibility for industrial competitiveness must lie with firms themselves.

Martin Bangemann warned that there would be no more nannying by the commission. He wanted to establish stable and long-term conditions for an efficiently functioning market economy and accelerate structural adjustment to enhance competitiveness. It no longer made sense to subsidize European champions. ICL had been taken over by Fujitsu; Bull had been nationalized and kept losing money despite the huge subsidies provided by the government; Olivetti had given up production of desktop computers and was selling Hitachi machines; Philips stopped production in 1993; only Siemens was still struggling to keep a tiny share of the market.

The Fourth Framework Programme (1994-1998) took cognizance of the fact that the European champions had thrown in the towel. The commission's technological policy would now shift from the development of new technologies to their use, their diffusion and application. It contained several innovations, such as a new program on socio-economic research. It was much broader in scope than its predecessors. The beneficiaries had also changed. The share of SMEs increased substantially while the share for large enterprises kept decreasing. A sum of 13.2 billion ecus was allocated to the program.

A group of industrialists publicly criticized the commission for emphasizing political-social concerns rather than the needs of industry, European and social cohesion rather than economic development. The programs were misconceived and had not achieved what they were set up to do; nor were they likely to. The subsidies had served to promote research far away from the marketplace. They wanted research to provide shorter term payback. The report proposed a policy based on direct contacts between researchers and industry, arguing that this would be more productive.

In reply, the commission blamed industry for failing to anticipate new trends and technologies, to manage innovation and in particular to commercialize new products. The commission also criticized the education and training systems for being too academic and lacking practical, technical and experimental content.

Since the large companies had put an end to computer manufacturing, the commission turned its attention to the small- and medium-sized companies. An Action Plan for SMEs with the purpose of providing seed-corn capital and loan guarantee schemes for start-up firms was set in motion. A vast number of new areas were to be investigated. At a Research Council meeting in March 1995, it was announced that several task forces would be created to concentrate on a new generation of airplanes, multimedia educational software, the car of the future, and the maritime industry of the future. [11]

Edith Cresson, a former French prime minister, had become commissioner for research. Like most commissioners, she was a professional politician without any scientific background. Allegations of corruption would force her and the other 19 members of the commission to resign. Surveying the performance of the technology policy, she estimated that results had been good, sometimes even excellent, for the promotion of scientific research, but disappointing when it came to the applications. The commission's experts were also perplexed by the paradoxical discrepancy between the excellence of research and the paucity of industrial output, innovation and commercialization. Scientists had published innumerable papers and a number of patents had been granted, but hardly any new product of global interest had come on the market. Instead of spreading community resources in a scatter-gun approach, they would in future be concentrated on fewer projects where they could have more impact.

In 1996, the Esprit Review Board issued a report recommending that the commission introduce greater flexibility in its procedure and reduce response times. Realizing that the European computer industry was practically extinct, the report recommended to focus research on niches such as applications software, integration issues, customization. By encouraging start-ups originating in academia and in the corporate sector, more commercial success would be achieved. The administration of the program needed drastic reform, and costs should be reduced. The current situation undermined the R&D effort, European competitiveness and long- term job creation. The Board intended to help bring an intolerable situation to an end. [12]

During 1994-98, subsidies were almost doubled; the national champions received about 85 percent. Yet they claimed this was not enough and kept clamoring for more, while using the money to prep up their finances and reduce their losses. [13]

From the core economic activities of the common market, the commission had expanded the range of its activities to embrace almost every conceivable area of political, economic and social life. Regulatory, distributive and redistributive policies kept thousands of researchers busy exploring new fields of action.

The Single European Act and the Maastricht and Amsterdam Treaties had established a time-consuming management and bargaining process that absorbed the administrative and political energies of several Directorates-General. At the Amsterdam Summit of 1997, it was decided that future decisions on the Framework Programme would be made by a qualified majority vote instead of a unanimous vote as in the past. The funding stream kept thousands of researchers in academia and in the industry busy with a vast number of projects. The policy of pan-European research seemed to have outlived its purpose. Both the national and European policies had failed. About

250,000 manufacturing jobs had been lost in the information technology industry. After 15 years, the commission rang down the curtain on Esprit. The Big Twelve and the European champions were part of history. But an inexhaustible nest egg was waiting to be distributed.

In 2000, a panel of independent experts from 11 countries undertook a rigorous evaluation of the Framework Programme and assessed the implementation and achievements of the research and technological development programs over the period 1995-1999. The report stirred up a hornet's nest by concluding that the program had achieved a major impact on co-operation between industry, academia and research laboratories, but that the industrial yield had been disappointing. The scope of Esprit had been too broad, and the objectives built into the program too numerous. The panel recommended a limited set of smaller, interrelated programs, each with a few key objectives.

In a communication "Towards a European Research Area", the commission painted an alarmist picture of Europe's international position. The average research effort in the Union, it pointed out, was only 1.8 percent of Europe's GDP, as against 2.8 percent for the United States and 2.9 percent in Japan. Moreover, the American lead had widened in absolute terms. The US was home to more researchers per capita and the world leader in key strategic areas such as information and communications technologies and biotechnology.

Cresson's successor, Philippe Busquin, launched ERA, the European Research Area, the most grandiose plan yet. He announced that he wanted to strengthen the position of European industry by a better coordination of research and development at both the national and trans-national level. He wanted to build a research and innovation area similar to the Common Market for goods and services and address a number of related issues, including the mobility of researchers, the renovation of Europe's research infrastructure, a standardized European patent, and so on. Busquin intended to integrate European research through increased exchange of information and more intense co-operation between member states. This would build greater trans-national scientific capacity for cutting-edge research, and less compartmentalization of national research programs. [14]

Busquin put spending on research and technical development policy at the heart of development strategies. During his first year in office, he crisscrossed Europe in an effort to garner support for his program. European business leaders cautioned against any reform that might increase subsidies for basic research at the expense of technological development, while the representatives of academia insisted on a policy of investment in line with European ambitions.

Busquin's ambitions can be summarized as follows: Esprit has been an effective instrument of integration for European scientific and industrial environments; R&D and technology policy have anticipated major developments in the building of the EU, on such vital areas as cohesion, enlargement, and majority voting. In addition to producing an impressive business return, that can be measured by the competitiveness of European products and services and the extent of exploitation, EC funded R&D have generated valuable intangibles, such as internationalizing and networking the research and industrial community in Europe, and creating cross border vertical alliances and synergies.

Framework 7 is due to run from 2007 to 2013. The commission has asked for a budget of €73 billion and plans a program based on four specific themes: Cooperation, Ideas, People and Capacities. As usual, the emphasis is on spending, not on results. There is no accountability, no audit and no procedure to provide policy-makers with reliable information about actual economic benefits of the research. The commission perpetuates the myth that government-funded science produces innovation, whereas experience shows that competition in the free market proves by far the most successful in stimulating the economy. Technological innovation is engineer driven as much a science driven. Transferring knowledge and skills from academia to entrepreneurs is a very complex process. The fundamental challenge in innovation is to convert an idea into a marketable product and commercial fruition. The various programs were set up with the aim of establishing a strong and competitive high- technology manufacturing industry. Contrary to conventional mythology, the strategic projects which would give Europe an additional competitive advantage have not materialized. The European Union has failed in the technology race. It is safe to predict that the European industry will continue to fall further behind.

EUREKA was the brainchild of François Mitterrand. In 1983, when President Reagan announced his Strategic Defense Initiative, the French government panicked at the idea that this would give America an insurmountable commercial, military and political superiority. Mitterrand decided that the European countries must pool and co-ordinate their military and civilian research projects to match the stimulus of the "Star-Wars" program. Instead of co-operating with the Americans as a junior partner in the arms race, Europe had to be technologically independent. Electronics was a major source of employment and a dominant component of military systems.

Mitterrand recommended the immediate creation of a European technological community to counter the imperialism of the United States. This would assure a coherent co-operation in research and development of new materials such as high-power laser, optoelectronics, artificial intelligence, superfast microelectronics and space travel.

The ten members of the Community and the candidate members, Spain and Portugal, would constitute the nucleus; the EFTA countries would be invited to join. Mitterrand's ulterior motive was to uphold national prestige and revive France's ailing high-tech industries through collaborative research and combine European resources in projects that France could not afford alone. The government was massively subsidizing the recently nationalized industry and wanted to avoid the meddlesome scrutiny of the commission's competition watchdogs by putting a European label on the operation.

French ministers toured the European capitals drumming up support for the president's project. They organized numerous meetings between German and French industrialists. It took some time to convince the Bonn government divided between Eureka protagonists and supporters of friendly relations with the United States, wary about getting involved in yet another technology policy. However, the idea behind the proposal was so vague that outright rejection was impossible.

The British and German governments disapproved of the interventionist character of the plan and of French preponderance in the program. They were very reluctant and maintained that public funds should be used only for projects that were beyond the financial resources of private industry. Transnational co-operative research should not become a disguised welfare scheme, but a support for near-market projects. Both gave expression of their misgivings about the anti-American character of the French project. The other European governments were surprised by Mitterrand's invitation, all the more so since the European Council had recently rejected the commission's proposals for increased spending on technology. The financing of the program also gave rise to controversy: France proposed the creation of a common fund and a centralized secretariat to co-ordinate the technical steering committees, but this was turned down.

On April 17, 1985, the French government announced that an agreement had been reached with the German government for the creation of a European Research Coordinating Agency that would be known as Eureka. In Mitterrand's mind, Eureka was to be a civilian project with military applications. It would stimulate co-operative research in key technologies. It was intended to be the main pillar of a concerted European answer to American industrial and economic dominance. The ambiguity of the French intentions was obvious. The government took great care to assuage its partners by claiming that a strong Europe would activate co-operation with the United States. This did not prevent the French minister of research and technology, Hubert Curien, from stating: "Eureka will have nothing to do with the Brussels muddle. We want to bring together the best industrialists of a given sector, project by project. They will define the programs and the prototypes to be selected for industrial production. Like in the Ariane program, each project will be managed by the most competent, whatever his nationality. And, whatever has been said, competition between Eureka and IDS has already started." [15]

Eureka was designed to correct the shortcomings of the Framework programs. National administrations working closely together would be more efficient than a vast conglomeration of bureaucracies. Eureka focused on promoting competitiveness through near-market research. The Eureka Declaration of Principles was drawn up at the first Eureka Ministerial Conference in Hannover in November 1985.

The objective of EUREKA was to raise, through closer co-operation among enterprises and research institutes in the field of advanced technologies, the productivity of Europe's industries and national economies on the world market, and hence strengthen the basis for lasting prosperity and employment.

Eureka was not a funding mechanism itself and had no central budget to support projects. The administration was coordinated by the commission and member states, and financed by the national governments. Every year, the chairmanship of the initiative was assumed by a different member, responsible for organizing the agenda and for supervising the further development of the initiative. From then on, the commission developed a two-pronged strategy: through its financial involvement in pan-European Eureka projects and through the EC's own Framework Programmes.

Eureka was geared toward industrial and applied R&D. Consortia of firms, universities and research institutes from 22 countries set up partnerships. They initiated collaborative schemes and prepared proposals on any project involving near-market R&D in advanced technology. The consortia had to contribute their own funds and applied for public support from their own governments. The commission provided for the costs of coordinating the research.

Eureka was an intergovernmental program. Each government determined its own policy. Each sector had its steering committee consisting of government representatives, industrialists and research institutions. This meant that while a project was in progress, new partners could be brought in. The ministerial conference was the highest political body in Eureka. It was composed of ministers of the member states responsible for research and development in their respective countries, plus a representative from the commission. The ministerial conference met once a year to formally announce the projects that had been approved.

The aim was the creation of partnerships between research teams from industry and academic laboratories who wished to co-operate in the field of advanced technologies. It was designed to promote near-market research leading to products, processes and services having a world-wide market potential in a relatively short period of time.

Participation in a research program required at least two partners from different countries, and 'an adequate financial commitment by participating enterprises.' Their commitment must extend over a period of several years. To submit a project, firms and researchers needed the support of their respective national authorities. The projects then had to be approved by Eureka's "high level" group.

The initiative for developing new projects began with the participants themselves who defined the topics of research as well as the content, type, extent and duration of the projects. The application process started with a proposal which was sent circulating and officially registered. A feasibility study analyzed the chances of realizing the project from a technical and economic perspective. Once this was achieved, the project was given 'announced' status, later transformed into endorsed or withdrawn.

In 1985, a "history-making" European summit in Milan endorsed Eureka. The decision to shift substantial policy resources to the European level committed every country to increase contributions to research. When the commission laid down the law, demanding that all member states deliver on their commitment to EU research, a series of wearisome and rancorous disputes erupted. Germany and Britain refused to endorse the commission's master plan. In the past, as long as it was a net beneficiary of community-funded R&D, the French government had championed the expansion of collaborative programs. Now France had become a net contributor to the EU's budget; a center-right coalition had replaced the socialists and the Framework program no longer served its original purpose.

Differences of opinion pitted the Big Three against a united front of the majority member states and of the commission. Italy was the champion of the coherence theory. The country had benefited disproportionately from the EU largesse; research had not led to any success stories, but was subsidizing a vast number of institutions and universities. [16]

The European champions faced from the beginning insurmountable handicaps. Production costs in Asia were considerably lower. Whereas American manufacturers started outsourcing at an early stage, the European governments and the commission wanted production to be located in Europe. Over a period of 20 years, €22 billion of taxpayer's money were spent on thousands of projects involving 11,000 partners from industry, universities and national administrations. The rationale underlying Eureka became increasingly heterogeneous and contradictory. Huge amounts of capital were indiscriminately distributed to subsidize undirected curiosity-driven research projects not connected to wealth creation. There was no follow-up, no control and no audit. It is fair to say that most of this money has been dissipated without making a significant contribution to EU competitiveness. François Mitterrand's dream of a pan-European collaborative research network that would give European high-tech industry a major presence on the world stage and improve its technological and commercial competitiveness ended in failure. [17]

JESSI (Joint European Submicron Silicon Initiative) was the quintessence and the most significant initiative developed by Eureka. The top three European semiconductor manufacturers, Siemens, Philips and SGS Thomson, were doing very badly. They were producing obsolete devices with dated processes. Capital investment was not keeping up and their share of world markets was slipping. Semiconductors were the critical drivers of the information age. Horst Nasko, a former senior executive of Siemens was made chairman of Jessi.

In 1984, Philips, SGS-Thomson and Siemens had launched the Megaproject with the purpose of producing a line of chips able to compete with the Japanese. Siemens was responsible for the development of the random access memory chips, SGS Thomson for the erasable programmable read-only memory chips, and Philips for the random access storage chips. Six months after signing the agreement, Siemens announced that it had agreed on a partnership with Toshiba for the development of its semiconductor technology. Philips continued for four years and finally decided that its 1-Mb SRAM would not sell, putting an end to the dream of a European microprocessor production. Because one of the triumvirate abandoned the project, the whole edifice collapsed. [18]

In 1988, Siemens and Philips came up with another project for the development of a super-chip. After some hesitation, the French-Italian SGS-Thomson decided to join. They approached their governments for support, and evaluated the costs of the program at 7.3 billion DM. It took some time for the governments to decide whether they wanted to spend that amount of money. [19] The commission reacted favorably, and let it be known that if a cooperative program was approved, Brussels would participate in the financing and coordinate the program. [20]

The management of Siemens and Philips had alerted the commission about the danger of American and Japanese technological superiority. The commission had failed to notice that

Intel and Microsoft had established near-monopoly technology standards, and that even IBM was running its computers on Intel microprocessors and on Windows software. The logic intensity of integrated circuits and the amount of information storable on a given amount of silicon had doubled every year, and then slowed down to 18 months. Intel had fought a dramatic battle with the Japanese and had won.

The European scientific community was given the task of developing a system that would beat Intel and Microsoft. Some observers whispered that Jessi was simply a massive waste of public and private money. But Jessi chairman Horst Nasko, vice-president of Siemens-Nixdorf, pointed out that Europe simply had to fund Jessi. Microelectronics was the most fundamental and promising industry in the world. Once its leverage effect on the electronic systems industry was taken into account, it would assure around eight million jobs. For Europe to give up would be a strategic blunder of immense proportions.

Launched in 1989, Jessi was an 8-year, 3.8 billion ecu project to develop and specify the processes, materials and equipment necessary for the production of semiconductors with geometries of 0.3 microns and below, so that the Europe would be a world class semiconductor competitor by 1996.

Jessi brought together over 220 companies and institutes from all over Europe and channelled subsidies into 103 projects. The cost was borne between the participants, the national budgets of 16 countries and several European research programs. The commission and the national governments funded each one quarter. Jessi was directed and managed by senior industrialists representing the entire European microelectronics industry.

The industry promised to furnish a proportionate contribution. Jessi came just in time to save Philips. The electronics division had incurred substantial losses, and restructuring led to 10,000 redundancies. It was rumored that the company intended to stop production of semiconductors, but this had not been confirmed. [21]

In 1992, Jessi was restructured and the funding reduced. By that time the debate was, in any case, largely out of the hands of the commission, and under control of the council of ministers, the real power in the Community. The attempt to mould European champions through EC-funded integrationist measures had failed. During the period of debate over the Maastricht Treaty ratification, the recession had cut deeply into employment levels in Europe.

Jessi became caught up in internal commission bickering about the EU's relationship with Eureka, and then in the budget cutting that followed German unification. The commission initially signalled that it could provide as much as half of all public funding. However, after an obtuse fight over legal rights to research results, the commission ended up contributing only a quarter. The Round Table vented its frustration publicly, and strong mutual incriminations ensued between commissioner Pandolfi and the heads of European IT multinationals. Another complication was the German decision to slash the public funding commitment to Jessi. Some participating firms pulled out as Jessi's budget for 1992 was cut by a quarter. With the project's future hanging on a knife-edge, the German government was pressed hard to resume its contribution. Eventually Germany came back on board and the project was seen through to conclusion in 1996.

Someone had suggested that co-operation with the United States might bring some benefits. In 1990, IBM was given permission to participate in Jessi, provided that this would lead to a rapprochement with Sematech for the exchange of information that could be useful to both parties. It is obvious that Intel was not going to reveal the status of its research; moreover, Congress was very allergic to any foreign contact with Sematech. There was disagreement about admitting ICL since it had been taken over by Fujitsu. While some were of the opinion that ICL had become a Japanese company, others argued that the research would still be conducted in Europe.

The perspective of public subsidies aroused the immediate interest of the industry, particularly in France. Companies such as Thomson, Aérospatiale and Matra announced their intention to start collaborative projects with companies from other countries. Next to a few very large "strategic" projects were a vast number of smaller ones. Among the major projects there was a "Europrocessor" intended to become the standard for the industry, and also a new type of integrated 64Mbit super-chip. Even before the program was finalized, a French company recommended the development of a programmable tractor for fieldwork. Another project recommended the development of a computer-aided driving mechanism that would fit cars with sensors and microcomputers, ready to warn the driver of any danger ahead or, if necessary, to override his controls.

The HDTV fiasco is a classic example of the wasteful extravagance governments and big companies can beget when they decide to cooperate in industrial projects. Launched in 1986, in haste to develop a new-generation cinema-quality TV system based on an analog technology, it was to become the European standard able to compete with the Japanese and Americans.

High Definition Television represented the next generation of television. For the first time in almost 50 years, the definition of television was about to change. The Japanese and European HDTV strategies provide instructive examples of the planning mentality. Both were determined to setting a home-made analog standard rather than achieving a global world-class standard. Under the administrative guidance of MITI, Japanese television was the first to transmit HDTV signals. In the early stages, competition was actively managed by the public broadcasting company, but industry ultimately decided on a single standard, and started marketing receivers. The Japanese transformed their image from followers to innovators in high technology.

Bosch, Philips, Thomson and Thorn-EMI engineered an analog HD MAC format under the umbrella of Eureka. Development costs amounted to the equivalent of $2 billion. The commission had issued a directive requiring all high-powered TV satellite broadcasts to use MAC, which made European manufacturers feel secure and protected. The commission had two main objectives in promoting MAC. One derived from a perception of European cultural identity which would benefit from frontier-free dissemination throughout the 12-nation territory; the second was commercial, since the commission has a mandate to support European industry.

The news that Japan had a revolutionary TV standard raised the alarm in the United States. The Federal Communications commission warned would-be standard-setters not to be satisfied with existing technology but to aim for a digital solution. In Washington, the Democrats considered television as one of the industries that had the potential to dominate the twenty-first century. HDTV became a controversial dividing line. The Bush administration had rejected the plan; but President Clinton argued that "it is both appropriate and necessary for government to directly support and accelerate the development of technologies critical for long-term economic growth "

Driven by market pressures, American engineers worked night and day to keep pace with the advances made in rival labs. Then General Instrument suddenly changed the rules of the game when it presented its digital HDTV system for FCC testing. Digital HDTV provided viewers with sharper images, better sound and more viewing options than the analog television standard. The other companies refused to be outdone, and within six months four digital HDTV systems were on the table for FCC consideration.

Meanwhile, technical advances and the launch of the Astra satellite made it possible to transmit TV signals from medium-power satellites which were not covered by the commission's directive. The commission tried in vain to dissuade commercial broadcasters from exploiting the loophole. Industry wanted above all to protect its investments, and refused to consider the incompatible digital systems emerging from American laboratories. Rather than suffer severe embarrassment, the commission resisted for three years while trying to make MAC compatible. The policymakers learned to their chagrin that by allowing industry to invest in an obsolete technology, they were compelled to adopt an authentic American standard. This did not prevent the Jessi Board from giving its 1996 award to "a project which has put Europe's consumer industry in the race for digital TV."

In 1989 media tycoon Rupert Murdoch's Sky Television, the first privately funded satellite service, started broadcasting in the conventional Pal format. The American digital standard made the MAC obsolete. Finally, Martin Bangemann decided to throw in the towel and bow to digital television. The MAC standard was abandoned in 1993.

The Japanese firms retreated in good order, although there was some bloodletting at the MITI top. As usual, the Japanese formed partnerships with American companies, focused on digital research and developed a common international standard. The industrial planners had underestimated the complexity of the high-tech chain and overestimated their ability to co-ordinate producers. In Europe, equipment manufacturers were unable to provide consumers with MAC receivers because the chip industry was slow in developing the components. In Japan, HDTV consumers were not interested, because HDTV programs were limited to eight hours a day and sets sold for $7,000 to $10,000. The HDT'V episode is just another example proving the superiority of free competition over coordinated high-tech planning and subsidized technology policy.

Eureka never came close to realizing Mitterrand's vision. In June 1991, the scheme was audited by seven senior businessmen. The program had backed 520 projects costing 8.2 billion ecus. Of the projects operative in 1990, the auditors found that only ten had brought new products to market. Eureka drew much criticism for its lack of openness. The commitment by participating enterprises to provide "adequate financial participation" remained forever beyond scrutiny.

During seven years of assistance and many billions spent to strengthen the scientific and technological basis of European industry and to encourage it to become more competitive at international level, Jessi helped the industry by improving the bottom lines, but did not bridge the technology gap. It turned out to be a costly respite. Jessi financed the survival of the computer industry for a few years and postponed the day of reckoning. The manna allowed European companies to latch on parasitically and sustain their investment levels in information technology. But by trying to protect them from the harshness of free-market competition, intervention simply accompanied their undoing. None of the participants ever questioned whether they delivered value for the money, and whether the costs to the economy as a whole were worth the benefits they granted themselves.

Jessi was to help develop new microchip technology. In 1990, after ten years of fruitless attempts to enter a market dominated by Intel, Philips pulled out of the static random-access memory chips research. Jessi's raison d'être was undermined 1991, when Siemens agreed to develop new chip technology with IBM and Toshiba. Jessi's managers sought to prolong its life beyond 1996, when it was to end. [21]

Jessi had attracted substantial public funding. A panel of experts judged the project's achievements 'positive and impressive', while criticizing its slow decision-making procedures, its lack of accessibility by SMEs and its unwieldiness. The EU Court of Auditors, responsible for inspecting EU expenditure also criticized the research programs for failing to generate concrete results: despite billions in expenditure, research activities between 1986 and 1990 had created only about 50 tangible inventions and 280 jobs. The Court also observed that, as projects neared completion, partners tended to execute the final stages separately.

European companies were unable to cope with the pace of change in the electronics industry. In 1996 Jessi was phased out. The Eureka managers felt that it was an unqualified success story for the European industry, since it enabled three of Europe's semiconductor companies to move into the world's top ten by outsourcing production to Asia. The Jessi Board made it an occasion to review the impact of the program. The president of the European research and development program, Horst Nasko, announced at a press conference in Strasbourg that the technology gap between Europe and the rest of the world had been closed.

The European champions had vanished into irrelevance, but the coffers of the European Union are overstocked and constantly refilled with disposable billions. The commission had already announced a new program and, as usual, thousands of researchers were lining up for a piece of the pie. Most are experienced solicitors, but for the newcomers, the Internet provides detailed instructions on how to write an application.

For years, Hyperion's Sean McCarthy has been teaching one-day courses all over Europe, telling researchers how to play the game. They learn how to write a competitive proposal, how to negotiate, manage, administer and audit a contract, how to write a technology implementation plan, how to identify the best research topics, how to select the most receptive evaluator, the best partners, the best instrument, and much more.

His first advice is: "Never go to Brussels asking for money. Instead, present them with the possible solution to a problem." The European Union has its own priorities, which are not necessarily the same as those of the applicants. The commission places high priority on cross-border collaboration with countries whose scientific infrastructure is underdeveloped. The trick is to fill out the grant application that appeals to the evaluators, while still allowing the participants to do what they want. This skill requires practice. McCarthy advises to concentrate on the integrated grants. They are easier to get approved, because the focus is on collaboration. Many researchers complain about the emphasis placed on technology over basic science, although the system is changing towards a more basic-science approach.

Another major issue that grant-writers confront is the unspoken aspiration to help researchers in less developed countries within the European Union. In order to succeed, by far the most important decision is choosing the right coordinator, who will be the main contact between the researchers and the commission, and who will do most of the paperwork. After selecting the coordinator, it is preferable to choose partners with whom it will be possible to stay in close communication.

If the proposal is approved, it enters the negotiations phase which requires time-consuming paperwork. Probably the most mind-numbing task is the technical annex, which is essentially a redrafting of parts of the proposal in a different format. This portion, however, does not have to be done until the negotiations phase. If there are any changes after this point, the technical annex must be redrawn. [22]

The Big Twelve and the European champions have vanished into the limbo of lost dreams. The billions spent to make them competitive, went up in smoke. The grandiose plans collided with the unpleasant realities of globalization. Europe has become dependent on American and Asian industry for its computer and electronics requirements. By supporting slow-moving companies and shallow research, European governments exempted the industry from facing up to global competition.

The disintegration of the computer industry signalled the erosion of the cutting-edge manufacturing base. The European economic model failed the test in its first major confrontation with the globalization of industry. Subsidies blunted emulation and stifled innovation by violating the rules of free and fair trade. Technology policy ushered the whole economy into medium-tech status, and aggravated the erosion of the European manufacturing base.

It is unlikely that the European Union will produce any champions in the foreseeable future. For too long the commission has overplayed and misplayed its hand. The best we may expect is that its commissioners, who tend to savor the power of telling others what to do, show more restraint when exercising their formidable powers over social, environmental and industrial legislation.

The major concern of the huge and powerful cadre of fonctionnaires, lobbyists, academics and politicians whose

lifeline depends on technology policy, is to assure its perpetu-
ation by permanently exploring new fields of research which
have not yet been investigated, but merit attention. They are
determined to preserve their ground by constructing new targets and new projects requiring expert research blessed with
government largesse. The programs overlap, and as the end of
one program is in sight, a spirit of renewed optimism and activ-
ism develops for the next.

Clueless bureaucrats keep funnelling tons of money into
institutions and businesses, hoping they will somehow come
up with a winner. They know nothing about the technologies
involved. Thousands of people constantly line up, all saying
they will find something if the commission gives them the
money. This money goes then into black holes where it will be
spent on whatever each handout recipient wants to spend it
on.

The original objective of building a globally competitive
European computer industry has lost its raison d'être, since
the industry is no more. The commission has now shifted its
attention from the submicron structures of silicon and cutting-
edge information technologies to the broad socio-economic
challenges. The Fifth and Sixth Frameworks were conceived
to help solve problems and respond to major socio-economic
challenges the European Union is facing. They focused on
a number of objectives and areas combining technological,
industrial, economic, social and cultural aspects. The research
programs have become larded with a broad set of additional
goals, such as environmental protection, sustainable development, and the protection of the European "social model". A
vast array of issues is the object of concern and study, in order
to determine the policies that will sustain the momentum for
European integration and contribute to the harmonious development of the European Union and of mankind as a whole.

At the center is the quality of life, the threats to the global
climate, and much more. Thousands of experts provide advice
to an overstretched bureaucratic infrastructure. They are
called upon to deal with the fundamental issues, to analyze the

intangible domain linking science and technology with industry and the social environment, to debate and write scientific reports, travel, and listen to speeches at colloquia and symposia. They satisfy the deeply human instinct to comprehend the order of the world in which we live. They will be long on theories and proposals; the outside world will pay no heed and will leave them to their devices.

Since the incubation period of new ideas resulting from basic research may take decades, since there is no monitoring of participants and since the benefits can never be quantified, as long as the coffers of the commission are replenished with public money, the future is theirs. The programs are fundamentally technology- generation schemes. Despite their disastrous cost/benefit ratio, they must continue because of their symbolic value as a cornerstone of the European construction.

In November 2004, a Slovenian economist Janez Potočnik was put in charge of European science policy. He has no background in the natural sciences and admits that he has a lot to learn. He will oversee Framework 6, as well as the development of Framework 7. He is very enthusiastic about the role of small- and medium-sized enterprises as drivers for scientific research. He considers that research is an indispensable part of the Lisbon Strategy, a 10-year plan endorsed by European leaders, that should make the European Union the most competitive and dynamic knowledge-based economy in the world. Potocnik intends to double the budget for the Framework 7 Programme. [23]

6

SINS OF COMMISSION

The acid test of any industrial policy is the measure of progress in creating new or better products, economic growth and new wealth. Success must be judged against announced objectives. For more than 30 years, European governments tried and failed to build up a computer industry able to compete with the Americans and the Japanese. European technology policy was intended to overcome a handicap by developing new technologies in the field of cutting-edge microelectronics.

R&D is one of the most important, yet least understood elements of the commission's budget. Science and technology are considered key drivers of economic growth. Considered an elitist technocracy, the commission proved its utter incompetence. Its research program was wasteful, misdirected and counterproductive. If one takes the industry's market performance as an indicator for the policy's success, the outcome of three decades of concerted efforts makes a mockery of the promise.

It was not the lack of money. European governments spent mind-boggling amounts to make the computer industry globally competitive. Instead of creating an innovative environment, they cosseted a vast number of research laboratories and the major companies with tax money.

The mistake was the belief that centralized planning would enable European industry to rival American and Japanese competition if the public authorities coordinated and mobilized resources and financed research. They overlooked the importance of close coupling between R&D, industrial production and marketing in a fast-changing industry. The cutting edge of invention has always been global. Rapid technological change requires up-to-date knowledge and understanding of industry and technology.

In a globalized economy, research, to be of any value, must be world-class. Computing technology is highly specialized. Any laboratory that engages in computing research needs several years to learn the basics. Moreover, a new idea requires a visionary appreciation of its potential applications, followed by imaginative and arduous work to turn theory into user-friendly gadgets and achieve commercial success. In the process, there are plenty of hurdles along the way.

European political leaders were convinced that their cumulative knowledge to elaborate a broad-based industrial policy would enable them to beat global market forces. The legitimacy of the commission and its regulatory authority are founded on the supposed technical and scientific knowledge of its personnel. Decisions are made by "experts" who are far removed from the world of business.

At the heart of the program was the assumption that cooperation between a vast number of academic research institutions and the industry across Europe would narrow the technological gap. They decided to fashion a distinctly European technology policy by emulating the industrial structure and the product mix they perceived from afar in the United States and Japan.

Cutting-edge research is by definition top secret. Its practitioners work in close professional communities of specialists and sub-specialists. European politicians entertain quaint ideas about research and development. Scientific research is considered a "public good" that would be underprovided if it was left to the market. Therefore, governments need to supply enough funds to make sure that the industry doesn't miss out on scientific breakthroughs.

Historically, in computing technology, the major breakthroughs have been achieved by scientists working alone or in very small groups. Research as it is practiced under the aegis of the commission is unaccountable, and does not reward excellence. Rather than gauging the research system's value by how much money is being awarded, the question is what kind of value the scientists have recently produced and what they may produce in the future. Industry concentrates mostly on applied research. In business, everything must be measurable and add to revenue. The laboratories take on assignments for which outcomes are prescribed and rely on patents that protect the company's intellectual property.

The emphasis on cognitive basic research was misconceived. The number of scientifically and technologically trained people able to understand the scope, the costs, risks and benefits of the research they were expected to conduct were extremely rare. Most of them were researchers for whom scientific inquiry was an end in itself, a matter of prestige and esteem in the academic community. They are in it for the intellectual challenge. European academia lacks the ethos favorable to technology transfer from the world of research to the world of commerce.

There is a clear distinction between engineering research where the goal is to produce a desirable outcome as quickly as possible and scientific research where the goal is to understand the relation between cause and effect.

Academic institutions concentrating on "classic" electrical engineering were not equipped to familiarize themselves in short order with the arcane domain of solid-state technology. Moreover, scientific discoveries resulting from research are seldom sufficient foundations for new technologies and economic growth; to be of any practical value, they must move out of the laboratory, into the production line and the marketplace.

Unaware of the burgeoning PC revolution, the commission pushed the European champions into an obsolescent segment of the market. The industry was in the midst of a groundbreaking restructuring; small start-ups were the prime agents in the commercialization of the new technologies. IBM and the other established computer manufacturers had been reluctant to adopt externally-generated technical advances representing a departure from their own architecture. Unable to break new ground with radical innovations, their leadership came to an end. Except for IBM, they closed their computer division.

Pre-competitive research is aimed at providing the tools, information and data that enable industry to develop future products and services. It may also be intended to develop industry standards and test procedures where no precedents exist. It is not catch-up work that allows laggards to reach a place that someone else has already taken. Nor is it intended to improve existing and successful products or their immediate successors.

In an industry with very short product life-cycles, pre-competitive research was the height of nonsense. In an age of extreme specialization in microelectronics research, the widely scattered approach was totally amateurish. The catch-up in a follow-the-leader game was impossible. To make matters worse, the political planners never had a clear concept of what they wanted. Their strategic priorities ended in disaster.

The legal and institutional basis of European technology policy emerged in the 1980s, as a response to the competitive problems of the European computer industry. It was Davignon's idea to co-finance projects. After the commission took the European computer industry under its wings, the Big Twelve were merged into five large companies. They had a substantial share of the European market and a modest global presence. Poorly managed, they were no match for their American and Japanese competitors.

The originators of the strategy stood on the sidelines of the action as spectators impervious to the intangibles. At the planning stage, the Round Table brought together commission officials, politicians, academics, plus representatives of the computer industry clamoring for subsidies. The policymakers, desperate for political credit by creating jobs, opened the taxpayers' wallets, determined to make industry achieve through subsidies what it had failed to stand up to in the market. A vast number of secure bureaucrats and researchers found interesting and pleasant employment; but the recipe for putting together teams that guaranteed outcomes was inept.

Each group had different priorities, interests and capabilities. The interlocking relations between economically inexperienced politicians and their academic assistants, the researchers and the industry, formed a nexus of power whose objectives cannot be said to be discretely economic or political or bureaucratic; they were all three. The belief that subsidies allocated to scattered researchers and industrial laggards would match the entrepreneurial drive of American and Japanese competition is one of the most ludicrous fictions of European technology policy.

Policy-making needs to be based on a sophisticated understanding of the ways in which science and technology interact and influence one another. European technology policy is a distributive system and not a development strategy. The welfare state rewards powerful lobbying groups unable to develop emerging sectors of the economy. Funding was programmed by government agencies ready to open the throttle of public money for companies so inefficient that they should have been told to close their computer divisions or wake up. Rather than allowing market forces to dictate competitive outcomes, they resorted to counterproductive practices by limiting rather than fostering international competition. Instead of producing an electroshock, subsidies simply postponed the day of reckoning.

The decision-makers fundamentally misperceived the technical dimensions of the business. They reasoned from the structures they visualized from afar to determine the strategies they wanted the firms to adopt. It is the nature of high-technology that it does not lend itself to empirical analysis. Any new development is out of date by the time it is assimilated by the outside observer. Bureaucrats could not take on the entrepreneurial role of imagining and inventing industrial futures. Firms were discouraged from finding their own distinctive technological avenues and consequently the possibility of innovative break-throughs that might have permitted them to create a few niches.

They were collectively out of touch with the real and fast-changing world of computerdom. They drew up a road map without knowing how to get there. They published long-winded reports whose exuberant rhetoric about the potential of the programs was intended to galvanize public faith in building a European high-tech industry. The structural funds were to bring the backward nations closer to the level of the more advanced. This is typical of the European egalitarian ideal, which puts equality far ahead of competitive efficiency. America celebrates the brightest and the best, because they are the ones who will keep the country ahead in the merciless global struggle for dominance.

The political justification for government-funded technology policy rested on the ability of firms to deliver tangible economic returns from their use of public money and spillovers for the entire economy. In fact, only a few companies and a large number of researchers, policymakers and bureaucrats, associated in cozy, self-interested, clientelistic complicity, have gobbled up the economic benefits at taxpayers' expense. The individual and collective capabilities came short of the proclaimed ambitions. The main achievement of European technology policy has been to delay for a few years the ultimate demise of the industry. The European manufacturers kept struggling until they finally closed their loss-making computer division. Paradoxically, European technology policy may have reduced the returns of capital investment to the European economy as a whole.

In Europe, the use of public funding to remedy market failure by private industry is warranted by the governments' economic and social responsibility. By playing midwife, governments are supposed to accelerate technology transfer and innovation and thus create new jobs. Research and development spending is high-profile. It represents the future. The proponents of funding programs, well ensconced in European institutions, kept warning that unless industry was given the means to develop new technologies, Europe would fall further behind, and become even more dependent on American and Asian competitors for the critical technologies of the future.

The European political establishment does not share the American and Japanese idea that the combined judgment of innovators, entrepreneurs and consumers is far superior to any form of centralized programming. Instead, they propose to solve economic problems by means of the greatest possible level of public-sector involvement.

In the 1980s, the commission decided to protect the semiconductor industry by imposing a 14 percent tariff on imported chips. As a result, the European computer industry had to pay higher prices for its most important raw material. The policy to protect its fledgling semiconductor industry had a negative impact on the much larger computer industry.

IBM's dominance of the global computer market was based on its quasi-monopoly of the design criteria for the hardware and software around which computer systems were built. In the 1980s, the commission and the council of ministers decided to establish a system of pan-European standards for public administrations in the European Community and to demand that the European computer industry clone the IBM system. The policy was self-defeating. The PC market was exploding, and with the major exception of Apple, the industry had chosen Intel and Microsoft as the *de facto* global standards.

Intel was in the process of establishing a practical monopoly after an epic battle with the Japanese to accelerate the ever-increasing processing speed and the miniaturization of printed circuits on silicon chips. Andy Grove had warned: "only the paranoid survive." The entry level was so high that European researchers could only extrapolate and tinker with existing technologies rather than search for really innovative lucky strokes. Moreover, as the price of memory chips declined, the cost of developing a new generation was exploding; every new hardware system required an adequate software program, immense financial resources and organizational ability.

Given the state of microelectronics, even the brightest crystallographers were at best marginal neophytes. Despite their number, in an industry driven by obsolescence and near-monopoly, they had neither the infrastructure nor the technological competence and skills required to design prototypes of a new generation of computers and microchips capable of rivaling the Americans and the Japanese, both astute at high-stakes corporate maneuvering in a game that is part chess, part cloak-and-dagger intrigue.

After Intel and Microsoft set their finespun standards, microelectronics had become a mature technology. Microchip capacities and miniaturization were increasing at breathtaking speed; prices were falling, while development costs increased exponentially. Competing with the Wintel duopoly presumed a world-class state-of-the-art expertise in electrical, mechanical, optical, chemical, biological, magnetic and other properties of semiconducting materials.

In information technology, standard-setting is a "winner takes all" contest. The companies able to master an innovative technology and to supply superior products that meet the expectations of the market are apt to set the pace of further developments, to take the industry with them and to establish a quasi-monopoly. Each company does its own R&D: every innovation is patented before it ever reaches the public. The Americans were best at innovation and marketing; the Japanese were best at mass-producing standardized products.

The European computer industry self-destructed by attempting to compete with IBM minicomputer technology, whereas IBM had adopted Intel and Microsoft microcomputer technology. Success in the computer market no more depended on research and development, but on production costs and marketing skill.

European researchers were given the task of competing with American technology and Japanese production prowess. Based on mistaken premises and conceptual errors, the European technology policy derailed from the beginning and sowed the seeds of its inevitable failure. The commission's concern was the harmonization of European standards at a time when the world was rapidly turning into a global market place dominated by the standards set by two American companies. The political ingredient of the strategy tended to distort the economic objective.

The commission proceeded by macro-level regulation and control through planning, rules and standards. Largely a political construct, the strategy lacked businesslike common sense and economic logic. Companies became accustomed to regular public-cash infusions and developed a dependency culture.

Ever since, many thousands of people compete to obtain money from the European Union. The commission gives away billions of euros. This enormous amount of cash inevitably attracts a great many applicants into a competitive bidding process. The money goes to those who best understand and address the pet projects of the fonctionnaires whose job it is to spend public money in order to achieve the priorities and the objectives of the ongoing programs. The EU's research and development program is entirely governed by successive four-year plans which determine strategy, action and budget. Priorities and objectives change with each new program.

The participants of Davignon's Round Table developed a consensus that the subsidizing of pre-competitive basic research and technological development would be the most efficient means to catch up and even surpass the Americans. Pre-competitive research was justified by the paradoxical principle of "collaborating to compete" and was supposed to close the gap. Collaborative research programs would promote the mobility of researchers and open new avenues in the integration of the European market. This would widely diffuse the results of academic research among competitors and create a trajectory that the computer industry could ride, setting the stage for commercial market penetration. Co-ordination of R&D became the central pillar of EC innovation policy.

The projects had to be "transnational", involving partners from more than one member state; the benefits would be shared among nations thus preventing any competitive distortion. The proposals were to be judged on technical and economic criteria by panels of experts or by some other independent peer-review process. The day-to-day decisions about which projects were to be funded and which were to be rejected were reached through compromise and often rancorous debate. Each committee tended to extend its field of competence, which resulted in duplication of efforts.

The focus was on spending, with slight concern for follow-through and for evaluating the commercial benefits. In the gaze of hindsight, the mission given to the European scientific community was beyond its capabilities. For several decades, basic and applied research in solid-state technology, carried out by theoretical and experimental physicists, mathematicians and chemists had yielded successive breakthroughs. The transistor, followed by the integrated circuit and the microprocessor had revolutionized computational science. The chemistry of computing had become so esoteric, sophisticated and costly, that it was accessible only to extremely few scientists. Very few people understand the work done by professional communities of specialists and sub-specialists conducting expensive experiments in secret laboratories. Moreover, making microprocessors was on the verge of becoming a multibillion-dollar proposition and the stakes were rising exponentially. But the commission founded its policy on the assumption that the European scientific community held a concentration of practical state-of-the-art expertise rivaling any on earth.

The Framework Programmes created dividing walls between invention, innovation and marketing; alongside such walls are moats in which good ideas sink out of sight. They could not be an efficient vehicle for the creation and transmission of useful knowledge. University laboratories and research institutes, unfamiliar with state-of-the-art microelectronics technology, could hardly ignite the fires of a technological breakthrough and come up with ideas that were beyond the grasp of Siemens' and Philips' research departments.

The commission tried to set up a procedure balancing competition and co-operation, and maximizing their symbiosis. Having overlooked the obvious contradiction, the masterminds fell between two stools. It was amateurish and naive to expect that advanced technology would diffuse across national boundaries. The logic of reciprocal access is incompatible with the antagonistic competitiveness of industry. While individual companies may cooperate for mutual benefit, regional diffusion of advanced technology was a pipe dream. Producers will sell or license proprietary technologies and know-how at arm's length.

What goes on in the industrial laboratories and on the production lines is kept secret. Scientists who are on the verge of discovering something new with commercial value, want to capture the benefits for themselves. Strict guard over intellectual property rights keeps technological secrets locked up in vaults. The gamesmanship of business is to make discoveries deliver payoffs before anybody else. In highly competitive industrial laboratories, urgency spurns creativity.

Politicians and bureaucrats lack the necessary understanding and focus relatively little of their time and energy on the issues, because they attract little popular attention. Jacks-of-all-trades, they have no first-hand understanding of what the IT world really is.

Academic research has produced immense expansions of mankind's knowledge and well-being. But, compared with the blistering pace of the industrial laboratories, and the cut-throat tactics of the IT boom-and-bust world, the scientific community is by and large a cozy, subsidized, closeted and highly regarded profession, pursuing research for its intrinsic value, and knowledge for knowledge's sake, without considering costs and practical benefits. The overriding driver of academic study is the fascination with the workings of nature. Routine is occasionally disturbed by in-house competition, disagreements and personality clashes. But the potential for wealth creation by commercializing academic research is not a priority. Moreover, European universities are no longer global players in the new technologies, and the gap is growing ever wider.

The great American colleges are predominantly private institutions with no assured source of income. An educational system driven by competition for financial support, must offer disciplines that produce commercially-useful knowledge. The university/industry interface is intensely active. Decentralized, market-driven and very competitive, American universities developed a high degree of responsiveness to changing industry needs; scientific research is more closely related to commercial potential. America's pre-eminence in software is due to the alacrity with which its universities turn out graduates with the necessary computer skills.

Japan's policymakers have traditionally seen to it that sufficient numbers of well-trained scientists are available to meet the needs of industry. Japan's universities turn out more engineering graduates than American colleges. The overwhelming majority is employed in large companies. University-industry interaction is very limited. Close collaboration is rare and professors in the national universities are prohibited from working for private companies. Government expenditure on research is quite small; much of it consists of loans and loan guarantees rather than direct grants. Public policies toward electronics have complemented the dynamism of private companies. The end effect has been effective mobilization of institutional and human resources.

In Europe, academic research is seen as culture. Basic science embodies longevity, thinks long-term and achieves its aims at its own pace. Industrial research stands under constant pressure and must closely interact with production, sales and marketing. The activities of the research lab must move symbiotically with the commercial activities of the company. The boundaries between research activities and product or technology development are often difficult to identify. In general, research programs are directly related to products which interest the company.

The logistics of such research programs must be coordinated; systems and designs must be compatible. The effectiveness of research depends not only on its internal functioning, but also on the way industry responds to innovation opportunities. A research and development program must clearly define the nature of the product, evaluate whether the objectives can be met within the original limits of time and cost, and whether the actors involved have the technical expertise and the incentives required to implement the program. The European research infrastructure was substandard and unable to generate a revolutionary innovation that would have created an alternative global standard, let alone the whole gamut of information technology.

Neither the evaluators nor the research community had the business sense to forestall the winners and the losers of the next generation. The scientific and engineering challenge was beyond their reach. Microelectronics was a relatively new science, confined to a few industrial laboratories where research was intense, driven and focused. It started with the production of the first transistors in 1948; then came into its own in the 1970s with the development of the microprocessor by a small company called Intel; to become an exploding new industry with the launch of the Apple Macintosh.

The processes involved in the fabrication of semiconductors are extraordinarily expensive and complex. There was no justification for pouring huge amounts of money into the design and development of such specialized devices. Moreover, university laboratories do not possess the expensive and specialized equipment nor the scientific expertise and access to proprietary information that is required to focus intelligently the research in the appropriate directions and respond to the needs of the industry. European academic research lagged far behind the American and Japanese industrial laboratories in the development of the technologies needed for next-generation information-processing systems. In cutting-edge research, the second-best are simply no good.

Basic research is exploratory in nature, addressing fundamental scientific questions for which ready answers are lacking. The structure of silicon had been explored for decades by generations of theoretical and experimental scientists. By 1985, Intel had become the sole source for the most advanced world-class microprocessors and had a stranglehold on the market. Whereas Intel chips were in short supply, the warehouses of the other manufacturers were full: an indication that something bizarre was happening.

Confusing quality with quantity, European governments spread huge resources across a vast number of projects that were too small in overall scale to have any impact. The policy ran into trouble for many reasons. Part of the problem was the gulf between the research community marked by inbreeding and influence peddling, and the real world of commerce and industry. In Europe, researchers are judged by their scientific publications which are of interest only to a very small community, and almost never pursued for wider consumption. Research financed by public funds is by its very nature non-competitive and is not expected to be concerned with costs, copyrights, and file formats. Much of it is correspondingly irrelevant to the business world, except when a smart entrepreneur picks it up and creates a new market.

The instinct of basic researchers is to explore the esoteric nature of matter, and to disseminate the findings in papers, seminars and colloquia, in order to gain status among their peers. Research is not primarily a means to develop a product intended to be manufactured and marketed; the thrill of discovery is an end in itself. Basic research involves substantial knowledge input from public research laboratories. It tends to be driven by its internal logic, rather than by the prospect of immediate commercial application. This gives them the enormous luxury of not having to worry about the problem of the duration of the project. Basic researchers are interested in a wide diffusion of their findings, while the industrial laboratories will defer diffusion until lead-time and learning-curve advantages give them an edge over competition.

When the Framework program started, it created a new manna for a vast number of research institutes. They had the patience to learn the labyrinthine processes, the time to write proposals and to attend preparatory meetings. Always short of funding, they became experts at grant-hunting, and could stand waiting a long time for the contract and even longer for the money. Cooperative projects between research institutions and SMEs have been very numerous. Small companies do not have the resources to carry out basic research; the research institutes "seeded" a project and submitted the proposal.

The commission has a moral duty to the taxpayers to see that their money is spent wisely. Too much money was spread around indiscriminately and wasted. Very few technology developments led to commercialization. Easy money often led researchers to squander resources on academic curiosities, and to re-invent technologies already created elsewhere. By promoting European research consortia, the commission fostered co-operation between European scientists; but it did so at the expense of links between researchers and the industry interested in taking ideas to the marketplace. Cooperation between researchers and research institutes throughout Europe has been intensified; but cooperation of researchers is not an end in itself. Technology policy must be measured by the extent to which its activities contribute toward innovation and improved competitiveness of European industry. In these terms, the technology policy of the European Union is a costly failure.

EU-funded research has contributed to the transfer of knowledge and skills and stimulated transnational collaboration. But the technology gap between the various countries has not narrowed. Moreover, the ivory-tower mentality has produced a vast number of expensive and unproductive programs. The beneficiaries of the funds generally expressed great .satisfaction, even if their projects failed. They complained, however, about the administrative burden of preparing and submitting proposals, the complex bureaucratic procedures, the slow decision-making and the delays in receiving funds.

European collaborative programs required industry to supplement public contributions. There was no way of verifying to what extent such prerequisites were met. The complex administrative structure of EU programs hindered coordination of goals and clarity in technical agendas. The policies failed to enhance the ability of European firms to respond to market signals and to direct R&D funding to promising fields.

Necessity breeds invention. Innovation is driven forward by scientific and technical knowledge under the pressure of competition, and by the capacity to exploit new technology. This requires the ability to react under intense pressure and to decide quickly. Production capabilities depend on industrial infrastructures. Capabilities range from organizational competencies in development and manufacturing to the availability of capital for investment and marketing.

Industrial innovation depends centrally on the components, materials, machinery and control technologies that are combined to create new products and processes. The task of integrating a new component into an existing fabrication line is highly complex. It was naïve to expect that the European industry could absorb the new technology in a timely fashion and produce computers at competitive cost.

Contrary to received wisdom, Europe did not quantitatively lag behind in R&D spending. But the funds were spread out over a raft of small-scale projects. The announced R&D budgets of Siemens or Philips exceeded those of many foreign competitors.[2]

In terms of publications, symposia or references in the specialist press, European scientific productivity is entirely satisfactory and equal to that of the United States. The specific European weakness appears as soon as one examines the transformation of this research into innovations and into marketable goods. The commission measures R&D investment by the amount of input, not by wealth creation.

The budgets of the Framework Programmes have grown exponentially:

First FP	1984-1987	3.7 billion ecus
Second FP	1987-1991	5.4
Third FP	1990-1994	6.6
Fourth FP	1994-1998	12.3
Fifth FP	1998-2002	14.9
Sixth FP	2002-2006	€ 17.5
Seventh FP	2007-2013	€ 50.5

The major objective of the early Framework program was the strengthening of the scientific and technological base of the computer industry to make it more competitive at the international level. The first Framework Programmes generated applications mostly from non-commercial institutes and universities which had neither the intention nor the money and the marketing expertise to commercialize the results. The program was based on a top-down supply-side academic approach targeting long-term results. It did not have the flexibility, the speed and confidentiality required to align or re-align in response to new developments in the marketplace. When it became evident that the researchers did not deliver any substantial technical breakthroughs, European firms turned to American and Japanese companies.

Driven by the need to acquire cutting-edge technology and state-of-the-art manufacturing skills, they went out and paid for it. The transfer of technology is, in most cases, not subject to tariff or non-tariff barriers. Globalization was a more powerful force than economic integration. In a globalized world, any industrial policy that runs foul of the laws of the market is bound to fail in the long run.

The "Fortress Europe" policy was counter-productive. It compelled American and Japanese companies to set up production in Europe. More efficient, they thwarted the policy-makers' attempts to favor domestic producers. They were easily able to outsmart protectionist plans by lowering their profit margin, leaving European manufacturers worse off than before.

The European political establishment considers public support of scientific research as one of the major functions of the state. In reality, the policy has created a self-sufficient and inefficient bureaucratic machinery. The main beneficiaries of the programs are the administrators, the firms at the receiving end, and the private and academic laboratories, sheltered havens where ivory-tower research is an interesting challenge and a salaried sinecure.

European technological policy was handicapped by complacency about governments' ability to successfully counteract the laws of the market. Wherever market dynamics have developed competitive advantages, public policy intervention is unlikely to alter them significantly. The lesson was learned the hard way, but it has not sunk in. The commissioners in charge of European research are politicians in limbo, able to give an enlightened opinion on any subject, but whose views are very hazy.

Hindsight shows that an overambitious policy designed and implemented by policymakers and bureaucrats without intimate knowledge of the industry and little experience of commercial realities had no chance of delivering substantial economic return. They had no idea of either the nature of the problems being addressed or of the direction in which solutions lied. The European scientific community was asked to invent hardware more powerful than Intel's and software more whizzy than Microsoft's.

Enterprise worth its salt would refuse public handouts. But the grab-bag nature of European policies mirrors the welfare-state mentality. Decision-making in the European Union involves successive rounds of inter-institutional and intergovernmental bargaining: the commission proposes, the European parliament amends, the Council disposes. This was too slow for the fast-moving, idea-intensive, permanently changing markets. They attempted to fashion a distinctly European technology policy that would allow Europe to compete with its global rivals. Instead, they failed to prevent the extinction of the European computer industry. It was at best futile and at worst a perverse form of charity, with taxpayers footing the bill for fruitless and expensive research.

The commission tends to overestimate its sapience and to oversell the potential of its programs. The exuberance may be excusable and necessary for sustaining faith in the benefits resulting from the European Union. But by raising false hopes, it aggravates one of Europe's major handicaps, namely the confident complacency about the ability of the European model to continue generating increased levels of wealth and quality of life.

Power has become increasingly centralized in a supranational institution around which an official mystique has developed. The role of the commission in technology policy has been largely exempt from critical scrutiny by the popular press and is opaque to public opinion. The technical complexity is a powerful deterrent to scrutiny by anyone trying to understand what goes on. The insiders quietly share the spoils. No reliable data are available for assessing the validity of technology policy programs, and much of what has been claimed was misleading and outright contrary to fact. The outcome of European technology policy belies its intended goals.

The reports evaluating the results of the commission's policies are consistently eulogistic. What is always absent from the literature is true evidence that links the enactment of the policies with success in their stated objectives of fostering domestic industry, much less whether such objectives truly resulted in a net welfare gain for society.

Evidence confirms a common-sense conclusion that European technology policy has wrought much damage by distorting priorities rather than letting economic forces run their course. The generous availability of public funds incubates schemes mostly of unpredictable and unsubstantial value.

The political establishment knows that EU-financed programs are among their most effective propaganda instruments.

Their unverifiable statistical data used to prove their case naturally have a high degree of public acceptance.

Evolutionary technologies inevitably generate creative destruction. Global competitiveness and success in world markets stems above all from entrepreneurial innovation and the ability of private firms to back the right technologies at the right time. Intended to facilitate the mobility of scientists, researchers, students and scholars throughout Europe and to create the feeling of belonging to a community without borders, the technology policy did not provide the dynamics that could have saved the European computer industry from extinction.

Moreover, it did not alleviate the acute shortage of computing engineers. Industry and the service sectors are experiencing a severe shortage of qualified personnel and skills to implement and manage IT solutions.

The Report of the Esprit Review Board 1996 sanctioned Esprit III as "a program contributing to the creation of an advanced skill base and helping to pave the way for Europe's advent into the Information Society. It has been very successful as an expression of R&D policy... The Board sees this as a matter for congratulation." In fact, Esprit III had presided over the extinction of the European computer industry. Having failed in information technologies, the Board called upon policy makers to shift R&D programs and reallocate resources to life sciences: user involvement, social demand and media synergies, best practice, training and diffusion. The Board also urged the commission to speed up its payments procedures "in order to enable participants to continue work in projects in which the coordinator has gone bankrupt, a natural and potentially not infrequent event in such a dynamic sector." [3]

The commission produces an uninterrupted stream of directives and papers: White Papers, Green Papers, Working Papers, reams of studies and analyses, futile resolutions, unproductive fact-finding missions, pandects of tautologies replete with sweeping generalizations. Several reports, based on answers to questionnaires, evaluated the efficiency of Eureka. The bottom-up character, the market orientation, the flexible and decentralized operational procedures were considered very positive. The negative points were a lack of transparency and insufficient synchronization. Industrial participants reported gains in know-how, improved product or process and skills. The report was very critical of the research institutions for their lack of market awareness and managerial competence. Another report indicated that academic researchers were more satisfied than industrial participants. While research institutes collaborated actively with industrial partners, universities gave priority to other universities for the exchange of information.

Business-cum-politics programs must cope with rivalries and the deadweight of bureaucratic centralization. Over the years, the visionary and idyllic pronouncements by the commission invariably continued to claim success and the need for pursuing them. When things go wrong, the scapegoat is to be found outside. Most decisions are the outcome of complex political bargains based on issue linkage. Even when things go awry, the bargains are maintained because undoing them is as complicated and laborious as getting them started.

At the commission, the opinion prevails that "public support continues to have a valid and strategic role to play before the information economy can safely be left to the full devices of the free-market forces."[4] In December 1999, the chairman of the program announced Medea+. He justified the continuance of government support: "In Jessi we closed the technology gap. In Medea we turned to embedded applications. In the next program Europe should be the leader in system-on-silicon integrated circuits." Every other major geographic region, he said, including the United States, Japan, Taiwan and Korea, support their national industry, so it is appropriate for Europe to do the same.

In fact, the US government does not support research conducted by Intel, Microsoft or their competitors. The recipe of the Asian governments to establish an electronics industry was simple: politicians should not get involved in industrial policy;

let the entrepreneurs attract foreign capital and technology; provide free industrial parks and an educated and diligent workforce; let companies operate tax-free: they will provide jobs with taxable incomes.

The Framework Programme is a slow and costly process. Occasionally, the life expectancy of a project is shorter than the time needed to complete the application file. Many proposals go through the procedure, only to be rejected in the last resort. Consultation with the European commission services made the procedures unwieldy. Every financial proposal is subject to interservice consultation and to approval by the college of commissioners. When speed and decisiveness are required, such a process proves fatal. Priority themes are rarely identified: a significant share of the funds was spread over secondary objectives; the constant concern for "cohesion" leads to a multitude of isolated objectives with very little coherence. The system of taxing and spending has created a downward economic spiral. The best way to end this symbiotic relationship between industry and government is to shut down the cash-dispensing programs. But if past is prologue, political-cum-business wealth destruction is bound to go on.

Corporate welfare is a cash-in-cash-out money-grabbing system that abuses government authority to confer privileged benefits to specific firms, specific industries and institutions. This is government hubris in the extreme. It unwisely converts the government into the role of the investment banker. When banks or venture capitalists allocate scarce investment capital to a company, they do this with their own money. If they do it poorly, they are out of business. Taxpayer funds should not be used to provide assistance to one specific industry. The burden of these subsidies is borne by the wealth-creating sectors of the economy forced to pay suffocating tax rates.

In speeches, reports and communiqués, the commission keeps stating that the EU policy framework is functioning well. Occasionally, suggestions are made to improve the research infrastructures. The working document entitled *A European research area for infrastructures,* notes that "there have been no success stories in the last ten years." In addition, there are no coordinated mechanisms to assess the main needs and priorities in European research. The present structures are complex and uncertain, and disciplinary fragmentation makes it extremely difficult to set priorities among infrastructures serving diverse research communities. Distribution of the financial burden is unclear and slow. The working document recommends the creation of a European research structure through new infrastructures involving pan-European scientific organizations to provide independent scientific advice. A permanent secretariat would assist this "high level panel." The commission would provide the financial resources. Research and development is still largely concentrated in the most prosperous regions. The poorer regions should not be left behind. [5]

European industrial policy has not benefited people with the brightest ideas and the most promising projects, but those most adroit in writing up a proposal and the most persuasive lobbyists. The results speak for themselves. The policy created a sort of techno-industrial complex, run largely by fonctionnaires. It has not prevented the demise of the computer industry and of the microelectronics industry in general.

One of the lessons to be learned is that successful merchandising requires an integrated approach, combining intellectual property-creation, design, manufacturing, marketing, customer support and service, and related non-technical factors. The world-view of the policy-makers, their unfamiliarity with the industry, the inherent inertia of big administrations, their paper-based inefficiencies, the encyclopedic work-programs, the slowness of decision processes, the strategic incoherence of the policies constituted obstacles to adapt to the rapid evolution of a fast-changing technology.

For fundamental scientific discoveries and technological advances originating in research institutions to make their way to the private sector for commercialization, it takes more than setting up a partnership between applicants from different countries.

Companies compete for government subsidies because they make a difference in the bottom line. They do what rational people do when governments afford them to be inefficient and give them free money and an exemption from the rules of the market. Relying on subsidies has obvious perverse effects, because it encourages dependency rather than self-help. Government assistance is no guarantee of success. Unless the project is viable to begin with and unless the scientists and managers working on it are competent and motivated, it will not succeed, subsidies or no subsidies.

A competitive meritocracy rewards the talented and the enterprising and leaves the indolent, the mediocre and the dimwits behind. Despite the huge amounts of subsidies poured into research budgets, the dream of national or European champions has been blown away.

One of the hidden costs of government interference is the inefficient use of human resources, knowledge and energy. Technology policy is contrary to competition policy. It inevitably favors one set of interests over another. State aid to selected companies distorts the playing field. Big companies were thought to be the sole drivers of innovation, and were favored to take on American competition. In the rush to bolster the national champions, the opportunity to create an environment where small and medium sized companies could develop, was overlooked. In the United States, the silicon revolution was spawned by start-ups.

The technology policy did not do what it was meant to do. The European countries and their taxpayers need a better way to keep - or strengthen - whatever global competitiveness they still maintain. Ultimately, competitiveness in the electronics industry depends on the efforts of individual firms. The prerequisites are capable people, capital for start-ups and for expansion, open markets and genuine competition, world-class research and business-friendly fiscal policies. Technology policy cannot make up for upper-level management failures, the unwillingness to compete internationally, overregulation of business, an anti-entrepreneurial climate and exorbitant wage and tax levels.

In the computer industry, innovative breakthroughs have usually been achieved by one exceptional individual or a small nucleus of people. Research and development as it is conceived and practiced in Europe should once and for all be thrown open to scrutiny and abandoned. [6]

European researchers have lost contact with the frontier areas of science, and are increasingly unable to move with times. The assumption that by creating a broad base of scientific knowledge, technology transfer will flow sequentially from science to industry through a natural process has been discredited by experience. Most projects produce nothing except reports.

Technological advance is the result of a never-ending cycle of entry by innovative firms, commercial application of new products or processes, displacement of incumbents. Each year, the World Economic Forum designates a number of start-ups who have recently put a truly innovative product on the market or have proven the practical application of their project. These pioneers are honored as standouts for visionary leadership and for the long-term impact their contribution will have on business and society. In 2002, 28 were American, three British, one Swedish, one German and one Dutch.[7] In 2007, 8 of the 10 laureates were American, one Dutch and one German.

For the European innovators, there is nothing to blow a trumpet. Nevertheless, the financial future of the research institutions is solidly assured. The commission bribes this highly regarded and influential community into "thinking European" by showering it with endowments amounting to billions of euros. Cordis, the European commission's research and development information service keeps the researchers up-to-date on projects and strategic directions through its web home page. The information anyone may need to participate in the sharing of the funding is just a few mouse clicks away.

Cordis provides advice on how to benefit from the European commission's Framework Programme, how to find partners and share expertise.

On March 20, 2002, the commission asked the scientific community to propose what they saw as the most promising topics for cutting-edge research in the 6th Research Framework Programme. On June 12, 2002, Cordis announced that European researchers had sent in more than 15,000 ideas for research projects. More than 100,000 groups and institutions were involved in drafting ideas; the proposed teams involved potentially several hundreds of thousands of researchers across Europe and beyond.

Research commissioner Philippe Busquin was encouraged by the massive response. "It shows that the European Research Area is becoming a reality", he said. "The strong response also demonstrates that our researchers have many good ideas; that much more funding for research is needed in Europe through a coordinated investment by Member States. It is an encouraging sign as we work towards the EU's target of investing 3% of GDP in research by 2010. Our researchers want to work together and share efforts with the best of their field in other countries. They want to work together in a new way at the European level, namely in projects or networks with sufficient critical mass to meet global scientific or technological challenges."

"Encouraging closer links between researchers all over the EU is a key priority for the European commission. EU action to pool resources, to bring together research teams in different countries and to share expertise is essential if the EU is to compete both scientifically and economically in the global marketplace. Without EU action, compartmentalisation of EU member state's research efforts, duplication of research efforts and failure to share expertise would continue to undermine EU competitiveness."

The European parliament and the European council decided on the main orientations of the 6th Framework Programme, which had a 4-year budget of €17.5 billion. The commission invited companies, universities and research centers to express their interest for research projects or networks in the fields of genomics and life sciences, information technologies, nanotechnologies, aerospace, food safety, sustainable development and social sciences.

The program ran from 2002 to 2006. It was designed as an instrument to help realize a European Research Area. It was based on four main principles: promoting scientific excellence, concentrating on a limited number of priorities with a true European-added value, structuring and integrating European and national efforts, and simplifying procedures. [8]

Europe has no computer industry anymore, but in 1998, three European companies, Philips Semiconductors, Siemens (today Infineon Technologies), and STMicroelectronics entered the top 10 ranking of the largest semiconductor companies. Virtually, these companies are Dutch, German or French-Italian. The planning, designing and marketing is mostly handled in Europe, but the overwhelming bulk of their operations takes place in Asia and in the United States. STMicroelectronics is headquartered in Geneva, Switzerland. Infineon keeps posting heavy losses despite substantial subsidies by the German government.

The materials and the manufacturing equipment are globally priced, which makes employment costs the determining factor for the location of production. With headquarters in one country, research facilities in many, and the productive base almost totally outside Europe, they are true multinationals. They enter joint ventures with competitors to gain access to critical technologies.

The semiconductor industry is dominated by multi-billion dollar giants psyched up to cycles of boom and bust, exacerbated by some of the semiconductor industry's own peculiarities. Slumps in sales are often due to a collapse in prices rather than to a decline in volumes sold. Cyclical overproduction and severe price fluctuations are a fact of life. Semiconductor chips are manufactured in sterile fabrication plants - or fabs - that use light waves to etch successive layers of circuitry on a silicon substrate. A fab takes two years to build and costs between $1bn and $3bn. The massive expense of re-sterilizing a semiconductor plant usually makes it uneconomical to suspend production once a fab has come into service. This limits the speed with which manufacturers can respond to a decline in demand. When sales dip, most chipmakers have little choice but to continue producing at full capacity, accepting whatever price they can get. They maximize profits and pay off debts during the upswings to make sure that they can weather the next slowdown.

In 2000, the industry had a record year. The year 2001 was the worst ever. Some companies will find it difficult to return to form, and more consolidation is likely. Only the companies that do less badly are apt to survive. Several Asian IT companies are well suited to thrive in a global down-market. The Japanese companies are part of a keiretsu, business groups that reduce each member's risks through weak members being supported by stronger ones in times of difficulty. In a tech recession, the lowest-cost producer is the winner. Chip firms will have to be consolidated. In the coming decade there will be less than a handful of giants.[9]

European semiconductor companies have been engaged for decades in a struggle for survival. The industry is cyclical and unpredictable. Every company needs billions of cash to stay ahead in the technological rat race. The interlinkage of technology development and high-performance management is crucial for the survival of even the strongest players. Philips Semiconductors, Infineon and STMicroelectronics are heavily subsidized by Medea+, but face financial trouble. Twice Philips has teetered on the brink of bankruptcy; Siemens has pushed off and renamed its money-losing semiconductor division; the French and Italian governments are major shareholders of STMicroelectronics. The three companies regularly announce substantial losses. Consolidation in the semiconductor industry is inescapable. For some, the specter of insolvency is on the horizon.

The commission is a virtual government in and of itself, with a staff of thousands of employees and a slush fund of billions of euros that go up in smoke. The asymmetry of costs and benefits is staggering. The commission will lavish billions of euros a year on scientific research. Nobody seems to question the usefulness of these programs, although they largely patronize and perpetuate research for the sake of research, instead of creating new industries and future wealth.

In the United States also, the biggest single source of funding for scientific research is the taxpayer. The Federal government dispenses about $20 billion a year to scientists and mathematicians through numerous outlets. But the purpose, the procedures and the beneficiaries are of an entirely different class. The National Science Foundation, the Department of Defense, the Department of Energy and NASA support a number of physics laboratories. The government invites leading physicist to Washington to read their colleagues' grant applications and make the judgments. The decision about who gets the money is made after this peer review process which guarantees competence, honesty and impartiality. Industrial policy can promote economic progress and can also have disastrous consequences. In the United States, military applications have been important drivers of new technologies. There is no agency to serve as a focal point for industrial policy, but some military research inevitably benefits commercial businesses.

National security, antitrust and macroeconomic policy has taken priority; competitiveness and economic efficiency have seldom been the concern of Federal agencies. Modern weapons systems and the space program placed a premium on miniaturization of circuits. Given the costs of research, development, and tooling for production, it is hard to imagine that the integrated circuit and the microprocessor would have emerged - at least as quickly as they did - without government support.

The failure of the command economy in the socialist countries of Eastern Europe to produce efficiently, innovate and create wealth resulted in their implosion in the late 1980s. Latin

America provides a case study of the catastrophic by-products resulting from policies which run counter to market forces and ignore the sobering effects of competition. In the 1970s, several Latin American governments decided to industrialize in order to produce domestically a vast number of manufactured products and make their economies independent from imports. They erected high import tariffs, subsidized exports, maintained uncompetitive exchange rates and poured money into heavy industry without ever exposing it to competitive pressures. The policies produced a number of "white elephants", huge budget and trade deficits, a burgeoning external debt and social unrest.

Japan is the prime example of an economy which has successfully implemented industrial policy to promote economic growth. An enlightened bureaucracy pursued sound macroeconomic policies with limited but effective levels of regulation. Economic growth in the other countries of East Asia is the result of active involvement by the government in the creation of a climate providing the right conditions for letting responsible entrepreneurs, namely a welcoming environment for foreign investment, restrictions on wages and union activity, and forced-savings schemes.

The European technology policy was determined by the role of the commission as centralizing institution, and by the welfare-state role of the governments. To what extent has it brought in a return to industry and to society? Private enterprise, in order to survive, must use its human and financial capital as efficiently as possible. How effectively can multidisciplinary, geographically dispersed knowledge workers collaborate on a project, without hierarchies and central management? The synergies and linkages European technology is supposed to generate, are hindered by innate limitations and roadblocks in communications. They waste away in bureaucratic sloth and unrealistic expectations. An end in themselves, these programs produce an interminable stream of meetings, reviews and reports, concocted by committees taking on a life of their own, and nurtured year after year with an inexhaustible cash pile, without delivering any tangible benefits for the citizens at large. Instead of solving the problems, they subsidize them.

The political planners see the markets in static terms. Revolutionary technologies bring off creative destruction. Genomics, information technology, nanotechnology and aerospace are esoteric and sophisticated disciplines requiring an expertise accessible only by very few extremely specialized and brainy individuals. What is the purpose of pouring huge amounts of financial resources into the development of highly exclusive technologies that may possibly be of use only to a very small number of manufacturers? To have any validity, such funding must be strictly targeted and research must be world-class.

Technologists and entrepreneurs, politicians, bureaucrats and social scientists live in parallel universes. The ethical oversensitivities prevalent in Europe drive the best researchers in biotechnology, bioelectronics and genetics into emigration. Sociology and economics are by no means "hard" sciences. Any 'intellectual' can express a valid opinion in matters of social issues and sustainable development. No need to spend public money. Instead of reliable feedback, such research programs can at best provide a broad and uncertain insight and guidance because the objects of interest are impossible to define scientifically and to measure with precision.

The rationale and the justification of European technology policy is the need to compete with the United States and Asia. R&D investment in the United States is overwhelmingly defense related. It has relatively little impact on the civilian economy and industrial competitiveness. The programs provide direct support mostly for key government missions, such as improving the nation's health and medical care, exploring space, and maintaining the nation's defense. [10]

The relative priority of different areas of R&D has varied over the years. Space exploration was dominant in the 1960s. Energy R&D gained priority following the oil shortages of the 1970s and then retreated as national attention turned elsewhere. Health R&D now represents the largest single share of the civilian R&D portfolio. R&D programs are not considered ends in themselves but means to the ends. The Office of Management and Budget attempts to provide co-ordination.

In 1998, the CEO's of about 50 Silicon Valley companies signed a "Declaration of Independence". They urged Congress to end corporate welfare "even if it means funding cuts to my own company." They claimed that the competitiveness of America's high-technology industry would benefit if corporate subsidies were eliminated altogether and the savings were devoted to reducing corporate income taxes, the capital gains tax, or the personal income tax.[11]

At the end of World War II, Japan's economy was in tatters. The objective that drove government R&D policy in the 1970s was to "bootstrap" domestic industries up to American standards. This effort propelled the Japanese electronics industry up to - and eventually beyond - US companies in consumer electronics. When Japanese companies attained world class status, they were no longer interested in sharing their market-focused R&D capabilities by participating in government-led consortia. The extent of MITI intervention and of government control has been greatly exaggerated. The MITI-sponsored R&D consortia fared poorly by almost any standards. In project after project, the government seriously misread technological trends or otherwise sponsored activities with unrealistic and overly ambitious goals. Companies became more and more reluctant to risk the loss of critical proprietary information that might result from participation in a joint R&D project. The Fifth Generation project's experience was typical for government-sponsored joint research. The reaction of Japan's computer manufacturers to the Fifth Generation project concept was highly negative. Japan's computer manufacturers had accurately forecast the trends in their industry.

At the 2008 spring European Council, the Commission announced that "we are on the right track: in recent years we have created 6.5 million new jobs, the unemployment rate has fallen to less than 7% and the foundations of the European economy are sound." No mention was made of the jobs that had been destroyed. Despite the creation of new jobs, unemployment is on the rise and the wealth-creating sector keeps shrinking. Industrial production in the euro area is down 1.7% against last year. In Switzerland it is up 6.1%; in Norway 2.4%.

The Lisbon Strategy is at the centre of European economic policy. It is a telling symptom of groupthink and collective incompetence. The oracular predictions that come out of these Councils are out of touch with reality. Its major attribute is the extent of self-deception. Words have no precise meaning. Despite the dismal failure to achieve its goals, its proponents reaffirm them time and again, hiding their failure behind a façade of misinformation. The EU establishment takes comfort in the fact that the "silent majority" has no way to make its voice heard. Any democratic government that manifestly fails to carry out its proclaimed mandate would be voted out of ofice. The European institutions - legislative, executive and judicial - constitute an unelected and unaccountable super-government immune from the pressures of public opinion. A self-centred, self-serving and self-perpetuating political class commutes between national politics and European institutions, and vice versa.

It is commonplace for governments to hold forth clear views on what is economically best for the country. When they do not succeed, they are generally unable or unwilling to read-just their strategy and reflexively redouble their unsuccessful approach. Authoritarian regimes do not have to justify their legitimacy by proving their competence.

The European Union functions in a virtual world of make-believe. The introduction of new and massive spending, taxation, regulation and redistribution schemes, on top of national legislation, imposes a heavy burden on the productive sector. The pursuit of political-ideological goals, such as equalisation and the distribution of wealth, turns a blind eye to the difference between what is socially desirable and economically feasible. The expectations prognosticated in Lisbon cannot materialise. After decades of working less and less for more and more and counterproductive legislation by the Commission, Europe has priced itself out of the market, currently leaving 19 million people unemployed, unable - or unwilling - to take a job. In the euro area, according to the latest official figures, the unemployment rate is in the euro area is 7.2%. In Switzerland it is 2.6% and in Norway 2.4%. Belgium ranks worst with 11.2%

At the heart of the Lisbon Strategy is the belief that scientific knowledge is the foundation of technological and economic progress. Financing research and development is one of the most important and least understood items of the Commission's budget. The approach is based on false premises and a misunderstanding of how R&D works. Common wisdom holds that the more money is put into the research pipeline, the more products will come out at the other end. The relationship between research and innovation is far more complex. No one can foresee what will result from a scientific discovery. Once a new invention rolls off the production line, management and some luck become the decisive factors of success.

Academic research at the cutting edge of knowledge seldom has an immediate applicability. The transfer of knowledge requires capabilities, infrastructure and relationships that extend beyond the traditional academic domains of research, scholarship and learning and teaching. We should not expect much cutting edge scientific discoveries to emanate from Europe's ivory towers. New knowledge is mostly produced in industrial research laboratories where scientists are confronted with specific problems and research is results-oriented.

Research conducted at the technological frontier is global, expensive and risky. To be of any value, it must have world class. The backwardness of European universities in the hard sciences leads most capable and ambitious students to complete their education in an American university. Very few come back. In a knowledge-based economy, losing the best and the brightest is proof of failure.

The culture of corporate America is integrated into its educational culture. Research is concentrated in a limited number of institutions with ample resources to invest in the best teachers and the most advanced facilities. The Commission scatters enormous amounts of public resources over a broad field of mediocre institutions and private projects. Programmes and results are evaluated in terms of expenditures rather than in terms of the goals achieved.

Random financing thousands of projects and SME's when only a few can be expected to be profitable, is a pure waste of taxpayers' money. The potential benefits are overwhelmingly outweighed by the huge expense of it all. *Science Magazine* recently published an article stating that a lot of research is being conducted in the EU for which there is no demand. The Seventh Framework Programme runs from 2007 to 2013 and has a budget of €54 billion. Thousands of researchers keep lining up to get their part of the manna. One should not expect any epoch-making invention to come out of it.

Hyperion's Sean McCarthy advertises on the web three-day courses which he teaches all over Europe. He lectures researchers about how to write a proposal, how to negotiate, manage, administer and audit a contract, how to identify the best research topics, how to select the most receptive evaluator, the best partners, the best instrument, and much more. The cost per participant is €475. His advice: never go to Brussels asking for money. Instead, present them with the probable solution to a problem. The trick is to fill out a grant application that interests the evaluators. Once you have the money, do as you like. Thus astronomical amounts ultimately evaporate into the pockets of smart researchers whose main concern is to "think European."

Private money goes where it is sensible to spend it. The Commission distributes research funds on the basis of the most cursory vetting. To qualify, there must be at least three participants from three countries. The Commission's bureaucrats have no way to evaluate the potential of the research applications they approve. The duration of an integrated project runs between 3 and 5 years. The problems of communication and coordination involved in multinational and joint research are obvious. Issues about the ownership of patents relating to jointly generated knowledge and the transfer of such knowledge for industrial or commercial applications require endless negotiations. The main result is a mountain of unread paperwork: 38% of world scientific publications originate in the EU, 31% in the US and 9% in Japan.

Ever since Jacques Delors Socialist ideology takes its toll. Setting up a business in Europe requires stamina, patience and personal money. Entrepreneurs who have a project face countless obstacles. They must devote many hours to comply with the paperwork imposed by their government and by EU legislation. Wages, taxes and social charges are the highest in the world. The balance between risk and reward is skewed towards risk. Professional venture capitalists are a rare breed and profits are blunted by punitive taxes.

Politicians play a major role in the extent to which markets are free or subject to regulation which penalises the business community. The EU makes it hard to be an entrepreneur. Economic growth is related to freedom from the constraint of bureaucracy. This postulate is not understood in Europe. Slow growth rates are linked to command and control bureaucracies, especially those that seek to impose social goals. The EU experience provides a chilling reflection: bureaucracy, when it takes command, defaults to interests and goals that are not congenial to productivity or to the operation of efficient firms in the global capitalist system.

The recipe for a growing economy includes a competitive industrial infrastructure and a competitive workforce; tax policies that allow saving and investment; a sound education system and welfare arrangements which provide a safety net but do not stifle initiative. The EU scores badly on all these fundamentals. In the latest economic freedom index published by the Fraser Institute, only the United Kingdom and Switzerland rank among to first 10. Maastricht and the euro may be part of the answer.

A government-knows-best approach ignores the process of, and the benefits from, creating long-term wealth through competition. The entrepreneur is the prime mover of economic growth that delivers the social goals. Much of the European economy has gradually come apart at its industrial seams, largely because of the Commission's mistaken policies. Case studies prove that economic vitality results mainly from the creative, disruptive and unpredictable action of entrepreneurs who bring new products and business methods to market. Entrepreneurial capitalism is competitive, dynamic, ruthless and occasionally nasty.

The governments of the "Asian Tigers" had enough commonsense to limit their role to the creation of industrial and educational infrastructures and to let the business community take care of employment, growth and development. Asian countries largely set the technological and industrial pace, because they have access to the most advanced technologies and work harder for less. Decades of Socialist rule inflicted untold misery upon the Russian and Chinese population. The changeover to unbridled capitalism produced a tectonic shift in global economic power while lifting millions of people out of abject poverty.

Globalisation augurs a new age in which emerging-market companies are increasingly out-competing European competitors. Work flows to places where it is done most advantageously. Obviously, Europe isn't working as it should. Its social model is in serious trouble. It may be morally superior; it is also economically disastrous. The world balance of economic power leaves Europe behind. The failure lies in the attempt to merge two competing and incompatible moral-political creeds: the liberal belief that the market economy is the most efficient to produce prosperity and the Socialist doctrine that the state is responsible for the well-being of its citizens.

Two centuries ago, the Industrial Revolution put Europe at the center of the global economy. The mechanisation of the economy did not require any scientific research. Entrepreneurs were left free to build and use their machinery and workforce so as to provide maximum profit. The IT Revolution has relegated the European Union to the fringes.

In a knowledge-driven economy, knowledge is *the* asset to be managed. The accelerated development of technology and the shorter life-cycle of products require novel knowledge-management tools. We stand at a moment in history when new learning and dramatic change is needed to rise to the next performance level. Miss the moment and decline is inevitable. Change can only be achieved by re-prioritising the economic-financial over the social-political.

7

EPITAPH FOR THE CHAMPIONS

For more than three decades, European computer companies tried to capture a share of the global market. They represented the European industrial aristocracy. Thwarted by the legacies and the environment that shaped them, by the mid-1990s, they had been driven out of business. Ever since, Europe is almost entirely dependent on American and Asian imports, after wasting huge amounts of human and financial capital on industrial laggards and feckless research, unable to deal efficiently with the challenges they faced and the tasks they were meant to perform. Their story provides a real-time documentation of the paths to competitive success and failure in high-tech industries.

The technological and institutional infrastructure of the computer industry was determined in the crucible of international competition between a dozen companies. The decline reflects the mistaken policies, but equally the traditions of corporate structure and the Old-World syndrome: managerial incompetence, the high cost of employing labor, misconceived premises and interventionist governments. The fortunes of the European computer industry are a mixture of political and industrial bungling. The lessons have not been learned. Confused by the ill-omened forebodings for the sustainability of the European economic and social model, politicians are perplexed and powerless in the face of globalization. In America and Asia the emphasis is on free competition and restricted government; in Europe the accent is on social justice, non-industrial priorities and regulatory interventionism.

A consensus developed between the political class and the senior managers of the industry that a state-business partnership was the most effective method for meeting the American and Japanese challenge. By establishing cooperation between the large computer manufacturers and academic researchers, it would be possible to develop a European technology able to compete in the global marketplace. State intervention took many forms: substantial R&D funding, nationalization, procurement and regulation policies, protective tariffs. The political establishment had no knowledge of the real world and of the microcomputer revolution that was unfolding in the United States. The protective strategy, aimed primarily at the preservation of existing jobs and the creation of job opportunities, ultimately destroyed the industry and the jobs.

The company executives were also on a steep learning curve: in an industry with ultra-rapid product and process innovation, they did not know where the game was going next. They were able to persuade the political class that they needed government help to compete in the global market, and were happy to take the money that was freely shed out. It assured a precarious survival of their computer division for a few years, but ended in total failure. Computing technology had changed beyond recognition, requiring entrepreneurs and business leaders to think and act globally. Despite high wage levels, American companies found the way to prosper. They outsourced labor-intensive production operations to low-cost Asia, whereas the European manufacturers were told to "think European."

Europe's unique institutional relationship between the state, labor and capital has not delivered the goods. Rather than letting the companies slug it out in an industry driven by American and Japanese entrepreneurship in a free-market economy, the way to industrial success was to be centrally directed by politicians and fonctionnaires. Government involvement in the industry was considered legitimate and necessary. For the industry, technology policy was an attractive and comfortable solution. It was much easier to collect government subsidies than to compete in the world markets.The European electronics manufacturers were not able to offer computing power at a competitive price and to develop a strong and viable industry. The competitiveness of the electronics industry is important not only intrinsically, but also because of the interactions with other segments of the economy and of job and skill opportunities.

Ultimately, it depends on the efforts of the individual firms and on the economic climate in which they operate. Unlike anywhere else in the industrialized world, European countries developed a tradition of government intervention in private investment decisions and in control over allocations of capital. The degree of interventionism was obviously influenced by the swings of the political pendulum, thus adding to the unpredictability of long-term strategic planning. The French government has sometimes chosen to allow, and even encouraged foreign ownership.

In the United States, practically every successful electronics start-up was originally financed by venture capitalists in search of greater returns than safer investments would yield. In Europe, companies able to show a track record of profit obtain their external financing from institutional lenders, securities and bonds. A network of venture capitalists ready to bet on young and promising entrepreneurs hardly exists. Experience shows that the successful stimulation of entrepreneurs requires an integrated system of positive legislation, freedom of enterprise and tax incentives. The entrepreneur should also be able to count on a positive relationship with the factory floor.

How an industry will fare in industrial competition depends on economic efficiency, which depends on factors ranging from the human resources - skills and aptitudes of technicians, vision at upper-level management - and to the conditions in which they operate. Competition is also a function of manufacturing costs themselves determined by wage rates, labor productivities and manufacturing processes. On every account, Europe was from the beginning on the losing end and has been completely marginalized. High-technology sectors such as microelectronics being the driving force for future economic growth, this brings up the question of where the economies of the various European countries are heading and where they should head. This will require a better understanding of how particular regulatory policies and legislation pieces of the national governments and of the commission have affected the competitiveness of the industry. Sooner or later they will have to adjust to the realities of globalization. The dream of the champions went sour. The European industrialists did not rise to meet the challenge. The following pages recall why they did not make the grade in the silicon revolution.

PHILIPS has been part of the Dutch landscape and a symbol of national pride for more than a century. In 1891, Gerard Philips started manufacturing carbon filament bulbs in Eindhoven and, with the help of his brother Anton, soon built his company into a major producer of lighting technology. When the depression of the 1930s disrupted international trade, the company established production units in several countries. For decades, the subsidiaries developed a high degree of autonomy, operating largely on a basis of self-sufficiency. Philips was not a multinational, but a collection of national companies jealous of their autonomy. They focused their strategy on their local markets, rendering impossible a cohesive global strategy. Within the executive board and between the various divisions and subsidiaries, the lines of authority were undefined, leading to power games and squabbles.

During World War II, the company made substantial profits, and after the war it benefited from the expropriation of German assets. During the post-war years of fast expansion, Philips produced a broad range of consumer goods. In the late 1950s, management decided to use its financial and technological power to enter the professional-products market and to manufacture a range of electric components for industry and telecommunications network operators. Philips was Europe's largest supplier of valves and vacuum tubes, but also managed the transition to electronic components, transistors and magnetic cores. With the profits earned from these activities, plus subsidies supplied by the government, Philips made a multibillion guilder investment in computer and semiconductor manufacturing. The first experimental mainframe computers were baptized Pascal and Stevin. The acquisition of Siemag, a relatively small German computer manufacturer, gave Philips its first competitive minicomputer range. In 1976, the P410 business system was launched. By 1980, the company had an 18 percent share of the European computer market.

The Philips Empire had several structural shortcomings: the bureaucratic style of management, the counter-productive system of promotions and rewards and the poor communication between the technical and commercial departments. The character of Philips' top management also constituted a structural weakness.

But its real problem was organizational. Until the beginning of the 1980s, each product division was headed by a technician and a marketing man who often held diverging views. Brilliant technologically, Philips had difficulty translating scientific innovation into success in the marketplace. More than once, its engineering prowess was ruined through managerial incompetence, arrogance, boardroom squabbles, erratic strategic moves and bureaucracy. Another problem was the non-cooperation between the laboratories and the commercial staff. Convinced of their technological superiority, the laboratory people repeatedly pushed products and standards that were doomed to commercial failure. Co-inventor, with Sony, of the compact disc, the Japanese electronics company ended up dominating the CD player market.

Philips became a powerful presence in US industry through acquisitions. The American Philips branch accounted for about 30 percent of the total turnover of the company; but less than 20 per cent of this was sold under the Philips label. The management openly ignored the directives from Eindhoven and did not contribute to the company's overhead and research expenses; it rarely paid dividends, but received substantial "dotations" from headquarters for the financing of acquisitions. When Philips launched its V-2000 video recorder, the US managing director refused to put it on sale, since Philips USA was already distributing the Matsushita recorder.

Without a share of the American market, Philips stood no chance of competing on a global scale. The American subsidiary was approached and requested to sell computers, but let it be known that it was a waste of money to invest in a marketing, sales and servicing organization.

Philips is largely responsible for Japan's achievements in mass-producing and mass-marketing high-tech consumer goods, by inadvertently turning two Japanese companies into the world's foremost commercializers of new technologies invented in Europe. The company played a critical role in providing the technical capabilities that Matsushita and Sony used to commercialize their new products. In 1952, Matsushita arranged to acquire the technical capabilities of Philips in return for 35 percent of the Japanese company's equity. It then concentrated on enhancing its functional capabilities in product development, production, and marketing. These capabilities permitted the company to enter related electronic commercial, industrial, and information technology markets. Philips was ultimately driven out of business by these same two Japanese firms and Sharp. The company's management had attempted to produce a CD for television, comparable to the earlier CD-ROM for computers, losing half a billion dollars in the effort. As a result, it lacked the funds necessary to build a DVD factory and exited the consumer electronics industry almost entirely at the end of the 1990s.

In the 1970s already, things had started to go wrong. Philips became very vulnerable to competition from Japanese manufacturers. Forced to give up its mainframe production, management decided to concentrate on the fast growing sector of medium and small office computers. Overwhelmingly dependent on preferential government procurement and state subsidies, Philips failed to develop an international sales force and a global strategy. The market share shrank as time went on, and by the end of the decade huge inventories of unsalable computers had accumulated.

In 1977, Nico Rodenburg became president and restructured the company by closing a vast number of small production units, against strong opposition from government and trade unions. Hard pressed by his critics, he resigned. Philips' management was convinced that the government would never let it fail. Between 1969 and 1980 the Dutch government subsidized the company with about 200 million guilders. In the 1980s, the European Community stepped in and gave Philips over four billion guilders.

Great hopes were invested in Wisse Dekker when he was appointed CEO in 1982. He was instrumental in convincing the European commission that a European technology policy and very substantial subsidies would allow the European electronics industry to compete globally. When the commission started funding the electronics industry, Philips was in the forefront of the campaign for subsidies and became heavily dependent on this additional largesse.

Philips continued to make major contributions in recording, transmission and reproduction of audio and video media: sound recording on wire, magnetic tape, video tape, the LaserVision optical disc and optical telecommunication systems. In 1985 the company produced about half-a-billion dollars worth of chips, making it number six in the world league. Dekker made Philips participate in a vast number of unsuccessful joint ventures.

His successor, Cor van der Klugt brought the American branch under control and laid the foundations for the restructuring of the whole company. His strong-arm tactics were effective for curbing the autonomy of the subsidiaries, but it soon became apparent that they also contained destructive elements.

During the decades in which the Japanese started to conquer the world with their cheap radios, television sets and hi-fi equipment, Philips failed to adapt to the changing market. The company's boardroom became the scene of excessive careerism and backstabbing. The structural weakness of the company was exacerbated by the lack of managerial know-how, the nepotism of appointments and the power games the executives engaged in, as well as by their character: Rodenburg's indecision; Dekker's megalomania and dislike of the Philips family; Van der Klugt's scandalous private behavior; the collisions between Eindhoven and the subsidiaries. In 1990, profitability collapsed and survival became doubtful. It was obvious that the company was in much deeper trouble than anyone had imagined. Cor van der Klugt was forced to resign.

His successor, Jan Timmer (1990-1996) had to announce a loss of two billion guilders. He immediately instigated a worldwide revitalization program in order to improve profitability. His restructuring entailed a loss of about 50,000 jobs. For a while, he was regarded as a saviour, but the company's results in 1992 showed that this was an illusion. He left much undone. He saved Philips from the brink but was unable to develop a new strategy. Partly thanks to large-scale divestments, the company's disastrous financial situation was redressed in the short term, but did not solve the fundamental problems. In 1991, Philips sold part of its computer division to DEC, leaving only the production of personal computers; two years later, production of computers completely stopped. The same year, Philips Semiconductors was set up.

In 1996, Cor Boonstra took over as chairman. He was the first outsider to get the job. He moved headquarters from Eindhoven to Amsterdam and decided to advertise Philips as a brand, with a global campaign built around the slogan: "Let's make things better." He decided to sell, close, or fix all underperforming divisions and to invest spare cash in building up the strongest parts of the firm. He got rid of a chain of video stores and of Grundig; he sold the 75 percent stake in Polygram and ended the disastrous joint venture in mobile telephones with Lucent.

Boonstra pledged to cut the staff at the head office by 45 percent. He eliminated 6,000 jobs in the consumer-electronics division and announced a new strategy focusing on high-volume consumer electronics. Convinced that the company's strategy should be attentive to the demands of the market rather than driven by the engineers, he proved to be an astute operator. He decided to selectively prune enough dead-wood from the long list of money losers to restore individual divisions to profitability by outsourcing to Asia and by directing research and development closer to customer demand. Labor unions were livid about the plant closings. His moves aroused enemies but produced no immediate payoff.

In November 1998, Philips announced that it would streamline its global operations by closing one-third of its manufacturing plants by 2002. The number of factories would be reduced from 269 to about 165. Expansion in the US would however continue through acquisitions. [1]

Philips never developed its brand name in the US. Its television sets are sold under the Magnavox label while its electric shavers are sold as Norelco. It even was selling short-wave radios under the Grundig name. The United States is the center for much of Philips' groundbreaking research in digital technologies. The company has a state-of-the-art office facility in Silicon Valley. Boonstra invested big money in designing and making chips for cell-phone-like devices. He paid $1.2 billion for Silicon Valley's VLSI Technology.

For years Philips' spokesmen blamed their difficulties on economic recessions, the dollar, the Japanese competition; but the decline was largely caused by the self-conceited and rash way in which the successive top managers misread the market, their megalomania and personal conflicts.

In 1998, Philips unveiled a new value-based management program that enabled it to analyze the company from an economic profit perspective. Every division was given its own cost of capital and told that it had to earn a return that exceeded it. In 2000, swept up in internet and telecom exuberance, Philips was riding high, posting record sales and profits. The year 2001 was horrible: the company unveiled record losses of €2.6 billion.

In 2001, Gerard Kleisterlee was appointed president and chairman of the board of management. Soon after, Philips announced a further 3,000 to 4,000 job cuts in its semiconductor operations, bringing the total number of staff shed for the year to 11,000. Mobile phones had been one of Boonstra's pet projects, but since labor costs in Europe were too high, Kleisterlee transferred production to China in a joint venture with CEC, a huge government-owned company.

Philips Semiconductor is one of the world's top semiconductor suppliers, but its production is overwhelmingly located in Asia. During the past few years, the company has established manufacturing facilities in the US and expanded aggressively in Asia. Among them: an LCD (liquid crystal displays) manufacturing facility in Shanghai; a joint venture with Shenzhen DIC Information Technologies Co., Ltd., a leading China-based set-top box manufacturer; a $1.2 billion logic fab in Singapore with Taiwan's Semiconductor Manufacturing and optical storage activities of its components division located in close proximity to several major universities, allowing Philips to draw from the local pool of technical and managerial talent; a joint venture with Korea's LG Group; a joint venture with Taiwan's Acer producing a range of silicon chips that will combine digital video, audio, graphics and Internet content into interactive program material; in 2000 Philips bought an IBM fab in upper New York State, geared for mainstream logic products.

During the past 30 years, Philips has outsourced much of its manufacturing and shrunken its workforce from 400,000 to 160,000. But the company remains one of the world's largest electronics companies with staff in more than 60 countries. About 60 per cent of the revenues come from consumer and communications industries. The rest is from chips for automotive, industry and smartcards. The company keeps closing factories in Western Europe while outsourcing production to low-cost countries.

In August 2006, Philips sold its computer chip department to an international finance syndicate for €6.4 billion ($8.2 billion). The company is gradually becoming a marketing organization. Its engineers develop product concepts, but production is outsourced. In the consumer electronics sector, about 90 percent of the appliances are produced entirely by subcontractors. Philips faces an uncertain future.

SIEMENS commemorated its centennial in 1947, in a country ravaged by war. In 1939 the company employed 153,000 people; in 1945, they were 38,000. Four-fifths of its capital had been lost or destroyed. Many of its factories had been completely wiped out whilst others were located in East Germany. Siemens was compelled to buy back the right to use its own brand name in countries where it had been confiscated. Production of rolling stock and other electrical goods was resumed, mainly for the Deutsche Bundespost and the railways. In 1949, because of the cold war, Siemens moved its headquarters from Berlin to Munich.

A century before, in 1847, Werner Siemens had invented the pointer telegraph for the transmission of messages. He also built the first dynamo machine which was used to power locomotives, streetcars, boats, electric automobiles and elevators. In 1891, the first telephone exchange went into service in Berlin. Combining engineering brilliance with entrepreneurial drive and a global vision, Siemens & Halske was a multinational almost from the start. By 1900, the company employed more than 25,000 people.

After the founder's death, expansion continued in a broad range of electrical technologies. Siemens' engineers invented the X-ray tube, the hearing aid, telex networks and much more. They laid a telegraph cable from France to Britain and the first direct cable across the Atlantic; they built an underground railway in Budapest; Berlin was the first city to be equipped with electric street lighting. [2]

Siemens also pioneered radio-acoustics. In 1923, the company started manufacturing radio tubes. Research into semiconductors began in the later 1930s. During the 1950s, Siemens developed into a global company in areas such as automation technologies, communication networks, as well as a number of medium technologies, such as electric wiring and lighting. Heinrich Welker was in charge of the solid-state division at Siemens-Schuckertwerke. A few days before the end of the war, he had lodged a patent application for a method of placing electrons on silicon crystals.

In the 1950s, the computer was seen as having a promising future. Siemens' management launched itself enthusiastically into developing commercial and automation-control computers and an array of peripherals. In 1959, the company presented its first fully transistorized mainframe computer, the Siemens 2002. By the early 1960s, after the rescue of Zuse and SEL, Siemens became Germany's leading indigenous computer company. In 1964, thanks to an alliance with RCA, a long-time technical partner, the company gained access to American mainframe technology. At the end of the 1990s, Siemens was the only major German IT company. AEG had been taken over by Daimler Benz. Most of the smaller German companies were absorbed by foreign companies: Mannesmann-Kienzle by DEC, Triumph-Adler by Olivetti.

When Fairchild started selling integrated circuits, and when Intel launched the microprocessor, Siemens lost the cutting edge of semiconductor technology and could only try to keep up with rapid process of miniaturization. When Intel's microprocessor allowed the production of personal computers having the same power as minicomputers, Siemens was definitely outclassed in high technology and confined to medium technologies. [3]

Although Siemens had the advantage of preferential procurement policies, the computer division never delivered any substantial profits. In 1989, the company lost one billion DM. As the German national champion in the computer industry, Siemens had for several years been hampered by competition from Nixdorf, a maverick company, unconventional and decentralized. Nixdorf had acquired an outstanding reputation by producing minicomputers that handled smaller processing loads and less onerous tasks than mainframes and were considerably less expensive. In the 1980s, Nixdorf did not recognize the consequences of the advent of open standards systems and expanded in the wrong direction, taking on an extra 5,500 employees to push its proprietary systems. Its stubborn refusal to pull away from proprietary architecture resulted in a sudden shrinking of sales. Nixdorf became an unqualified disaster for its shareholders. In 1989, the company lost DM 1 billion. In January 1990, pressed by the government and the Deutsche Bank to provide a "German solution", Siemens stepped in to rescue Nixdorf.

Welding into one coherent organization the sales and marketing of two very different corporate cultures proved to be far more difficult than expected. Siemens was accustomed to working with large customers, while Nixdorf was used to smaller ones. Siemens was solid, technically excellent and financially sound, but slow-moving. Nixdorf had prospered in fast-growing markets, but had been unable to adjust to changing production methods. Instead of rationalizing the various ranges of computers, the company maintained a disparate product range. Nixdorf's heavy losses upset Siemens employees, while the Nixdorf staff resented their subordinate role. [4]

The management of each half tried to maintain its technology and kept putting off the decision to combine and rationalize. Potential customers hesitated to buy equipment whose future was uncertain and moved to other suppliers. In the first year after the merger, orders dropped substantially, particularly among Nixdorf customers; losses amounted to DM 780 million. The company announced 3,000 job cuts. In 1992, another 6,000 jobs were lost, followed by an additional 5,100.

According to Heinrich von Pierer, chairman of the Siemens group, the company's major disadvantage was inherent in the German economy: the high social cost of employing people. The Wall Street Journal observed that "if Germany cannot be competitive in computers, the economy will rapidly fall behind. In order to remain a major player in the key sectors of the information technology industry, it is necessary to reduce the labor costs and to establish alliances with foreign companies while remaining independent as national champion". [5]

In 1998, Siemens made an unsuccessful attempt to remedy its cost problems by selling its computer manufacturing operations to Acer, but that deal collapsed because of disagreements over the price. The immediate candidate for an alliance was Fujitsu, Japan's largest computer manufacturer. The two companies had a long-standing relationship dating from before the Second World War, when Fujitsu sold Siemens' products in Japan. By the mid-1970s, Fujitsu had turned the tables and was supplying Siemens with mainframe technology. In June 1993 the two companies intensified their co-operation, extending it well beyond the mainframe sector.

Fujitsu acquired its second major landfall in Europe, following the acquisition of ICL. Consolidating the two businesses in Europe provided the opportunity to create a cost-efficient and competitive PC enterprise. Under a 50-50 ownership with equal board representation, the Siemens-Fujitsu post-merger restructuring went smoothly because the two companies had shared technology for many years. The division of responsibilities was relatively straightforward. Size and partnership were intended to help the German company put an end to years of frustration with its troubled computer operations.

In June 1999, the European IT landscape changed for good when Siemens, the last remaining major computer manufacturer, tossed its computer business into a joint venture with Fujitsu Ltd. Fujitsu Siemens Computers was registered in the Netherlands, with headquarters in Amsterdam, and soon became the second-largest European vendor, behind Compaq in terms of unit shipments.

Siemens is still the largest European electronics company. Products range from light bulbs to x-ray equipment, to mobile phones. The breadth and depth of its scientific, technical and manufacturing expertise ensure its presence in nearly every sector of electrical and electronic engineering, from hydro-electric and nuclear power generating stations to medical electronics and telecommunications. About one-third of the company's revenues are derived from public procurement contracts. Its high cost-base and low margins make it vulnerable to more efficient players in the world market.

The United States is Siemens' single largest operations center, with 80,000 employees and sales approaching $20 billion. China with its huge need for power transmission and distribution, transportation systems, and telecoms, comes next. [6]

In December 1998, Siemens announced that it was to shake up its loss-making activities. Semiconductors were the biggest drain on company resources. Siemens Semiconductors was spun off in April 1999, to form a separate legal entity, Infineon Technologies AG, with headquarters in Munich. Siemens had moved up from the 19th largest semiconductor manufacturer in 1993 to the 10th largest in 1998.

In 2001, Siemens posted substantial losses. The company offered worker "timeouts" to save cash, and in August 7,000 more jobs were cut. Toshiba Corp. announced it would end its alliance with Siemens to develop third-generation handsets, opting instead to sell its own phones in Europe. In December 2001, Siemens reduced its stake in its money-losing semiconductor manufacturing spin-off Infineon Technologies AG to less than 50 percent by selling some shares and placing others in an irrevocable trust, so that Infineon would no longer be consolidated in Siemens' financial reports. In the financial year ending 31 March, 2004, Fujitsu-Siemens reported its first-ever annual net profit, of €38.3m, after posting a loss of €9.6m the year before and €7m in 2002.

Siemens employs so many people abroad that it is reasonable to ask whether it is still a German company. It is Germany's fourth-largest private employer. Germany accounts for 23 per cent of sales, while German workers currently account for 40 per cent of the workforce. Germany's labor market is one of the most costly and rigid in the world, but more than just labor costs are at issue. The company faces a crisis in its train-building business and suffers from low margins, particularly in mobile phone handsets. Increasingly, the company is booking orders in China and elsewhere. Management has warned workers that they must make concessions to avoid that more production be shifted to India, Brazil, Hungary, Czechoslovakia and other low-cost locations.

In 2006, Siemens became embroiled in the biggest bribery scandal in German corporate history. Munich prosecutors had uncovered evidence that Siemens' managers bribed foreign politicians and civil servants around the globe in order to land contracts. The company paid for nonexistent consultant services and then channelled the money into off-the-books slush funds. The prosecutors raided the company's headquarters and conducted inquiries the United States, Greece, Liechtenstein, Italy and Austria. They confiscated a huge amount of electronic data and printed material. About 300 people were involved in the investigation.

When the company embarked on a housecleaning, its legal and financial investigators identified 1.3 billion euros ($2.1 billion) in suspicious payments. The scandal forced the resignation of former Siemens CEO Klaus Kleinfeld and former Chairman Heinrich von Pierer, though both denied any wrongdoing. In May 2007, Peter Löscher succeeded Klaus Kleinfeld as chief executive. Under Löscher's leadership, the company underwent a radical reorganization. Executive committees were pared down and several divisions were merged.

The investigation grabbed the attention of the Securities and Exchange Commission in the United States. The Siemens case was an opportunity for US authorities to show they are serious about pursuing foreign companies violating US anti-corruption laws. The Justice Department and the Securities and Exchange Commission are investigating the case. Siemens faces U.S. penalties that will exceed any existing records. Siemens hopes to settle the case as soon as possible. But before they devise a fitting penalty, the US authorities want to determine how much profit Siemens earned from its bribes; an inquiry that could take several years. [7]

OLIVETTI was founded in 1908 by Camillo Olivetti who set up a small typewriter factory in Ivrea. The company grew rapidly, broadened its assortment and established sales subsidiaries in many countries. By 1940, Olivetti had become a major supplier of office equipment. In 1959, the company acquired Underwood, a leading US typewriter manufacturer, and introduced Italy's first electronic mainframe computer - Elea 9003 - which was moderately successful. After Adriano Olivetti's death in 1960, the company continued research in electronics technology and produced its first mainframe equipped with vacuum tubes, followed by two transistorized models, of which 105 units were sold. These machines had to compete with the American computer industry and required substantial finance for research and development. In 1964, Olivetti sold its computer operations to General Electric. Two years later, the company established a niche for itself with a range of highly innovative programmable desktop computers.

Olivetti's destiny is typical of the fate that hit the European micro-electronics industry. The company had acquired an international reputation for advanced design and was Europe's major contender in the global computer market. Family-owned, management had to cope with serious financial difficulties. In 1978, the company went nearly bankrupt. It was rescued by Carlo De Benedetti, an ambitious young businessman frustrated by the suffocating grip the government and the industrial establishment exercised on Italy's business and commercial life.

In 1978, he acquired a shareholding of Olivetti and took over as chief executive officer. He transformed the company from a loss-making producer of typewriters into one of Europe's leading microcomputer and data processing equipment makers. His arrival marked the start not only of a long period of restructuring, but also of a new cycle of growth. He shifted production of mechanical typewriters to Brazil, and cut 4,000 jobs at a time when this was unheard of in Italy. Rather than spending massively on research and development, he bought technology from American, French, Japanese and Canadian firms, and broadened his product range from electronic typewriters to medium-sized and small office computers, terminals linking office machines through telecommunications networks, and ultimately personal computers.

The large Italian industrial and financial companies were concentrated in the hands of a few powerful families and individuals. De Benedetti was the first to stand up to the country's corporate hierarchy dominated by Fiat's Agnelli dynasty. He challenged the status quo and the old-style elitism by using techniques such hostile take-over bids or public-share offers. He established a reputation as a very skilful manager and rose to fame in the international business community. He became the archetype of a new breed of European business tycoons who foresaw Europe as a single market and decided to build conglomerates that would become the giants of this new economic space. His critics called him a raider; he said he was a builder.

In 1980, he contracted with the French industrial combine, Saint Gobain, a manufacturer of ceramics and glass which wanted to branch out into information technology. However, the two partners had quite different understandings of what the deal involved. Saint Gobain intended to gain majority control of Olivetti, while De Benedetti openly stated that control of the company would forever rest in Italy. When the Mitterrand government nationalized Saint Gobain in 1981, management was ordered to sell its shareholding in Olivetti at a loss. Originally De Benedetti had used the alliance to lighten his debt burden and recuperated his shares at the expense of the French taxpayers.

Carlo De Benedetti seemed destined to shake the European community out of its Eurosclerosis and was hailed as Europe's champion in the global battle for supremacy in the promising field of information technology. In 1982, Olivetti launched its first personal computer. The company expanded operations in the information technology field and pursued an international acquisition and alliance strategy, leading to an agreement with AT&T in 1983.

De Benedetti concentrated on developing a niche for medium-sized and small office computers, often based on technology licensed from others companies and supplemented by a range of office products. Olivetti was the only European company able to stand up to American competition. During the late 1980s, the computer division was expanded by adding office equipment such as printers, calculators and cash registers.

De Benedetti built a many-faceted empire and went on to become one of the world's best known businessmen, securing a reputation as a smart horse-trader. He orchestrated the company's growth by responding to market needs and by negotiating alliances with other companies in order to gain access to new technology, marketing and finance. He displayed remarkable flair and creativity in deal-making.

One of his most celebrated deals was struck with the giant AT&T. In 1983, after a long antitrust suit, the company had been forced to divest itself of its telephone operations. De Benedetti persuaded management into taking a 22 per cent stake in Olivetti and to sell Italian-made microcomputers in the United States. Between 1984 and 1985 Olivetti shipped about 600,000 units. However, when AT&T realized that the operation did not give them any substantial access to the European markets, the board of directors became disenchanted with what was clearly a one-way deal. By the late 1980s, AT&T's interest in the relationship had cooled considerably. De Benedetti's final coup was to persuade AT&T to exchange its shareholding in Olivetti for a share in his holding company CIR. He nearly doubled CIR's stake in Olivetti without spending a lira in cash, and substantially increased CIR's shareholders' equity through the AT&T investment.

Until the mid-1980s, Olivetti prospered. De Benedetti used his newly acquired power and reputation to build up a vast industrial empire. He acquired Acorn, a British microcomputer manufacturer and Triumph-Adler, a German office equipment company. Olivetti became a major European contender in the information technology; but the bid for the champion's belt did not last long. The company started to show symptoms of weakness. Research and development was insufficient to introduce new models. Profits collapsed even though turnover was up. The response was restructuring and a search for alliances to expanding his empire.

In 1990, Olivetti gave up manufacturing of PCs. In 18 years, De Benedetti had turned the company temporarily into Europe's largest information technology company, but when technologically more advanced American and Japanese manufacturers started slashing prices and shortening the product cycle, the company raked up huge losses.

In May 1993, De Benedetti was accused of having paid bribes to the Italian Post Office and of overcharging for the equipment provided. At first he denied the allegations, but he ended up admitting that he had 'reluctantly' authorized the payments. He was arrested and spent 24 hours in custody. For a while the company was not allowed to enter tenders to the large Italian companies, which undermined its position when competing for contracts abroad. Convicted for having been involved in the fraudulent bankruptcy of Banco Ambrosiano, he was sentenced to six years in prison, but appealed.

In a face-to-face talk with the prosecutors who interrogated him, he broke omerta and described the ins and outs of business kickbacks. He confessed that his company had paid huge bribes to politicians and civil servants. Even the computers used by the prosecutors were purchased under a government contract influenced by payoffs. Most of the money, he said, went to the Socialist and Christian Democrat parties in return for contracts to sell computers and printers to the national postal service. When he decided to stop the kickbacks, the response was both immediate and predictable: Olivetti was automatically excluded from lucrative state contracts. "You pay what you're told or you're not allowed to work", he said. "Our managers were no longer welcome at the Ministry for Postal Services." To protect the company from further damage, he reluctantly authorized payments to the civil servants, who delivered the kickbacks to the political parties. He felt his confession might be useful: "If we can complete the liberation of the country without excessive turmoil, I will feel extremely comfortable as a citizen about what I've done. I believe I've accelerated the process of reform, and that at last our country is climbing out of the hole."[8]

De Benedetti decided to enter the nascent mobile telephone business, and joined forces with some of the world's top telecommunications operators, to form a mobile communications start-up named Omnitel. Omnitel became operational at the end of 1995 after bidding successfully for an operating license. The telecoms strategy also led to the formation in 1995 of Infostrada, a wireline telephone operator. In a very short space of time, his new venture turned out to be a mistake.

After having presided over a disastrous run of losses, disappointments and almost constant restructuring, he resigned when complaints turned into full-blown mutiny. The company had lost money every year since 1990. A new breed of shareholders, institutional investors from the US, Japan and Britain, exasperated by five straight years of losses, demanded his resignation. The day he left, the company announced a pre-tax loss of $291 million for the first half of the year. De Benedetti was the victim not just of his stockholders but also of a Europe-wide phenomenon: the inability to compete in the industries of the future. He was faulted for the steady erosion of Olivetti's market position in personal computers.

De Benedetti was replaced by Antonio Tesone, a long-standing legal consultant to Olivetti. Effective control of the group was in the hands of 39-year-old Francesco Caio, appointed sole managing director. A former personal assistant to De Benedetti, he had acquired shareholder support to topple his former boss when they disagreed on basic strategy. Caio first won recognition for his stint as manager of the thriving mobile-phone unit Minitel-Pronto, owned 41 percent by Olivetti, the rest by German and American partners including Mannesmann and Bell Atlantic. De Benedetti retained his 15 per cent interest in the company and his Cerus holding company. His son was named to a new executive board, and Antonio Tesone took over as chairman.

Mobile phones proved to be salvation. Within two years, Olivetti transformed itself into a telecommunications company. After a remarkable financial recovery, it launched the boldest hostile take-over bid in European corporate history with a highly leveraged offer for Telecom Italia, its much bigger telecoms rival, the privatized Italian telecoms group five times its size.

By the end of 1996, it was rumored that Olivetti was holding discussions with several parties about the sale of its PC division. The company's sales had been steadily falling, but it still claimed 17 per cent of Italy's market share. [9]

In 1997, the loss-making computer manufacturing operations were sold to a group led by a London-based American lawyer, Edward Gottesman. Olivetti exited from the PC business to focus on software and system integration in banking, office information systems, and distribution. In addition, it entered forcefully in the mobile phone market. By the end of 1998, the company came close to bankruptcy. In March 1999, Olivetti presented a formal request to go into controlled administration in order to protect itself from its creditors. An administrator was appointed by the court, and the company continued to operate normally.

Its debt was reduced as a result of the cash payment, and the company began to focus on its growing investments in telecommunications. Cellular telephone operator Omnitel Pronto Italia, in which Olivetti was the largest shareholder, had 700,000 subscribers since its start-up in December, 1995, one of the best growth records in Europe. [10]

In 1999, the Luxembourg-based company Bell S.A. acquired a controlling stake in Olivetti but sold it to a consortium including the Pirelli and Benetton groups. In 2003 Olivetti was absorbed into the Telecom Italia group, while maintaining a separate identity as Olivetti Tecnost. Currently, the company has operations in Italy and Switzerland, and sales associates in 83 countries.

ICL has a special place in the history of computing as a descendant of the company that sold the first commercial computer. During the 1950s and early 1960s, a number of British companies entered the computer industry. Electronics firms, such as Ferranti, English Electric, Elliott Brothers and EMI were joined by punched-card-machine manufacturers BTM and Powers-Samas. The catering firm J. Lyons & Company pioneered the commercial programmable computer, LEO. The National Research Development Corporation tried to foster the industry by advocating consolidation in order to reduce duplication and increase financial strength.

The first major merger took place in 1959, when BTM and Powers-Samas joined to form International Computers and Tabulators (ICT) which became the largest data-processing-machine manufacturer in Europe, with over 19,000 employees. ICT inherited a range of incompatible machines, but intended to compete with IBM in the market of punched-card based office equipment. In 1964, the face of computing changed when IBM launched its System/360 range, a general-purpose machine offering several radical innovations. This compelled every competitor to follow up with ranges of comparable performance. In response, ICT announced its 1900 series, derived from a design developed in Canada. It rapidly gained a substantial share of the market and proved to be a considerable commercial success.

The number of government bodies involved in Britain's industrial policy provides one explanation for the "stop-go" random approach to programs in electronics. Since the beginning, British industrial policy has been a hodgepodge of government-directed reorganizations and changes in direction.

When Harold Wilson's Labour government came to power in 1964, it was decided to rationalize the industry. Government policy reflected the dominant belief in both economies of scale and the need to respond to the American challenge in kind. In 1968, ICL was established under the Labour government, through the merger between International Computers and Tabulators and English Electric Computers. It was the culmination of a series of mergers and acquisitions. The mergers were complicated affairs because of the incompatibility of the machines and tensions between both product strategies and corporate cultures. The government provided £13.5 million for the development of a new computer range. With a workforce of 34,000, ICL was the largest computer manufacturer outside the United States and was to be Britain's national champion for the next 22 years.

Protected behind a 15- import surcharge and preferential treatment, it achieved a regular annual growth of about 20 per cent. ICL tried to develop a new range of mainframes based on in-house technology, but its research and development resources were totally insufficient. Many computer pioneers worked for ICL. Some of the most brilliant minds of that computing generation shattered their dreams by running into brick walls created by well-meaning politicians who were desperately struggling to do the right thing without any idea of what the right thing was.

In 1970, the newly-elected Conservative government, ideologically committed to withdrawing from state intervention, decided to put an end to funding. When ICL faced a huge financial loss, 3,400 workers were laid off. This threw ICL into crisis, and management appealed for help. Severely criticized, the government finally yielded and granted ICL a loan of £40 million for the development of a new range of machines.

In 1971, ICL brought out the New Range, which was well received. But dependence on preferential procurement policy and the mergers of companies whose architectures, systems and philosophies were incompatible weighed heavily. Without government support, research grants and indirect help, it would have crumbled. The country had a national champion, but IBM continued to increase its sales to British companies and even to government agencies. In 1974, IBM secured a £2.5 million order for a computer for delivery to the Post Office. [11]

In 1973, ICL made a very effective entry into the small-business systems market. Its computers sold very well. The company launched a new series of mainframes based on advanced technology; but clumsy management and software breakdowns spoiled the effort, giving the whole series a bad name that lasted for well over a decade.

Labour government's Ministry of Technology had been dismantled by the Conservative government, but when the Labour Party returned to power in 1974, the emphasis was again on government intervention and industrial rationalization. The National Enterprise Board (NEB) was set up. In the late 1970s, technological innovation shortened the life-cycles and competition escalated with the arrival of plug-compatible mainframes and time-sharing pioneered in the United States.

ICL was unable to keep up with the speed of change, and had to reassess its long-term strategy. The alternative was further expansion and a high-risk strategy, or a more modest move towards becoming a niche supplier. ICL opted for a high-growth course. When the Japanese and IBM started a price war, profits tumbled and the R&D budget had once more to be substantially reduced. In the spring of 1979, ICL announced a substantial increase in turnover and in orders. Shortly afterwards, production was halted when the workforce went on strike demanding a 15 per cent wage increase.

Meanwhile, several companies disappeared from the scene. Business Computers Ltd. collapsed into receivership. Ferranti was rescued by the government, which provided an unspecified cash hand-out to tide the company over while it searched for a long-term solution. [12]

In 1979, IBM introduced its 4300 range, using a new generation of processor and memory chips that offered a four-fold improvement in price/performance ratio. ICL kept falling further behind in processor chip technology. Its chips were obsolete almost as soon as they hit the market. Between 1981 and 1985, the workforce was reduced from 33,000 to 20,000.

In 1979, the Labour government was once more replaced by a Conservative administration. The 1980-81 recession drained lCL's profits; management once more turned to the government for aid. The Thatcher administration took the view that the finances of ICL were the concern of its shareholders and bankers. Eventually the banks provided funds after the government agreed to provide loan guarantees up to £200 million. The period 1981-84 was the most traumatic in ICL's history. The company was fundamentally restructured and the R&D program was reduced. ICL held discussions in view of collaborative ventures. A link with Fujitsu gave access to Japanese state-of- the-art semiconductor technology.

The question arose: should management find a partner for a merger? Discussions with Siemens, Bull, Olivetti, Philips, Nixdorf and several other manufacturers foundered on the questions of ultimate control and on the consequences of ICL's agreement with Fujitsu.

In 1990, the unthinkable happened: Britain's ICL sold to Fujitsu 80 percent of its shares. This gave ICL the financial staying power it lacked. In return Fujitsu established a solid foothold in Britain, with the prospect of getting access to a wider European market. ICL was thrown off the European roundtable of national champions and branded as "Fujitsu's Trojan horse in Europe." Fujitsu's chairman announced this was only the beginning and that he was interested in a joint venture with Siemens. [13]

Comforted by the ample finances and the technology provided by Fujitsu ICL decided to expand its sales in continental Europe. But apart from France, where it gained important customers in the retail sector, its marketing effort failed to overcome the disadvantages of size. ICL depended entirely on Fujitsu's goodwill and there was doubt about the long-term ability to sustain its profits if Fujitsu were to increase the price of its co-operation.

ICL was no more a national champion. But the operation was generally well accepted in Britain. Several British IT companies had recently been sold to foreign competitors. While in Britain the operation did not meet with much criticism, on the continent the take-over was taken as a grave danger. The commission's vice-president called for a boycott. ICL was expelled from most high-level consultations between the commission and industry. The vice-president of Siemens-Nixdorf stated that ICL was no longer a European company. In 1994, in a complete volte-face, the commission appointed the chairman of ICL to its High Level Group on Information Technology.

Fujitsu bought the remaining shares and in 2000, ICL incorporated Fujitsu into its logo. In June 2001, ICL was unceremoniously relegated to the history books. In 2002, the European IT industry lost a well-known brand name, when British computing became Fujitsu Services. The once proud flagship of the UK computer industry and standard-bearer of British technology became the services arm of a Japanese company. From a position of leadership forged by its scientists who developed the first stored-program computers and of the largest European computer manufacturer of the 1960s, Britain became almost totally dependent on imported information technology. The legacies provided by the brilliant achievements of its scientists were dilapidated by clumsy mismanagement and misgovernment.

BULL has suffered and profited more from the dead hand of government sponsorship than any other European computer company. In 1919, Frederik Bull, an employee of a Norwegian insurance company, filed a patent for a punched-card data processing machine. A French paper manufacturer bought the patent and set up the Compagnie des Machines Bull. Its punch-card machines pioneered several significant innovations, notably alphanumeric printing, which gave the company a reputation for high-quality equipment.

In 1950, Bull produced its first electronic equipment, a photo-reader able to read pencil marks. Its electronic calculator, the Gamma 2, followed by Gamma 3 performed extremely well and was highly successful. It established Bull as a major supplier of the French banking sector. In the late 1950s and early 1960s, Bull had 45 percent of the French market and was the only company able to hold its own against IBM, although its machines were somewhat more expensive. By 1959, Bull had about 5,000 employees and subsidiaries in several countries.

Management became convinced that the time had come to compete with IBM and other American manufacturers in the world market and to develop a high-speed supercomputer. The result was the Gamma 60, an innovative machine using germanium transistors and magnetic core memory. But the price was too high; only 17 units were sold.

When IBM started leasing computers rather than selling them outright, Bull was unable to finance a leased park. Sales collapsed, and management turned to the government for help. But President de Gaulle rebuffed the request because Bull had continued its activities under German occupation, and also because its owners adamantly refused to participate in defense research, leaving government contracts to a small company, SEA.

In 1964, General Electric announced its interest in acquiring a controlling interest in Bull. The government refused permission but, unable to find a French solution, the takeover was authorized. The new management immediately cut 650 jobs. It soon became evident that General Electric was not interested in Bull's technology, but rather in new markets. The French-designed computer technology was abandoned, development projects underway in France were scrapped and Bull-General Electric became a fully integrated subsidiary of General Electric.

The French government became very concerned about the domination of the American multinationals. President Johnson's refusal to let Control Data sell the supercomputer which was needed for the development of nuclear weapons upset de Gaulle. He decided to create and finance a computer industry that would be authentically French and able to insure France's strategic independence. Plan Calcul and a Délégation à l'Informatique were set up, directly responsible to the Elysée, with the assignment of federating the French electronics companies. Several small firms, including SEA and CAE, as well as subsidiaries of electronics and electrical combines were merged into the CII (Compagnie Industrielle pour l'Informatique).

In 1968, CII delivered its first medium-sized computer, the Iris 50. It was largely based on American technology brought in by CAE. A second system, the Iris 80, was incompatible with the first. The political administrators saw no harm in this incompatibility. They were convinced they could design a French mainframe computer system to compete technically and commercially with IBM. The company grew rapidly, mainly due to the preferential treatment it received from the government. Within four years, employment increased to 6,000. But it soon turned out that the technology did not live up to the ambitions.

Meanwhile, in 1970, General Electric sold its computer division to Honeywell, and the company was renamed Honeywell-Bull. The French government had a 20 per cent stake. Year after year, Honeywell-Bull lost huge amounts of money and survived only thanks to massive subsidies. CII and Honeywell-Bull decided to cross-license their patents and to set up cross-distribution agreements for all products in several countries. The government pressed the management of CII to merge with Honeywell-Bull. In 1976, the merger took place after a year of negotiations, and the company was renamed CII-Honeywell-Bull. [14]

The plan was to manufacture a French-designed computer using French semiconductors and other components. The objective was to allow the company to develop, by the end of 1971, a volume of activity, profitability and technical potential that would allow it to hold its place in the home and foreign markets. But the basic economics were changing: globally, the cost of electronics went down while French wages went up.

In 1978, CII-Honeywell Bull acquired R2E, the tiny pioneer that built the Micral, the world's first computer based on Intel microprocessors. Unable to develop a market, the owner had been forced to sell out. Bull-Micral developed a multi-terminal operating system named Prologue that essentially targeted business applications. A database system called Dialogue and a macro-assembler application language BAL completed the Prologue system. A line of computers based on Intel 8080 and 8086 was also developed.

In 1980, Saint-Gobain took a controlling interest in Bull. In 1981, a major conflict developed during an attempted take-over of Olivetti by Saint-Gobain. Jean Pierre Brulé was PDG of Honeywell-Bull and CII-HB. He was dismissed with the agreement of Honeywell, and the government negotiated with private shareholders. Honeywell being the largest one, received cash in exchange of shares. The government reorganized the industry by merging the activities of other nationalized companies, essentially Thomson and CGE, and made Groupe Bull an independent company.

In 1981, François Mitterrand was elected president and a socialist-communist government took over. Mitterrand considered the electronics industry as strategic. He decided to implement a grand national program of state intervention, with the objective of making France "the world's third leading technological power by the year 2000, behind only the US and Japan." French industry would produce a wide range of products: chips, computers, software, industrial automation, scientific instrumentation and telecommunications. The government would provide funds for research and development and for the education of thousands of engineers.

The government restructured the electronics businesses of the five big industrial groups: Thomson, CII, Honeywell-Bull, Saint-Gobain and Compagnie Générale d'Electricité. Electronic chips became top priority. The government was confident "that the state is more easily ready to take the big risks involved in seeking new-technology leadership than profit-hungry private companies." [15]

Then, in the early 1980s, American PCs made their appearance in France. The government wanted Bull to take up production, in competition with American world-class technology and cheap-labor Asian manufacturing. Bull built a highly automated factory. Unable to sell enough machines to make production profitable; the plant was closed down.

The government considered Bull as essential to the military arsenal. Bull became the national champion and was granted substantial financial support, so that it could continue its head-on struggle with IBM. The supercomputer Isis was intended for defense and related applications. But

France's socialist governments were also fascinated by the potential and the promise of scientific research, convinced that it would do for France what it had done for Japan: develop an electronics industry that would combine innovation and productivity, capture a substantial share of the consumer electronics and mini-computer mass market and create a vast number of new jobs. This required massive spending on research with the emphasis on electronics and microchip technology. Under previous governments, the ministry responsible for research had been a modest affair; now it was to be substantially expanded.

In its early years, Bull had been an outstanding pioneer, but was unable to create a market for its revolutionary machines. While the management of the company often made the wrong decisions, government intervention proved in every case disastrous. When the government nationalized the electronics industry and decided to make it an emblem of technological prowess, Bull became a refuge for unviable projects and a bazaar with innumerable and incompatible products. The management structure was totally inefficient and production costs were out of line. The government was forced to foot the bill, and Bull's survival was financed by public funds and the sale of assets. [16]

In 1982, CII-Honeywell-Bull was nationalized. The government put together several companies whose individual survival was uncertain because of high production costs. Bull became a plaything of politicians and the hobbyhorse of the government, while the taxpayers were called upon to make up for the losses. The strategy of national prestige, guided by political rather than commercial considerations, backfired. The architectures of the various companies were incompatible and became rapidly obsolete. [17]

J.-P. Chevènement, minister for research and industry, proudly announced his intention to "make France the Japan of Europe." He intervened frequently in the management of the companies to redirect their industrial policies, and instructed them to stop investing abroad except for compelling reasons.

Thomson had to abandon the large and medium-sized computers in favor of CII-Honeywell; Saint-Gobain's drive into computer manufacturing was halted. [18]

Bull had so far focused on the French market. An aggressive strategy of international development was now initiated. In 1989, Bull acquired the microcomputer division of Zenith in order to gain a foothold in the US market. Zenith had a reputation for technical excellence. The company had important contracts with the US Department of Defense and was a key supplier to the government. Shortly after the takeover, Zenith started losing money. When Bull took over, orders stopped abruptly. Zenith turned out to be a disaster.

In the early 1990s, Bull's losses kept increasing. Personal computers were increasingly replacing mainframes. Bull had a global distribution network and very heavy overhead. It was the start of a long and painful series of restructurings. The government undermined the company's efforts to reform itself by intervening to prevent harsh measures from being implemented.

In 1991, the government asked the telecommunications operator, France Telecom, to take an equity stake in Bull. Since the request sounded like an order, France Telecom reluctantly gave in. In March 1991, the government was forced to inject another FFr.4 billion. Management was instructed to look towards the US and negotiations were taken up with IBM and Hewlett-Packard. The government expected that the deal would give Bull access to IBM's mid-range computer technology. IBM was permitted to take a 5.7 shareholding.

Since 1989, over 14,000 jobs had been lost and financial deficits had continued to pile up. The government decided to reverse the nationalizations of the 1980s; Bull was on the list of companies to be privatized. This, however, was only feasible if the company became profitable. In 1994, after an injection of Far. 7 billion and the nomination of a new chairman, the search for partners was on. It took several months of discussions with American and Asian companies before the objective of reducing the government share to below 50 per cent could be achieved.

In 1993, a conservative administration under Edouard Balladur came to power. The government prepared for yet another capital injection and another chairman, who was soon replaced by Jean-Marie Descarpentries. He launched an austerity program and transferred the company's headquarters from the prestigious La Défense to barracks in Louveciennes. His successor, Guy de Panafieu, was unable to find foreign partners willing to take over the government shares.

Once more management asked for an ultimate subsidy, after which Bull would become a company like any other. But the losses kept accumulating, and management was forced to cut 17,000 jobs. Most of 1994 was taken up with discussions in view of reducing the government share to less than 50 percent; the search for a partner was resumed.

In 1996, Bull and Olivetti started negotiations in view of a possible co-operation. Both companies were in the red. Bull's Zenith Data Systems was losing money and the company was looking for a European partner. Olivetti was in principle interested but had its own problems. The same year the government privatized Bull, while retaining a 30.5 percent interest; the rest was taken up by Motorola, NEC, France Telecom, and Dai Nippon Printing. In 1996, it folded its Zenith Data Systems subsidiary into Japanese-controlled Packard Bell NEC, while retaining a minority stake. The following year, the company posted positive net earnings for the first time since 1988. [19]

Bull has been working to mold itself into a software and services company concentrating on Internet technologies. In 1998, it set up a software division in an attempt to build a global software business focusing on systems management and network security products.

In 1998, Bull and NEC signed an agreement for the distribution in France of the NEC range of SX-4 supercomputers. NEC decided to take advantage of Bull's local infrastructure in order to respond to the special needs of corporate users in

France. This, however, is a limited market. The same year, Bull launched TwinCash, the smallest color-screen cash dispenser in the world. Bull is strong in the field of secured financial transactions and a leader in electronic purse cards. In 1979, Bull's Michel Ugon, in collaboration with Motorola, invented the world's first micro-processor card.

In 1999, the government announced its decision to relinquish the 17.3 percent interest it still maintained. Sales and shares continued to fall. The management decided to sell whatever could be sold; anything that could be outsourced would go that way. The company was divided into several independently operating subsidiaries with the purpose of giving them more entrepreneurial freedom and making them financially more attractive for an eventual partner.

In 2000, de Panafieu decided to split the company into several autonomous subsidiaries that would have greater freedom of action and be more interesting for potential buyers. The software division Bull Soft operates under the name Evidian. In November 2001, de Panafieu resigned as chairman. The government, which still owned 16.3 percent, had granted a loan described as "a repayable shareholder advance." The announcement fuelled expectations that Bull would eventually be totally dismantled.

De Panafieu's strategy had been to pare back to the company's 'core' business, mainframes, Unix boxes from IBM and NET systems produced in partnership with NEC. In the 12 months to December 31, 2001, Bull's net losses widened to €253 million. Bull sold its CP8 smart card business to Schlumberger Ltd.

In 2001, it was uncertain whether Bull could make a comeback or whether the end was nearing. Motorola and NEC were potential candidates, but they had their own problems and lacked staying power. The purchase of the PC division of Zenith and the co-operation with Packard Bell and NEC in the expectation of gaining a foothold in this market was expensive and without results.

Pierre Bonelli was made chairman, with the mission of developing a survival strategy. Being realistic, he commented: "I believe Bull has a future, but this must still be proven." He decided to lay off 1,500 staff and to improve co-ordination between the group's many divisions. Once more, the government pulled the company from the brink by injecting huge amounts of subsidies. Each time Bull announced huge losses, it was granted another rescue package.

In March 2002, afraid of labor unrest in case of bankruptcy, the French government threw a €350 million euros lifeline at Bull. The flagship of the French computer industry had seen its workforce shrink from 46,000 in 1988 to 10,700 at the end of 2001. Its shareholders, France Telecom, NEC, Motorola and Dai Nippon Printing had refused to inject more money. It was still uncertain for how long Bull could survive. [20]

Since the 1960s, Bull survives on state-sponsored life-support. The French government has given Bull the equivalent of more than €7 billion. The state indirectly controls some 32 percent. The company's managers have tried to save the company by reorganizing and selling non-core assets. Even the smart cards business, which is one of the few areas of high growth, had to go. Given the scale of the reorganization, more layoffs are almost certainly in store. As major shareholders, the government and France Telecom, faced with falling revenues and heavy losses, can only watch as the clock is ticking. Bull has enjoyed exactly one year of profitability since 1988. It should have been liquidated years ago, but the government keeps postponing the decision because it would provoke a violent clash with the trade unions.

8

SILICON VALLEY

Santa Clara County, California, has long been known for its blue skies, its mild climate and lush orchards. Within a few decades, this bucolic Garden of Eden where perpetual sunshine and fruit trees symbolized a leisurely way of life, has been metamorphosed into the birthplace of the global electronics industry. San Jose, the capital of Silicon Valley, is a vibrant community with a population exceeding 800,000. About 4,000 IT-related companies are located along Highway 101 from San Jose to San Francisco.

Silicon Valley came into existence during the late 1930s through the relationships between Stanford University and a small group of entrepreneurs devoted to the pursuit of innovation and its commercialization. Stanford University was founded in 1891 by railroad magnate Leland Stanford, who donated millions of dollars in remembrance of his son who had died of typhoid fever. He wanted a teaching and research institution with a more practical bent than the elite private universities back East. From the start the focus was on sciences and engineering and the building of ties with local industry.

The seeds of the Valley were sown in 1909, when David Starr Jordan, president of Stanford University, put up $500 to fund research on Lee de Forrest's vacuum tube. De Forrest is considered the founder of modern electronics: his vacuum tube which could amplify an electrical signal within its airless confines is the cornerstone of all the electronic marvels that followed. Thereafter, the relationship of intellectual brilliance and capital would be forever entwined.

During the Depression of the 1930s, the vision of Frederick Terman, professor of electrical engineering, laid the foundations of the Valley's industrial development. He was concerned with the lack of opportunities for his students to find jobs in the area and wished to develop institutional links between science and business, so that inventors could commercialize applications of their research. Terman was also convinced that the engineering schools needed to reassess their proper social role. The laboratories of the big industrial companies worked independently from the academic world, but the supply of technically trained young men could come only from the universities. He decided to develop Stanford into a center of engineering education and to foster strong links with the business world. He envisioned what he called "a community of technical scholars." He succeeded in persuading the administration to turn a tract of land into an industrial park.

Terman thought that the university, particularly the research university, is a central institution in a modern society. It does not exist as an ivory tower; the advances in basic knowledge made by scholars should be commercially exploited. America's prestigious universities were strong in basic sciences, social sciences and humanities, but lacked the ethos favorable to technology transfer from the university to the world of commerce. Stanford was to be a confluence of academic ardor, industrial intensity, unbridled imagination and money.

Faculty members were actively encouraged to work in industry, which gave corporations access to the university's research while scientists had a chance to try out their ideas in the real world of business. This program had no parallel elsewhere. The absence of an industrial structure and of an established business culture, as well as the inexistence of trade unionism made it possible to create an environment conducive to risk-taking, innovation and growth. From the conditions offered by this academic and economic environment emerged a new partnership between institutions, firms and individuals which would evolve into Silicon Valley.

What made Stanford unique was its infectious entrepreneurial spirit. Its country-clubbish campus soon attracted some of the world's best engineers, scientists and managers, the smartest faculty and also the brightest students. They found not merely interesting jobs, high incomes and a stimulating intellectual atmosphere, but a community of high-achieving professionals, determined to market the bounty of their knowledge.

One of Terman's most important achievements was to have two of his former students, William Hewlett and David Packard, build a business around an audio oscillator they had developed and to house it on the campus. It was an instrument for testing sound equipment that seemed to have great commercial possibilities. Terman even invested $538 of his own in the operation.

Hewlett and Packard formed a partnership. They transformed a small garage into their workshop. Using the few tools that were available, they produced an audio oscillator which sold for $71.50. When Walt Disney ordered eight oscillators for the production of his film *Fantasia*, Hewlett-Packard Co. was on the road to success.

Hewlett and Packard adopted a company policy that included share options, profit-related pay and profit sharing, decentralized decision-making, open door policy, management by wandering around and by objectives, the recognition that a company is responsible to its customers, employees, shareholders and also to the community in which it operates. Based on the assumption that people are eager to do a good job and will work most efficiently when given the autonomy to carry out their tasks, the company considered them as partners. Blending work with play, business with pleasure, extravagant Christmas parties and other ritual celebrations of collective well-being kept the workers happy.

HP became known for the fair treatment of the people they hired, for their high business ethics and integrity. Employees had access to equipment rooms in their off hours; they were encouraged to tinker with new products and to work with their hands as well as their minds. The company set the tone for the individualistic and visionary makeup which epitomizes the Valley and put an indelible stamp on the way it operates. Hewlett and Packard achieved one of the most dramatic success stories in American business. Both were known for working in their austere, linoleum-floored offices. The "HP way" has largely become synonymous with corporate integrity.

Hewlett-Packard's success was an inspiration to technologically sophisticated entrepreneurs, and within a few years the Stanford Industrial Park was thriving. Over the next decades the Valley developed a unique ecosystem and a mystical culture that attracted and bred a motley collection of students, entrepreneurs, start-up companies and venture capitalists, all having a dream, and eager to take risks. Unheard-of companies sprang up to reap fortunes from newfangled products; then, almost without pause, most of them quietly disappeared. Each successful product and service they developed became the inspiration for future innovations.

Over the years, HP has faced problems resulting from the ups and downs of the economy. In 1970, when an economic downturn sharply reduced sales, all employees, including executives were asked to agree to a 10 percent cut in pay. No one was laid off. Six months later, business picked up and things went back to normal. At Steve Packard's death in 1996, the Packard Foundation's endowment amounted to $6.6 billion, making it America's third largest charity.

The second founding father of the Valley is William Shockley. Persuaded by Terman to establish a plant in the university's vicinity, he founded the Shockley Semiconductor Laboratories. His company was short-lived, but eight of his engineers left him to create Fairchild Semiconductor that was to become a training center for entrepreneurs and the crucial catalyst in the development of Silicon Valley.

With the establishment of Stanford Industrial Park, the character of Silicon Valley took hold. Land was leased on long-term leases, providing substantial income to the university. IBM set up a huge research center; General Electric, Sylvania, Westinghouse, Philco and many other companies established facilities. Terman fostered and supported local industry with new programs that allowed engineers to take graduate courses at the campus.

During World War II, several aircraft companies, attracted by a sunny climate which allowed year-round production and testing, set up production in California. The area became the nation's busiest producer of jet fighters, guided missiles, smart bombs and other sophisticated weapons systems. The impetus for the early growth of the industry came largely from the military. During the post-World War II boom, the orchards were plowed under and replaced by laboratories, office buildings and homes. A number of technologically sophisticated young entrepreneurs moved in and set up new companies. Their products were based on the semiconductor and its silicon chip, giving rise to the name Silicon Valley. Santa Clara County became the birthplace of microprocessors, followed by pocket calculators, digital wristwatches, cordless telephones, laser technology, video games and personal computers.

Thus was created a technically gifted community that understood the need to invest in ideas with money-making potential, and believed that electronics could usher in an age of human empowerment. The structure of Silicon Valley is unique. It houses the densest concentration of innovative industry that exists anywhere in the world, including companies that are leaders in computers, semiconductors, lasers, fiber optics, robotics, medical instrumentation, magnetic recording, educational and consumer electronics. The combined effect is electrifying, and the resulting wealth is staggering.

Stanford graduates and associates set the tone for the individualistic, visionary makeup which epitomizes the Valley's mindset. A culture that worships intelligence, determination, hard work, innovation, money, talent and opportunity attracts ambitious people. They come from the heartland of America and from many countries to learn from its culture of success. Nowhere else can they get access to such a concentration of the professional skills required to bring innovation to the marketplace. This web of local services, from chip designers and specialist software writers, to patent lawyers, public-relations experts and venture capitalists, combined with the communal spirit, the intellectual brilliance and blundering, the assortment of naiveté, noble purpose and greed, and the determination and boundless energy for discovery, made it the heart and the cradle of a new economy. Mental capacity and risk-taking are hallmarks of the distinct culture that eventually became identified with the Valley and transformed it into the quintessence of the American Dream: a good idea that turns into a gold mine.

The cluster of electronics firms grew rapidly during the 1960s and 1970s. Lockheed Aerospace, Westinghouse, Ford Aerospace, Sylvania, Raytheon, ITT and XEROX were among the most important. By 1974, over 150 firms operated in Silicon Valley, with Stanford University investing a portion of its own endowment in venture activities. The region's high technology enterprises employed over 100,000 workers. Stanford, Berkeley and San Jose State University graduated large numbers of engineers, while the region's six community colleges offered specialized technical programs oriented specifically to the needs of the area's firms.

Many people believe that Silicon Valley was built by the American government. The Internet began as a government project, and several companies, including Netscape, have arisen directly or indirectly from state-funded research projects. But there is a clear difference between being a big customer and intervening in the industry.

Originally, the government was the principal user of semiconductor devices. Between 1958 and 1974 the Pentagon paid $1 billion for semiconductor research for military applications. By the early 1970s, the military's role in the development and purchase of electronics diminished, as the electronics industry expanded. Venture capital came to replace the military as the lead source of financing for novice entrepreneurs and cash-strapped young companies who needed money to finance expansion. Venture capitalists became part and parcel of the Valley, plunging billions of dollars into start-ups.

Actively seeking risk makes sense for venture capitalists. Many of their gambles do not come off, but some of those that make it deliver huge rewards. In the technology industry, a company that establishes an early lead may set a standard and end up scooping most of the market. This nimbleness is prompted by fear. The technology market changes so quickly that any company which fails to adjust quickly will get pushed out. The innovator's curse is to be transitory.

On one occasion, in the mid-1980s, when the memory-chip industry was overrun by suspiciously cheap imports from Japan, the industry appealed for government protection. Between 1984 and 1987 the computer industry went into a tailspin; high-tech employment plunged to less than 200,000 jobs. Japanese companies twisted free trade by charging much higher prices at home to absorb the losses on exports, expecting that their American competitors would be brought on their knees. America's vaunted leadership in high technology, the wellspring of innovation for the entire industrial sector, was eroding rapidly in every major electronics market and creating a crisis in US high technology.

Chip demand continued to climb, but bloated inventories caused pain. Intel slashed employment by 900. America's high-tech sector was in danger of losing its world leadership position. US high-tech manufacturers turned increasingly to Japanese suppliers for electronic components they could not buy competitively at home. The electronics industry, one of the country's largest employers, with a workforce of 2.6

million, was in jeopardy of being gradually transformed into a distribution business for Asian manufacturers. The severity of the problem was masked by the fact that American brand names continued to dominate computers and scientific instruments markets, but many of their components were imported.

The industry called for a strategic partnership between the electronics industry and government. Computer makers, software houses, telecommunications companies and chip producers urged Washington to help bolster competitiveness by relaxing antitrust regulations, recasting fiscal and tax policies, and adopting a more pragmatic stance on trade. Many company executives who once were rabid free-traders now beseeched Washington for protection. The electronics industry associations were determined to force the Administration to rethink its priorities and to do something to counter the government-industry colossus known as Japan Inc.

Some executives considered competition from Japan unfair, and called for a surcharge on imports. In 1985, the industry submitted a report to the White House criticizing US performance in several essential areas: American industry had not kept up with the new realities of world competition; the tax system was biased against investment; the Justice Department's antitrust investigations were wrongheaded in the face of the gigantic integrated companies in Japan and South Korea; American workers were still mired in adversarial relationships with management that "may no longer serve the best interests of both parties and the public"; the educational system was not providing engineers in the numbers required by high-tech industries; the cost of capital was double what it was in Japan, because the tax system was biased against investment.

The report urged revising the tax code to stimulate savings and long-term investments, because "tax policy is one of the most important de facto industrial policies we have," Japan had subverted the US industry by first supplying cheap parts, then sub-assemblies, and finally finished products labeled with American-sounding brand names. Eventually key engineering and production skills in consumer electronics would dry up, leaving the US extremely vulnerable in all electronics markets and put in jeopardy long-term economic development. In reality, American industry was largely responsible. When one company started outsourcing part of its production to a Japanese subcontractor, others were induced to follow.[1]

The industry lobbied successfully and obtained $1 billion to support a semiconductor industry consortium, called Sematech. But most companies quickly dumped the subsidy while hundreds of millions of dollars were still available. The current charter of the Semiconductor Industry Association called for "free and open markets", and the SIA board of directors announced that it would not lobby for government subsidies. The Semiconductor Trade Agreement provided temporary protection, but many in the Valley still view it with shame. Ever since, the prevailing attitude has been that the government, however well-meaning, should stay out and simply maintain an environment - such as a favorable tax structure - giving business the freedom to succeed or fail.[2] The American government has made a powerful contribution by not doing things that would have messed it up.

Ever since, Silicon Valley has risen and prospered in an environment of governmental non-interference and without any strategic planning. Its industry leaders are convinced that the further they stay away from the federal government, the better. The high-tech community has a deep understanding of the process that has generated its success and looks askance at Washington, simply expecting to be left alone. They feel money is extracted from Silicon Valley and then wasted by government. The government should let every company fend for itself, and keep out. State intervention is contrary to the value the industry sets on free market forces as the final judge in the competitive struggle. Industry should

be free to set its own standards, develop the best products possible, and let the customers pass final judgment and decide what they want.

Silicon Valley is a tightly coupled network of talent, resources and opportunities. Each new successful start-up attracts another start-up, which in turn attracts more capital and skills and yet more start-ups.

The glass-fronted buildings along the length of El Camino Real, the 50-mile-long corridor reaching from San Jose to San Francisco are crowded by people who aim to dominate the world of computing and know they can do it. They are willing to work 60 to 80 hours a week for it. Flamboyant entrepreneurs and capable managers, some of whom lost fortunes and then made them again, live alongside computer freaks, hackers, and super-specialists from the exotic research world.

Silicon Valley has developed a corporate culture that values freedom, initiative and fun. Work is play, not toil. Companies value their human capital and treat employees as peers; the jobs they create provide scope for ambition and creativity. Engineers and programmers behave increasingly like independent entrepreneurs, moving from company to company, always ready to switch to a more exciting or better-paying job. Wages are higher than in any other industry, on average over $50,000 a year.

A dozen new firms and hundreds of new millionaires are created each week. With a population of 2.3 million, Silicon Valley is world of strangers and newcomers. It is a self-organizing system, made up of numerous interacting specialist companies that come and go. Nobody directs it. The companies and their products are mysterious; the technology is difficult to grasp without an understanding of basic concepts of physics. Engineers busy themselves developing products that were unknown when they were in college.

The Valley is basically a one-industry town crammed with some 7,000 electronics and software companies. There are no factories, only facilities, modern, low-slung and clean buildings, complete with immaculate landscaping, lawns and greenery. Some have swimming pools and tennis courts. The astonishing variety of companies, from chip designers and specialist software firms is ready to provide anything that a start-up might need. It is adaptable and can instantly cope with change.

Silicon Valley does not set agendas for technological development. It represents a distinctive and seemingly enduring model of business innovation and success. One of its secrets is the presence of thousands of small firms who must compete but also cooperate with each other in order to stand up against the giants. The complacency of large corporations frequently leaves gaps open for young entrepreneurs to exploit a new idea. Brash upstarts create products or services overlooked or neglected by established companies. Two or three engineers working together in a laboratory decide to quit their job; they set up a business of their own, raise finance to start it, beaver away night and day practically sleeping under their desk to get a new product on the market before competitors catch up. In this world of restless insecurity and civilized warfare, crushing competition is the name of the succeed-or-bust game.

At the center of this unique habitat are the entrepreneurs, the idea generators and the financiers, surrounded by specialized lawyers, accountants, consultants and human resource experts. Each wave of entrepreneurs spawns new venture capitalists who plow some of their profits and technical skills into start-up companies, keeping the cycle going. Silicon Valley has spawned an elitist culture of achievers for whom long-term job security is not an issue. One rite of passage to gain status is to quit a job and start a company to make something different and better. Money is one motivation. But what drives them is need to create new and innovative products, to imagine new solutions, new companies, the feeling of doing something significant. Having fun is compatible with hard work.

A knowledge-based economy requires large public investments in education, infrastructure, and research and development. Innovation and creativity require an entrepreneurial culture, the passion to invent something new, risk-taking, vision, effort, adventure, venture capital.

The Valley has developed a culture that rewards those who can live with creative chaos and adjust quickly to change, taking risks and trying new ideas. One of the secrets of its success is the management philosophy for running a business: informal, broadly egalitarian relationships, entrepreneurial teamwork, coordination, minimal bureaucracy, equal opportunity and authority pushed down into the ranks. The employment seekers are often the ones who do the interviewing.

But it doesn't always work out. The line between being a millionaire and being a down-and-out can be very thin. Everything is accelerated: the business cycles, wealth creation, and the rate at which life can fall apart. Failures are regarded as being part of the game. Should a start-up fail and come to a sticky end, jobs await a seasoned entrepreneur at large. Silicon Valley does not penalize those whose efforts do not come up to expectations. Initial failure in charting a start-up does not lead to ostracizing. Failure is not only inevitable, but valuable for what it teaches. Doing something that hasn't been done before is a learning process.

Silicon Valley clearly has something special going for it. The ability to transform an idea into a company has reached an art form. The mixture of technology, optimism and money has created and developed an ecosystem for producing something extremely valuable from virtually nothing. It is a modern version of the quest for the philosophers' stone, which allows the capitalist ferment to constantly spin out new companies and new products.

The Valley generates a persistent optimism that overrides life's minor problems. This diffuses a sense of infectious enthusiasm and energy, and nurtures a creative risk-taking atmosphere and an entrepreneurial culture eager to make most of science, education and know-how. Information and innovation combine to produce economic value. Silicon Valley is high-technology capitalism run wild. [3]

The Valley's employment market has several characteristics that define its particular brand of social capital. Plentiful employment opportunities and the industry's norms of career advancement allow people to change jobs frequently. The average employee becomes a mini-capitalist willing to embrace uncertainty, flexibility and negotiability in daily life. Each year an estimated 30 percent of the employees switch companies. Job-hopping, temporary work arrangements and pay pegged purely to performance tend to become the norm. The geographic proximity of so many firms within the same industry contributes to this fluidity. You can change your job without changing where you park your car.

Secrets and staff are hard to keep. Virtually every big firm is a spin-off from another one. The place is a strange mixture of rampant individualism and collaboration: staff are borrowed, ideas shared, favours exchanged. Much of the Valley's value lies in the round-the-table chat in restaurants, the buzz in bars. Jealousy is rare because most people believe that they, too, have a chance of becoming rich.

Commitment to the craft of innovation is more powerful than loyalty to any particular employer. This results in rapid turnover from one company to the next creating information-sharing networks. As individuals move from one project or one firm to another, their paths overlap; they take with them the knowledge they carry around in their brains, creating networks of information-sharing that accelerate the diffusion of technological capabilities and know-how within the area.

People go back and forth from academia to the business world; many faculty members have part-time jobs in industry; many senior executives have part-time faculty appointments. Admission to this exclusive community requires at least a bachelor's degree in electrical engineering, physics or computer science from one of the nation's reputable universities. To move ahead, one must conceive a new product idea, gather a skilled team and convince venture capitalists to invest, leave a job and set up a new corporation. The Valley's greatest rewards come from being the owner of a successful new enterprise.

Meritocracy is the essence of the work ethic: the single criterion of performance is success. The victims of this work ethic, those who didn't make it, outnumber by far the successes. The vicious side is that the downward spiral can spin just as fast as the sudden-wealth machine. For people whose starting salary is $100,000, life can be exciting, although competitors can occasionally make it miserable. Morale suffers when shares suddenly plunge, and with them the plan of buying a two-million-dollar house in Palo Alto. Then the dream becomes a cruel letdown.

The men and women of the IT industry form an esoteric fraternity. They are disciplined; they work long hours, even on weekends. Many of the young men go to work at eight in the morning, work right through lunch, leave at six-thirty or seven, drive home, play with the baby for half an hour, have dinner with their wife, may get in bed with her, then leave her there and return to the office two or three more hours, or have a drink and gossip and brag.

Living together without marriage was at one time frowned upon, but is now generally accepted. Family life suffers when two working parents drive themselves to exhaustion, and come to resent their inability to give their small children the nurturing they require. Many have endured the pain of divorce, which inhibits them from establishing another formal relationship. In a world of independent newcomers, every one of them has gone through personal battles, with ups and downs.

They all have scars to show, but they keep psyching a world where you have to suffer to get tougher. These recurring spasms of gloom and euphoria tend to be self-fulfilling. Instead of viewing themselves as an integrated person, they see themselves as a collection of components that can be upgraded. They are the visionary heroes and the villains, risk-takers whose life is full of suspense, anxiety, of brilliant ideas and near-disasters. They thrust themselves forward between elation, exhaustion, occasional legal fights, and sometimes wealth beyond anyone's expectations. They keep changing the world. As America moves forward in the Information Age, the values of competition, faith in technology and political conservatism make up for the darker side.

Silicon Valley thrives on creative destruction and anarchy. It is a gigantic pressure cooker of ideas, generating cumulative, self-sustaining and continuous advance in technology in an environment accustomed to fierce competition. Chaos is a key ingredient of its success. Technological innovation requires a certain state of mind and the Valley has it. New companies come up with better products that kill off existing ones, allowing people, ideas and capital to be reallocated. An ecosystem that stimulates bright young brains on ego trips and unleashes the power of their individual creativity, it is based on the coalescence of a multitude of brilliant, ambitious and impatient young entrepreneurs, on a sizeable and flexible labor pool, a vast network of specialized suppliers, access to venture capital and the excellence of the education facilities and research institutions.

The assurance of being able to leave one company and move to another with an increase in salary provides a form of security. Each shift means a raise and perhaps a move up the management ladder. For the employer, job-hopping can be a major problem: it means the loss of experienced employees; staff turnover also creates problems in establishing consistency in internal operations. When an engineer who is essential to a design project leaves the company, much of the thinking behind the project leaves with him. There is no legal way to erase what is in his head. On the other hand, he may later return and be even more valuable to the firm.

Marketing skills are valued as well as engineering skills. People with specialized know-how can literally walk across the street and find a new job. Employers like it because they can fill important vacancies without suffering extended and costly searches, even though they may lose key personnel to competitors. This leads to a virtuous circle of positive feedbacks. While companies can protect their formal trade secrets, they can't prevent employees from taking tacit knowledge learned at one company to another. Like bumblebees pollinating flowers, these employees speed up the innovation process. The move of key employees from firm to firm creates cross-fertilization.

Sometimes a couple of young engineers who have been working on a project decide to set up a company. Driven by entrepreneurial urges they cannot fully satisfy, blue-jeaned youngsters who want to rule cyberspace and change the world burst from nowhere to conquer a niche in the market. Those who see the near-future more clearly and understand better than their competitors how to exploit it are those who come out on top. The Valley has spawned whiz-kid business heroes and stock market stars. Hundreds of specialized services support the industry. This is the place where new products that will fill the unexplored needs of the 21st century are being thought up.

With pay linked to performance and management techniques pushing workers to the limit, employees strain under exceedingly high levels of pressure and put in long work hours. Many eventually "burn out" and leave. To thrive in this big-stakes, high-tech, cut-throat community, survival depends on keeping ahead. Anyone who falls behind may find himself out of business. Survival of the fittest is the law, and the community does not apologize for it. The atmosphere is intense, the competition ruthless. This causes people to get more mature and more effective. Competition makes savvy and crushes. People who are unable to adapt move away for an easier life in less expensive areas. Some are not up to the test, or fear that the pursuit of money will prevent them from leading full and meaningful lives.

The Valley's liberal stock-option culture and vesting programs also make the difference. Start-ups use them to attract the best engineering and management talent without having to pay top salaries. They allow employees to buy shares at prices below market value, with the prospect of cashing in big when the stock takes off. Stock options reward success with giant payoffs. They also extend loyalty and employment tenure of key employees for the several years of the option holding period. When the options vest, some beneficiaries cash them in and use the proceeds to start their own companies or to invest in other start-ups. Capital gains from stock options add hugely to the valley's wealth accumulation, not just at the very peak of the income distribution, but quite a way down into the engineering, professional and managerial ranks, and occasionally even lower.

In established firms, stock options stretch from the boardroom to the reception desk; they play a vital part in the commercial success of a company. By allocating shares to engineers, accountants and secretaries, employees become part-owners and associates whose stock may one day be worth millions. Making employees work hard and making them rich fast creates a natural pool of managers, ready to use their bankroll to fund the next big idea and stay at the cutting edge by investing in start-ups.[4]

The bulk of high-tech wealth rests in the hands of entrepreneurs, bankers, venture capitalists and senior executives. But an increasing number of lower-level employees at successful start-ups elect to take part of their paycheck in equity, on top of stock options. For those who are in the right place at the right time, unbelievable things may happen.

Many of the Valley dwellers are there to make money; others, believing they are going to change the world for the better, want to find out what they are truly capable of. For them, piling up personal wealth becomes secondary. They have a dream, a goal, work night and day to reach for it, and hope for the best. They possess the nerves of champion poker players. With some luck and a blast of genius now and then, some become billionaires, while others go broke. Many dreams and hopes are realized; most are shattered. The push to come up with bigger, better, faster and cheaper technology fills entrepreneurs with ambition and vision. They create a new product to crush a rival product, or retaliate by offering some software free of charge or slashing prices sharply.

Retirement plans are virtually unknown, although a few companies have them. The younger employees do not expect to stay with the same company until they retire, and do not consider retirement benefits when making a job change. Jobs are perceived in terms of months or years, not in terms of life-time employment, health insurance or retirement security. The benefits packages of many companies even exclude a pension plan. The high-velocity of the labor markets creates a climate of uncertainty and insecurity that seems to contribute to the dynamism and growth. There's nothing like a little fear and urgency to force creativity.

Status, keeping up with the neighbors, requires the display of wealth: a comfortable home with a big pool and money to do whatever one wants. Newly hired young engineers drive Porsches or BMWs; the older ones with families generally prefer Mercedes or Jaguar sedans; the most extravagant like to be seen in Lamborghinis or custom-built sports cars. A few have a golf course in their backyard or a place to land their helicopter. Another symbol marking exactly where one stands comes from owning condominium or a house in one of the fashionable hot spots such as Malibu, Palm Springs, Aspen or the Caribbean, and commuting on weekends in a private plane.

In a community where hard work becomes an all-consuming passion and the ultimate gratification, wealth has not generated a leisure class. For a surprising number of young millionaires, there's no time for relaxing or celebrating. They do not have much spare time, nor do they appear to want any. They lead a strenuous, fast-paced life of long hours and intense pressure, leaving little time for family, friends or entertainment. They put in long hours and cope with the job-related stress. Some of the work intensity is self-induced. But on the other hand, life and work in Silicon Valley never gets dull.

Trust is the foundation of relationships between firms and individuals who compete and co-operate within a congregation where a checking account can be opened on word or a building rented without showing an ID card. People who have to deal with one another will tend, in their own interest, to gain and maintain a reputation of honesty and reliability, by living up to the norms for fair dealing. It is a tight-knit community, both cooperative and competitive. Work and social life are intertwined; friendly relations are mostly assessed for the value they can add to one's career; but many lifelong friendships have endured periods of tension. Some people play rough: the frenetic pace of high tech and the testosterone levels of its power players may occasionally generate an endemic nastiness.

Most inventions are not patented because the inventor must disclose the invention at the time of the patent's issue. Disclosure may encourage competitors to copy the invention or invent around a patent, making legal recourse difficult or impossible. Patent infringement suits are expensive and lengthy. Most microelectronics firms have company secrecy policies; but employees and firms utilize various information strategies to circumvent this mandated secrecy. Job mobility of R&D workers is one means of technological information-exchange, while information-exchange may be one reason for job mobility.

Like success, failure has its own style. The problem is not to get started, but to keep up once established. Many entrepreneurs do not make the grade, because they overreach themselves or get bogged down in the transition. A brilliant engineer-inventor starts a company based on an innovative idea; the product catches on and the company grows; new staff is hired at a rapid rate. Then company policies, formal procedures and adequate monitoring must be established. The process of growth follows a typical pattern: a firm starts small with a few employees in a rented building. Within a year or two, if all goes well, it expands rapidly, adding facilities and employees. When a business grows to a significant size, the problem is to get professional help.

Fast growing high-technology firms soon reach the phase during which size outgrows managerial ability. Transition problems occur at around 500 workers. At this size a firm must have personnel, advertising, and accounting departments, as well as a training division. The growing company can no longer operate effectively as an informal and dedicated group clustered around a charismatic entrepreneur-engineer. Not all engineer-founders are able to make the transition to successful managers. Some start-ups crash with a big thud, others just quietly fade away.[5]

Bankruptcy is treated like a duelling scar. Many of the new Internet companies are headed by entrepreneurs who went bust before starting again and making a huge success. Silicon Valley likes to forget mistakes.

Money is the least of Silicon Valley's problems. While living quarters, office space and roads are inadequate, venture capital is overabundant. No other place in the world hosts so many investors eager to finance the untested ideas of young entrepreneurs. Venture firms compete fiercely to put money in what they hope will be the next success story.[6]

High-risk investment offers tax advantages and the opportunity to make outstanding returns. Wealthy individuals, pension funds, universities, banks, insurance companies and other large corporations are encouraged to place money in new or young high-technology companies with a promising potential for very rapid growth. At the core of this is an all-things-are-possible attitude, an unerring belief that a new technology, an entrepreneur's vision of the digital future is the right one. And if it isn't, the next one will be.

In 1969, Congress increased the maximum tax on long-term capital gains from 28 to 49 percent. The incentive to invest in new companies melted away. The effect was devastating. In 1978, after intensive lobbying by Silicon Valley and high-tech firms elsewhere, the maximum capital gains tax was rolled back to 28 percent. In 1981, it was further decreased to 20 percent, generating a flood of venture capital for the nascent electronics industry.

Northern California has the largest concentration of venture capitalists and incubators in any place in the world. The Valley's venture capitalists have created a new and different kind of financial institution in which technological and business expertise, equity stakes and direct involvement in the firms they finance are the hallmark. They become central actors in the establishment of networks incorporating finance, entrepreneurship, innovation and troubleshooting. The venture-capital industry and start-ups are so intertwined that neither can exist without the other.

Venture capital firms are heavily involved in the strategic and managerial decisions of the companies they back. They often demand an active role in setting the course for the new company. They provide experienced executives at critical moments of a firm's development, strategic and operational advice, links and leads to potential customers and partners.

Another peculiarity is the market for initial public offerings of small companies. For entrepreneurs and for the venture capitalists who fund their ideas, selling stock to the public is a critical phase and the ultimate kick of the delicate ecosystem that sustains the Valley. The venture-capital firms and their investors can make a bundle by taking a company public and selling stock of companies that have never made a profit. But not all IPOs are successful. Many start-ups boom briefly and then fade. Some downfalls can be downright crushing. A growing number of companies chose instead to sell to one of the established companies that are constantly scouring the field for promising new technology by acquisitions and partnerships.

The paragon of Silicon Valley's venture capitalists is Arthur Rock. In 1957, he helped the "Traitorous Eight" start up Fairchild Semiconductor. The idea that a few engineers, however technically talented, could start their own company was considered too risky for the banking industry. Unable to get financial support from the banks, Rock convinced Sherman Fairchild to back them with the $1.5 million they needed. Eleven years later, Rock helped Noyce and Moore leave Fairchild to found Intel. The two main qualities he looked for when he invested were: intellectual honesty and drive.[7]

By the late 1970s, Silicon Valley had created more high-tech jobs than Route 128, and it proved far more resilient. The big East Coast companies such as Digital Equipment Corporation and Data General were self-contained empires that focused on minicomputers. Silicon Valley is a networked economy that relies on creative destruction and can adapt very quickly. An essential ingredient in this is the presence of entrepreneurs and a culture that attracts them.

The Valley's venture capitalists understood the technical dimensions of the business far better than their East Coast counterparts. Venture capitalists prefer to be seen not as financiers, a term they disdain, but as company builders who work closely with the entrepreneurs. Because no one knows which technologies will be profitable, some put their eggs in as many baskets as possible. Some demand a "liquidation preference", meaning that in case of sale or insolvency, they get a guaranteed return, prior to the shareholders.

Most venture capitalists have experience with technology firms in the region. As a result, they understand the technical dimensions of the business. The personal connections are forged by the shared business and technological experience and by the deep trust upon which relationships between entrepreneurialism, innovation and financial backing flourish. As a result of their unique relationship with technology firms, they are embedded within the broader fabric of high technology development.

Small companies founded by a group of scientists who cut loose from their university laboratories, assemble their brainpower and strike out for commercial success suddenly appear from nowhere and skyrocket. One of the crucial problems of rapidly growing high-technology firms is the adolescent transition, the phase when they have to build for the next stage, during which size outgrows managerial ability. Most entrepreneurs are engineers, poorly trained in business management, financial, and legal matters.

This is where the lawyers able to deal with refined legal issues come in. The Valley's leading law firms are not there for litigating, but for arranging marriages between businesses.

They are crucial intermediaries in deal-making and business counseling. They set up contracts linking the engineers and scientists with venture capitalists, or helping new companies to form joint ventures or take on licensees. The attorneys are information brokers for the inventors and for venture capitalists. They play a central role in the culture of the community and its resource structure and base. They define the nature of the relationships between venture capitalists and entrepreneurs and help to structure these relationships to reduce conflicts and antagonisms. They know the ins and outs of software and patents; they specialize in areas important to high-tech companies such as intellectual property rights, technology licensing, encryption law as well as tax and corporate matters.

The lawyers know the venture capitalists; they both know large numbers of experienced technology executives who can be called in to help deal with an organizational or strategic problem or opportunity. They sit on boards of companies that can be key customers or partners for new firms. There is about one lawyer per ten engineers.

Silicon Valley is no paradise. It is home to a huge number of families on welfare. In the summer of 2003, the richest US state had the largest budget deficit in its history and was officially facing bankruptcy. Its finances follow the ups and downs of the electronics industry. In boom years, the party in power indulges in lavish spending combined with tax cuts. When a downturn hits the economy, the budget gets drastically out of line.

Victim of its own success, overcrowded and expensive, it is a land of haves and have-nots. From the beginning, the community has been characterized by extreme income inequality. Nowhere is the gap between rich and poor as flagrant. The Valley's vaunted wealth does not trickle down to the manual workers in the microelectronics plants, who constitute the proletariat of the information society.

Lured by a booming technology-driven economy and jobs with stock-option laden compensation packages, people flocked to Silicon Valley. By the late 1970s, it became financially more attractive for cities to develop commercial property than residential. As the Valley's economic structure changed, the number of employees per acre increased dramatically, while housing intensity did not keep up with job growth. Between 1992 and 2, about 250,000 new jobs were created while only about 40,000 new housing units were built.

The region never had any coordination of city decisions on land-use planning. New urban centers have emerged in areas where land prices were still affordable. But this means spending at least a couple of hours a day commuting. Traffic congestion is one of the aggravations on the jam-packed roads and keeps getting worse. In the morning, afternoon and early evening, speedy Jaguars and Porsches inch along bumper to bumper with hordes of old Chevrolets and Toyotas, making commuting a chore.

The housing crisis exacts a toll; competition for living quarters is fierce and costly. A single-family home is out of reach for 70 percent of the residents. The median price of a house in the Valley is double the median price in the rest of the state. People earning what would be considered comfortable incomes almost anywhere else, cannot enjoy comfortable housing. Households headed by medium-skilled workers and those outside the tech industry - administrative assistants, teachers, nurses, custodians, espresso pourers and mechanics - people who in other regions would be middle class, live in tiny rooms renting for $1,200 a month. Many are forced to live in converted garages or to pay $400 a month for an unheated room in a house with cracked walls. Some families crowd together in a small apartment. Many hard-working people with a full-time $10-an-hour job spend their nights in a homeless shelter, because even a modest room is out of reach.

Future trends suggest no self correction for years to come. People earning six-figure incomes frequently buy mobile homes because that is all they can afford. In the Valley's toniest neighborhoods, "starter" homes begin at $800,000. Whenever a "For Sale" sign goes up, potential buyers start bidding over it, offering well above the asking price.

Beneath the high-tech sparkle of the Valley lays a hidden underbelly which should not be given a blind eye. Nor should it stand accused or vilified. The power relationship between capital, management and labor is built upon extremes of talent and income among the workforce. This leads to grinding poverty amidst fabulous wealth. At the bottom of the rung, immigrant production workers toil under sweatshop-type conditions, exposed to health and environmental hazards. More than 70 percent of the 200,000 people laboring in the production line are of Asian and Mexican origin. Many work 10 to 12 hours a day in insalubrious rooms. They make $7 to $14 an hour in the most unaffordable area to live; but they stay and more keep coming.

After taxes, a low-skilled worker brings home about $1,000 a month. The top pay for maids or janitors, the people who empty the trash, and wipe down the work areas, is $17,000 a year. They have no job security, no health insurance, no options or retirement benefits. Most of them are Mexican, Filipino, Chinese or Vietnamese immigrants. African-Americans are frozen out almost entirely. Real wages for the lowest-paid 25 percent of workers have dropped since 1989.[8]

Networks of small firms, called contract assembly houses, compete by cutting prices and wages to the lowest levels. By offering flexibility and speed, they fulfill essential functions in the production process. Many immigrants have started their own companies employing immigrant workers. Overcompetitive subcontracting leads to poverty-level wages, piece-rate compensation, chemical and ergonomic hazards, routine health and safety violations, absence of medical benefits, precariousness.

By contracting out production, the big corporations avoid accountability for workers' wages, benefits or working conditions. By fostering intense competition between the contract houses, they are able to drive down costs to rock bottom. A loose network of immigrant families assemble electronics parts at home in violation of labor, tax- and safety laws. They are paid by the piece. Without them, much of the Valley's subcontracting would simply have to move to Asia.

Silicon Valley's homeless mock every common mythology about the place. In entrepreneurial circles, failure is said to be a valuable, and even laudable, experience. It can be the source of vital business lessons and proof of a pioneer's willingness to take chances. But the pioneer's mentality of Silicon Valley imposes perverse interpretations on personal failure. There is a kind of failure that no one in Silicon Valley likes to think about. Technology workers who lose their job in a mass layoff or for whatever reason, become unable to pay their rent. They inevitably have a baser notion of failure.[9]

Some executives and companies spread part of their wealth around for the benefit of social, educational or environmental organizations. But by and large the low-skilled are left behind and the upwardly mobile are not concerned with the social issues of inequality or injustice. Silicon Valley believes in the absolute correctness of free competition and in technological solutions to social problems. The poor are poor because they are intellectually and mentally inferior. If they are downtrodden, it is their fault rather than the side-effect of the system. Some companies are beginning to focus on social issues such as closing the gap between the Valley's digitally connected and the unconnected; and some of the high-tech industry's money is flowing into community philanthropy.

Silicon Valley is a bastion of profit-driven capitalism and the citadel of America's most anti-union industry. Unionization is anathema, simply because it runs counter to the entrepreneurial spirit. In the early days, Bob Noyce of Intel laid down the rule: "remaining non-union is an essential for survival for most of our companies. If we had the work rules that unionized companies have, we'd all go out of business. This is a very high priority for management here. We have to retain flexibility in operating our companies. The great hope for our nation is to avoid those deep, deep divisions between workers and management, which can paralyze action."

Production employees are told they are part of the family, and that if unions are established and wage rates rise too high, they will not be able to compete with low-cost, non-unionized labor in foreign countries. The AFL-CIO has tried in vain to get a foothold; all tentative efforts to unionize the workforce failed, and unions have come to consider the electronics industry unorganizable. Moves to establish unions are opposed by the workers themselves; employees found out to be union organizers have been fired. Companies are able to operate unencumbered by collective bargaining agreements covering wages, hours, benefits, and work rules. As long as they are so convinced, Silicon Valley firms will continue to treat their workers with a high degree of paternalistic care.

Toxic chemicals pose serious problems to the health of production workers and to the environment of the region as well. For years the industry has stored chemical wastes in underground tanks. Eventually these substances enter the soil and groundwater where they now threaten the water supply.

Silicon Valley has become a major destination for foreign scientists and entrepreneurs eager to study its accomplishments and emulate its methods. Ambitious educated people, mostly young, come from all over the world to take their chances. They stay because they feel the place is full of opportunity. Many remain in the area after attending one of the local universities. The promise of the good life continues to draw precocious computer nerds, aspiring and ambitious high achievers. Foreign-born entrepreneurs run high-tech companies and spawn hundreds of start-ups. Others are attracted by the openness of the labor market to talented foreigners, one of the region's most valuable assets.

Silicon Valley is a magnet for people with aspirations to high-tech specialization. Nowhere else in the world can they get access to such a concentration of the professional skills needed to bring new products to the marketplace. About one-fourth of the residents come from abroad. Hungarian-born Andrew S. Grove, CEO of Intel, is the most famous. Technically savvy Indians, Chinese, Israelis and Europeans keep the area at the forefront of global technology. About 10,000 French citizens live in the Valley, at least twice as many Taiwanese, thousands of Indians and a few thousand Israelis. People come and go; some pass through quickly, but many work for years and become citizens. They are a transmission belt diffusing technology and market knowledge, sometimes establishing off-shore facilities. Asians represent 31 percent of the jobs. They also own nearly a quarter of the start-ups. Almost a third of the Valley's scientists and engineers are Asian-born. Indians and Chinese created 27 percent of the 4,000-plus high-tech businesses founded in 1991-1996.[10]

Taiwan-born scientists are among Silicon Valley's most successful. But a growing proportion of these entrepreneurs come from the mainland. They are among the best and brightest. Ethnic Chinese are at the helm of about 2,000 Silicon Valley companies. They are driven by intellectual curiosity or personal ambition. Some are spies who may put America's technological secrets at risk. But pulling the noose too tightly would choke off a promising market for US computers, chips and satellites in China and threaten the vitality of a local community.[11] Japanese firms have established what are disparagingly referred to as spy shops to tap technological know-how. It is estimated that each year the Russians get more than $1.5 billion worth of high technology through dummy companies, espionage, and simple theft.

Stanford's high-tech incubator system has created and developed a process for producing something valuable from virtually nothing, and put the Valley on the world map. Upper-class residents like the wonderful climate and the scenery of the Bay and the Pacific Ocean. They value Silicon Valley as a place to live and work. They like the intellectual and creative energy that challenges to a continual higher standard of excellence.

They like the breadth of jobs, the high wages, the safe environment and the educational opportunities. They enjoy working
with talented and visionary people and perceive the Valley as
the place where things happen first and as the epicenter of the
global economy. They like the Valley's culture of money and
celebrity, and the feeling to be part of the creative forces that
change the world. For anyone who is talented and eager to
work hard, the sky is the limit. This is where they want to live.

To this day, Stanford University remains the engine room
and the catalyst of the Valley's growth, churning out almost as
many new start-ups each year as it does engineering and business graduates. Stanford supplies the talented young people
who generate the ideas and the skills that create wealth and
perpetuate America's industrial supremacy: engineers, bankers, venture capitalists and lawyers. Stanford provides the
environment for commercializing research and encouraging
entrepreneurial risk-taking. The strategic importance of education and its close link to high technology is recognized and
understood.

America's high-tech industry was not planned. It happened
when thousands of scientists and entrepreneurs migrated to a
sunny valley with a sophisticated financial system and a culture
of inventing things and making money. In America, people
with good ideas can usually find the means to put them into
practice. American venture-capital funds have bundles of cash
to invest in risky projects. High-tech firms can raise yet more
money by listing their shares on Nasdaq. Sometimes investors grow over-enthusiastic and cause a bubble; when it bursts,
it hurts. The booms and busts of Californian capitalism can
be alarming. But no other system is able to channel so much
money into technology so quickly, nor pulls the plug so quickly
when an idea proves to be a dud.

Silicon Valley went through several boom-bust and job-loss
cycles. In 1970, when it was hit by cuts in defense spending,
the industry shifted to commercial applications and entered
a huge growth phase. Each time, from these down cycles -
overcapacity and Japanese competition - emerged the "next"

Silicon Valley economy. Adversity helped stimulate the industry to major innovations, including the commercialization of the integrated circuit in the 1970s, the development of the microprocessor and personal computer in the 1980s, and application of the Internet in the 1990s.

At the turn of the century, Silicon Valley faced an unprecedented set of challenges. The boom slowed down and the high-tech sector felt the pressure. Share prices, which often take the place of wage increases, dropped sharply. Mergers and acquisitions became a major pre-occupation. But Silicon Valley has a long history of re-inventing itself. It possesses the combination of ingredients that inspires start-ups with ideas that create new products and new markets. As long as it does, the land of dreams, breakthrough technologies and fast fortunes will keep its innovative verve. Despite periodic downturns, the region has shown a remarkable ability to catch the latest technical wave. It appears well-positioned to be at the forefront of future waves of innovation.

Silicon Valley, the birthplace of the electronics industry is an existential creation that has become the high-tech center of the world. Without Shockley's managerial heavy-handedness, it might never have existed. It evolved from a unique, historically-conditioned local culture. Founded by engineers who were fascinated by technology, and who felt that there is more to life than making money, it was neither planned nor programmed. It keeps thriving in permanent anarchy, on a combination of vision, relentless drive and inexhaustible brainpower. It has much that is unique and admirable: its emphasis on merit, its openness to new ideas, its tolerance of disparity between different levels of success, its fabulous ability to re-invent itself, its common desire to make the world a more exciting place.

A number of individual inventors or entrepreneurs have revolutionized the technological history of the region and changed our lives, but innovation is largely the result of a collaborative process. A line-up of aggressive specialty firms that is unmatched anywhere, keeps innovating at a ferocious pace. The pathway from ideas to innovation occurs along networks of communication through which the economic and institutional actors engage in relationships to solve problems. These innovation networks constitute the region's resource base of social capital. They emerged from a combination of local conditions and institutions, national historical trends, and competitive choices.

In comparison to other regional economies, Silicon Valley is a latecomer. Instead of posing a challenge for industrial development, this actually conferred certain advantages. In the absence of an existing industrial structure and of an established local business culture or industrial practices, the economic actors in Silicon Valley were able to create a unique economic environment conducive to risk-taking, innovation, and growth.

Farsighted individuals within academic institutions provided the catalyst for entrepreneurship. The role played by Stanford in the formation of the industry provided the initial threads of the Valley's networks of innovation. Forged on the basis of linkages, these networks lie at the foundation of the region's social structure of economic development. Relationships between the Valley and Stanford, U.C. Berkeley and U.C.S.F. remain at the heart of the Valley's continuing success.

Like the West of earlier generations, the Valley represents the American state of mind of the late twentieth century. Thousands of companies squashed into a small space have managed to create a critical mass of ingredients for entrepreneurial explosions. Scientists, entrepreneurs, financiers, lawyers, academics and the mass of people who do the dirty work keep the place going.

Successful entrepreneurs heading multi-billion-dollar enterprises become role models for hungry upstarts. They act as mentors and angels to guide a rising generation of entrepreneurs, and help them bring their innovations to the global marketplace. Greed is a magnificent motivator. Never in the history of capitalism have so many become so rich, so young.

The Valley derives its edge from a spirit of adventure and a willingness to take risks. It is tuned to turn ideas into products and be the first to take them to the market. What makes it different is the easy way to create new businesses, the presence of research universities that interact with industry, an exceptionally talented and highly mobile work force, experienced support services in finance, law, accounting,   headhunting and marketing, all helping new companies start and grow.

The elements of this habitat are packed into a small geographic area. Networks of specialists form communities of practice within which ideas develop and circulate, and from which new products and new firms emerge. Feedback processes are strongly at work: the successes of individual firms strengthen the habitat and the stronger it becomes the more new firms are created.

Electronics came into the Valley first, followed by semiconductors, computers and software. In the 1990s came biotechnology, networking and the Internet. This extraordinary ability to keep adding new industrial sectors will determine Silicon Valley's future. It will continue to export technology, much of which will reshape the world. Its scientists and engineers will search to extend what we know, until eventually the impossible becomes possible.

Silicon Valley is crowded with people who might be called working-class millionaires. Many of them are at their desk by 7. They work 12 hours a day and log an extra 10 hours over the weekend. They do not think of themselves as very wealthy because they are surrounded by people having much more money. When chief executives are routinely paid tens of millions of dollars a year and a hedge fund manager can collect $1 billion annually, those with a few million dollars see their wealth as puny.

The Valley is based around technology and entrepreneurship. It draws talent from all over the world. Most of the inhabitants were born elsewhere. People flock here from all over the world to be part of something very special. It became an icon with the PC revolution and the arrival of Apple as a glamour company. When the Internet exploded, it became even more meaningful as the paradigm of creative destruction.

The basic building block of the economy is the entrepreneur. Every individual likes to think of imself as an entrepreneur rather than an employee. The system has to some extent fulfilled Lenin's rule that the workers should be the owners of the means of production. Silicon Valley is like America, only more so. For all its faults and shortcomings, it is hard to think of a place as well prepared to face the future. President David Starr Jordan would be proud of his $500 investment. Professor Terman, who passed away in 1982, would have loved to see what Silicon Valley has become.

9

THE SILICON DREAM MACHINE

In the 1950s, computers were huge, rare and very expensive. Moreover, they required a large maintenance and support staff. IBM dominated the market, followed by Honeywell, Burroughs, General Electric, RCA and NCR. The advent of the transistor in replacement of the vacuum tube as a signal-amplifying device augured a radical transformation of computer technology. But mainframe manufacturers saw no need for small computers, since anybody who wanted to, could hook into their time-sharing systems.

None of the large established computer companies saw value in an inexpensive product line that would replace the profitable computers they were selling. Computer scientists had been working on incremental ways to reduce the size of mainframes for more than a decade, though few believed customers would buy such devices.

The world of computing changed dramatically when a few scientists who were far ahead of their time, came up with entirely new concepts. One of them was Ken Olsen, an engineer at the Massachusetts Institute of Technology, who was serving as liaison between MIT and IBM. He anticipated the possibility of building computers whose performance would almost equal mainframes and be small enough to be installed in offices where several individuals could interact with them.

With $70,000 invested by a venture capitalist, and in association with Harlan Anderson, he set up Digital Equipment Corp - DEC.

In 1961, Digital Equipment Corporation announced the PDP-1, the first interactive computer and the first of a series of commercial machines commonly referred to as minicomputers. Two years later, DEC introduced its PDP-8, priced $18,000. It was based on the integrated-circuit technology developed by Jack Kilby and Robert Noyce. Minicomputers gave quick feedback to the user and allowed hands-on computing. Thus a computer culture developed that would later become a major factor in the growth of the personal computer industry.

At its peak in the late 1980s, DEC was the second-largest computer manufacturer the world, with revenues of $14 billion. By 1985, the company had installed over 500,000 machines. But when dozens of lower-cost manufacturers, such as Hewlett-Packard and Honeywell took up production, deficits kept increasing. In the end, DEC was acquired by Compaq. [1]

.In 1961, IBM introduced small systems for technical and professional users starting with the Model 1620. Four years later, the company released Model 1130, a single-user system with an integrated disk-based operating system.

Hewlett-Packard produced stand-alone minicomputers. The HP 2114A minicomputer was released at a price of $9,950. The HP 9100A has been described as a "computing calculator." It was a predecessor to the programmable calculators released in the early 1970's.

Other companies competed with DEC, HP and IBM for a share of the small system market. The most important were Computer Control Corporation, Control Data Corporation, Data Machines, Honeywell, Scientific Control Systems, Scientific Data Systems and Systems Engineering Laboratories.

The computer industry of the 1950s was concentrated in the Route 128 area, near Boston. Stanford Research Institute was the major pioneer of computing technology. In 1946, the 30-ton ENIAC had been installed, and its engineers immediately began downsizing the monster. When the USSR launched

Sputnik, the American government established the Advanced Research Projects Agency (ARPA). The most brilliant scientists in the country were given the task of re-establishing US leadership.

Douglas Engelbart was one of them. A pioneer of human-computer intercommunication and symbiosis, he formulated concepts about allowing machines to perform the mechanical part of thinking and idea sharing. His vision of using computers and software to augment human intellect led to the development of the graphical user interface, the mouse, and many other computer constituents. As a radar technician, he had seen how information could be displayed on a screen. An article by Vannevar Bush in *Atlantic Monthly*, titled *"As We May Think"*, had made a profound impression on him. Bush wanted science to reach beyond developing instruments of war and concentrate on creating a system of global communication that would benefit all of humanity. He envisioned computers that could store and manipulate words and pictures, not just numbers. Computers would have screens on which material could be projected. And he predicted that one day there would be computers that would be owned and operated by individuals.

Engelbart dreamed of taking technology beyond mathematics and decided to devote his life to this challenge. At the Stanford Research Institute, he began conceiving the computer as an 'augmenting tool', capable of empowering the intellect rather than simply automating number crunching. A visionary and a pioneer in the area of human-computer communications, he sought to boost people's collective ability and to confront complex problems at an increasingly faster pace. His seminal work added major contributions to the technology that revolutionized the way the world communicates. His team crafted a set of "user-friendly" tools that enabled computers to store, process and communicate ideas.

In the early 1960s, he headed the ARC (Augmentation Research Center) where a number of revolutionary concepts and devices were developed: the combination of computer, keyboard and video screen; word processing software; the mouse and the principle of pointing and clicking; multiple windows; hypertext software; outline processing, cross-file editing; integrated hypermedia e-mail; hypermedia publishing; text-based computer conferences between connected machines, and much more. While at Stanford Research Institute, he earned a dozen patents working on magnetic computer components.

In 1968, he demonstrated how the computer could be used to deal with everyday tasks and how users could participate in live video and audio conferencing by using a keyboard, screen, mouse and a head-mounted microphone. Engelbart was 20 years ahead of his time. He was ridiculed and ignored. His groundbreaking inventions are now credited with the creation of the communications tools that launched the Information Age.

Throughout the 1960s and 1970s, his laboratory pioneered an elaborate hypermedia-groupware system called NLS. In 1967, it was announced that all the ARPA-sponsored computer research labs, including Engelbart's, would be networked to promote resource sharing.

The Xerox Palo Alto Research Center gathered computer scientists and programmers who wanted to develop a sophisticated architecture for the future. A group of extraordinarily talented people were creating the foundations of personal computer technology.

In 1972, they developed a very small computer, the Alto. A 64K machine with a bit-mapped screen, it incorporated most of Engelbart's ideas: a mouse as pointing device, a keyboard for data input and a video-screen as an output device, icons, windows, menus, and so on. The operating-system was no longer a command-line interface but a graphical user interface, based on the idea that pointing to something is a natural and intuitive gesture, easy to learn. A mouse equipped with a trackball pointing to icons is much easier to use than having to remember key words to operate a system. The graphical desktop is a metaphor of an office desk, with files on a screen, making it easy for users to be read, copied or printed. Xerox PARC did not market the ideas developed by its scientists. The graphic interface was picked up by Steve Jobs and later copied by Microsoft. [2]

In the late 1960s, the idea of the computer on a chip was in the air, but the technology to make it work was not available. Ted Hoff was the first to recognize that Intel's new silicon-gated MOS technologies might make a single-chip CPU possible if a sufficiently simple architecture could be developed. He had created a program that could be implemented within the technological limitations of the day, but not much was known about designing random logic using silicon gate technology.

Federico Faggin envisioned it might have many applications beyond calculators. Together with Stan Mazor and Ted Hoff, he developed the 8008 microprocessor and positioned it as a replacement for calculators. NASA bought a few samples, but there seemed to be no commercial market for it. Intel was still a small company struggling to increase its market share for integrated circuits. Its president, Robert Noyce hesitated to push anything that could be construed by his customers as a competing product. Microprocessors were untested and might hurt sales of memory chips.

In April 1972, when Intel announced "a new era" in electronics, few people gave it any attention. Computer technicians viewed Intel's ad as marketing hyperbole. In the corporate world, the advertised prophesy of a new era met with skepticism. [3]

Noyce decided to test the response of the European computer industry. Federico Faggin visited Philips, Siemens, Olivetti, Nixdorf and several other customers. It was an unpleasant experience. Years later, he recalled: "they seemed bitter that we had a microprocessor... they were particularly obnoxious to me... I mean they were really angry... and they were very critical about it."

Faggin himself didn't think much of the 8008. He considered the 8080 as the real breakthrough. "The 8080 was the microprocessor that made the industry... And, it was really the first microprocessor that broke the performance barrier. And a lot of that was because it was in 40 pins and it used n-channel technology instead of p-channel technology. It was a better microprocessor, of course, than the 8008 but it was compatible with the 8008. I wanted to maintain the machine code compatibility. And it had more registers... it was a cleanup of the 8008. Particularly the interrupt structure was quite a bit better, because the one in the 8008 was totally useless. It was really useless." [4]

The 8008 was designed as a terminal controller. A general-purpose processor, it could be programmed for various uses. Intel's engineers envisaged that the 8008 could actually function as a central processing unit, but they were not sure. They had accumulated know-how in semiconductor processing and memory, but had no experience in logic design. No software was available, but an engineer capable of writing an adequate program would make a computer automatically control a paper tape reader, store and locate the data in memory and feed them out.

Several programmers took up the challenge of writing usable code, but without success. Two young computer buffs, Paul Allen and Bill Gates, purchased an 8008 and developed a device to count the traffic flow from a rubber tube strung across the highway. According to Bill Gates, "the 8008 is basically an 8-bit machine with no programmable stack. Doing traffic analysis software was pushing the limits." [5]

Intel had a sales office in Paris. The manager sent out information to his customers describing the 8008 as a miniature electronic device that contained the arithmetic, logic, and control circuitry necessary to perform the functions of a digital computer's central processing unit. The microprocessor would considerably reduce the size and cost of the computer.

Francois Gernelle, a young engineer employed by Intertechnique, a manufacturer of medical and nuclear applications, was fascinated by the idea of an inexpensive automat that would perform most of the functions of a minicomputer. He had studied physics, chemistry and electronics. He also held a doctorate in applied mathematics. Having experimented with Varian 6201, Multi 8, Elbit and other minicomputers, he was familiar with the intricacies of programming. [6]

When he saw the preliminary data sheet of the 8008, he "started dreaming". He tried to interest his superiors in building a small computer around the new device, but was told not waste time meddling with useless projects. Disappointed, he joined a small company, located in a Paris suburb. It had been founded the previous year by André Truong Than Thy, a Vietnamese immigrant who had also left Intertechnique to set up an electronics consulting company, which he called *Réalisations et Etudes Electroniques* (R2E).

Gernelle had hardly settled down when he noticed a newspaper ad published by the National Institute of Agronomic Research (INRA), inviting tenders for an inexpensive computer. Alain Perrier, a researcher in bioclimatology was toying with the idea of a portable device capable of automating the hygrometric measurements in the Maghreb arable areas, and of programming the irrigation of crops. The computer would capture data on humidity and temperature and an automatic sprinkler system would maintain sufficient humidity for the crops to grow, while dispending a minimum quantity of water. A minicomputer PDP-8 would have done the job, but the INRA could not afford it. Moreover, Perrier wanted a battery operated machine, light and solid. François Gernelle called him and offered to supply a small computer for a fraction of the price of a minicomputer. Perrier immediately agreed. François Gernelle's dream of changing the computer from a giant electronic brain that was the exclusive domain of engineers and scientists to a device that could be purchased and used by an individual could now be put to test.

II THE MICRAL

The computer was to be delivered to the INRA by the end of 1972. Truong approved the project and put François Gernelle in charge. Together with Jean-Claude Beckmann, Alain Lacombe and Maurice Benchetrit, he set to work.

The microprocessor had to be programmed by a mechanical language providing instructions and data to perform specific tasks. In order to develop a new conceptual framework, they needed a thorough understanding of the operating system and an in-depth knowledge of all the aspects of the technology, as well as a variety of software and hardware issues. [7]

The 8008 microprocessor required 20 or more additional devices to function as a central processing unit, plus a very large amount of external logic to support it. The software was written on an Intertechnique Multi-8 minicomputer using a cross-assembler. The programs had to enable the computer to automatically control the paper tape reader or paper punch, accept the data electronically as the information streamed in from the tape, store and locate the data in memory and feed them out to the paper tape punch. The computer also had to manipulate data in memory, and keep track of which spots were available for data storage and which were in use at any given moment.

Since no software was available, Gernelle asked Beckmann to develop the architecture and to design the input/output channels able to communicate with external terminals, acquire digital and analog data, connect and drive peripherals, store information, print reports, etc.

It took six grueling months, working 18 hours a day in the window-less basement of a low-rent apartment building, often sleeping on the spot, for Gernelle and his team to write, test, debug and troubleshoot a programming language.

They formalized the basic concepts and invented the core logic which married the 8008 to a complex operating system: 32/32 I/O board (32 digital inputs, 32 digital outputs); 64 Digital input board; 64 Digital output board; high voltage relay output board; low voltage signals Hg relay router; 8" and 5" 1/4 floppy disk driver, SD & HD (Shugart, Sagem, Memorex, etc.); Cynthia D120/140 hard disk controller; 64KRAM battery backupped memory; Sync/Async V24 modem and current loop controller; Sync/Async four channel V24/V28-V32 FIFO;

HDLC/SDLC communication controller; Xtal controlled clock to timecode BEARN application. [8]

They called it Micral, meaning "small" in French argot. The first model, the Micral N, initially functioned with perforated cards. It had no keyboard and no screen. Two Kbytes of random access memory could only be programmed in binary. But it was rugged, well designed, easy to use, and required no maintenance. The execution time for an instruction was 20 microseconds. The central processing unit recognized 8 interrupt levels. The entries were assured with the assistance of switches and posting was carried out on indicators located on the front panel. The software of the Micral was Prologue, a very efficient and powerful multitasking and multi-user operating system.

The heart of the Micral was the internal communication unit Pluribus. It had the shape of a printed circuit card equipped with 11 sockets which could receive 11 cards. This circuit made it possible to route 60 bits in parallel. Each socket was entirely unspecialized; it could receive a coupler card or a memory card or a channel card, thus insuring an optimum filling capacity as well as a great modularity. The Micral was provided with programmed channels having their own buffer memories which were thus to be compared to peripheral processors. These channels were connected to the Pluribus but were totally asynchronous. They were also asynchronous between one another.

The Micral-N was working at 500 KHz, running approximately 50,000 instructions per second. It was set on a bus, did have a MOS memory, parallel and serial I/O cards, a real-time system. It had all the features of the minicomputer, but cost only one-fifth. It sold for 8,450 French Francs -about $1,300.

Delivery was made in January 1973 and the INRA was entirely satisfied with the results. Over the first six years, about 2,000 units were sold to public and private institutions. Bernard Francina was responsible for the manufacturing engineering, the production planning and control and delivery. The French government installed the Micral on the highways to control traffic and in its colonies to collect demographic information. Several laboratories used it to control their experiments.

Gernelle applied for two patents. Since the Micral was a microprocessor-based device, he coined the word 'microcomputer'. The patent attorney refused to include the term in the application because it was not mentioned in the dictionary. According to French law, Bull owned the rights. In 1979, Bull transferred the intellectual property rights to IBM in exchange of a license to manufacture the RS600 minicomputer.

The next generation, the Micral S was based on Intel 8080 microprocessor. In 1973, an 8-inch floppy disk reader was added. In 1974, a keyboard and screen were added. A hard disk became available in 1975. The following Micral computers successively used the Intel 8080 at 1 MHz (Micral G and Micral S), Zilog Z80 (Micral CZ) and Intel 8088 as microprocessors. The Micral M was a multiprocessor. The original SYSMIC operating system was renamed Prologue in 1978.

Since 1975, several Micral S development tools were available such as ASMIC assembler and MOMIC monitor, concurrently application run-time and development tools, both written by Maurice Benchetrit. Michel Joubert then started developing a third generation language, BAL (Basic Algorithmic Language), similar to BASIC. Available at end 1975, BAL was an interpreter producing an interim very compact code, compatible with the size of the available memory (8K).

In 1975, Michel Joubert and Jean-Marie Ackermann joined the company. Ackermann developed real-time MTZ-based monitoring, which became the kernel of the multitasking and multi-user operating system Prologue. This kernel was perfectly adapted to run BAL and other applications. It included multi-tasking/multi-users features allowing to it run simultaneously several applications and federate system resources. The main difficulty was the s/w code optimization, to retain the essential features into the reduced size memory and maintaining sufficient space for the applications. The s/w code being such compressed also helped to optimize the CPU resource, the chip being very low speed. To save space in the memory and avoid creating a file management system on disk, the programs were simply identified by a figure quote instead of a file name. Although this s/w version to be bundled and sold with the unit, they considered this it incomplete and simply called it PROTOCOL.

In 1975, R2E introduced the MICRAL M, a federal system of up to 8 independent microcomputers, each having its own input-output bus, its memory and interrupt system. The processors operated simultaneously and did not require a task management monitor. The Micral M used the software and the interfaces developed for the Micral S.

Each microcomputer could initiate an interrupt on any processor. Such an organization had several advantages: no memory conflict between the various processors as long as they operated on their particular work. No slowing down, since all the processors operated in parallel; the tasks transmitted their parameters through the common memory. The sharing of common programs, made in common memory, was transparent; natural re-entrance; each unit offered flexibility and safety. A dual redundancy system made it possible to palliate the failures of the program as well as those of the processor.

The MICRAL M had the following technical specifications: 1 to 8 MICRAL S microcomputers; 6 K to 510 K bytes of central memory per distribution between local memory/common memory and the number of processors; up to 64 main interrupt levels and 512 sub-levels; up to 64 channels of each 1 million bytes per second; about 2.5 million instructions carried out per second; inputs addressing: 16,384 bits; outputs addressing: 6,144 bits; 'test and set' instruction of mutual exclusion.

In enlarged configuration, the MICRAL M was capable of solving problems normally handled by large real-time computers. In small configuration, it decreased the cost of a system calling upon several minicomputers. The enlargement of the configuration could be performed in situ, without interfering with the existing software and equipment.

By the end of 1976, the second release of the software was much more accurate. It included an improved disk manager and was enriched with innovative tools to optimize the memory allocation. Thanks to the availability of improved hard disks, they developed "overlays" functions, mainly used into ERP oriented software. Much more powerful than the previous ones, this release was named MTZ, the « Z » being taken from the Zilog Z80. [9]

Micral C - September 1977.
Bernard Francina, F. Gernelle, J. C. Beckmann, M. Joubert.

The company gradually developed a series of computers based on the most powerful processors of the time: 8080, Z80, 8088, constantly adding improvements like a monitor-keyboard in 1974, a hard disk in 1975. Until 1978, the Micral was managed by a Sysmic monitor, which became Prologue. The Micral transformed the computer into a tool for which no technical training was required and demonstrated that a small computer could be used as a business machine. For several years, the Micral was the smallest and the least powerful computer on the market, but also the least expensive.

A number of machines were in use on the French auto-routes until 1991, when they were scrapped and destroyed. On December 10, 2003, the *Association pour l'Histoire des Télécommunications et de l'Informatique* (Association for the History of Telecommunications and Informatics) organized a meeting at the Musée des Arts et Métiers to celebrate the 30th anniversary of the Micral. During the ceremony François Gernelle handed over his own Micral N, which seems to be the only surviving example.

ILL BULL TAKES OVER

For several years, Truong had within his grasp a global technology and patent monopoly. While technically years ahead, the Micral did not attract the interest of the French business community. Gernelle and his team produced a succession of machines, each model being more sophisticated than the previous ones. But Truong's clumsy and erratic management and poor marketing compelled him to enter bankruptcy proceedings. An ambitious entrepreneur who, by his own admission, was unable to read a balance sheet, he had led his company into trouble. Unable to finance further expansion, he tried to sell it. [Why You Never Heard Of The Man Who Built The First Computer. New York Times, 4 Sept. 1985.] In a Los Angeles bar, the boss of Honeywell offered $2 million for the company and for the rights to use its software. When Truong asked for $4 million, the man left the table.

The first microcomputer in history, born of an encounter betweenagronomics and informaticsDuring the 1970s, Alain Perrier, a researcher in bioclimatology at INRA, designed a new apparatus to measure the evapotranspiration of crops and thus pilot their irrigation. He also had an idea which was novel at that time, which was to call upon a computer specialist, François Gernelle to automate this system, and the first microcomputer was born.

In December 2003, to celebrate the 30th anniversary of the Micral, the INRA issued the following press relea **Press release.**

In the past, evapotranspiration measurements were taken by weighing the soil. In an attempt to design a more reliable measurement system which could be applied to any soil type, Alain Perrier[1] had the idea of measuring the water which had evaporated in the air. Sensors sited 40 to 70 cm above the soil measured variations in the water content and temperature of the air, thus determining rates of evaporation over large surface areas (up to 2500 m²) with considerable accuracy.

Alain Perrier's second original idea was to enlist the help of informatics to manage the mechanical functioning of sensors and data storage. It was in response to his call to tender that in 1973, Francois Gernelle designed the first microcomputer in the history of informatics, the Micral (as slang for small).

After fruitful collaboration for several years, during which the agronomist and the computer specialists developed their own programs, the system called BEARN *(Bilan d'Energie Automatique Regional et Numerique, or Automatic Regional and Digital Energy Assessment)* became operational and received the French Academy of Sciences Prize in 1978. A considerable advance towards automation, this apparatus comprises both physical and informatics components and can record data in the open, in the middle of a field, for 3 months, using a complex calculation method to supply evapotranspiration values every 15 minutes.

BEARN has enabled measurements in crops of luzerne, maize and wheat in France, in pineapple plantations in Ivory Coast and in sugar cane fields in Guadeloupe. The thousands of data recorded have contributed to the development of models which are now being used in meteorology and take account of the participation of plants in global assessments of water circulation and, more generally, of energy.

Alain Perrier was one of the first people to emphasise the importance of the continental regions of the Earth to energy flows. Indeed, two-thirds of condensed water, the source of continental rainfall, arise from evapotranspiration of the soil and plant canopy. A reduction in evapotranspiration, for example by deforestation, would contribute to reducing rainfall in large areas and cause warming and desertification.

On December 10, 2003, at the Musée des Arts et Métiers, the AHTI *(Association pour l'Histoire des Télécommunications et de l'Informatique,* or Association for the History of Telecommunications and Informatics) is organising a meeting to celebrate the 30th anniversary of the first microcomputer, the Micral N. During this event, Francois Gernelle will hand over his personal model of the machine to the Museum.

The company was put into receivership. In 1978 CII-Honeywell Bull purchased the majority of the R2E shares and set it up as an independent subsidiary under the name Bull-Micral. CII-Honeywell Bull was the result of several mergers and acquisitions. In 1974, General Electric announced its intention to acquire a controlling interest in Bull. The company was not interested in Bull's technology, but in developing its presence in the European market. Bull-General Electric became a fully integrated subsidiary of General Electric. In 1970, General Electric sold its computer division to Honeywell. The company was renamed CII-Honeywell Bull.

When CII-Honeywell Bull acquired R2E, the company was set up as a separate division under the name Bull-Micral. André Truong remained in charge. Bull-Micral developed an improved multi-terminal system of Prologue that essentially targeted business applications. A database system called Dialogue and a macro-assembler application language BAL completed the Prologue system.

The management of Bull did not anticipate the potential of the Micral and decided to further concentrate on minicomputers. However, the Micral gradually became almost as powerful as the minicomputers and sales kept increasing. In order to limit competition between the two systems, Bull ordered the management of R2E to limit the power of the Micral. The takeover of R2E could have given Bull a head start in the global computer market; but the success of the Micral annoyed the company's management. When Truong was able to sell 300 machines to a large bank in competition with the Bull minicomputer, the decision was made to market the machines under the name Bull-Micral. [10]

In 1981, when IBM entered the PC market, Truong realized that Bull did not have the slightest chance to stand up against the emerging open systems. He developed a clone prototype based on the IBM PC architecture, but the management of Bull disagreed about the strategy to follow. They did not understand that the IBM PC powered by Microsoft's operating systems and Intel's microprocessors had become the standard of the personal computer market and inaugurated a new global electronics era. Over a period of 18 years, about 90.000 Micral computers were produced. In 1991, the 150 microcomputers still in service at the toll gates of the autoroutes were dismantled.

When Bull adopted the MOS standard, Gernelle resigned. In 1983, he set up his own company, Forum International. Several colleagues from the research and development department and from the commercial network joined him. Forum International was a multipost system. Essentially targeting business applications, it became an immediate success. Within a very short time, the company had a substantial share of the market and became very profitable. Three years after its foundation it was listed on the stock exchange.

Forum International sold about 60,000 machines through a network of 40 distributors. But when American and Japanese manufacturers started selling lower-priced computers, Gernelle was unable to compete and was taken over by Goupil. Shortly thereafter, Goupil ran into financial trouble and was liquidated. The Micral faded away, not to be heard of again.

François Gernelle had been granted worldwide patent rights. According to French law, Bull owned these rights. In 1979, Bull transferred the intellectual property rights to IBM in exchange of a license to manufacture the RS600 minicomputer.

Truong moved to the United States and became a consultant. In 1986, the Boston Computer Museum recognized the Micral as the first microprocessor-based personal computer and the first microcomputer to be commercially distributed. One day in 1994, François Gernelle saw his former boss present himself on French TV as the inventor of the microcomputer. He filed a lawsuit against Truong accusing him of a false claim. After more than four years of litigation, the court of appeals of Versailles decided that Gernelle is the inventor of the microcomputer.

In May 1974, Truong and Gernelle showed the Micral at the National Computer Conference in Chicago. It was a very disappointing operation. The fair attendants passed their booth without looking. Those who stopped were puzzled. The only one who seemed interested was the technical director of the magazine *Popular Electronics,* Leslie Solomon. He picked up the leaflets describing the various components and features. Shortly after, he flew to Albuquerque, N.M. where Ed Roberts - a country doctor and former US Air Force officer - had a small store that sold radio transmitters for model airplanes. He told him to put together a computer kit having the size and the external appearance of the Micral.

Six months later, *Popular Electronics* published an article announcing the Altair as "the world's first microcomputer kit to rival commercial models." Roberts had no experience in computing. The Altair was a crude do-it-yourself hobbyist's toy that fascinated thousands of people. A shoebox-sized machine with rows of switches and blinking lights, it had enough power to be potentially useful. It was designed around an expandable system that opened it up to all sorts of experiments; but it took a seasoned solderer to assemble it and make it work.

The Altair created a sensation in the hacker arena. Bill Gates and Paul Allen were among those who were fascinated by the idea of owning a computer. Being skilled programmers, they knew that the Altair opened the world of computing to a vast number of people. Before they even had an Altair to work with, they began writing software for it. Computer clubs sprouted up throughout the US, generating an enormous amount of creative energy, enthusiasm and exuberance. These clubs became breeding ground of the personal computer industry.

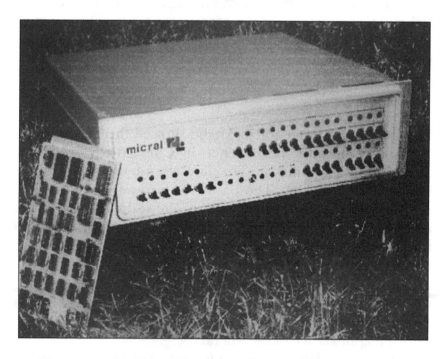

The Micral shown at the NCC in May 1974

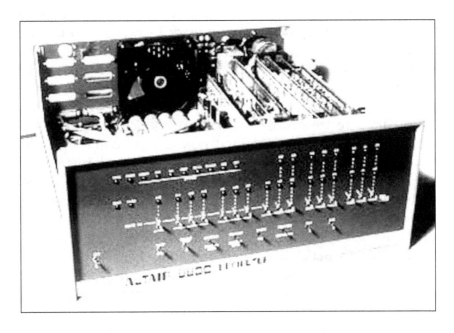

The Altair kit in 1975

The Silicon Revolution ushered in on February 15, 1973, when the first Micral was delivered to the INRA. Several years later came Apple, Compaq, IBM PC and the many brands of word processors that built the multibillion-dollar microcomputer industry. The history of the Micral is one of the more egregious oversights of the Information Age. The personal computer transformed the face of the global economy, created huge fortunes and millions of jobs. The names of its inventors are unheard of and the Micral itself came to a dead end. The concept was picked up by hobbyists who sensed its commercial potential. The wheel of fortune spun in the direction of entrepreneurs who accidentally accumulated ineffable wealth. The pioneers who fundamentally revolutionized the computer industry came out empty-handed and are practically unknown.

The Micral represents one of the most fundamental milestones of the Information Technology value chain. The technological prowess and the paradigm shift achieved by a small team of engineers ended in commercial failure. Their pioneering

329

work delineated the architectural and technological choices that were to be adopted by the industry. By demonstrating the feasibility of building a commercial computer around a microprocessor and developing a market for it, the Micral gave Intel its future. Today's personal computers trace their lineage back to the Micral.

In an interview with a journalist of the magazine *01 Informatique,* Gernelle explained how he had come upon he idea of a microcomputer. While working with minicomputers at Intertechnique, he became convinced of the necessity of smaller less expensive machines able to do the same job. Besides, it would create a new market. When INRA placed the order for a machine intended for one specific purpose, he decided to make it a programmable electronic machine capable of performing high-speed mathematical and logical operations and of assembling, storing and processing information. Rather than tinkering with the microprocessor to see how it worked, he decided to go all the way and build a machine around it.

He expected that microcomputers would be used in laboratories and in the universities. He did not foresee a market for personal computers, because no software was available. In business and industry, robotics would bring about a technological revolution. Industry would have computer automated production systems, from design engineering to manufacture, while numerical control programming would automate material handling.

He estimated that only a dozen people, all American, would determine the future of micro informatics. Looking into the future, he foresaw a revolutionary restructuring of the computer industry and predicted that the winners would be those who were first to develop and commercialize the new technologies. The big ones would be reluctant to restructure their manufacturing process and leave the way open to upstarts. [11]

Passed over by history, the Micral was the spark behind the evolution of the original microprocessor, the archetype and the genetic ancestor from which all the following PC generations derived. It served as a model to the Altair which in turn led to Microsoft, Apple and the IBM PC. Bill Gates, Steve Jobs, Michael Dell and many of today's billionaires and millionaires owe their fortune, status and fame to Gernelle and to a team of unknown engineers who developed the microcomputer technology. Without the demonstration of the Micral at the Chicago Computer Conference, Bill Gates would not have written the software; nor would Steve Jobs and Steve Wozniak bought an Altair kit.

André Truong, the owner of R2E, had for several years a world monopoly created by his employees. Clumsy management forced him to sell out to CII-Honeywell Bull. The patent rights were included in the price. In 1979, Bull transferred these rights to IBM in exchange of a license to manufacture the RS600 minicomputer.

The engineers who designed the Micral laid the foundations of the modern electronic computer industry. Without François Gernelle, Maurice Benchetrit, Michel Joubert, Alain Lacombe, Jean-Marie Ackermann and Jean-Claude Beckmann, the PC would eventually have come about. But the history of the Information Age would have taken a very different course.

THE ALTAIR SAGA

In January 1975, *Popular Electronics* published an article announcing the Altair kit. The Altair created a sensation in the hacker arena. Sold by a small company called MITS, it included an Intel 8080 microprocessor. Bill Gates and Paul Allen were among the thousands who were fascinated by the idea of owning a small computer. Being skilled programmers, they instinctively knew that the Altair opened the world of computing to a vast number of people. Before they even had an Altair to work with, they began writing software for it.

The era of the 1960s was a special time in America. The civil rights struggles of the 1950s had generated a vast number of committed radicals and counterculture iconoclasts. Resenting the fact that immense power resided in the hands of a few and was jealously guarded, they wanted to abolish the hegemony of IBM and other large companies.

The counterculture's scorn for authority provided the philosophical foundations of the personal-computer revolution. They saw themselves as the bards and the pioneers of a new technology. A small contingent of 'hackers' set about transforming computers into tools of liberation. In the 1960s and early 1970s, hackers emerged in university computer-science departments.

Palo Alto was at the center of the Left Alternative movement. IBM was seen as the enemy. In the early 1970s, America faced a political crisis. At the height of the Vietnam debacle, governments and institutions of all kinds were detested as instruments of oppression. Social unrest generated an anti-establishment counterculture, anti-war protests, Woodstock and long hair. The young put into question the development of war-orientated technologies. IBM had a monopoly position on hardware and software sold to business and programmed by IBM technicians on IBM punch-cards. Computers exemplified the technological arrogance of big business and big government. The movement developed out of the spirit of the age and the frustration of technological rebels who understood and knew something about computers and wanted to own one.

It could not be done through the existing structures, nor by the government. A book written by Ted Nelson, *Computer Lib/Dream Machines* became a cult classic of the student revolt demanding the liberation of communication. Nelson had a BA in philosophy, a Masters degree in sociology and a PhD in Media and Governance. In 1960 he started working on a word-processor type program that would enable multiple documents to be linked together. He coined the word hypertext. His ideas were far ahead of their time. He named his system Xanadu.

Xanadu was conceived as a huge repository of published information. It could contain music, reference material, stories and movies. Users would connect to it from outside and read or download as much or as little information as they liked.

They would automatically be charged for their usage, and a royalty would automatically go to the author.

Hobbyists had wanted a computer all by themselves to play with at home. But the price of a standard minicomputer was way beyond the pocket of the average amateur. A former Air Force officer, Ed Roberts, would make their dreams come true. In January 1975, the cover of *Popular Electronics* featured the picture of a computer kit with a caption reading: "World's First Minicomputer Kit to Rival Commercial Models - the Altair 8800." Inside, an editorial promoted the Altair as "a full-blown computer whose performance competes with current commercial minicomputers." The article vaguely promised "manifold uses we cannot even think of at this time". An insert listed some possible applications for the computer, stating that "the Altair 8800 is so powerful, in fact, that many of these applications can be performed simultaneously." The possible uses included an automated control for a ham station, a digital clock with time zone conversion, an autopilot for planes and boats, a navigation computer, a brain for a robot, a pattern-recognition device, and a printed matter-to-Braille converter for the blind. It sold for $397 as a kit, and $498 assembled. Putting it together and writing a program was said to be made easy with the aid of a manual. Free consultation service was available. The low price was the actual sensation, because Intel was charging $360 for the 8080 chip alone.

The ad had been placed by a company, called MITS - Micro Instrumentation Telemetry Systems - located in Albuquerque, New Mexico. Ed Roberts, the owner, ran a small hardware store selling radio transmitters for model airplanes, instruments for model rockets and kits for programmable calculators. In the early 1970's, MITS was doing fairly well. But when Texas Instruments swept the market with their low cost calculators selling at less than half the price of his kits, he was stuck with a large surplus inventory. Having accumulated a substantial debt load, he was desperate for a new product and had to think of something quick or go broke.

In June1974, shortly after the National Computing Conference in Chicago, he suddenly started thinking and talking about a computer kit based on Intel's new 8080 microprocessor. He even asked the people who worked with him, but had no idea about how computers functioned, to think about how to assemble such a kit.

Roberts, however, had a problem. With $300,000 in debt to his bank, he was practically broke. Yet, surprisingly, he was able to convince the local loan officer of Fidelity National to lend him an additional US$65,000. This allowed him to buy a supply of the various components needed to make up the Altair. He was even able to talk Intel into selling cosmetically blemished 8080's for $75, when they normally sold for $360.

In June 1974, with the help of two engineers, William Yates, who had a degree in aeronautical engineering, and Jim Bybee, an electronics engineer, he sketched out the general plan. He wanted the computer to be expandable so that the user would be able to install additional circuit boards for particular functions. He also wanted the boards designed to plug easily into the computer. If different elements of the computer were to reside on physically distinct circuit boards, the boards had to be able to communicate with each other. [12]

As soon as the ad appeared, MITS was deluged with orders. Computer buffs from all over the country sent in their $397. The small MITS crew was totally unprepared to process the thousands of packages. They did not even have enough parts on order. There was no way they could deliver. However, when people were asked if they wanted their money back, no one asked for a refund. To a large extent, they didn't know what they were going to do with a computer kit, but they knew that they wanted one.

The flood of money catapulted MITS back into business. Roberts started to advertise in *Byte, Creative Computing* and the various emerging computer magazines. The company was flooded with money. The Altair saved Roberts from bankruptcy. In a few weeks, MIT's balance went from $365,000 in the red to $250,000 in the black. Within three months 4,000 people sent in pre-paid orders. It took almost a full year to catch up. During the first quarter of 1975, MITS received over $1 million in orders. More than 10,000 units were ultimately sold.

For $397 the customer got a box of parts that included a power supply, a bunch of lights and switches, an 8080 microprocessor and 256 bytes of RAM. The cabinet looked nice; on the front panel the name ALTAIR 8800 had been stencilled. An 8-amp power supply consisting of a transformer, switch, fuses, some rectifiers, controller chips and a group of electrolytic capacitors had to be assembled. After installing the bus card, the front panel and CPU had to be connected by inserting the parts into the tiny little holes, applying solder without bridging the connections. Every solder connection was a potential source of trouble.

Even if you were successful in assembling the computer and didn't bridge any of the hundreds of solder points, the computer did nothing. The input was the row of switches on the front panel and the output was the row of lights just above the switches. Programming was accomplished by entering the program into memory in machine code, one byte at a time. If you wanted something that we might recognize as a computer, you were going to spend more money. You would need a memory board, a serial interface, and a Teletype terminal. If you had 4K of RAM you could run the BASIC written by Bill Gates and Paul Allen.

The typical early PC was a motherboard that the hobbyist soldered all the components onto. The front panel of the Altair used small toggle switches to program the computer in binary machine language. Ones and zeros were represented by switches "on" or "off". He would program the computer via these switches; he would then save the program he had created on an audio cassette. The avant-garde of the engineers would find a refurbished teletypewriter unit with a keyboard, printer, and a paper tape reader and punch.

Those who felt unable to put together a kit could buy an assembled Altair for $498. Waiting time, however, was much longer. The kit contained a cabinet, a transformer, switch, fuses, some rectifiers, controller chips, a group of electrolytic capacitors. The 8080 had ten times the performance of the 8008. The 8080 created the microprocessor market. The 4004 and 8008 suggested it, but the 8080 made it real. For the first time, several applications that were not possible with prior microprocessors became practical. The 8080 was immediately used in hundreds of different products. The microprocessor had come of age.

The Altair turned out to be just a box with toggle switches and rows of red LEDs (light-emitting diodes) decorating the front panel. The switches were its only input device; the LEDs were its output, glowing and darkening in patterns that showed what you had input from the switches and what the computer had done as a result. Both operated at the same simple-minded level as the computer itself, in binary numbers built up of 1s and 0s. A "1" was entered by raising a switch, a "0" by lowering it. The corresponding LEDs glowed for each "1" and darkened for each "0."A one-byte program instruction, nothing more arduous than STOP, took eight switch settings.

Computers don't communicate with terminals until a program has told them how to do it. There was a program that could be translated into binary and toggled in from the front panel. Unfortunately, well over a thousand switch-flicks were needed before the program was in the machine. Since a computer's random access memory became amnesiac the instant its power was shut off, the program had to be toggled in every time the machine was re-started. And if just one of those thousand switch-flicks went wrong, the program wouldn't run.

A shoebox-sized machine with rows of switches and blinking lights, the Altair had enough power to be potentially useful, and was designed around an expandable system that opened it up to all sorts of experiments. But it took a seasoned solderer to assemble an Altair and make it work. The front panel and central processing unit had to be carefully put together by inserting the parts into the tiny little holes, applying solder without bridging any of the connections. The CPU, front panel I/O board, and one memory board filled it completely. To add another bus board, the computer had to be completely disassembled and 100 jumper wires had to be soldered to connect the new bus board to the existing one. Then you had to install the connectors into the bus board, making 100 solder joints for each connector. Finally, you had to solder the 100 new wires to the additional bus board. For every bus extender board, you had to solder 100 wires at each end.

The front panel and central processing unit had to be carefully built by inserting the parts into tiny little holes; solder had to be applied so that it did not bridge any of the connections. It required a good deal of time, application and care to make it work. Too much heat ruined the chips; too little resulted in a cold solder joint which stifled the operation. Some would go at it night and day, seven days a week, until they collapsed with exhaustion at their workstations.

When assembled, the Altair was a blue, box-shaped machine that measured 17 inches by 18 inches by 7 inches (approximately 43 cm by 46 cm by 18 cm). There was no keyboard, video terminal, paper-tape reader, or printer. The only way to input programs was by setting switches on the front panel for each instruction, step-by-step.

Since no program was available, the hobbyist could try to write one in 8080 machine language and enter it by flipping switches on the front panel, with one flip of a switch for every binary digit. Results were indicated by a pattern of flashing neon bulbs on the front. It was not of much use, applications were very limited, but it was a computer. The challenge of hands-on experience and its unique do-it-yourself character captured the imagination. The limitations of the Altair were in fact a fabulous asset as they created the opportunity for would-be entrepreneurs to upgrade the machine and turn their hobby into a start-up business. The really avant-garde experimenter would try to plug in a refurbished teletypewriter unit with a keyboard, printer, and a paper tape reader and punch.

The Altair was the ultimate gadget, a game machine and an educational device. A tool – or a toy - to learn about computers, it forced the hobbyists to be creative. They became fascinated by their own capability of putting it together, making it follow their commands and correcting its deficiencies. It inaugurated a mass learning experience in digital electronics. This was the zero hour of something new and very big, and they wanted to be part of it. They would spend all their free time with soldering irons and wire strippers, assembling, improving and learning arcane languages, just for the pure joy of seeing their own computer work to their own commands. The game consisted in guessing which front panel light would come on and trying to flick the switch before the light went out again. This was the indication that the computer was functioning.

The Altair inspired extensive support of user groups driven by a desire of sharing technical insights, informal newsletters, commercial magazines, clubs, conventions, and retail stores. It generated a quantum leap in computing technology and started the micro-electronics revolution. Very soon, hobbyists were able to purchase off-the-shelf parts and devote their free time building a machine.

All the Altair could do was blink its lights; but just the fact that it was there turned on the computer aficionados. They wanted to see how far they could go in solving the problems involved in running their computer. Presenting their work at local computer clubs created a first marketing opportunity. This was supported by the electronics companies: larger programs would need a lot more memory to run than was normally provided with the early microcomputers like the Altair 8800, so they expected to be able to sell extra memory with a high margin of profit. They assembled a few machines which sold as fast as they could turn them out. Most nerds remained indifferent to the commercial potential of their creation. A few measured their satisfaction in dollars. The thrill of designing a new program and watching it spring to life is of a different nature than starting a small company, finding ways to expand by undercutting and outmaneuvering competitors. Hobbyist-entrepreneurs kept right on launching companies; some produced microcomputers, but most of them turned out components and add-ons like screens, keyboards, disk drives, and printers. And with an increase in the power of the early microcomputers, more machines could be sold - which increased the demand for new and better software.

The saga of the Altair is largely clouded in mystery, a mixture of fact, fiction, implausible details, false claims and unanswered questions. Most of it is based on anecdote. A web of deceit was deliberately woven around the event. As memories blur, confusion has passed into folklore and became history. How the Altair project got started is a major bone of contention. It has not been critically examined or challenged and is regarded as self-evident. The few people closely connected with it have told a different story while leaving much unsaid.

The clue to the riddle is that in May 1974, a French company demonstrated a microcomputer, the Micral, at the National Computer Conference in Chicago. It was powered by an Intel 8008 microprocessor and was selling in France with great success to government agencies and business companies. Shortly after the NCC, Les Solomon flew to Albuquerque to discuss with Ed Roberts his idea of a computer powered by a microprocessor.

He suggested that it be powered by the recently developed Intel 8080. Ed Roberts put together a computer kit which he intended to sell for about $400. It had a front panel with lights and switches and was housed in an attractive Optima cabinet to meet Art Salsberg's requirements that the computer be attractive as well as practical·

We do not know which arrangements were made, but Stan Veit who was very close to Solomon, is categorical: "The external appearance of the Altair was dictated by Popular Electronics." This leads to the reasonable conclusion that Les Solomon and Arthur Salsberg had visited the show, picked up the advertising material for the Micral and told Roberts to assemble a computer kit similar in appearance to the Micral.

Why did Salsberg and Solomon pick Ed Roberts and MITS to undertake the computer project? He had never seen the innards, less programmed, a computer. There existed no such machine and supposedly there was no market for it. No one at MITS had ever built a computer before.

In July 1974, *Radio-Electronics* magazine had published a construction article for the Mark-8 computer. It was simply titled: "Computer," with a subhead "Build the Mark-8, Your Personal Minicomputer". Anyone interested who sent in $5 received in the mail a set of instructions, tutorial experiments, schematics and diagrams containing circuit board layouts. The design was purely on paper, requiring the builder to track down and gather the various electronics parts from different sources, one at a time. Although it seemed difficult to assemble the components, about 7.500 plans were sold. The Mark-8 was the first computer built around a microprocessor to be written up in a national magazine. Converted into a kit design, it allowed expert electronics hobbyists and experimenters to test their ability.

The construction article was written by Jon Titus, a computer scientist whose PhD work had involved instrument design, computer-interface design, and software for high-speed real-time data acquisition. He used minicomputers, particularly the DEC PDP-8/L, and became adept at creating minor programs for the system. In 1973, he purchased three 8008 chips for $125 each. The 8008 contained 3,500 transistors. It provided the ability to manage alpha-numeric data. The microprocessor was the heart and soul of this novel machine and almost everything has to pass through it. He had built a working model around the new Intel 8008, a little box decorated with a bunch of toggle switches and flickering red lights. The front panel had switch controls and indicators. The switches acted as individual bits. By manipulating the switch array, he could create small programs to allow the use of a keyboard or display device.

The Mark 8 was soundly designed, but it proved too challenging a project for most people, who ran out of skill before the project was completed. The article and the idea of a small and inexpensive machine lit a fire. Newsletters and clubs sprang up where computer hobbyists began to exchange information, construction tips and ideas about improving and programming.

Solomon and Salsberg realized that something important was in the offing. Eager to trump *Radio-Electronics* and the Mark 8, they concocted a response to the Mark-8 and contacted Ed Roberts. The Micral leaflets they picked up in Chicago, the data sheets of the new 8080 sheets together with the construction plan for the Mark-8 gave them all the information they needed to tell Roberts which components should be included in the kit and how it should look.

The outer appearance - the size, the rectangular construction - of the Altair are almost identical to that of the Micral. The front panels look like twins. The difference is in the innards and the performance. The Micral had an assembler and an operating system which supported a teletype and a cassette recorder. It was battery-operated, portable, and required no maintenance. It had been installed at a number of toll gates of the French autoroutes. By January 1974, when the Altair kit was first advertised, about 1.200 Micral computers had been sold in France to public and private institutions.

The announcement of the Altair in *Popular Electronics* in January 1975 spawned the home computer revolution. In April 1972, Intel announced "a new era" in electronics. Few people gave it any attention. Computer technicians viewed Intel's ad as marketing hyperbole. In the corporate world, the advertised prophesy of a new era met with skepticism. The applications were marginal and very limited. The idea of a single-user computer seemed far-fetched.

The Altair became the stuff of high-tech dreams and opened the floodgates. But the wonder-working toy had many short-comings. The novelty wore out quickly. To do something useful with the Altair it was essential to add plug-in boards to expand it. In order to turn it into a useful tool, it needed software, and none was readily available. A program would enable users to operate the machine without having to go through a daunting series of switches. For the Altair to really become successful, it needed a language that people could use to write applications. A computer language is a set of commands a computer can recognize and to which it can respond.

THE SHAPING OF THE PERSONAL COMPUTER

When Intel's 8008 microprocessor came out, Paul Allen tried to interest Bill Gates into writing a BASIC interpreter - a translator that would convert statements from BASIC input into sequences of 8008 instructions. Gates was skeptical. The 8008 was the first 8-bit microprocessor. It had severe limitations. But he eventually agreed to lend a hand, and came up with the $360 needed to buy one.

They decided to construct an apparatus able to collect traffic flow statistics by using a sensor installed in a rubber tube strung across a highway. They figured there would be a sizable market for such a device. Allen wrote the development software, which allowed them to simulate the operation of their machine on a computer; Gates wrote the actual data-logging software the machine required. It took almost a year to complete the project. In 1972, they set up a company called Traf-O-Data. They sold a few units, but their venture was not the success they expected.

One day, walking around Boston, Paul Allen spotted the *Popular Electronics* cover featuring the Altair. He bought a copy and showed to his friend who immediately sensed a business opportunity. Allen called Roberts telling him that he had written a version of the BASIC programming language to run the Altair. Roberts suggested that he come to Albuquerque and demonstrate it. BASIC was a computer language developed at Dartmouth and released into the public domain. It was easy to learn and was widely used in commercial time-sharing systems and on minicomputers. It was possible to take bits and pieces from various dialects of different versions of BASIC and come up with a program to run on the Altair.

A Harvard sophomore, Gates was allowed to use the PDP-10 in the school's computer lab at night. He surreptitiously smuggled in his friend and programmed the PDP-10 to make it behave like the much simpler 8080 processor. Then they wrote 8080 code using the tried and true programming methods they had learned over the years. After several weeks of late-night code-writing sessions, Paul Allen flew to Albuquerque with a paper tape of the version of BASIC. Without ever having seen or touched the Altair, he entered the language program onto the machine. It took some adjustments but, to his surprise, it worked.

Roberts was still sceptical, but he hired both of them. Allen quit his job at Honeywell and was given the title of director of software development. Gates dropped out of Harvard, moved to Albuquerque and went to work as a freelance software writer.

They authorized MITS to sell BASIC software as part of the Altair kit, under license and on a royalty basis, while retaining the right to market it themselves. Gates and Roberts often clashed. Roberts was very authoritarian; while he respected Gates' technical abilities, he resented his confrontational style.

After more than two years of bickering, their relationship came to an end. Later on, when Roberts sold his company to Pertec Computer Corporation, Pertec's management expected to get the rights to BASIC. Allen and Gates disagreed. The case went to an arbitrator who decided that Microsoft was the owner of BASIC. Gates had learned a lesson he would later remember when dealing with IBM.

MITS sold about 50,000 units, most of them pre-assembled, together with keyboards and monitors. Ed Roberts was on his way to fame and fortune. He spent an increasing amount of his time trying to knock off competition instead of improving the

Altair. Inevitably, others tried their luck in this new business space. By 1976, several machines were available on the market. The most successful was the IMSAI 8080, which was very similar to the Altair but of much better design. It included a keyboard, monitor and a floppy disk controller.

When Roberts demanded that retail stores sell only his machines, they turned to competition, thereby squeezing MITS out of the market. When he saw competitors springing up all around him and when Pertec Computer offered to buy MITS, he decided to sell. Pertec paid $6 million. Having become wealthy, Roberts returned to his home state of Georgia and bought a 900-acre farm. He studied medicine and, after receiving his degree, he established himself as a medical doctor in Cochran, Georgia.

Pertec ambitioned to become a major computer company but felt the name Altair was too identified with "hobby computers." The line was discontinued, and the Altair vanished from the market. All that was left was the memory of MITS, a small hardware store owned by "the father of the microcomputer", who accidentally sparked the Personal Computer Revolution, spawned Microsoft and changed the world.

The Altair was the catalyst of an industry that transformed the global economy. A bunch of self-taught electronics wizards, learning by doing and bartering their latest strokes of genius in a world of autodidactic communalism, spawned the silicon revolution. Their labor of love caught commercial fire. Many people and many manufacturing companies got their start in computing by assembling a kit. The synergy between progress and information sharing was a key factor in the spectacular growth of the computer industry.

The Altair started a grassroots movement in the San Francisco area, an eclectic mix of computer nerds, aficionados and potential entrepreneurs. It brought into existence the Homebrew Computer Club, an extraordinary gathering of people with engineering expertise and a revolutionary spirit. They wanted to have their own machine, just the way they designed it. Many of them were to start companies which built Altair add-on devices as well as competitive machines.

They dreamed of a future when everyone could enjoy having a computer, and have fun with all the fascinating things that could be done with it. Some saw computers as a way to pull the world together; others wanted to use personal computers for political organizing. Thousands of people sank their money into learning about computers by trying to build or program them from barely adequate components. Hundreds of people attempted to produce new hardware and software. They strove to do what had never been done, to exceed their known limits and to share their success and efforts with each other, hoping that all would gain.

The technology was primitive. Being with people sharing the same interest and goal of solving a technical problem or impressing friends was a thrill in itself. Everyone picked everyone's brain. Nobody thought of protecting his intellectual property. They were not money motivated but idea motivated. They built a computer for themselves and their friends. They wrote software programs for themselves. They were fascinated by the complexity and by the challenges of problem solving. If it was going to be easy, it was no fun.

Some bought an idea and put it into production. The economic future of the technology was appreciated only by the few who ultimately created the industry. The Altair spawned a cottage industry of small companies that made machines running on programs written for the Altair; some made attachments that would plug into the various kinds of micro computersThe Homebrew Computer Club drew together the initial corps of engineers, programmers and computer fans who would launch the personal computer revolution. Among the participants were a couple of adolescents named Steve Jobs and Steve Wozniak. They bought the essential components from Intel and Microsoft and put together a computer they called Apple, Jobs' favorite fruit. Apple Computer Company was to become the fastest growing business in American history.

The microprocessor had been developed in 1972, but Intel never applied for a patent. Within a short time, its major architect, Federico Faggin founded his own company, Zilog Inc. and set out to improve on the 8080 but still maintain compatibility with it. After two years of research and experimentation, the Z80 was put on the market. It offered real improvements over the 8080 at a much lower price. It was a powerful chip that immediately became the microprocessor of choice in many applications. The Z-80 sold in huge quantities and was at the heart of most of the microcomputers of the era. More than one billion Z80s were eventually sold. The chip was in production for over twenty years. Despite its success Zilog remained a relatively small company. Faggin never managed to accumulate enough cash flow for a smooth running of his business. In 1981, Exxon Enterprises, which had supplied Faggin with venture capital, acquired Zilog. A few years later, the management team and the employees decided to buy the company back.

Many companies started producing microcontrollers and microprocessors. One of them, Motorola, was a major manufacturer of car radios and transistors. In 1974, the company launched the 6800 to compete with Intel's 8080. Much of the design was based on Intel's 8008. The most significant application of the 6800 was in automotive engine-control systems and video games.

When the personal-computing industry exploded, the pattern for its future structure was set. The industry splintered into an array of specialty companies, each focusing on a different part of the value chain: chips, disks, distribution, data-base software, customer service, and so on. As a whole, computing power fragmented, but the system proved much more efficient than integrated manufacturing. The new technology was produced and commercialized almost accidentally, but it was the initial customers - the computer fans - who shaped its development.

Their companies started and folded on a shoestring, but they kept coming and gradually established the infrastructure of the industry. By the late 1970s, the transition from mainframes to PCs created a vast new market whose access was easy and barriers to entry low. The initial catalyst was the availability of standard components, which allowed for experimentation in computer design. Most personal computers were assembled from standard off-the-shelf components, using common architectural interfaces, largely determined by Intel and Microsoft. PC makers could no longer gain an edge by virtue of design and manufacturing, as everyone had access to the same supply base and technical information. The difference among PC companies was determined increasingly by the structure of outsourcing, manufacturing and marketing skills.

To ensure competitive success in this field, the key was proprietary control over an essential component of the system. This depended on the knowledge associated with setting, maintaining and continuously upgrading a de facto market standard through improvement in product features, functionality, cost and quality. Microsoft became dominant in system software, Intel in microprocessors, Novell in network software, Sun in network hardware and software, Adobe and Hewlett-Packard in printer protocols. These companies managed to establish the codes and standards for their products as industry norms. New options emerged for outsourcing, transforming an erstwhile integrated industry into horizontally disintegrated, yet closely interacting market segments which became rapidly globalized.

Hundreds of computer hobbyists or young computer professionals started assembling personal computers all over America. Within months of its launch, the Altair 8800 was eclipsed by dozens of new brand produced by companies such as Applied Computer Technology, IMSAI, North Star, Cromemco, Vector.

Lots of "personal computers" sprang up during this time. Some were based on the Commodore 6502 which was by far the most popular; others used the Z80, Intel's 8080 or the Motorola 6800. The very first systems were all aimed at the electronics enthusiast who wanted to assemble them from a kit of parts. Thus was born a generation of computer programmers and hardware experts. [13]

UNDERSTANDING SILICON VALLEY

In April, 1977, at the First West Coast Computer Faire in San Francisco, attended by nearly 13,000 visitors, Apple and Commodore demonstrated their first computers which met with tremendous success.

The same year saw an explosion of companies producing personal computers and the introduction of a long succession of machines. Apple, Commodore and Radio Shack were the most important. Dozens of start-ups tried to define a unique combination of power, price, performance and features. Most of them disappeared almost as quickly as they rose, and only a few survived beyond the mid-1980s.

Some of the machines introduced during this period, such as Commodore's Vic-20 and 64, Atari's 400 series, and Texas Instruments' TI 99, were intended for home and hobbyist users. Tandy/Radio Shack and a host of computers that ran Digital Research's operating system CP/M were business-oriented.

Between 1975 and 1977, the microcomputer was transformed from a techie's toy to a consumer product with a useful function. Computer magazines such as *Byte* and *Popular Computing* contributed enormously to the exponential growth of the fledgling industry. They were important vehicles for selling computers by mail order. A number of computer shops such as the Byte Shop and ComputerLand were initially hobby shops full of government-surplus hardware and electronic gadgets. Within two years, ComputerLand was transformed into a nation-wide chain.

In 1976, Cray Research introduced the Cray-1, the fastest computer in the world at that time, but also the most expensive. This was probably a significant reason for its success. Customers bought it even though their problems were not vectorizable, purely for its fast performance. Whatever the reason, the Cray-1 was the first successful vector supercomputer; it created a whole new market for high-end vector machines and vectorizing compilers.

The industry exploded in 1977 when Jobs and Wozniak introduced the Apple II for $1,298. Apple II was a color computer with expansion slots and floppy drive support. It had a built-in keyboard, graphics display and BASIC; it used an audio cassette drive for storage. In 1978, Apple introduced the floppy disk drive.

Up to 1976, there were only a handful of software firms; the most popular were Microsoft's BASIC and Digital Research's CP/M. With the arrival of consumer-oriented machines, the market for "applications" software took off. There were three main markets: games, education, and business. Initially the biggest market was for games software, followed by educational programs. The first application to receive wide acceptance was the VisiCalc spreadsheet developed for Apple II by Daniel Bricklin. VisiCalc revolutionized accounting. It was a simple spreadsheet, but it allowed people to change one number in a budget and watch the effect it had on the entire budget. It was something new and valuable that could only be done with a computer. When it was launched in December 1979, VisiCalc was an overnight success. Not only was the program a breakthrough as a financial tool but its users experienced for the first time the freedom of having their own affordable machine on their desk. VisiCalc transformed the home computer into a business tool for which no prior technical training was needed. The potential of the personal computer as an office machine became clearly recognizable. More than any other development, it made the microcomputer a business tool and started the application software industry. It reduced the time to calculate financial projections from days to minutes.

Radio Shack was the first to produce a portable with a vast combination of features in battery life, weight, and price. The $800 TRS-80 Model 100 had a reflective LCD screen, supplied read only memory based applications including a text editor and a communications program, a built-in modem, non-volatile random access memory and a keyboard. Weighing under 4 lb, and with a battery life measured in weeks, the TRS-80

Model 100 became the first popular laptop, always in standby mode, ready to take notes, write a report or go online.

In the late 1970s, researchers at Xerox PARC developed the basic ideas of a graphical user interface along with all the associated innovations: the mouse, the desktop metaphor, icons, windows, menus, and so on. The concept of the Xerox Star was revolutionary, but the price tag of $50,000 made it a commercial failure. Xerox had invested in Apple, and invited Steve Jobs and his staff to a demonstration of the extraordinary features the engineers had developed. Many of the ideas were so exciting that Jobs decided to integrate them into the new Macintosh product line.

The Macintosh featured a graphical user interface (GUI) using windows, icons and a mouse, which made it relatively easy for beginners to use. Instead of a set of complex commands, all the operator had to do was to point to a selection on the menu and click a mouse button. The GUI was embedded into the operating system. Once a user became familiar with one application, it was easy to learn new applications. Launched in 1984, it was a huge success and inaugurated a new age of graphics-based applications and operating systems. The Macintosh became a paradigm for human-computer interaction.

Microcomputers were made possible by the microprocessor which permitted the miniaturization of memory circuits. The demand was immediate and overwhelming. Scores of small companies started producing computers for this new market. The first major electronics firm to manufacture and sell personal computers, Tandy Corporation introduced its model in 1977. It was popular because it could be programmed and the user was able to store information by means of a cassette tape. It soon dominated the field because of the combination of two features: a keyboard and a cathode-ray display terminal.

In 1976, Tandy designed what eventually became the TRS-80 Microcomputer System. In the first year, about 55,000 were sold. In 1980, Tandy released Model III which could be used in businesses and schools. By 1983, computers and accessories were its biggest single category of revenue. But when the company introduced the Tandy 2000 which was not IBM compatible, although considerably faster, it failed.

Commodore International was a pioneering innovator producing a series of low-cost, easy-to-use machines that introduced millions of people to the personal computer. In 1977 the company unveiled the Personal Electronic Transactor, known as the PET. Priced at $795, it immediately became a huge success. The PET featured a built-in monitor, keyboard and tape drive housed in a compact case. In 1981 Commodore introduced the VIC 20, a color computer selling for about $300. The Commodore 64 launched the following year, brought computers to the masses. Another first was the VIC 20, a stripped-down model combining a keyboard with a built-in central processing unit. Low-priced, it was an enormous success, although it often ran out of memory before users finished writing their programs.

A billion-dollar company in the early 1980s, Commodore seemed destined to dominate the global computer market. Introduced in 1985, the Amiga 1000 was the first multi-media computer. It was by far the most advanced system available for home use. It was so futuristic that nobody - including the Commodore management - really understood its potential. It was viewed as a games machine. It could display 4,096 colors, and had built-in video outputs for TVs and VCRs. The operating system included preemptive multitasking, a graphical user interface, shared libraries, messaging, scripting, and multiple simultaneous command line consoles. For nearly a decade, a combination of mismanagement and poor marketing caused Commodore's position to steadily erode. While practically all manufacturers built compatible systems, Commodore's engineers continued to devise brilliant new systems that were too expensive and did not appeal to a large public. This, combined with poorly coordinated marketing, led to the company's downfall.

Companies that once produced software for Commodore became more interested in supplying IBM and Apple. The company became marginalized, while continuing to upgrade and expand the Amiga series through the 1980s and early 1990s. Although each model had its loyal customers, Commodore lost its market share to IBM and Apple. In 1994, Commodore closed its doors forever.

In April 1981, Adam Osborne set up the Osborne Computer Corp. and launched the first commercially successful portable personal computer about the size of a suitcase. It included 64K of memory, a monochrome monitor, a keyboard and a disk drive. Collapsible, it turned itself into an easy-to-carry attaché case. The Osborne 1 computer included practically everything a business executive needed. It sold for $1,795.

It was also the first computer to be sold with bundled software packages. Until then, hardware and software companies had served the same clients but had never offered their services together. Osborne expected he could attract buyers by packaging desirable software programs, for example word processing and spreadsheets, with the computer. By September, 1981, Osborne had its first million-dollar sales month.

Over the next two years, the Osborne Computer Corporation would go from nothing to a company with $70 million in annual revenue. Several companies brought out products that duplicated or approximated Osborne's pricing, packaging, portability and software offerings. Even with all of the competition, the Osborne 1 became one of the top-selling computers, quickly reaching a peak of 10,000 units per month.

But the harsh economics of the personal computer swept computerdom. IBM and Apple became the main players, and one by one the other companies fell by the wayside. On September 13, 1983, Osborne Computer Corporation declared bankruptcy.

By mid-1981, Apple was selling 15,000 to 20,000 computers a month, ahead of Commodore, Hewlett-Packard, Tandy and Zenith. The rapid growth of the market inspired a large number of entrepreneurs to enter the field. In the mid-1980s, the introduction of a powerful 32-bit computer capable of running advanced multi-user operating systems at high speeds placed enough computing power on an office desktop to serve small businesses and most medium-sized companies.

IBM and the major computer companies were busy developing mainframes and improving computer systems for industry. They still ran vertically integrated organizations, building their own chips, circuit boards, disk drives, terminals, printers, tape drives, software, and even the boxes. Running a mainframe computer installation required systems programmers and systems analysts, operators, engineers, applications programmers. Tens of thousands of employees, dozens of plants and huge investments in research and development were involved. Every major change represented an overhaul of machinery and staff.

The IBM top management was out of touch with developments in personal computers and paralyzed by its corporate bureaucracy. They couldn't really see why people would want home computers. Mainframe computers were the market. Over the years, IBM had developed a corporate hubris and a rigid hierarchy, proud of itself and fond of rituals. Complacent executives failed to spot the significance of the personal computer, while upstart companies reinvented the industry, nimbly opening new markets. When Apple released its Apple II in 1977, IBM engineers cobbled together a comparable machine, which contained no IBM parts and ran on a Microsoft operating system. Friction between the creative individuals and the central bureaucracy grew endemic, but management backed away from destroying its existing mainframe business to build something new. [14]

The personal computer gradually pulled the plug on the foundation of IBM's hegemony. The inexpensive desktop computers were quickly becoming as powerful as the multi-million-dollar mainframes. For a time it seemed as if the company that had defined technology in the workplace for much of the 20th century was facing its most formidable challenge ever.

IBM saw its dominance threatened and was compelled to learn the new rules of the game. Management decided to take the plunge and develop an IBM PC. It had to be a state-of-the-art machine. In order to reduce development time, they decided to buy existing components. They approached Microsoft under pretense of doing a market survey. Gates and Allen wanted desperately to write the operating system, but realized that the program they had put together for the Altair would not be adequate for IBM. They began to panic, but then remembered that a Seattle hardware hacker had already built a computer using the Intel microprocessor and written his own operating system for it. They bought the operating system SCP-DOS (Disk Operating System) from Seattle Computing for $50,000. They revised it, renamed it MS-DOS and delivered it to IBM, while keeping the rights to the software.

IBM could have easily bought them out, but their decision to buy the microprocessors from Intel and the software from Microsoft came back with a vengeance. The contracts with Microsoft and Intel allowed them to sell respectively their software or microprocessors to IBM's competitors who in turn developed 'clones' based on Intel chips and Microsoft software. Thus IBM created the standard, but lost control of it.

On August 12, 1981, the computer was released as the IBM PC. In six months, IBM sold 50,000 machines, and within two years it had surpassed Apple in sales. Big Blue had put its stamp on personal computing, and personal computer became a burgeoning industry.

Technically, the IBM PC was something of a breakthrough: while previous personal computers had processors that worked with only eight bits of data at a time, the Intel 8088 chip could handle 16 bits. It accommodated four times as much memory as competing hardware. The machine was no bargain. The least expensive configuration cost $1,565. The original business plan for the PC anticipated sales of about 240,000 units over five years. In fact, sales topped that total within a year. IBM's entrance popularized the term PC and marked the transition of the computer from a novelty item to a household appliance. The IBM PC created a watershed in the computer industry.

It set the standard architecture of the desktop computer and defined its open architecture.

IBM gave the world the acronym PC which caught on as a shorthand name. By putting IBM's stamp on the concept of desktop computing, it opened the door to widespread adoption of the technology in the business world. When IBM introduced its first PC, it set the de facto standard and became the technological fountainhead for a new industry. IBM's personal computer was an open system to be licensed by any applicant. Within a short time, 200 clones poured into the market. While few of them survived, the personal computer transformed the computer industry.

The PC makers wanted to clone IBM's computer design, but they were forbidden from using IBM's proprietary RAM BIOS chip standard. The three essential building blocks of any computer are its processor, its operating system, and its BIOS (Basic Input/Output System.) The BIOS provided the communication protocols used between the operating system, the processor and the other components. IBM didn't own either the processor or the operating system inside its PC. When Compaq created its own BIOS chip that worked with IBM's BIOS standard without infringing its patent, it was the turning point that opened up the market. Consumers and businesses knew that lower-priced computers could operate identically to IBM computers, affording them the unprecedented option of buying from multiple PC vendors.

IBM transformed little-known companies - Microsoft and Intel - into billionaires and made computer hardware and software the most lucrative products in corporate America. Through the use of clever marketing, the company soon captured a large share of the market. The IBM PC had a tremendous impact on the future of the PC. For many people, even those who prided themselves on being able to operate mainframes, if IBM was making PCs then the small desk-top units were worthy of respect. IBM validated the desk-top computer as a legitimate business tool.

Now that the PC had been validated, it began to be used in the offices of large and small companies. Jim Harris and Rod Canion were among the first to seize on the idea. They founded Compaq Computer. In 1982, Compaq introduced the first IBM compatible machine. Compaq's portable almost single-handedly created the PC clone market and became Apple's major competitor. Compaq quickly gained a reputation for quality and set a record for the largest first-year sales of any American business. It reached the Fortune 500 list and surpassed $1 billion in revenue faster than any other company. Nine years after Compaq was founded, the company employed more than 10,000 people and operated in 65 countries. Many clone makers also emerged in Taiwan, Korea and Japan: Daewoo, Epson, Hyundai, Acer, and scores of smaller companies. In 1983, US firms held an estimated 88 percent of the world-wide computer market; by 1992, their share had fallen to around 56 percent. Over the same period Japanese market share in the computer industry increased from 8 percent to 30 percent.

In 1983, Apple brought out a machine that failed to sell but nonetheless showed consumers and manufacturers a new direction for the PC. The Lisa, an expensive machine with a graphical user interface (GUI), hit the market with a thud. At $10,000, it had few buyers. Immediately after the failure of Lisa, Steve Jobs rebuilt the machine and in 1984, Apple revolutionized the personal computer business with the introduction of the Macintosh. Known affectionately as Macs, the Macintosh was the first to feature a graphical user interface (GUI) that utilized windows, icons, and a mouse, thereby making it easy for most anyone to use a computer. Rather than having to learn a complex set of commands to type, a user could point to a selection on a menu and click a mouse button. Moreover, the GUI was embedded into the operating system, so that all Mac applications had a similar appearance. Once a user became familiar with one application, he or she also understood other applications. The success of the Macintosh GUI inaugurated a new age of graphics-based applications and operating systems.

The Mac was introduced to the world in an extravagant television commercial that was shown only once during half-time of the NFL Super Bowl. The commercial changed the advertising industry almost as much as the Mac changed computing. After suffering from the failure of the Apple III and Lisa, Apple was literally saved by the Mac. The GUI allowed the user to click a mouse button on an icon to launch a program, print a document, or copy a file. No longer did users have to know combinations of keys or special codes to get the computer to do what they wanted it to do. The Mac was 'user friendly.'

When Apple came out with the Apple LaserWriter in 1985, it was with Adobe Systems Inc.'s PostScript page description language and printing. Desk-top publishing was born. WYSIWYG meant that a person could format a document with special fonts and spacing and be assured that what came out of the printer would look like what had been created on the screen.

In January 1984, the introduction of Apple's Macintosh computer, with its graphical user interface, generated even more excitement than the IBM PC had three years earlier. Apple's R&D people were inspired by the concepts developed at Xerox PARC (and practiced on the Apple Lisa) but Apple programmers also added many of their own ideas to create the final polished Macintosh. It was the Macintosh that changed the way people used computers.

By 1986, IBM and Apple were the major players in the marketplace, followed by Commodore and by the Tandy Leather Company, later known as RadioShack. IBM's estimated combined PC sales were around seven million units, Apple claimed five million, Commodore four million, and RadioShack around two million. In 1986, Compaq computer beat IBM to the punch and introduced the world's first 80386-based PC, using an Intel processor which had the power and design to run a GUI-based operating system. IBM's PC sales were overtaken by clone PC sales. [15]

In 1991, IBM set up the Personal Computer Co. Small groups within the company followed each market individually and adjusted products that met those needs. IBM introduced the low-end lines of PCs, the PS/1 and the ValuePoint line, aimed at homes and small businesses. They were sold through retail outlets, superstores and by phone.

American firms excelled not only at volume manufacture but at the international transfer of technology. Coordinating technical activities with volume manufacturing across national boundaries became standard practice for the industry. By shifting assembly off-shore, American firms were able to learn the organizational technology of international co-ordination and production: research and development concentrated in the US; labor-intensive assembly in low-cost Asia; somewhat more skilled assembly activities in Singapore.

For computer customers, the late 1980s were a time of frustration. No sooner had they learned to run their new PCs and Macs than a new, better and faster model was on the shelf. New versions of software, printers, and modems made it impossible to have the latest of anything.

In the early 1990s, IBM and Apple dominated with almost one-third market share. Other big names like Compaq, Dell, AST, Packard Bell, NEC, commanded approximately 30 percent. The rest belonged to obscure clone makers. Among the Japanese companies, Toshiba was the market leader in the fastest growing segment of the industry: laptop and notebook computers.

The shake-out of the decade-old personal computer industry came earlier than expected. Starting in 1990, several companies cut prices drastically on their existing product lines while promoting lower-priced models. Personal computers had become commodity products, and price was the main force in competition in the low end of the market. In 1992, Compaq dropped its prices by up to 32 percent and entered the low-end market with an inexpensive line. This compelled other computer manufacturers to respond. In September 1992, IBM brought to the market its PS/1 line aimed at homes and small businesses. IBM and Compaq now sold at prices matching those of the nameless clones, leading consumers to move to the high-end brands.

The price war bolstered strong companies and ruined vulnerable manufacturers. PC makers competed to keep customers loyal by providing on-site service warranties, money-back warranties, technical support, toll-free telephone and fax services, bulletin boards, and forums. Smaller manufacturers could not follow suit. Companies such as Everex Systems filed for bankruptcy. Tandy Corp., one of the original personal computer pioneers, was bailed out and sold its computer operations to AST Research Inc. Apple was able to command premium prices for its Macintosh machines because their graphical interface was much easier to use. But improvements in Microsoft Windows 3.1 and the price freefall of Windows machines forced Apple to lower its price as much as 50 percent.

The computer industry has its ups and downs. In the summer of 2001, a steep downturn triggered a price war led by Dell. Margins collapsed and analysts were wondering which firm would be first to throw in the towel and quit the business. A vast number of foreign employees, mainly from India and China, were active in the industry as temporary workers; as soon as their visa expired, they were laid off. But many of them refused to go home; some found a job in one of the numerous companies founded by Americans of Asian descent; others set themselves up as consultants; some even sued their former employer for failing to help them obtain a permanent residence permit, which would have allowed them to remain unemployed without being deported.

The Information Revolution has driven the US economy and changed the world. In the early 1970s, Massachusetts' Route 128 was as well known a center of the computer industry as Silicon Valley. Both grew strong on defense contracting, but diversified into civilian production. Route 128 was dominated by a few self-contained, vertically integrated companies using proprietary systems. Silicon Valley's electronics industry was spread among many small firms, horizontally integrated companies differentiated by component. Both employed workforces of roughly equal size. Silicon Valley decisively passed Route 128 in the 1980s. Between 1975 and 1990, California generated three times as many jobs as Massachusetts. During those years, Silicon Valley-based producers exported electronics products worth more than twice as much as Route 128's.

What accounts for the comparative advantage and the difference? Silicon Valley has a regional network-based industrial system that promotes collective learning and flexible adjustment among specialist producers of related technologies. The region's dense social networks and open labor markets encourage experimentation and entrepreneurship. Companies compete intensely, while at the same time learning from one another, through informal communication and collaborative practices, about the latest development in the markets and technologies. Loosely linked team structures encourage horizontal communication within the company and with outside suppliers and customers. The PC industry is driven by rapid technological improvements in components particularly microprocessors and storage devices. It is also an industry where customers are willing to pay a premium for the latest technologies and reward quality by repeat purchases.

As computers became commonly used in the workplace, new ways to harness their potential developed. As smaller computers became more powerful, they could be linked together or networked to share memory space, software, information and communicate with each other.

The personal computer is probably the greatest disrupter of all time. Initially, it offered little in the way of performance and was ignored by the industry's established leaders until it was too late. Dismissed as a plaything, it single-handedly tore the mainstream computer industry apart, pushing even IBM to the brink. The PC is a prime example of a disruptive technology. In terms of cost, convenience and ease of use, it appealed to a different and much broader class of customers, creating wholly new markets for itself before taking on the industrial giants. In the past 60 years the computer was invented and continuously reinvented, transformed into something different: from a device that decoded military secrets or solved complex mathematical problems, into a machine for business data processing; and, more recently, into a global information and communications network.

During the late 1980s, IBM went through the most difficult and challenging period in its history. In the early 1990s, the company lost money for three consecutive years. The descent was unexpected, swift, and brutal. In 1993, 25,000 employees lost their job on top of the 40,000 in 1992, which had reduced the workforce to 300,000 from a high of 407,000 in 1986. Lou Gerstner was named CEO. Tough-minded, market-driven, he infused a sense of urgency into a company which had begun to consider aggressiveness undignified. Gerstner stopped the financial hemorrhaging. He turned a profit of $6.3 billion for the year 1998. In 2002, he turned over the reins to Sam Palmisano.

Today IBM has an impressive array of new products and its business is booming. IBM is still a powerful company: the world's largest Dram producer; it is also the world's dominant mainframe supplier; it has market leading products in minis and workstations. Thanks to an extraordinary mixture of luck and the intuition of a new boss, IBM is back as a power to be reckoned with. But the company *is* no more the computer industry. IBM went through a wrenching change, and suffered until Lou Gerstner came along. As a truly great company, IBM reemerged in a different but equally powerful form. IBM bounced back, but doesn't rule anymore. [16]

Half a century ago, a few outstanding individuals laid the groundwork for computer technology as we know it today. A few of them stand out. John Backus invented the Fortran programming language; Dan Bricklin developed the VisiCalc spreadsheet; John G. Kemeny and Thomas E. Kurz developed Basic Programming Language; Bob Metcalfe invented Ethernet; Dennis Ritchie developed the UNIX computer operating system. In France, François Gernelle and a small team of engineers built the world's first microcomputer. Unknown for more than three decades, they deserve a prominent place in the history books.

In the space of two decades, the personal computer has led a tumultuous existence. In 2001, its 20th anniversary was no occasion for celebration. The previous year, high-tech shares slumped as the bubble burst. Times were grim: the industry was suffering a serious slump. Manufacturers slashed costs and slugged it out for market share by driving prices downwards. They shed tens of thousands of jobs, and planned to cut tens of thousands more. Hewlett-Packard and Compaq merged to become by far the biggest computer manufacturer in the world. IBM was able to maintain its profitability, but Gateway suffered its third successive quarter of heavy losses. Only Dell recorded a year-on-year increase in shipments.

In 2005, IBM sold its computer division to Chinese computer maker Lenovo for $1.75 billion. It was expected to quadruple sales of Lenovo Group Ltd. Lenovo would create a company based in New York, with offices in Beijing and Raleigh, N.C. IBM had an 18.9 percent stake. Partially owned by the Chinese government, Lenovo is China's biggest computer maker. It was founded in 1984 by academics at the government-backed Chinese Academy of Sciences. Set up to distribute equipment made by IBM and other companies, by 1990 it was selling PCs under its own brand name.

The computer business is now tightly consolidated: the top five manufacturers - HP, Dell, Acer, Lenovo and Toshiba -account for more than half of world-wide PC shipments. They are the survivors of a brutal shake-out. Half a century ago, IBM sparked the computer age. Shaken and bruised for a while by a bunch of upstarts, the company had to reinvent itself in order to survive. It has again become one of the most resilient of the big computer firms, thanks mainly to the revenue it earns from consulting and services.

10

THE BEST AND THE BRIGHTEST

"America is not a land of money, but of wealth;
not a land of rich people, but of successful workers. "
Henry Ford

Having sold his company, Ed Roberts went back to his native Georgia, attended medical school and became a doctor. The Altair generated a number of clubs where electronics aficionados could talk about their new toy, swap components and programming tips. The Altair was frustrating, but it incited the fans to experiment in order to find real uses for the box by turning it from a curiosity into a useful machine.

A community spirit permeated the computer clubs. As soon as somebody solved a problem, he would proudly let it know to impress his friends. The sharing of information was a major factor in the development of the technology. Thousands of people absorbed it by osmosis. They learned in the hardest and surest way - by trying to build or program from elements that were barely adequate; by modifying the hardware, and by the kick of an incredibly thrilling experience when it worked. Most of the components were available: keyboards, screens, disk drives. It was just a matter of soldering the parts together. Two years after the appearance of the Altair, the personal computer had become a business machine.

Newly launched magazines, such as *Byte* and *Popular Computing* were the major catalysts of the new computer culture. Initially, they were the essential vehicles for selling computers by mail order. Computer shops such as the Byte Shop and ComputerLand opened all over the country. About 150 companies making computers were set up in 1982 alone; only a few survived.

It was a kind of group sport whose reward was technical achievement, not money. Companies sprang up, blundered and folded. Others kept coming, gradually creating the infrastructure for the personal computer industry. Student entrepreneurs banded together in screwdriver shops. Growing technological savvy about how computers worked and the widespread availability of technical magazines and components made it fairly easy for enterprising hobbyists to assemble a generic computer. To keep costs and prices low, they incorporated parts from low-end suppliers.

They built castles in the air, and then put foundations under them. They were fascinated by electronics and technology, and their flair turned their hobby into an industry that changed the world. They are also known for their brashness. Work and experiment were the primary forces that drove their lives, and anything that interrupted was wasteful. Among those who were present at the creation of the personal computer, a few stand out as the most brilliant and the best. Their life stories exemplify the impact one enterprising individual can have on the world.

APPLE is the stuff of legend: the first US microcomputer company was started by two high school dropouts who were passionately interested in electronics. Steve Wozniak was the technical wizard and Steve Jobs the visionary who saw computers as a business. Jobs was an adopted child grown up in a working-class family; Wozniak's father was an electronics engineer who had interested his son in computing. Jobs worked for Atari; Wozniak had a job at Hewlett-Packard.

AT&T's long-distance trunk lines had become a playground for hackers, known as phone phreaks. The two youngsters had developed a pocket-size telephone attachment that allowed the user to direct the phone company into switching calls anywhere in the world for free. A brilliant technician and an engineer with a passion for inventing electronic gadgets, Wozniak had perfected the "blue box" as it was called. Jobs had sold a few of them. One day, they decided to call the Pope; they dialed the number of the Vatican and got the call through. "This is Henry Kissinger" said Jobs, "and I'd like to speak to the Pope about the summit trip." After a while, a voice told him that he was not Henry Kissinger, and the line was cut.

Wozniak dreamed of building his own computer, and the Altair proved it was possible. For working capital, Jobs sold his Volkswagen minibus for $1,300 and Wozniak sold his programmable calculator. They named their company Apple Computer. The cost of microprocessors, memory chips and other parts having been reduced, they decided to build a prototype in Jobs' garage. The first Apple computer was cobbled together by Wozniak on a preassembled circuit board. When it was finished, he went to see his supervisor at Hewlett-Packard, but the man saw no future in the idea of a microcomputer, and pointed out incidentally that he didn't have a college degree or the formal qualifications for computer design.

Realizing that thousands of people were interested in owning a computer, but unable to put one together, Jobs and Wozniak visualized the opportunity for starting a new type of business. The problem was that they needed capital for tooling the hardware. Mike Markkula agreed to invest $250,000 in the new company and was for many years the real power behind the scenes as president and head of the board of directors. When they showed their prototype at a meeting of computer hobbyists, a local dealer saw it and ordered 50 units. About two hundred computers were built and sold over a ten-month period.

Wozniak upgraded the machine and introduced it as Apple II: a complete microcomputer with keyboard, monitor, floppy disk drive, and an operating system. Its open architecture allowed anyone to design plug-in cards, and to hook up to a TV set. The Apple II was launched at one of the West Coast's microcomputer shows. The show drew thousands of attendees and dozens of exhibitors, many of them members of the Homebrew Computer Club. Steve Jobs had negotiated a prime spot by the entrance, where he showed the Apple II. It fascinated all who saw it. Dealers and distributors were mesmerized and lined up. Priced within the reach of the enthusiast amateur, it became an instant success. The Apple II inaugurated the home computer boom. Fully assembled and pretested, it included 4K of standard memory. The price was $ 1,298, without a screen.

The Apple II was highly innovative and immensely popular with computer enthusiasts because it offered the opportunity to engage with the machine by customizing it and using it for novel applications. It did exceptionally well in the graphics industry. It also helped to demonstrate that small computers could be used as business machines. Like the Apple I, it could be connected to a domestic TV set and programs could be stored and retrieved using an ordinary cassette recorder. The two young partners turned their business from a garage-bench operation into a Fortune 500 corporation.

The Apple II was the first mass-produced microcomputer. Jobs and Wozniak developed a unique hardware and software configuration and a unique operating system and philosophy. Their machines were fully proprietary: anybody who tried to copy was sued. Business took off beyond their wildest dreams. Within a year, 50,000 units were sold. Dozens of developers began writing software for it: games, home programs, even business accounting programs. The next two years Apple's growth was explosive, with thousands of customers literally coming to the doorstep of the tiny office in Cupertino, California. By the early 1980s, Apple was one of the fastest-growing companies in the history of American business.

With its sound, graphics, and sleek design, Apple II was a technological marvel, Small and portable, it was a complete business solution. Dan Bricklin and Bob Frankston decided to use the Apple as the platform for creating a computerized electronic spreadsheet program and created VisiCalc, short for "visible calculator."

VisiCalc was a financial planning tool known as a spreadsheet. It transformed not only the fortunes of the Apple II but also the world of micro-computing by demonstrating that small desk-top computers could be powerful business machines handling stock control, word processing and payroll. The benefits of computing were no longer confined to large companies which could afford large computers. Office managers could buy an Apple II with Visicalc, bring it into their departments, and immediately increase their productivity. Budgets and forecasts that traditionally took weeks could now be done in hours. By 1980, Apple netted over $100 million and had more than 1,000 employees. The day the company went public, 4.5 million shares were sold within a few minutes. Computer companies were sprouting like mushrooms to meet the enormous demand, but Apple took 50 percent of the market and its network grew to 300 outlets. In 1980, assembly plants were established in Ireland and in the Netherlands.

Apple's hegemony, based on proprietary technology, ended when IBM entered the PC market in 1981. Within two years, IBM passed Apple in dollar sales. IBM's dominance made its operating system an industry standard which was not compatible with Apple's products. Jobs knew that in order to compete with IBM, he would have to introduce new computers that could be marketed in the business world controlled by IBM.

By 1982, more than 100 manufacturers were making personal computers. The market became saturated. Wozniak was injured in a plane crash and took a leave of absence. He returned briefly, but left definitely to become a teacher. Jobs became chairman at the age of 27, with a fortune worth $100 million. But the corporation was vulnerable; it had cutting-edge technology, but lacked business experience. Incoherent marketing strategy and a reluctance to make its peace with an IBM-dominated world led to layoffs. Another failure was the mouse-controlled Lisa. It should have been a success: Lisa was the first personal computer controlled by a mouse which gave it a user-friendly interface. But priced over $10,000, it did not sell. Apple had entered the Fortune 500, but the company came close to bankruptcy.

The entrance of IBM into the personal computer market seemed the death knell for Apple. Steve Jobs rethought the Lisa, and in 1984 he launched the Macintosh. What made the Macintosh different was the mouse developed by Douglas Englebart of the Stanford Research Institute; a point-and-click interface that replaced the cumbersome commands of MS-DOS, it offered an elegant means of interaction. Its user-friendly design had an operating system that allowed moving screen icons instead of typing instructions. The Macintosh was capable of such astounding tasks as desktop publishing and editing of sound and pictures. Part of its special quality derived from its electronic hardware; but much more of it came from the Macintosh operating system. Macs were a fairyland of pictures, animation and work tools. The Macintosh was reasonably priced and portable. The advanced graphics capabilities soon established it as the standard computer for the publishing industry.

The strength of Macintosh design was flexibility and adaptability to perform creative work. Apple was saved by Macintosh enthusiasts who loved its simplicity. They clicked a mouse button on an icon to launch a program, print a document, or copy a file. No longer was it necessary to know combinations of keys or special codes. Initial sales of the Macintosh, however, lagged far behind expectations. It was not IBM compatible, and big corporations where IBM territory.

In 1983, Jobs met John Sculley, then president of Pepsi-Cola and persuaded him to take the presidency of Apple. Sculley tried to change the discipline of the company by controlling costs, reducing overhead and rationalizing product lines. As the Macintosh took off in sales and became a big hit, Sculley felt Jobs was hurting the company, and persuaded the board to strip him of his power. Jobs decided that he would not be a part of Apple's future and resigned. What began as a three way partnership of engineering, marketing and corporate funding soon became a one-man show. In 1985, both Jobs and Wozniak were gone and actual control of Apple was in the hands of the president and the board of directors that appointed him, headed by Mike Markkula.

Jobs decided to form his own company. He sold over $20 million of his stock, and founded NeXT Software. The NeXT was his first major computer after leaving Apple. It was released in late 1989 and featured a Motorola processor, greyscale graphics and the first commercial magneto-optical drive. Unfortunately, the NeXT had critical flaws. The primary programming style was correctly chosen to be object oriented, but the primary language was a hybrid mix.

Meanwhile, Sculley had become the de facto head of Apple; but the company posted a loss and was forced to lay off a fifth of its workforce. Sculley became locked in a battle with Bill Gates over Windows 1.0. When Apple introduced two ideal tools for inexpensive publishing, the LaserWriter and the PageMaker, Macintosh became an overnight success, and put the company once more on the right track. In 1987, the Mac II, built with expandablity in mind made the Macintosh line a powerful family of computers. By 1990 the market was saturated with PC-clones, while Apple remained the only company selling Macs. Sculley lost interest in the day-to-day operations and was replaced by Michael Spindler.

Apple broke from its long-standing rule of selling only to dealers who could offer full support to customers, and allowed Mac systems to be sold through retail outlets and mail-order companies. This was a golden age for Apple; the company's revenues approached $10 billion, and it sold more than a million computers a year. But its market share kept falling despite the technological superiority of its products. Consumer sales suffered as the company discouraged game development out of fear that the Mac would not be taken seriously in the business community. Moreover, Microsoft, after an unsuccessful attempt to secure an agreement to market the Mac OS on the Intel processor, introduced Windows, its own graphical operating system. Apple litigated in vain for years to stop Microsoft from copying the 'look and feel' of its operating system.

Although he was not the right man for the job, Spindler oversaw several accomplishments. In 1994 Apple launched the PowerMac range, the first to be based on the PowerPC chip, an extremely fast processor co-developed with IBM and Motorola. The PowerPC processor surpassed in several ways the speed of Intel's processors.

But Apple's production line was disorganized. Large unsalable inventories of some models accumulated, while simultaneously huge orders for other models could not be met. Quality control problems and some highly-publicized dangerously combustible portable computers brought an end to Spindler's reign. When Microsoft launched Windows 95, which emulated the Mac GUI, Apple took its worst plunge ever. In January 1996, Spindler was told to resign as CEO and was replaced by Gilbert F. Amelio, the former president of National Semiconductor.

Amelio tried to bring Apple back to profitability, but largely without success. He split the company into seven separate divisions, each responsible for its own profit or loss. He reduced the number of Macintosh motherboard designs from five to two, and consolidated Apple's six hardware architectures into a single core Mac system. He also reorganized Apple's corporate structure into two fundamental divisions, the Macintosh group (in charge of hardware) and AppleSoft (in charge of software).

In the decade since Jobs had been ousted, the company had run into a wall about every 18 months, generating losses, inventory gluts, morale-sapping layoffs, restructurings, precipitous plunges in the value of stocks, and the firing of three CEOs. In December 1996, Apple announced that it would acquire NeXT and that Steve Jobs would return to the company he set up. Apple spent around $400 million to buy NeXT Software, hoping to fuse its powerful operating system with its flagging Macintosh software. Jobs had been serving as an advisor to Apple's executive management team several months prior to the announcement. Apple's board of directors formalized the role of Steve Jobs by naming him interim chief executive officer. A few months later, Gil Amelio resigned, following another multi-million dollar quarterly loss.

Jobs became the undisputed boss of the company. He announced a new direction for the corporation, with radical changes in the way it would design, build and sell computers. Having taken over in mid-1997, Jobs accelerated the company's restructuring. He shed several products, closed plants and cut thousands of jobs. He instilled new confidence among investors, and shares rebounded. He enlisted a new executive team of computer-industry veterans.

Historically, one of Apple's greatest weaknesses had been its supply chain because managers did a poor job of matching production to demand. Apple's huge losses could be attributed to sloppy inventory management. Part of the production was outsourced to Korea, Taiwan and Singapore. The assembly was transferred to Asia. Instead of building hundreds of thousands of computers in advance to meet a sales forecast, Apple now projected sales each week and adjusted production schedules daily. In mid-1997, the company started reducing the number of its national reseller chains, and began selling computers via the Apple Store on its Web site.[1]

It was the alliance with Microsoft that caused the real surprise. In exchange for $150 million in Apple stock, Microsoft and Apple agreed on a patent cross-license and, more importantly, on the settlement of the GUI argument. This gave Apple new life. But Jobs went further; he felt that clone vendors such as Power Computing were cutting into Apple's high-end market. He announced his intention to buy out Power Computing's MacOS license, and much of its engineering staff. Power went out of business a few months later, with Apple taking over its product support. Jobs also bought out its licenses from Motorola and IBM.

In November 1997, Apple announced a new form of retail sales, the Apple Store. It is a World-Wide-Web-based system by which customers can order Macs electronically with customizable specifications, instead of having to buy from a set range of models and subsequently add additional memory, hard drives and so on. The Apple Store was a runaway success. The first day, Apple reported half a million dollars worth of sales.

Apple holds the lead in schools, where some of the original computers sold in the late 1970s are still in use. Cost-conscious administrators have been swayed by Dell. But Apple is preparing for the day when wireless-networked laptops with Internet access will replace textbooks and chalkboards. In many schools teachers have traded in their briefcases for wireless Apple iBooks. They can grade, take attendance, and post homework on the fly; changes are immediately posted through PowerSchool on the school's Web sites.[2]

Since its nadir of the mid-1990s, Apple has been unable to regain its previously long-held five-percent of the market. A continual parade of innovative products has won the company popping eyes but has failed to increase market share. In late 2001, the industry went in the worst slump in 20 years. Apple and Dell were the only two PC companies still making money. Apple had learned to master cost control while surprising the market with stylish and useful innovations. Its new iBook was a huge success.

In 2002, Apple launched an ad campaign to turn Windows users into Mac converts by making them feel like intelligent people who have fun and are creative with computers. Jobs reshaped Apple's outlets into flashy digital playgrounds of dream machines, such as working iBooks, cameras, flat-screen monitors and iPods. Microsoft dominates corporate and home computing. Apple is the instrument of choice for writers, musicians, visual artists and publishing. Windows' domination of PCs has little to do with innovation. Microsoft excels at commercialization of the innovations of others, primarily Apple. As long as Apple keeps a step or two ahead of Microsoft it will remain the stylish innovator of computing.

Jobs and Gates both know that, for better or worse, their fates are entwined. The Mac couldn't run without Office and Internet Explorer. Graphic designers, the most ardent of Mac aficionados, write their invoices using Microsoft Word. The Mac version of Office is among Microsoft's most profitable products. Apple is Microsoft's major research and development team. Nearly every innovation pioneered by Apple has been eventually incorporated into Windows. Gates also needs Apple for political cover. They get along well in public; but both have also demonstrated a glee in stomping on each other's foot at every opportunity, shaking hands one day, trading punches the next.[3]

Jobs has made a career out of trying to stay ahead of the curve. A steady parade of new products has refurbished Apple's image as a trend-setter. His innovations filter into the rest of the PC world, eventually mutating their way into the whole industry. When he correctly judged technology and consumer taste, he grabbed a substantial share of the market. No one understands better than Jobs how to use timing, luck, and innovation to stage a comeback.

The history of Apple has been littered with brilliant innovations which were ruined by poor marketing strategies. The company's tumultuous history exemplifies the ups and downs of many Silicon Valley corporations. No other company contributed as much to get the personal computer to the public. After several years wandering in the wilderness, Apple is back. While it may never regain the influence it held in the early days of personal computing, Apple Computer is again turning out fascinating products and breaking the mold. Evidence of Apple's comeback as a major force in design was the iMac. Beyond its futuristic appearance, it represents a clean break with the past.

In five years, Jobs brought Apple back to health and turned it into a lean and mean, highly profitable computer company. Since May 2001, the company has opened retail stores in high-traffic malls across the country. For the first time in ten years, Apple has a solid look and set to make a run in a lucrative future.[4]

Jobs still indulges his obsession to fashion and market the world's most stylish and clever computers. He was worth about over a million dollars when he was twenty-three. He always claimed he is not interested in money. The 2,000 hardware and software engineers of the company he founded keep coming up with stupendous design innovations. Vice-President Phil Schiller is charged with turning Jobs's brilliant ideas into world-wide sales. The iBook is probably the most popular consumer notebook available. Jobs is still able to tantalize potential customers with visions of magical computers. Apple wants to attract people who are interested in something better and willing to try something different. Today, Apple has its best executive team ever. Jobs and Apple understand better than anyone that the difference between men and boys is the price of their toys.

COMPAQ Computer Corporation was founded in February 1982 by Rod Canion, Jim Harris and Bill Murto, three Texas Instruments engineers who had developed a disk-drive and wanted to start their own company. They presented their idea to Ben Rosen, president of a high-tech venture capital firm. Ben Rosen had made his name as an analyst at Morgan Stanley, where his electronics newsletter became the industry bible. He told them to come back in six months with something salable. When they brought him a design for an IBM PC compatible computer, he was impressed with the idea and agreed to fund the new company, with himself as chairman.

Compaq's beginning was unique; in those days, most computer companies were set up in garages. The team patiently reverse-engineered the IBM PC chip for software compatibility. It took 15 senior programmers several months and cost one million dollars. In July 1982, Compaq announced its first product, the $3,000 Compaq Portable PC, powered by an 8088 processor and sporting a single 5.25-inch disk drive and a 9-inch monitor. The main selling point was IBM compatibility. The Compaq was an instant hit. In the first year, on the strength of being exactly like IBM but a little cheaper, the company sold 47,000 computers.

Compaq went public in 1983, raising $67 million with a public offering at $11 a share. It quickly became one of the fastest-growing companies in American history. Within five years, Compaq went to a $1 billion business. The young company had a major competitive advantage: its overhead was low. By shrinking margins and expenses, Compaq could easily outsell IBM while making fabulous profits. Three years after it was founded, Compaq rose to Fortune 500 status.

One reason for its growth was its network of authorized dealers and the fact that it targeted primarily the business market. Most of its contemporaries from the early days of personal computers, companies with names like Osborne, Sinclair, Commodore, were unable to maintain themselves. Compaq lasted because Rod Canion focused on building high-quality, high-end PCs. He mastered the art of making IBM clones that were better than the original.

With Rod Canion in charge, Compaq moved to the top, and continued moving upward, because it evolved and took the industry with it. By 1991, the line that had firmly separated the home computer from the business computer was blurred and fading. One of the major problems was the dearth of new models. The company was heavily centralized, and decisions were made by consensus-building. Canion decided that smaller, separate units with their own staffs of engineers and marketers would stand a better chance. But he resisted pressure to slash overhead, and costs continued to rise.

In 1991, Rosen replaced Rod Canion by Eckhard Pfeiffer. The company had lost $70 million in the last quarter of 1991 and was preparing to lay off more than 1,400 of its 11,600 employees. Pfeiffer slashed payrolls and streamlined manufacturing. He used the savings to launch new lines of lower-priced PCs. He restructured the company into two divisions, desktops and systems, and set goals that seemed unattainable. He reduced the sales staff by one third; products were re-designed to share components, and snap-together construction was used for assembly. In one year Pfeiffer managed to restore the glitter to the company.

In 1992, Compaq introduced its first low-cost PCs. Two years after Pfeiffer took over, sales in the US had more than doubled. In 1994, Compaq became the world's leading manufacturer with a global market share of about 13 percent. Having convinced its suppliers to store their parts and components in Compaq's warehouse until needed. Pfeiffer's goal of building each computer as it was ordered became reality.

To accelerate sales to consumers and home owners, Compaq vastly increased the number of retail outlets carrying its products, including Wal-Mart and Sears. The company expanded its manufacturing in Houston and Singapore and added facilities in Brazil and China.

Compaq entered into a partnership with Mattel to develop interactive computer toys, pre-school peripherals and educational software for children, called Wonder Tools. The Wonder Tools Cruiser put children behind the wheel of a driving toy where they could interact with characters, solve puzzles and invent games. Wonder Tools Keyboard gave children a fully-functional keyboard, mouse and software designed for them to use.

In February 1996, Compaq launched its Presario home computer and the CEBus technology to automate telecommunications, entertainment, lighting, energy utilization, security, and kitchen appliance control. The Netelligent line of products included network interface controllers, repeaters and switches. The company also began shipping each of its servers with Internet capability and announced a partnership with Raptor, a software publisher that specialized in firewall security to protect servers connected to the Internet from intrusion and unauthorized access.

Present in virtually every sector associated with electronics, Pfeiffer reorganized the products into three groups: Enterprise Computing for server, network, workstation, and Internet products; PC Products for desktops, portables, and small business products; Consumer Products to develop and market its expanding array of home PC's, entertainment, and educational products.

Under Pfeiffer, Compaq became the world's most important manufacturer of PCs. The company purchased Tandem Computer, which made super-fast computers used by large companies. That was quickly followed by the purchase of Massachusetts-based Digital Equipment Corp. in a $9.6 billion deal in June 1998. Digital had been suffering through its own problems, unable to come to grips with the client-server era of computing and the rise of the PC. Compaq bought Digital largely for its services components, but the merger of the two corporate cultures proved more difficult than first thought.

Compaq again had problems adjusting to a shifting market as prices drifted ever downward, and the promised benefits of the Digital acquisition failed to materialize. Pfeiffer seemed well on his way to making good on his goal of $50 billion in sales by 2001. But Rosen felt the manufacturing costs had to be reduced, and when Pfeiffer disagreed, Rosen fired him.

After overcoming bloated PC inventories in early 1998 and completing the initial stages of acquiring Digital Equipment, Compaq management was optimistic. But in April, the company issued major first-quarter earnings warning, which Pfeiffer blamed on industry-wide PC sales slowdown. But in reality PC sales surged industry-wide. When the company's chief financial officer disclosed information about the company's financial crisis to select analysts, he was forced to resign. Compaq's board took three months to look for a new chief executive, and in April 1999, after a series of earnings disappointments, Pfeiffer was ousted and replaced by Michael Capellas.

Rosen took temporary control, and in June, Michael Capellas stepped in as chief operating officer, a few days before Compaq released second-quarter results. Capellas took over day-to-day operations and implemented broad restructuring breaking Compaq into three business areas: personal computing, enterprise computing and services.

In 2001, a world-wide slowdown in demand reduced earnings very sharply. The company reduced its staff by 4,900 employees world-wide. Compaq had superb technology and a sound foundation for developing new products, but was unable to produce and distribute them cheaply enough to compete with Dell. In June, AltaVista was sold for $2.3 billion. The move marked the first in a series of divestitures as Compaq sought to unload business units that were either loss makers or a distraction.

In September 2002, it was reported that Hewlett Packard and Compaq had agreed to merge. The two companies had held strongly to No. 2 and No. 3 positions, but needed sufficient clout to potentially unseat Dell. Hewlett-Packard was a veteran stalwart technology company, standing for first-rate products and for a company culture with an unmatched employee loyalty. Compaq carried the image of a brash Texan upstart, although the company had shed the pejorative connotations of the word "clone" as it unseated IBM in sales. Compaq was strongest in PCs; HP focused more on corporate servers and printers, which should result in stronger group performance. One acquisition rationale cited by HP executives was to acquire the heft to compete against IBM. Another was to strengthen their position vis-à-vis suppliers who often leveraged HP and Compaq against each other.

Dell was the largest and most feared company in the industry. HP and Compaq were almost clones of one another, strong in most mature and most competitive parts of the business. Cost savings would be generated by combining the companies, but much time would be consumed with integration issues.

In sharp contrast to Compaq enthusiasm for the tie-up, Hewlett-Packard shareholders - including the company's founding families - bitterly opposed the deal. Walter Hewlett, eldest son of William Hewlett, led the opposition to the merger. But the management of both HP and Compaq said the deal was essential for their survival in the personal computer industry.

After months of headlines and expensive ad campaigns about the shareholder vote, Carly Fiorina won by just three percent. The merger would result in about 15,000 layoffs. It followed one of the meanest and most expensive battles in corporate history. For a while Hewlett-Packard became the world's largest PC maker, but by mid-2003 Dell had recaptured the lead in units shipped.

The computer business is now tightly consolidated: the top five manufacturers account for more than half of worldwide PC shipments. There is not much scope for another merger on the scale of HP-Compaq. A takeover of one company by another would probably run into collision with the antitrust division of the Department of Justice.

MICHAEL DELL is the typical precocious American wunderkind and the quintessential entrepreneur. At age 12, his father asked him what he wanted to do; "compete with IBM", he replied. At age 14, his parents gave him an Apple II, which he took apart and rebuilt a number of times to check out the motherboard. At 16, he made money by selling subscriptions to a local newspaper. At the age of 19, while studying premedical at the University of Texas, he founded a company with the purpose of selling computers. Michael Dell had no capital, no experience, no image, and no product to call his own. But he had a novel idea: sell PC's directly to the final customer.

With less than $1,000, he started his business by running ads in newspapers and magazines. He bought obsolete IBM PC's from local retailers, upgraded them, and sold them as IBM clones at a 40 percent discount. He quickly realized that instead of upgrading outmoded machines, he could buy the components, assemble them and sell new computers under his name. The build-to-order and sell-direct strategy appealed to a growing number of customers and demand was astounding. Bypassing the traditional retailer, he was able to sell at lower prices, take higher margins, gauge demand more accurately, and deliver virtually custom products. Thus Dell, all by himself, revolutionized the PC industry.[5]

He dropped out of college and never earned his degree in biology. Working 18-hour days, often sleeping on a cot in his office, he set up an assembly line, and within a few months 40 people were putting together Dell computers selling at a 15 percent discount to established brands. In 1986, he began providing a one-year guarantee of free on-site service. For this, he contracted with local service providers. The company became the disruptive force that helped unhinge companies like Digital and Compaq. By the end of the year, sales reached $33 million. He never had to share profits with a venture capital partner. Wall Street took notice. In 1988, the company became a glittering Wall Street star, raising $30 million in an initial public offering.

Business grew extremely fast, and the young company showed signs of spinning out of control. Design flaws emerged in some models, and the dearth of experienced managers began to show. In 1993, Dell shifted course and began selling through retail outlets. Revenues grew rapidly, but problems arose. In the first six months of 1993, the company had a $65 million loss. Skeptics declared the Dell dream over; but the close call was transformed into a lesson on the dangers of growth at any cost.

Dell decided to withdraw from the retail market and return to his roots. He also brought in a new chief operating officer, Mort Topfer who reorganized internal operations and tightened the integration with suppliers and other business partners. Having matured, Dell decided to take the company to the next level by recruiting experienced managers to assist him in his day-to-day operations and delegating authority to them. Within 12 months the company was righted, and the following year profits climbed to $149 million.

The company's meteoric rise was due to a unique strategy modeled around a number of core elements: build-to-order manufacturing, mass customization, partnerships with suppliers, just-in-time components inventories, direct sales, market segmentation, customer service and extensive data and information sharing with both supply partners and customers. PCs are not produced for inventory; the incoming orders are directed to the nearest factory and built to match customer specifications. The distribution system allows the order to be shipped within a matter of days. The customer pays for the finished product weeks before Dell pays its suppliers. PCs are built from standard components, using common architectural interfaces determined largely by Intel and Microsoft.

The company has long-term contracts with top-class suppliers and stays with them as long as they maintain their leadership in technology, performance, and quality. Most suppliers have plants or distribution centers within a few miles of Dell's assembly plants. After an order is received, Dell notifies each supplier about the components needed; delivery takes place within an hour and a half. The process is called "pull to order". Once the parts are delivered, the assembly line can begin preparing components, and assemble the computer. Dell is able to achieve a four-hour production cycle time and generally fulfils customer demands within five days. The Texas assembly plant can deliver daily or even hourly if needed.

Selling PC's directly to the final customer and building them only when an order was received enabled him to know the ultimate user and to provide better service. Direct sales and build-to-order production are simple concepts, but execution is very complex. Each order must meet customer specifications, a process that puts heavy demands on shop floor employees, suppliers, logistical systems, and information systems.

The just-in-time method demands a very disciplined assembly-line process. Delays or errors in the delivery of components can be costly; if a part isn't there, production stops. With thousands of phone and fax orders daily, and close contacts between the field sales force and customers, the company is able to detect shifts in sales trends and any problem with its products. Dell's ability to respond quickly gave it a significant advantage over competition. About 90 percent of Dell's sales are to business or government institutions, and to large corporate customers who buy hundreds of units at a time.

Michael Dell serves as chairman and chief executive officer. The company has sales offices around the world, and approximately 33,000 employees. Dell is acknowledged as the largest online commercial seller of computer systems, with $50 million per day in online sales. The company has been included on Fortune's list of most admired companies since 1995, ranking No. 3 in 2000. In 1998, *Business Week* named Dell the best performing information-technology company. The value of Dell's stock has risen nearly 50.000 percent over the past decade, and in 1999, *The Wall Street Journal* named Dell No. 1 in total return to investors over the past three, five and ten years.

Dell Computer's direct sales strategy has even taken root in China, paving the way for the company to win a piece of the country's booming personal computer market. With a manufacturing and sales force in nine Chinese cities, Dell has replicated its strategy of targeting multinational corporations and government enterprises as prime customers.[6] Dell is Ireland's largest multinational employer. More than 4,000 people are employed in Limerick and Bray. From its factories in Ireland, Dell supplies the European, Middle East and African markets.

Dell spends little on research - about $250 million annually - 1.5 percent of revenues. Research and development concentrates on sorting out new technology coming into the marketplace in order to determine whether, when, and how to incorporate it into new products. The company's R&D unit also studies and implements ways to control quality and to streamline the assembly process: improve product quality and reliability from components through finished product; reduce cost throughout the value chain and improve the speed of assembly, repair, and servicing; on listening carefully to customers' needs and problems incorporating the latest and best technologies, on making products easier to use, and devising ways to keep costs down.

Dell was the first PC maker to sell online. About 50 percent of the company's sales are made this way. Suppliers are plugged directly into its customer database, so they will instantly know about any changes in demand. Customers are plugged into its supply chain via its website, which enables them to track the progress of their order, making inquiries unnecessary. This helps the supplier to better manage its inventory and avoids missing out on sales opportunities. It also achieves virtual integration with suppliers and customers by real-time information sharing. The company has thus extended its reach to millions of potential customers at low marginal cost through the use of the Internet. Other direct sellers such as Gateway and Micron have not come close to Dell's performance. Execution is the key factor in differentiating companies with similar business models.

With operations in 12 Asian countries and customers in two dozen others, Dell's Asian revenues are growing at 50 percent a year; profit margins are approaching those of other regions.[7] Dell makes PCs for the Japanese market at a factory in the south-eastern Chinese city of Xiamen. Japanese companies are compelled to move part of their production to China. For the Chinese market, Dell has developed a PC called Su Ma, which means Speedy Horse. There is plenty of room to grow in Asia. The region generates only $3 billion of Dell's global sales of $31.2 billion.[8]

In 2001, when the downturn in the computer market gained momentum, Dell started a price war, because he knew he could survive longer than anybody else. The brutal reality became apparent almost immediately, when he made a profit in the first quarter and all his competitors lost money. His price-war timing is particularly clever. Competitors are well aware of Dell's strategy. They have yet to catch up in terms of operating efficiency.

Like a living organism, Dell is constantly adapting and changing in search of ways to master its environment. The company has retained its start-up mindset. Deliberately and decisively anti-hierarchical, there are no fancy corporate offices. Employees thrive on change, on creative thinking in combination with hard work and determination. Despite its growth, it has remained obsessively focused on execution. Dell's secret is simply managerial brilliance.

Dell acknowledges that he is not in computer technology at all, but in distribution and marketing. He is set up to excel in two areas: handling orders and queries from customers, while providing an endless supply of new models and options. Dell does no real manufacturing - only final assembly and testing. And in many cases, it doesn't even design the machines it sells: Dell engineers, using input from a vast customer base, create specifications for new computers and hire subcontractors to build them.

Ever since he hit the computer scene, Dell has shaken up the whole industry by taking efficiency to new highs, squeezing every last cent out of the cost of building and selling PCs. His competitors have struggled to keep up, but he remains the undisputed low-cost leader.

Dell is a tough boss. When top managers in Europe didn't deliver big market-share gains, they were shown the door. In less than 20 years, Michael Dell amassed a personal fortune of $16 billion and built a $25 billion company. His build-to-order model has blossomed into a new manufacturing paradigm. The priced-to-move strategy cuts deep into profit margins. The discounting cuts profits for competitors who can't afford a long price war, giving Dell a chance to gain even more market share. The low-cost producer may be the ultimate winner.

MARC ANDREESSEN is a cyberspace folk hero whose programming savvy made the resources of the World Wide Web available to anyone with a computer and a modem. He is the visionary whose dream of creating an easy-to-use Web browser revolutionized information technology, sparked the Internet boom of the 1990s and laid the groundwork for one of the fastest-growing companies in US history.

The Internet has produced a communications miracle that could not have been programmed. The seeds were planted by the US government in the wake of a nationwide concern over the Soviet Union's Sputnik, long-range bombers and atomic bombs. The Pentagon needed a secret and reliable interactive communication link, able to resist interruptions caused by a nuclear attack. The government also wanted to promote the sharing of super-computers amongst researchers working on military contracts. Developed for the Department of Defense, ARPAnet was a communications network which allowed computers to exchange military and national security data by using existing telephone lines. ARPA stands for the Advanced Research Projects Agency, a branch of the military that developed top secret systems and weapons during the Cold War.

The network was assumed to be vulnerable, and was designed to transcend its own unreliability. To send a message on the network, a computer broke its data into IP (Internet Protocol) packets, like individually addressed digital envelopes. TCP (Transmission Control Protocol) making sure the packets were delivered from client to server and reassembled in the right order.

The messages were divided into packets, each packet separately addressed and able to wind its way throughout the network, moving from node to node until it ended up at its proper destination. The messages were put into an electronic "envelope" of a computer to be addressed to another computer. The method of packaging and shipping electronic messages became known as the Internet Protocol or IP.

In the following years, the use of networks spread from defense research to general scientific and academic use. Universities and research groups developed in-house networks known as Local Area Networks. With IP software a LAN could connect with other LANs. It was fairly easy to link one of these computers to the other. Since the software was public-domain and the technology was decentralized, anyone could barge in and link up.

Word of its existence came to be known by academics; soon hundreds of universities and research labs were using it to communicate with colleagues around the world. During the 1980s personal computers had become affordable, and modems allowed them to be connected up over telephone lines to commercial "on-line" services and "bulletin boards". Networking became a tool for expanding information access to the research community. Large corporations also began to use the Internet to communicate with each other and the customers. In the early 1990s, the Internet's pace of growth was spectacular mainly because it was also a bargain. The ARPANET became a high-speed digital post office as people used it to collaborate on research projects.

It was Tim Berners-Lee who laid the groundwork for the Web. A British physicist working in Geneva, at the physics research laboratory CERN, during the 1980s, he felt the need for a central database where scientists could place and find information on the Internet. He had always been interested in programs that dealt with information in a "brainlike" way. He wanted a clearinghouse for scientists to share information, while he and his colleagues were working in diverse international environments.

He designed an addressing system that gave each web page its own tag or URL (universal resource locator). He also worked out a set of rules called HTTP (hypertext transfer protocol), that would allow files to be exchanged across the Internet. He even constructed the first browser. The system, known as HTML (hypertext mark-up language), became the web's lingua franca.

Acting as pitchman, he convinced a number of people to adopt the standards he developed. CERN released the basic Web code and protocols into the public domain, and released them via the Internet for free. It became soon apparent that HTML documents were an ideal medium for publishing and annotating scientific papers, research materials, reference works, and the like. Within months, there were literally millions of Web documents, but no simple way to find and view them.

Berners-Lee had devised the hyperlink system of document linkage and access; but the problem remained how to hook up and standardize the numerous proprietary networks competing for corporate and consumer business. He was hailed by Time magazine as one of the 100 greatest minds of the century.

In 1993, Marc Andreessen, a 21-year-old undergraduate at the University of Illinois came upon the idea of combining the existing Internet framework with the multimedia applications made available by the World Wide Web. He had discovered programming at age 12. Recuperating from an operation, he persuaded his parents to buy a computer. He taught himself Basic by reading books at the local library. By the time he'd reached sixth grade, Andreessen had created a virtual calculator to do his math homework. By the seventh grade, he was writing his own games and playing them on the family computer.

At the University of Illinois, he got a programming job which earned him $6.85 an hour. Most of the browsers available then were very expensive. Used mainly by engineers and academics who had access to Unix machines, they required practice and experience.

With his friend Eric Bina he created a prototype for the Mosaic browser that was simple to install and use. Bina had undergraduate and master's degrees in computer science. The two wrote Mosaic at night and on weekends. Bina was the master programmer, while Andreessen played team leader, bringing in other programmers to write their own version of Mosaic. It was much more sophisticated graphically than other browsers. Mosaic could not only track down HTML documents on the Net, but also display them in a consistent way. The Mosaic browser allowed users to travel through the world of electronic information, by using a point-and-click interface, and to load their own documents onto the Net. Mosaic offered an easy to use point and click method of navigating the Internet. It was an instant success.

Suddenly the World Wide Web was accessible to everyone. Andreessen expected that it would spread quickly as free-ware on the Internet. The idea was simple: link up existing networks and let anyone use them for free. There would be no central computer, no master plan and no company to run the system.

The graphical interface opened up the Internet to novice users. It exploded as people were allowed to 'dial-in' to the

Internet using their computer at home and a modem to ring up an ISP - Internet Service Provider - to get their connection. Millions of copies were downloaded by users all over the world. By adding pictures, sound and video, navigation was made easier.

The Internet developed on the principle that it would be owned and controlled by nobody, and cost next to nothing to use. Andreessen headed for Silicon Valley to write programs for Enterprise Integration Technologies. There he received an e-mail message from Jim Clark, who had recently left Silicon Graphics after losing a fight over the direction the company he had co-founded. Clark's story is an American classic: a high school dropout, he got a PhD in the then-new discipline of computer science. He had developed a computer chip called the Geometry Engine, which enabled the user to produce computer-generated three-dimensional graphics. Clark wanted to create software for interactive television, and he thought the browser might serve as the interface. But as Andreessen explained the World Wide Web to him, Clark decided they should focus instead on browsers and servers for the Internet.

They decided to start a company together. Andreessen recruited a number of people from NCSA that had helped him create the first browser. Clark contacted a venture capital firm which readily agreed to back the fledgling company. In April 1994, Mosaic Communications Corporation was founded with seven people on the payroll. After a property rights battle with NCSA, the name was changed to Netscape.

Netscape launched the Navigator browser, a program permitting anybody to browse on the Internet. The company dug no trenches and laid no telephone lines; it simply leased the existing world-wide cable networks, becoming automatically and overnight a global network. Netscape Navigator, the first commercial Web browser set off the Internet frenzy.

Netscape's revolutionary Web navigation technology allowed users to experience the Net as pictures, texts and sounds with a click of a button rather than having to enter arcane programming codes. Clark became chairman; Andreessen became vice president of technology, and James Barksdale became its CEO and president.

They decided the browser would be free for students and educators, while everybody else would pay $39. In fact, nearly everyone had free access. Andreessen did not worry much about selling the browser. He expected to make money by selling advertising.

At a trade show in December 1994, people crowded around Netscape's flashy booth and around the 23-year-old programming star. When the company went public in 1995, after less than two years in operation it was still far from posting any profits. In August of 1995, sixteen months after it was formed, Netscape became a publicly traded company. The initial public offering was five million shares for $28 per share, but trading opened the first day at $71. When the stock market closed, Andreessen, then just 23, was worth $58 million. By December, the value of his stock had risen to $174 million. By 1996, Netscape had 80 percent of the market and a value of $6 billion. At 24, Andreessen appeared - barefoot and wearing a crown - on the cover of *Time*. He had transformed his programming project at the University of Illinois into a multi-million-dollar company that challenged the world's software giants.

The number of Netscape personnel grew dramatically. In June, 1994, Netscape's development group comprised about 25 individuals. By December 31, 1994, Netscape employed 115 people. By the time of its initial public offering in August, 1995 the company numbered 257 employees and the number grew to 1.400 by mid-1996. Early in 1997, Netscape had expanded to nearly 2,000 employees.

In 1995, Bill Gates set out to rule the Internet. He launched Windows 95 with a web browser, Internet Explorer. Since the browser was free of charge, Microsoft gained a major advantage over Netscape. The strategy worked so well that it threatened to level Netscape, unable to mount a convincing counterattack. From then on, the two companies tried to outdo each other by releasing a better version. Gradually Internet Explorer gained market share and also caught up technologically. Netscape's market share diminished from its once-towering percentages. In January 1998, Netscape announced that its browser would thereafter be free, and that the development of the browser would move to an open-source process.

Netscape's dominance in web browsers prompted a vicious and victorious counter-attack from Microsoft. With this aggressive marketing strategy, Microsoft gained ground on Netscape, forcing the smaller company to also start giving away its browser. The confrontation between Microsoft and Netscape not only drained Netscape of a revenue stream from its browser, but also led to sagging morale. The release of Windows 98 in June 1998 with the Microsoft browser well integrated into the desktop showed Bill Gates' determination to capitalize on the enormous growth of the Internet.

Quality problems had crept into Netscape's new products. Through most of Netscape's early days, Andreessen occupied the relatively insulated and cushy post of chief technology officer. But as troubles mounted, Andreessen was promoted to executive vice-president in charge of a 1,000-person product-development group. The move gave him a crucial role in the company's battle for survival.

As the company's CTO and resident visionary, he felt sidelined by his absence of direct management responsibilities. Andreessen was no longer the programming wunderkind. He had to learn how quickly fortunes can change in a cut-throat industry and needed to prove himself all over again as a market-savvy manager capable of making the right product choices for Netscape to regain momentum.

As Netscape lost its market dominance, Andreessen faded into the background, and Barksdale emerged as the driving force of the company. He brokered a deal with AOL in 1998 to sell Netscape for $4.2 billion. Under the terms of the buyout, Andreessen was named chief technology officer of AOL, the world's biggest Internet-access provider. Andreessen stayed on at AOL for a few months; but in September 1999 he left, along with three other Netscape veterans.[9] By the age of 28, he had suffered slings and arrows and made a fortune. His glory days had been brief; but, as usual, he was restless and itching to jump into another ambitious undertaking.

The legacy of Marc Andreessen is firmly entrenched in the annals of online history. He set the standard for Internet browsers, providing an "on-ramp" to the Web for computer users and changing the way millions of people access and use the Internet, while paving the way for e-business and e-commerce. He brought the World Wide Web to the masses, but became involved in a battle over market share against Microsoft, and lost.

LARRY ELLISON is undoubtedly the most controversial chief executive in the high-tech industry. The flamboyant chairman and CEO of Oracle, he is one of the richest men in the world. His software is the core of operations in corporate America and around the world. Born to an unwed mother who abandoned him to her relatives, Ellison has never known his father and met his mother only once. He attended the University of Illinois and the University of Chicago, but was not a great student and quit.

In 1977, he went to San Francisco and worked in several high-tech companies. He met Bob Miner and Ed Oates who had acquired experience designing customized database programs for government agencies. They had set up a company called Software Development Laboratories to commercialize the relational database language SQL (Structured Query Language) developed by IBM. Ellison joined the company and became the driving force. In 1979, the company changed its name to Relational Software Inc., and released the first version of Oracle.

A database is a collection of information organized in such a way that a computer program can easily detect desired pieces of data. To access data, a database management system is needed. Databases existed, but they were static and could not interact with each other. They depended on a team of programmers to extract meaningful information.

In 1970, while routinely scanning the IBM Journal of Research and Development, Ellison discovered a research paper that described a working prototype for a relational database management system. It allowed people to analyze, rather than just store, computer information. It was the first relational database which allowed different types of computers from different manufacturers to work together. He realized there was tremendous business potential in the relational database model which had been overlooked by IBM. Ellison picked up the idea to exploit its potential in the emerging market for UNIX systems.

Sales grew gradually and the company was renamed Oracle. By 1982, annual revenues amounted to nearly $2.5 million. In 1986, Oracle made its first public stock offering, selling one million common shares. Oracle's customer base included 2,000 major international firms operating in such fields as aerospace, automotive, pharmaceutical and computer manufacturing industries, as well as a variety of government organizations. Under Oracle's system, computer users could access data stored on a network of computers in the same way and with the same ease as if all a network's information were stored on one computer.

In 1987, Oracle established the VAR (Value-Added Reseller) Alliance Program, aimed at building co-operative selling and product-planning alliances with other software manufacturers. Most hardware manufacturers broadly accepted its database product standard. In 1988, it introduced a line of accounting programs for corporate bookkeeping. That same year the company introduced its Oracle Transaction Process Subsystem (TPS) and opened up a new market niche for the company, targeting customers such as banks that needed software to process large numbers of financial transactions in a short period of time. The same year, Oracle unveiled its initial family of computer-aided systems engineering (CASE) application development tools.

Oracle kept doubling its size every year during the 1980s to become a $970 million company by 1990. But sloppy accounting and a general plateau in database sales caused a series of revenue shortfalls. Ellison fired several top managers and brought in people who knew how to run a billion-dollar company. Oracle once more became a lucrative consulting business.

Oracle's traditional rivals, Sybase and Informix, gradually dropped back in market share. Microsoft, whose enormous resources enabled it to absorb the cost of pricing its own database programs below its competitors, was positioning its SQL Server database to eventually compete head on with Oracle.

Oracle provides services that offer a range of programs, enabling customers to select whatever matches their requirements for on-site, telephone, and electronic support. The value Oracle delivers is mainly from its Internet-enabled applications which help customers reduce operating cost, improve information access and accuracy, integrate resources easily, increase future productivity and create competitive advantage. These are advantages its customers are willing to pay for. The subscription-based model charges a monthly fee based on the number of users and selected application services.

Currently, Oracle is the world's second-largest software maker. The company owns 40 percent of the market share in database software industry compared to IBM's 18 percent in 2000. Virtually all major electronic-commerce sites use the Oracle software. It allows them to take various segments of their operations and streamline them by sifting through the sales, financial, and customer data, and then distributing them to managers and employees in usable packages. Thanks to the Internet, salespeople on the road have access to the corporate data.

In 2001, the group recorded a profit margin of 44 percent, despite the downturn. Larry Ellison predicted further casualties in the software sector. BEA Systems and Siebel looked particularly vulnerable to him. He expects his own company, IBM and Microsoft to ultimately control the market.[10]

Oracle and Microsoft are placing their bets on different computing trends. Oracle foresees thick servers and thin client models, while Microsoft predicts more of a balance in the client/server computing power. Future computing trends could determine which software company will dominate the market.

The corporate-software market totals $50 billion. For every Oracle product, IBM has a counterpunch: but the companies' philosophies are very different. Oracle offers its customers a package of software with everything a company needs to manage its financials, manufacturing, sales force, logistics, e-commerce, and suppliers. IBM stitches together a quilt of business software from various companies, including itself. Ellison has predicted that within a few years most PCs will handled at the server level, while Gates insists that computer manufacturers should move devices away from the increasing "master-slave" relationship between servers and PCs.

Today, Oracle's 74,000 employees serve more than 275,000 customers in over 145 countries. The expenditure for research amounts to about 13 percent of revenue. Oracle sells very expensive database software products, while Microsoft's is inexpensive. Oracle is second only to Microsoft, but is first in supplying databases to governments and big companies. Ellison claims that Oracle will soon supplant Microsoft as the world's dominant software company. If that occurs, he may supplant Bill Gates as the richest man in the world.

For years, the two top software firms were fierce rivals. Oracle, for example, supported a US government antitrust suit against Microsoft. But in May 2004, Microsoft and Oracle announced a software development agreement, signaling an improved relationship. The accord would enable software developers to work with Microsoft's tools to write programs for Oracle's databases.

GATEWAY is **A** struggling computer maker. Founder and chairman Ted Waitt dropped out of college to go to work for a computer retailer in Des Moines, Iowa. After nine months, he quit to form his own company. Operating out of a barn on his father's cattle ranch, he sold add-on parts by phone for

Texas Instruments PCs. In 1987, using his own PC design, he started selling fully-equipped PCs at a price lower than other PC makers. Sales took off, and Gateway became one of the nation's fastest growing private enterprises.

Gateway went public in 1993, achieving sales of $1.7 billion and earnings of $151 million. Like Dell, Gateway built to order and sold direct over the telephone. But its market strengths were concentrated in home users, small businesses and schools, where it outsold Dell. It was the market leader in the education segment. At the beginning of 1997, Gateway's consumer line of desktop PCs was priced on average 12 percent below comparable Dell consumer models. One of Gateway's strategies to boost profit margins was to strengthen its appeal to medium-sized and large corporations.

Over the years, the company offered a comprehensive range of technology products and solutions to consumers and businesses through about 300 stores. Gateway stores, introduced in 1996, are a unique blend of product showroom, personalized service center and learning facility to demystify the technology. Most of the Gateway stores offer not only the latest technology solutions and services, but also broadband Internet access, in-home wireless network installation and other services. People can come to try out new technology in a relaxed setting, participate in free learning clinics, get free advice and access the Internet at broadband speed. Customers are attracted to Gateway's 90-day same-as-cash plan. No payment is due for three months. Pay in full before 90 days, and avoid a finance charge.

Gateway ranked number one in US consumer PC revenue in the second and third quarters of 1999 and was rated among the top ten best corporate reputations in America. In early 1999, Ted Waitt resigned, but he returned in January 2001, to implement a new strategy of lowering prices in order to increase volume. In December 2001, Gateway delivered its 25 millionth PC. In 2001, sales declined 36 percent to $6.1 billion. Gateway keeps computers on hand for walk-in customers, and has not learned to move its products quickly. In an industry where goods left on the shelf lose up to two percent of their value each week, this represents a big handicap.

In 2002, Gateway forecasted a loss of $200 million to $250 million. With more than $1 billion in cash reserves, the company can survive for quite some time, even if revenues slide. Because of its expensive stores, it is an unlikely target for takeover. Waitt is trying to transform the company into a branded integrator. The PC will remain the most important part of the business, but he wants to add other product lines. The PC business moves very rapidly whereas consumer electronics tends to have longer product life cycles and not as much change.

At Gateway's annual shareholder meeting on May 20, 2004, it looked as if Wall Street had left the struggling PC maker for dead After two years of losses, a risky merger with rival eMachines, and a subsequent shutdown of all Gateway Country stores, the future of the company seemed uncertain.[11]

In April 2005 Microsoft and Gateway agreed to cooperate. The agreement provided for periodic Microsoft payments to Gateway totalling $150 million over four years. The funds will be used to market, develop and test new Gateway products that can run Microsoft software. In exchange, Gateway dropped all antitrust claims against the software giant. Gateway's claims arose from the government's antitrust suit against Microsoft in the mid-1990s. Gateway had been identified by a federal judge as being hurt by Microsoft.

These men and many others have turned the computer into the quintessence of the American Dream. They are visionaries, dealmakers, and rip-roaring capitalists. Some have a Ph.D. while others dropped out of college. Some created stunning technologies; others just seized the opportunities thus created, or picked up a concept and improved upon it. They work with each other and compete with each other, creating a synergy with exponential effect. They thrive on risk, on ideas that go from dream to reality, and on inventions. Most of them suffered setbacks and self-doubt. Throughout America there are plenty of young, smart and ambitious entrepreneurs who, with perseverance and luck, could become the future golden boys of computing history.

11

WINTEL POWER

*"The balance between American and Japanese producers
now depends on their relative capacity to endure pain."*
Andy Grove

In 1980, IBM brought together Intel and Microsoft and established the IBM PC standard. Intel supplied the chip and Microsoft the word processing program. Microsoft was then three dozen people and Intel several thousand. From that accident has arisen a remarkable domination of their respective sectors. At the time, IBM had a 20 percent stake in Intel. If it still owned the shares today, Big Blue's market value would be substantially greater than it is. Gates proposed that IBM buy 30 percent of Microsoft, but was turned down.

Intel and Microsoft define the technological parameters of the industry. They have established a standard-based quasi-monopoly by running a treadmill of product obsolescence and upgrades. They keep their dominance, while making a graceful transition from one standard to another. Both have developed enormous strengths, including superb technology laboratories, and enough cash to acquire any hot company that has hit upon the latest thing they wish they had discovered on their own. Wintel - a concatenation of Windows and Intel - is at the heart of the computer universe and has a tollbooth on the world's information highways. The two companies operate in tandem, consolidating their position as leaders of the computer industry and as the most unusual and lucrative business relationship in American history.

Microsoft's operating system and Intel's microprocessors run close to 90 percent of the world's PCs. The two companies co-operate to assure technical compatibility. They are defining examples of companies whose complementarity and mutual dependence makes them unique. It is the interface between the application program and the underlying operating system which constitutes the standard. Chips and software must be compatible to deliver a useful result, and they know more about each other than any potential competitor.

What Microsoft is to software, Intel is to hardware. The two firms' core products control the two most fundamental technologies that make PCs work, and account for the largest chunk of the cost of most personal computers. They make the rules, and the rest of the world adapts to them. They have developed a choke hold and an extraordinary grip on the market. Practical monopoly rewards them for past effort and risk. A key to their rapport is constructive confrontation. Even though they have been locked in this symbiotic relationship, the partners in the Wintel marriage often find themselves pursuing different business interests.

The duopoly occasionally hits a rough patch, when one deals with the other's competitors. But they are staying together for the sake of the hundreds of millions of PCs based on Intel chips that run Microsoft software. Squabbles in the partnership are public knowledge. In early 1995, a rift arose over software developed by Intel known as NSP. Intel publicly declared that NSP would boost the popularity of PCs by improving their video and audio performance. Gates estimated that NSP intruded into Microsoft's operating system domain and advised PC makers not to use Intel's NSP. Microsoft's pressure tactics won the day: by the time Microsoft released Windows 95, Intel had abandoned NSP as a platform-level technology. The Wintel family feud intermittently heats up; for example, when

Intel publicly supported Linux, an operating system that takes up the challenge against Microsoft's Windows NT; or when Andy Grove praised the innovations in Apple Computer's iMac home computer.

Competitors complain that both companies abuse their near-monopolies. The US government has filed an anti-trust lawsuit against Microsoft and against Intel alleging that they use their grip on the market to choke off rivals. But the unifying technology standards they developed have been beneficial to consumers, and have helped spread PCs world-wide.

Intel's biggest rival is Advanced Micro Devices (AMD). Other chip manufacturers, National Semiconductor and Cyrix have also made inroads. Microsoft is facing increasing competition from Linux. Even though Intel and Microsoft face very similar challenges of extending their dominance of the PC into new spheres, their strategies differ markedly.

Both have unmatched power over the direction of the PC industry as well as unmatchable financial resources. They keep accumulating money by making computers work better. We wouldn't have had the World Wide Web phenomenon if Microsoft hadn't standardized, evangelized and engineered the PC into ubiquity. Gates' Microsoft popularized computing and brought brain power to the world. Their dominance helps maintain a certain order and structure in an otherwise chaotic industry. They dominate PCs, but they cannot be certain that PCs will be the salient choke point in the future as Internet access moves onto portable devices, and all manner of every-day objects get connected to the Net.

The relationship between Microsoft and Intel is not entirely symbiotic. Although they are the foundation of the personal computer, each company views the world from a different perspective. Microsoft is happy to see Intel's competitors challenge the market leader. If chip prices are driven down, more people will buy computers with Microsoft's software. Similarly, if the freely available Linux operating system becomes more widely available, Intel can sell more chips.

Software is a somewhat easier business to enter than semiconductors. All it takes is a PC and programming skills. In contrast, making world-class microprocessors is a multibillion-dollar proposition. The Next Big Thing, however, may be created by another whiz kid, inventing an unexpected technology that nobody in the industry has yet heard of.

INTEL INSIDE. In 1968, Bob Noyce resigned as head of Fairchild Semiconductor; Gordon Moore went along with him. Noyce had developed the integrated circuit, while Moore was regarded as one of the great chemists in the emerging field of solid state electronics. They were frustrated, and wanted "to regain the satisfaction of research and development in a small, growing company." Andrew Grove and five other Fairchild engineers joined them. Grove took responsibility for building the organization, and largely shaped the culture of the company. Born in Budapest in 1936, András Gróf escaped to Austria after the Russian army invaded Hungary in 1956. He sailed to New York, moved in with an uncle, changed his name to Andrew S. Grove and enrolled at City College of New York, where he received a degree in chemical engineering. During summer he worked as a busboy. A brilliant student, he earned a PhD at the University of California.

Grove was trained as a fluid dynamicist. His first assignment at Fairchild had been to work in materials chemistry. He set out to make silicon usable, and discovered that when sodium was introduced into the chips, it soured the semiconductors. The discovery solved a fundamental problem in materials science and set the stage for the semiconductor revolution. Noyce contacted venture capitalist Arthur Rock and told him what he wanted to do. Even before the company had a written business plan, Rock raised $2.5 million on the telephone in two days.

They named the company Integrated Electronics, which was soon shortened to Intel. Work started in an unoccupied concrete building. Research concentrated on data storage, the most unexplored area of computer technology. Magnetic core memory had supplanted the vacuum tube and had been for over two decades the dominant computer storage technology, but its performances were very limited. The first year was devoted almost exclusively to research; sales totaled $2,672 and the workforce numbered 42. Within two years, they developed a semiconductor memory chip containing 4,000 transistors. Demand was immediate and overwhelming. Intel was able to set prices based upon demand rather than costs. In 1970, sales totaled $4.2 million, and more than doubled the following year.

The production line consisted of rows of women sitting at tables in an air-conditioned cube of vinyl tiles, stainless steel, fluorescent lighting and backlit plastic. They engraved the circuits on the silicon photographically. Because a single speck of dust could ruin a circuit, they wore antiseptic suits, headgear and gloves. By 1973, the 1103 chip was the world's largest-selling semiconductor. Sales amounted to $66 million and the workforce increased to 2,500.

Intel's culture was shaped by the character and the behavior of its founders. Noyce, Moore and Grove made the major decisions by consensus. Noyce brought vision; he dealt with the government and the rest of the industry. Moore focused on planning the technology and the products. Grove was the man of action, intensely competitive and intimidating, who saw it as his job to instill discipline in the company.

An environment emerged in which scientific knowledge and financial expertise combined to create technical excellence focused on results. The boundary lines that symbolize the traditional corporate hierarchy were abolished. There was no top management other than the eight partners themselves, and no gradations of status. In an egalitarian meritocracy, knowledge power was not to be subjugated by position power. Every employee was made to feel that he could go as far and as fast as his talent would take him, which presumed a tolerance for error. Failure carried no stigma, but it was better to bring up failures and discuss 'what's gone wrong' rather than to compound a problem by allowing it to continue.

They all worked in one big room without partitions, and there were no reserved parking places. There were no rules of dress, except that it should be modest, neat and clean. Everyone was expected to be at work at 8 AM. Anyone arriving late had to sign what came to be known as the late list. Underperformers were told to shape up or get out; the procedure was strict, but it created a company-wide standard of performance.

According to Noyce, Intel was seen as a community of common interests. "It was much more a co-operative venture than an authoritarian structure, a community rather than an army. People came here because of their abilities, and we knew we would all prosper or fail together." Each division was run like a separate corporation. If the marketing division had to make a major decision that would affect the engineering division, the "councils" of the divisions that were affected would meet and work it out themselves.

Noyce believed that the great flashes of genius come to the young, particularly if the environment is right. Major decisions were made at weekly meetings where everyone was encouraged to come up with an idea or make a suggestion. These meetings covered matters of marketing or production as well as broad philosophical principles. Noyce set the agenda, but after that everybody was an equal. Issues were discussed openly and directly. A young engineer who had an idea he wanted to get across, was expected to speak up and challenge anybody who didn't understand him. Issues were dealt with aggressively, but when a decision had been made, everyone had to fall in line. Intel came to be known for its "constructive confrontation" and "management by objectives." Results against those objectives became the basis for measuring individual performance. A "ranking and rating" process was applied by each manager to each of his/her direct reports.

Noyce considered stock options a more powerful incentive than profit sharing. They were part of compensation for all employees, not just for management. He wanted to tie everyone, from janitors to bosses, into the overall success of the company. People sharing profits tend to concentrate on proven products, rather than risk their future on untried research. A share bought at $20.80 in 1972 is worth more than $50,000 today.

As the workforce grew and the profits soared, labor unions attempted to organize the company. Noyce made it known that labor-management battles had no place at Intel, and that unionization would be a death threat to the semiconductor industry. A company divided into workers and bosses, with the implication that each side had to squeeze money out of the other would lead to work rules and grievance procedures and smother motivation. Intel's corporate culture and style of management was intended to develop enthusiasm about technology's potential and a common determination to keep the company at the top. The upshot was remarkable freedom of action, and a corresponding burden to perform.

The invention of the microprocessor was not planned. In 1970, a Japanese company named Busicom contacted Intel. They wanted to build a high-performance programmable desktop-printing calculator for scientific use, and needed a dozen different types of semiconductor. Ted Hoff, who had recently joined Intel after doing research at Stanford University, was assigned to the job. He doubted it was possible to manufacture the chips within the imposed cost limits, and proposed to pack all the functions, instructions and data on a single memory chip, a central processing unit that could be programmed via software to perform the 15 functions, plus a wide variety of other operations.

The idea of a central processing unit had been around since the mid-sixties. It was only a question of time to refine the process technology so that a vast number of transistors could be put on a chip. Intel and a few other companies envisioned semiconductor memories as the wave of the future that would replace the magnetic-core memories then in use. Since the invention of the integrated circuit in 1959, the semiconductor industry had doubled the number of components integrated into a single chip every year. It seemed obvious that the printed circuit boards would soon be replaced by something entirely different.

Intel had no experience with random logic and nobody had done random logic with silicon-gate technology. An Italian engineer, Federico Faggin, had recently left Fairchild and joined Intel. At the age of 19, he had co-designed and built a digital computer, the size of a cabinet, at Olivetti in Italy. Then, after studying solid-state physics and receiving a doctorate in physics at the University of Padua, he became the MOS group leader of SGS-Fairchild in Milan. There he discovered the potential of silicon and developed the MOS (metal oxide silicon) manufacturing process called silicon-gate technology. The company had an exchange program with Fairchild, Palo Alto, and sent him to the United States for a six-month period. He decided to stay.

Hoff believed that Faggin's silicon-gate technology might be used for the development of a central processing unit on a single chip. Faggin was convinced that silicon-gate was the only way to do it cost-effectively. Once the decision made, Faggin refined the required manufacturing process. It took nearly a year to convince the Japanese that it would work. Finally, an agreement was reached to develop the project jointly, and Busicom paid $60,000 in exchange of the exclusive proprietary rights. It took another eleven months for a team of engineers, led by Andy Grove, working from twelve to fourteen hours a day, to implement Hoff's ideas and to turn them into hardware. Stan Mazor who had worked at Fairchild as a programmer wrote the software for the new chip which came to be known as a microprocessor.

A microprocessor - also known as a CPU or central processing unit – is a computing device that is fabricated on a single chip. The first microprocessor was introduced in 1971. They called the chip the 4004, which was the approximate number of transistors the single device replaced.

The 4004 was not very powerful. all it could do was add and subtract, and it could only do that 4 bits at a time. But it was amazing that everything was on one chip. Prior to the 4004, engineers built computers either from collections of chips or from discrete components (transistors wired one at a time). The 4004 powered one of the first portable electronic calculators.

The 4004 paved the way for embedding intelligence in inanimate objects. It was a silicon-based chip measuring 1/8th of an inch long by 1/16th of an inch wide, and containing about 2,300 transistors. The surface was etched with the initials F.F. for Federico Faggin. It executed about 100,000 on-off switches per second and performed basic addition and subtraction. This represented approximately the same computing power as the wartime ENIAC which weighed 30 tons, occupied 3,000 cubic feet of space and used 18,000 vacuum tubes. The MOS process allowed Intel to become the first successful producer of DRAMs, and to use the technology for seven years without competition.

When Busicom became involved in a price-cutting war that led to financial difficulties, the management asked Intel for price reductions. Hoff believed the new device had a vast potential in many applications ranging from cash registers to street lights. It seemed desirable to renegotiate the rights to the design. Noyce and his crew flew to Japan and bought back the rights for $60,000. Shortly after, Busicom went bankrupt.

The 4004 is considered the world's first single-chip microprocessor, although this may be an overstatement. Not so much an invention as an evolution, it was the most complex man-made creation in history. The 4004 took the integrated circuit one step further ahead by placing the central processing unit, as well as input and output controls, on one minuscule chip. Whereas previously the integrated circuit had to be manufactured to fit a special purpose, now one microprocessor could be manufactured and then programmed to perform complex mathematical calculations. Hoff now had a rudimentary general-purpose semiconductor that not only could run a complex calculator, but also be programmed to control an elevator, a set of traffic lights, or perform many other tasks.

This breakthrough paved the way for embedding memory in silicon. The microprocessor was destined to become the brains of the computer. One of the first Intel 4004 was installed in the Pioneer spacecraft launched in March 1972. Today it continues to operate 13 billion miles away, sending its signals to the earth and heading to the outer edges of time and space, to infinity and beyond.

In April 1972, Intel announced the 8008 microprocessor with a price tag of $360. It had been commissioned by Computer Terminal Corporation for use in a programmable terminal. When Intel failed to meet the specifications and the deadline, the order was cancelled.

Now the challenge was to market the microprocessor to customers other than calculator manufacturers. A number of ads in periodicals, as well as educational seminars and manuals describing the many potential uses of a programmable chip produced no response. The manufacturing and R&D facilities of the industry were geared toward producing mainframes and minicomputers.

The 8008 had a single 8-bit bus and required a very large external logic to support it. A few were tested by NASA, but Intel found no market for it. The invention met with skepticism among professionals. In the boardrooms the microprocessor was perceived as a threat because it meant a technological revolution and would compel the computer industry to restructure.

Several programmers had tried to implement BASIC language on the 8008, but had found it to be an excruciating process. Intel's management became convinced that the microprocessor was only good for calculators. For several years they were used primarily as microcontrollers in automobiles, appliances, automated production lines and many other applications. During the second half of the 1970s Intel's revenues from microcontrollers were much greater than those from its microprocessors. Microprocessors are Intel's defining business area but for the first 10 years, they were just a sideshow. Intel temporarily lost the battle. The 6502 produced by MOS Technologies and Zilog Z80, along with Motorola's 6800 remained for several years the main suppliers of microprocessors.

Bill Gates and Paul Allen were among the very few who found any use for the 8008. Paul Allen wanted to build something around it by writing a translator that would convert statements from BASIC into sequences of 8008 instructions. Controlling the chip directly via its instruction set was an appealing idea. But Gates was convinced that it was built only for calculators, and that writing a program would be a painfully laborious process. Despite his skepticism, he came up with the $360 needed to buy one. A third enthusiast, Paul Gilbert, joined in to help with the hardware design. The machine they built was not a computer, but an automatic calculator intended to generate traffic flow statistics by using data collected by a sensor installed in a rubber tube strung across the highways. Each time a car crossed the hose, the box increased its count. Allen wrote the development software, which Gates used for the actual data-logging software. They expected there would be a sizable market for it. After almost a full year, when they got the device running, they set up their first company called Traf-O-Data. It was not a commercial success.

In March 1974, Intel introduced the 8080 which really created the microprocessor market. Able to perform 200,000 operations per second, it was ready for use in many applications that were not possible with previous microprocessors. The 8080 was immediately used in many different products. Soon after Intel's success with its 8080, several competitors entered the market and began to erode its position. At the time, Intel's primary competitors were Motorola and Zilog, a company co-founded by Federico Faggin who had defected from Intel after leading the design teams for the 4004, the 8008 and the 8080. Texas Instruments, Advanced Micro Devices and other semiconductor companies followed.

Innovation in production processes and memory design led to steadily increasing performance, decreasing cost and increased demand. Intel had an exceptional research and development group that generated new concepts and improvements. Every three years or so, a new generation was introduced with four times as much capacity as its predecessor. After the launch of a new chip, Intel could enjoy margins as high as 80 percent for a few months; as soon as a clone entered the market, Intel dropped the price drastically and came out with the next generation chip at a high margin.

In the early days, manufacturing lots were occasionally affected by problems. They manifested themselves when power was applied to the devices and their characteristics changed as they were tested, until they eventually became totally useless. Dov Frohman, a young scientist was given the task of solving the mystery. He proved that because of some improper steps in the manufacturing process, certain areas that were supposed to be connected in the device structure were actually disconnected. His findings allowed the laboratory to make the necessary modifications in the manufacturing process.

In 1975, a small company called MITS sparked the silicon revolution by advertising Altair kits which allowed amateur computer hobbyists to build their own microcomputer. The main component of the kit was the 8080 microprocessor made by Intel. In 1981, when IBM selected Intel's microprocessor 8088 as the brains of its first PC, the company was on its way. From thereon, microprocessor development was rapid. Copied by scores of clone manufacturers, Intel quickly established itself as the standard for business computing, and was soon selling tens of millions of microprocessors every year. The Intel architecture has been the PC industry standard ever since. IBM and IBM-compatible PCs became the leading PC platform, and the Intel architecture became the highest volume microprocessor architecture by a wide margin. The cost and complexity of microprocessor development increased dramatically with each new generation.[1]

A microprocessor is made of quartz purified into metallurgical-grade silicon in electric arc furnaces. The silicon is converted to a liquid, distilled and re-deposited in the form of semiconductor grade rods 99.999999 percent pure. Broken into chunks and packed into quartz crucibles, they are melted at 2.593 degrees Fahrenheit. A monocrystal seed is introduced, and as the seed rotates in the melted silicon, a crystal grows. After a few days, a 5-foot-long ingot of silicon is extracted. These pure silicon ingots are then sliced by diamond saws into wafers, which are washed, polished, cleaned and inspected both visually and mechanically.

Chipmaking is a combination of repeating steps consisting of the application of a thin film, followed by photolithography and then etching, in which the mask acts like a negative. Of paramount importance is the precise alignment of each mask: if one mask is out of alignment more than a fraction of a micron (one thousandth of a millimeter), the wafer is useless. The ability to develop and manufacture is the supreme test of a company's standing in the advanced technology race.

Today's chip plants run round the clock, usually two 12-hour shifts per day, seven days a week, in order to wring out as much production as possible. Because a single speck of dust could ruin a miniature circuit, workers are placed in "clean rooms", encased in bunny suits that cover them from head to toe, in order to keep minute particles from contaminating the microscopic circuits. They wear helmets that pump their expelled breath through a special filter package. They work with computer-controlled robotic devices, and never touch a wafer. Powerful pumps in the ceiling continually pour filtered air into the fab to keep the dust level at an absolute minimum. Temperature, barometric pressure, and humidity are controlled to extreme tolerances.

Some critical elements of the microprocessor are still laid out by hand. No tool can optimize the operation as well as trained workers. The machinery requires considerable skill and fine gradations of judgment. Because pencils generate dust, only ball-point pens are used. Report forms are made of lint-free paper.

The line-operators are female; the only men are engineers and maintenance personnel. Each chip is tested throughout the entire process both while part of a wafer and after separation. Microprocessor-controlled robots whisk the wafers between process stages and operators are called on to keep the complex equipment working at peak efficiency. In addition to more consistent handling, automation isolates workers from physical and chemical hazards. At each step of the process, wafers are tested with specially designed equipment under computer control. When the metallization process is completed, the chips on a wafer are tested again. Those that pass the rigorous electrical tests are then cut from the wafer with high-speed, water-cooled diamond cutting saws and mounted in metal or plastic packages, called modules. These modules are then tested again. Wafers are cut with a diamond saw into individual chips, referred to as a die. Each die is then placed on a static-free plate to be transported to the next step and inserted into its "packaging." With quality control done, the chips are ready for market. From wafer to chip to market, the process takes up to 45 days.

The microprocessor is the bedrock of the computer industry and probably the most important technological breakthrough of our time. No invention in history has spread so quickly. It is used in televisions and VCRs, microwave ovens and dishwashers. Without it, stereos would grow mute, most clocks, cars, airplanes, and the telephone system would stop. The microprocessor, the computer on a chip, has turned technology into magic.

The chip industry is the most extraordinary money-making machine ever. Compared with Intel's Pentium, any industrial product is low-tech and low value-added. Staying ahead in such a business requires continuous investment simply to keep up with technology. A new plant requires super clean air-conditioning facilities with state of the art equipment. It costs up to $4 billion and may be obsolete within three to five years. Commissioning and building a new plant can take up to two years. The company that runs it must squeeze as much out of it as possible. By the time it is completed, demand may have dried up. In an industry that can swing from feast to famine, this is a risky undertaking.

For several years, microprocessor production grew steadily. Office automation became America's most competitive high-tech industry and its biggest revenue-earner abroad. Relatively autonomous business groups were run by general managers; research and development teams generated many new ideas and product innovations. The sales force provided input about the market and customer needs, and gave feedback to the product planning groups. The chip market met the textbook requirements of perfect competition. A few firms controlled nearly 80 percent of the American market.

The boom lasted till the early 1980s, when the Japanese moved in. Hitachi, Sony, Fujitsu, Nippon Electric Company (NEC), Toshiba, Mitsubishi and other Japanese electronics companies started manufacturing semiconductors under license, acquiring chip-design capabilities in the process. They copied the technology and targeted semiconductors as a strategic industry, leading to considerable capacity expansion and aggressive price competition. They viewed success in the American market as crucial to their global strategy. Soon they were making microprocessors on par with American technology, but their prices were lower. Fujitsu acquired a stake in Amdahl and American Telecom.

The competitive nature of the market favored low production costs. This was an area where the Japanese had the advantage. Japan's lower wages and a workforce trained to exacting quality standards constituted a major trump. Ferocious competition drove prices down. From freeloading imitators and industrial latecomers, the Japanese built up a huge chip industry and soon became pacesetters challenging American manufacturers in their own market.

The Japanese high-tech industry was invading lucrative areas, thereby threatening the last remaining American bastion of technological clout. By 1982, American chipmakers were losing money. Most of them were small firms perpetually short of cash. For years, they scoffed at Japanese competition, but were careless with quality standards and with customers. Few of them had the financial resources to keep up with investment by Japan's diversified electronics giants, used to ploughing a substantial share of their sales revenues back into R & D and new plant. Japanese chipmakers were divisions of diversified conglomerates making a wide variety of products; they seemed better equipped for an endurance test.

The Japanese decided on an all-out fight for hegemony. They dumped their products on the American market, selling them not only below the price they charged in their home market, but also well below their manufacturing cost. Japanese companies also paid more attention to quality and spent more effort trying to perfect their manufacturing processes. Gradually, Intel began to fall behind in the memory chip business it had created. In 1984, Hitachi and NEC had a combined DRAM market share that was eight times greater than that of Intel. In the late 1980s, it looked as if Japan's great companies would replicate earlier triumphs in home electronics.

Shareholder-value was the responsibility of Intel's finance group. Its prominent position within the company was felt during the 1981-82 recession, when the company instituted the "125% solution", requiring all salaried employees to work an additional 10 hours per week without additional compensation. When the recession persisted, the company imposed a 10 percent pay cut. This allowed management to minimize lay-offs.

By 1984, Intel had 25,000 employees, but the Japanese were flooding the American market. America and Japan, the world's two technological heavyweights, proud of their industrial skills, were determined to fight it out. The country that commanded semiconductors, computing and communications would assuredly command the mightiest industrial bandwagon of the 21st century. The decline of the global market share of the American semiconductor industry seemed to indicate that the days of American dominance of science-based industries might be numbered. The electronics industry called for temporary import quotas and countervailing duties. Washington tried to force the Japanese government a guaranteed 20 percent share of its own market for American semiconductors, and to "voluntarily" restrict exports.

Sematech, a research consortium of the 14 largest American semiconductor manufacturers was set up with government funds. Sematech was the US government's major foray into "saving" the semiconductor industry. It was a consortium of large chipmakers. Half of its funding was provided by the Pentagon. It was launched in 1988, after the mass exit of US producers from the DRAM (dynamic random access memory) market. The Japanese had chased all but two American companies away from making DRAMs; the American share of the world market had fallen from 100 percent a decade earlier to ten percent. Sematech's supporters believed that commodity memory chips like DRAMs were the key to overall semiconductor competitiveness. They feared the loss of DRAMs would lead to the eventual collapse of the whole US industry.

On several occasions, Andy Grove warned that protective measures would provide temporary relief, but would ultimately be fateful to American industry. The only way to offset Japan's efficient production methods was to counter with American creativity. In order to survive, Intel had to keep ahead of Japanese technology and fight it out in the world markets. Convinced that Intel could out-invent any competitor, he decided to raise the technological stakes, focus on intellectual leadership rather than production costs and turn the game into ultra-tech. "The balance between American and Japanese producers now depends", said Grove "on their relative capacity to endure pain".[2]

Grove's survival instincts turned the plant into a sweatshop. But Intel survived, and from then on was able to impose its microprocessor as the global standard on which operating systems and application software are based. Andrew Grove recalls: "There is at least one point in the history of any company when you have to change dramatically to rise to the next performance level. Miss the moment and you start to decline".[3] At Intel the moment came in 1985. Intel's three major development areas were DRAM, EPROM and microprocessors; each

413

of the three groups had about the same number of personnel and budget allocations.

The depression in the chip business was the worst in the industry's history. Prices and sales dropped, and the company came close to being destroyed. After months of agony, Moore and Grove made their toughest and smartest business decision: they surrendered commodity-type memory chips to Japan and concentrated all their energy on making more design-intensive types of logic chips. Intel still defined itself as a memory company; a significant percentage of its research, development, and engineering resources were devoted to memory products. Competing in the microprocessor business required different competencies. Transforming the company and shifting the focus and direction required strong strategic leadership. Grove was in charge: the people who did not support the change of direction were removed from positions where they could impede progress. Several of them left.

The strategic retreat enabled the company to commit itself fully to microprocessors and to restore its leading position in the world market. Intel's decision to focus on the microprocessor business, combined with its excellent execution, propelled the company to become the number-one semiconductor manufacturer in the world. In 1985, Intel stopped licensing and became the *de facto* monopoly supplier for the most advanced world-class microprocessors. Ever since, Intel's strategy has focused on technology leadership and first-mover advantage. This has enabled it to maximize profitability with premium priced products.

Back in 1965, *Electronics Magazine* asked Moore to predict the course of component technology. He observed that so far the number of transistors and resistors that fit onto a chip had nearly doubled approximately every 18 to 24 months. Extrapolating from this observation, he predicted that this rate of progress would continue in a similar pattern, and that by 1975 microchip complexity would increase a thousand-fold, to some 60,000 components. His prediction is known as Moore's

Law, a law that became a postulate and has governed the industry ever since.

Moore's Law is not a law of physics. It is a law of technology. As computer makers and software companies develop new features and programs that require more power, Intel creates new chips to meet those new demands. The impact of Moore's Law has led users to expect a continuous stream of faster, better and cheaper high-technology products. Moore expected his law to last until it got to the point where it approached the physical limitations of atomic nature of matter. On the other hand, he did not see any new technology coming along that would replace the microprocessor. So far, each time the company approaches a technical wall, it makes it crumble.[4]

In 1987, Andy Grove became chief executive, while Gordon Moore remained chairman. During his 11-year tenure, Grove built Intel into the world's largest chip maker, generating huge returns for its stockholders. Intel rose to dominance by constantly upgrading its microprocessors, and maintained it against competitors through aggressive marketing, ruthless business tactics and liberal use of patent infringement lawsuits.

Grove attributes much of this success to Intel's culture and to the strategy of its management. In *Only the Paranoid Survive,* a classic of managerial and leadership skills, he describes how a sudden menace can become a challenge and a source of increased market power. His prescription: constantly watch out for the signals given by the market; develop new products and new needs; anticipate the bad news and be ready to face it; focus on the most probable alternative and concentrate on the essential; set the strategy; make harsh decisions, but resolve any problem swiftly; adapt quickly to sudden change; be constantly alert to what might go wrong; complacency is the primary obstacle to progress. The greatest gratification of the business game is in being one step ahead of every competitor. But then, he says, "you do a lot of things instinctively, without knowing why you're doing it."

With each new generation, scale and complexity of microprocessor development increased dramatically. The products are offered to the industry by a talented technical sales force that provides input about the market and customer needs and gives feedback to the product planning groups. Intel focuses on stimulating the supply of and demand for high-performance content and applications. Customers are persuaded to demand ever increasing processing power. Intel management has continually exploited opportunities and addressed challenges to its core business, while pursuing new opportunities outside the core business.

The *Intel Inside* policy initiated in 1991 was the first comprehensive effort geared toward turning the Intel name into a consumer brand. It was intended to make customers specify that they wanted Intel microprocessors when they purchased a PC. The company realized that the ultimate way to keep competitors out was to make consumers associate the Intel name with high quality and reliability. It marked the transformation of Intel from a component supplier targeting the manufacturing industry to a branded products company that sent a message directly to the mass market.

In 1994, Intel produced a Pentium microprocessor that was flawed. The engineers had known about the defect but kept quiet, hoping that only a few of the millions of users would ever notice. When a mathematics professor discovered the flaw, Intel's attempt to play down the problem angered customers and provoked a storm of criticism in the press. The company kept insisting that no corrective action was required. The computer manufacturers, fearing that they would be compelled to replace the microprocessor, stood behind Intel with press releases telling customers that there was nothing to worry about. For some time, they seemed to succeed; but when IBM announced that it was withholding delivery of machines equipped with Pentium chips until the issue was resolved, the media unleashed a new round of criticism. Intel was forced to reverse its position, and announced that it would offer a no-questions-asked exchange to anyone who owned a flawed Pentium.

To cover the costs, the company set aside $475 million, more than half its earnings during the last quarter of 1994. Very soon, public confidence in the corrected Pentium chip returned. Customers appreciated Intel's commitment to getting things right. The name became more renowned than ever. Confronted with another disaster, scarred and chastened by the experience, Intel survived.[5] By 1996, Intel had record earnings of $5.2 billion on sales of $20.8 billion. Since Grove took over as CEO in 1987, Intel's average annual return to investors had been 44 %.[6]

Intel is constantly on the lookout for manufacturing sites outside the United States. It looks for locations that minimize overall operating costs, including tax and duties, the total cost of the workforce, the cost of the infrastructure, logistics and local supplies. The company's selection committee has a checklist of essential criteria: political and economic stability, the quality of the country's construction industry, the maturity of its infrastructure, the efficiency of local suppliers, the availability of qualified people willing to work in 12-hour shifts, three- and four- day weeks, including Saturdays and Sundays. It also insists on a non-union workforce. Only if these criteria are satisfied, does Intel look at costs, which does not mean the lowest labor cost.

Government incentives are low on the list of criteria, because they are generally intended to compensate for a country's disadvantages, such as high wages or lack of infrastructure. Ireland has been exceptions to the rule. Eastern Europe is presently considered for possible manufacturing: Poland, the Czech Republic, Hungary offer varying degrees of low-cost manufacturing, a well-developed supplier base and healthy local markets.

Realizing that housing costs in Silicon Valley would force them to locate new plants elsewhere, the company set up fabs in California, in Oregon, Arizona, and New Mexico. Production facilities were also established in countries where labor is cheap: Malaysia, Manila, Barbados, Puerto Rico, and Israel.

In 1998, Grove relinquished his job as CEO but remained as chairman. He decided that if he hung on until he was 65, his successor would not have time to put his own imprint on the company. Craig Barrett took over at a time when Intel was putting itself through another dramatic process of mutation. The emergence of the Internet as a powerful driving force in high technology constituted a challenge to adapt the organization in the face of major change.

Demand for Internet connectivity had become the primary driver of PC sales. Processor power was not important to a user of Internet, and this threatened to devalue desktop processing power. But there was a potential opportunity for Intel as well. The Internet caused more processing power to be needed in high-end servers that distributed content and processed on-line transactions, and this was a potential growth market for high-end Intel processors. Craig Barrett wanted Intel to become the building block supplier to the economy by focusing on four areas: client platforms, networking infrastructure, server platforms, solutions and services.

A new class of lower-cost PCs with less powerful processors from AMD and Cyrix captured a significant percentage of consumer sales, causing Intel's overall market segment share to drop. In January 1999, for the first time ever, AMD chips outsold Intel chips in the US retail desktop PC market segment. In the high end of the microprocessor market segment, Intel faced competition from Sun, IBM, HP, SGI, and others. Despite gains by Windows NT and Intel systems in the low end of the workstation and server markets, they continued to hold market share on the high end. Craig Barrett did not believe that the company's historical growth rates and profitability could be sustained solely with microprocessors, and began actively pushing Intel to diversify into new businesses.

By 1999, NCG had become a sizeable and strategic business for Intel. NCG consisted of 4 distinct businesses: home networking, network adapters, small to medium sized systems for business, and communications silicon. In addition to the popular Pentium® processor, Intel manufactures networking and communications products as well as semiconductor products used in automobile engines, home appliances, and laser printers. The secret of its power lies in its ability to constantly reinvent itself, to "obsolete" its own products and to relentlessly raise the bar to the next level. Virtually all of Intel's sales and profits derive from products developed within the past three years.

Intel mirrors its leaders: brilliant, ferociously competitive, pugnacious and driven. Intel is as much criticized for its monopolistic behavior and exhaustive use of the legal system to thwart competitors as it is admired for its ability to design, manufacture and market processors.[7]

In 2000, Intel had 70,000 employees. The company keeps introducing new microprocessors based on breakthrough technologies. The Federal Trade Commission has charged Intel with illegally using monopoly power to harm rivals. The agency has also probed whether Intel unlawfully uses its chip dominance to muscle into new markets. The FTC probe has looked at how Intel uses intellectual-property "blackmail" to keep customers in line. The company's most obvious weapon here is the famous Intel Inside marketing program.[8]

Intel reaches out to Asia for some products, but keeps manufacturing of its world-dominating microprocessors in-house. The company has a strict policy of pursuing anyone or any company that appropriates its intellectual property, design capability or process, and has filed a vast number of patent infringement lawsuits. There are many in Silicon Valley who would love to see something nasty happen to the Wintel duopoly - Microsoft and Intel - if only for the change of pace. To meet the challenges ahead, Intel's corporate culture allows the company to set objectives, communicate them swiftly to its workforce, and make a good attempt at achieving them. Its compensation system, which rewards hard work and loyalty with stock options worth millions, but checks underperformance with regular reviews and corrective action, is highly successful in motivating people to give their best. And its lack of hierarchy makes it easier for the company to respond swiftly to change and to make rational decisions. Through a mix of extraordinarily hard work, attention to detail, ruthlessness, Intel's management has made it the world's prime chipmaker. The brain drain has immensely added to the company's success. Jean Hoerni's planar process provided the engineering edge that put them in the lead of integrated circuit technology. Federico Faggin led the design and development of the world's first microprocessor. The software developed for the 8008 in 1972 by François Gernelle and a team of French engineers led to the 8080, to the Altair and to the computer revolution.

MICROSOFT was founded by the man who stands atop the list of the world's wealthiest. Bill Gates was the scion of a family with a rich history in business, politics and community service. In 1968, he attended Seattle's private Lakeside School, when a mother's group decided to familiarize the children with computer technology. With the $3,000 they raised, the school bought an old teletype; hooked up to a telephone line, the machine gave access to a DEC minicomputer located in downtown Seattle and owned by General Electric. The school dialed into this computer at a scheduled time and was charged for the usage. The practice was called time-sharing.

The idea was that the teachers would figure how to operate it, and then tell the students. It worked the other way around. Two of the youngsters became instantly obsessed with the fabulous prospect of being able to dial into a computer located miles away, type in commands, and have the answer instantly typed back. One of them was 12-year-old Bill Gates, the other 14-year-old Paul Allen. They learned to master a computer language named BASIC which had recently been developed at Dartmouth College by John Kemeny and Thomas Kurtz. BASIC stood for Beginner's All-purpose Symbolic Instruction Code.

Kemeny was a brilliant mathematician intent on philosophizing about the relation between man and machines.

He spent his boyhood in Budapest, and accompanied his parents when they moved to the United States. A brilliant student, he had been Einstein's mathematical assistant, and also taught philosophy at Princeton. Based on the work of Alan Turing, he visualized a machine equipped with a simple code enabling it to perform automatically any operation mechanical calculating machines could do.

Kemeny and Kurtz designed a language in basic English for the computer to translate into binary code. This enabled the inexperienced user to learn a few instructions and write his personal program. Easy to use, it could be assimilated after only two hours of instruction. The boys became addicted to computer technology, and soon knew more about it than their instructor. They stored BASIC on a cassette tape and started making money by selling it.

Then another time-sharing company, named Computer Center Corporation, made a similar agreement with the school. Computer time, however, cost a lot of money, and the boys soon ran up very high bills. To alleviate the problem they hacked into the company's secured accounts and changed the processing time, causing the system to crash. On time-sharing computer systems, many users share the same machine simultaneously. Safeguards are built into the system to prevent one user from invading another user's data files or "crashing" a program and bringing the whole system to a halt.

The boys became experts in subverting computer system security and became masters in electronic mischief. They were amused by their exploits. They got caught, but the management felt they could be useful and gave them free time in exchange for finding bugs in the software programs. The boys would cause a program to crash, make notes of what they had done, and the company's programmers would fix the problem. In 1970, Computer Center Corporation went bankrupt. Bill Gates and his friend lost their free computer access, but continued to experiment with different languages and operating systems.

In 1972, Intel came out with a chip, called the 8008. They bought one for $360, developed a primitive microcomputer for recording automobile traffic flow on busy intersections of the highway, and set up their first "company" called Traf-O-Data. They sold some to several municipalities, but it was not a big success. Gates spent the next couple of years teaching himself machine language. While studying law at Harvard, he applied for a summer job at Honeywell together with Paul Allen. Pursuing their dreams of starting their own computer company, Gates soon dropped out of college and set up a partnership with Allen, called Micro-Soft.

Paul Allen was an avid reader of electronics magazines. In January 1975, *Popular Electronics* featured on its cover an ad that caught his eye. A company called MITS offered a microcomputer kit called Altair 8800, using the new 8080 Intel microprocessor. The Altair came without software, and would only be of interest to hobbyists who bought it for the fun of assembling it. To be really successful it needed a language.

The boys called Ed Roberts, the owner of MITS, and told him they had a program that could be used for the Altair. In fact, they hadn't even begun writing it; but after working day and night for seven weeks converting BASIC for the 8080, without having an Altair to test it out, they had it ready. Allen flew out to Albuquerque. After some adjusting, amazingly, both the hardware and the software were compatible. The Altair now featured a software language which turned a fascinating toy for hobbyists into a real computer. Allen and Gates licensed BASIC to MITS. Allen was offered a position as director of software and was soon joined by Bill Gates. Both traveled around the country in a big van, demonstrating the Altair computer to enthusiasts, thus jump-starting the computer-hobbyist movement that set the course for the personal computer revolution.

In 1975, Gates and Allen founded the Microsoft Corporation. Immediately, a vast number of people became interested in Microsoft's software, since it was easier to buy to than to write their own. In 1979, Microsoft and its 16 employees moved from Albuquerque to Seattle. As business expanded, new staff was gradually recruited. Gates asked his long-time friend, Steve Ballmer, to help with the business side, and establish policies and procedures in the financial, organizational, and resource allocation areas. By the late 1970s, BASIC had been ported to platforms such as the Apple, Commodore and Atari computers.[9]

In 1980, IBM's top management recognized the inescapable reality: the company needed to introduce a personal computer quickly. IBM employed capable software builders, but was essentially a hardware company that bundled software and services with its machines. Management decided to break with tradition and outsource virtually the entire project, including the operating system. An IBM team approached Microsoft under pretense of doing a market survey, and requested Bill Gates to sign a non-disclosure agreement which would enable them to disavow the meeting ever happened. They asked him for advice about the desirable features of a microcomputer. Gates suggested that in order to have better graphics and the best possible performance, IBM use the new Intel 8086 16 bit processor. IBM soon returned with the admission that they intended to build their own computer, and were interested in using several of Gates' ideas. The IBM people thought that Microsoft had an operating system. Gates said he had the language, but not the operating system and suggested that they see Gary Kildall who had written the most efficient system on the market.

Gary Kildall had invented the concept of a Basic Input Output System (BIOS), the core logic which marries hardware to the operating system. He had written CP/M, the first mainstream desktop operating system that could accept and interpret operator commands using less than 4 K of memory. The purpose of the operating system was to control the storage and retrieval of information on floppy disks. CP/M proved to be just what was needed for the personal computer.

Kildall was a brilliant programmer, but was out for a good and easy life. He had formed a company called Digital Research, and soon became a multimillionaire fond of piloting his own plane. Following Bill Gates' suggestion, the IBM people went to see Kildall, but when they showed up on the doorstep, Mrs. Kildall was in a hurry, preparing to go on vacation. Annoyed by the reception, IBM wrote him off as a potential partner, and went back to Microsoft. Bill Gates had been open and sincere, but he was not the man to give a competitor a second chance. He saw the opportunity of a lifetime.

He knew that when Intel brought out its 8088 and 8086 chips, Kildall had been slow to bring out a CP/M upgrade to run it. Tim Paterson, a boardmaker at Seattle Computer Products, got tired of waiting and wrote his own operating system, a cloned CP/M called Q-DOS (Quick and Dirty Operating System). The Q-DOS had the same command structures and directories as the CP/M; the only obvious external difference was the label. Gates felt that this would be the best bet for IBM, but it would need to be upgraded to work on 16-bit machines. He bought Patterson's Q-DOS for $50,000 and renamed it MS-DOS for Microsoft Disk Operating System. It took four months of adjustments to make a working version for the 16-bit IBM PCs. Twenty-five year old Bill Gates then turned around and sold it to IBM for a fixed fee of $80,000.

In one of the most remarkable deals of the century, IBM contracted with Microsoft to purchase a license for non-exclusive rights to the operating system, instead of buying it outright. IBM misjudged, believing that the "real money" was in the hardware. They conceded to Gates' request that he retain the rights to the code he wrote for them. Before long, Gates was selling his operating system to IBM's competitors.

The introduction of the IBM PC, a machine with 16 kilobytes of memory, that sold for as little as $1,565 transformed the founders of Microsoft and Intel into billionaires and made software the most lucrative product in corporate America. Gates had retained the right to license the operating system to other computer manufacturers. IBM thus handed over the keys of the kingdom, and ceded control of the PC operating system to Microsoft. The agreement set the technical standards that fueled the growth of the personal computer industry.

Within a year, Microsoft's MS-DOS was licensed by about 50 computer manufacturers. Two years later, the number had increased to 200. Instead of taking a one-time licensing charge, Microsoft collected a fee for every PC sold. Incorporated in 1981, Microsoft gained a solid foothold in the nascent PC industry. In 1982, *Time Magazine* named the PC "Man of the Year". Allen left his full-time function at Microsoft, while remaining on the board. He started a venture capital firm that has been one of the biggest funders of high-tech companies.

There is a large random factor in the success of any company and any man. Thanks to IBM, Bill Gates became the world's wealthiest billionaire. Microsoft has been the beneficiary of one of the most spectacular blunders in the history of business, and Bill Gates was smart enough to steer IBM into making it. If IBM's management had understood the game he was playing, Microsoft's future would have been very different. If IBM had required an exclusive license, Bill Gates would still have signed the deal, since it would have meant a lot of money. Instead IBM gave him control of the PC standard. From there on, all he had to do was to collect licence fees and update his operating system.

On November 10, 1983, at the Plaza Hotel, in New York City, Bill Gates announced Microsoft Windows 1.0, a next-generation operating system that would provide a graphical user interface (GUI) and multitasking environment for IBM computers. He promised that the new program would be available by April 1984; in fact, it took until November 1985 to make the first shipments. Windows 1.0 was crude and slow; the selection of applications was sparse, and sales were modest. The launch was complicated by a warning from Apple's lawyers that it infringed on copyrights and patents.

When Apple Computer released the Macintosh, Gates was aware of the superiority in both ease of use and functionality. He approached Jobs, requesting to license some of the key interface elements. When Jobs declined, Gates threatened to discontinue development of Macintosh applications, which would have been a major blow to Apple, since Microsoft was the dominant software provider for the Mac. Apple and Microsoft then entered into an agreement by which Microsoft was licensed to use the icons and windows. In exchange, Microsoft was to develop software for the Macintosh platform. In December 1987, Microsoft released Windows 2.0 which had icons to represent programs and files, improved support for expanded-memory hardware and windows that could overlap. The agreement held until Microsoft released Windows version 2.03. Apple claimed the "look and feel" was "too Mac-like", and challenged Microsoft in court but was rebuffed.

With IBM's business firmly in hand, Microsoft's revenues soared, and on 13 March 1986, the company went public on the Stock Exchange. Bill Gates became an instant millionaire. The IBM PC, built on open hardware, set the *de facto* standard for computing technology; but IBM held a copyright on BIOS, a chip that controlled low-level functions of the PC. Customers looked at IBM as the summit of computer technology and started buying its PCs; the small computer makers risked being destroyed. Some tried to clone the architecture, but they were prevented from using IBM's proprietary BIOS chip standard.

The secret was reverse engineering. The first company to reverse engineer the IBM-PC was a start-up called Compaq. Soon dozens of clone makers sprang up, using Intel microprocessors and Windows software.

For several years, Gates took great care of IBM, his most important customer. But soon Compaq and other brands became available that would function like an IBM PC, but at a considerably lower price. This spawned an industry of PC clones that would soon outpace IBM. When the number of small PC makers kept growing, IBM lost its hold, and the IBM PC standard became the Intel/Microsoft standard. From then on IBM was relegated to the sidelines.

IBM had not envisaged that Bill Gates would sell Windows to anyone else. When Compaq, Commodore, Tandy and other manufacturers kept eroding IBM's market share, management decided time had come to regain control of the PC business by developing a proprietary technology. Gates had expected that IBM would forever use his software, and had built much of Microsoft's long-term growth strategy around his association with IBM. But in 1986, IBM announced that it would design its own program. After some argument it was agreed that Gates would work with IBM's engineers to improve Windows. The result was the Operating System OS/2.[10]

Windows 2.0 introduced several changes, including enhancements to the keyboard and mouse interface, particularly for menus and dialog boxes. It was more popular than the original version. About 2 million copies of Windows 2.0 were sold. Microsoft grew dramatically, and by the end of 1989 the company employed some 4,000 people.

So far, Microsoft and IBM had co-operated. In the early 1990s, tensions arose. Gates wanted to further develop Windows, while IBM wished future research to be based on OS/2. IBM became Microsoft's most bitter opponent in the software market.

In 1990, when Microsoft released Windows 3.0, the face of computing changed almost overnight. Preinstalled on most PCs, it sold around ten million copies in two years. Since there is no cost of manufacturing or support for software, Gates only had to recover the cost of development and overhead. IBM's operating system OS/2 was better than Windows, but it cost $400.

Windows 3.0 spelled the end of Microsoft and IBM's collaboration. Both companies went their separate ways. Gates continued shipping Windows to a vast number of computer makers. Software programmers started writing programs that ran on Windows and hardware makers created devices that made it run faster. What started as a lead became an unassailable franchise. Microsoft developed its monopoly by creating a new market and by offering a product at an acceptable price.

In 1992, IBM released OS/2 version 2.0, a powerful and easy-to-use operating system. In response, Microsoft developed Windows 3.1 which quickly became the *de-facto* standard for consumer software. It included several significant features, sound and music, and common dialog boxes. Within 50 days, the sales of Windows 3.1 reached one million and gave Microsoft domination of the software market. By the end of 1993, 40 million packages were sold, making Bill Gates a billionaire. Despite the technical superiority of the OS/2 system, Microsoft firmly took center stage.

While Apple had more technologically innovative machines than the DOS-based PCs, the Macintoshes were more expensive and therefore never gained much market share. The sweeping success of Windows compared with the lackluster OS/2 changed Microsoft from a junior partner into an equal negotiator, and later into a rival with a dominant position. After gaining strength from affiliation with IBM and capitalizing on the PC's success, Microsoft was now able to successfully compete with IBM. By holding on to this relationship, Gates gained the exclusive position of writing software for the architecture that was to become the market domineer. This provided him with a unique market share, financial power, and expertise in developing for the predominant hardware architecture. It also prepared him for his break-away from IBM. The IBM-Microsoft collaboration ended with a complete reversal of fortunes. After ten years, the partnership disintegrated. IBM became an also-ran in the PC business, while Microsoft was on its way to conquer the world.

IBM learned the hard way it could not do without Windows. Much of the smarting took place when Microsoft was preparing to release Windows 95. IBM had bought Lotus and announced that it would make Lotus SmartSuite its primary desktop offering. Gates asked IBM to drop OS/2 as well as Lotus SmartSuite. IBM refused. Immediately Microsoft cut off negotiations for the delivery of Windows 95. At the time, an accounting firm was conducting an audit because IBM had allegedly underpaid Microsoft, and Gates wanted to know how much IBM owed him. Microsoft offered to settle the underpayment problem if IBM would agree to drop SmartSuites. When IBM disagreed, Microsoft responded by refusing to supply the Windows 95 code. The agreement was signed 15 minutes before the deadline; but IBM missed the back-to-school season, and was late for Christmas sales. IBM learned that from now on the relationship with Microsoft was to be co-operative.

In June 1998, Microsoft released Windows 98, which was a minor revision of Windows 95. It integrated the Internet Explorer into the Windows GUI, prompting the opening of the Microsoft antitrust case. Microsoft's dominance indeed turned into a quasi-monopoly. The company devised a licensing agreement that required any company wishing to use MS-DOS on some of their computers, to pay Microsoft for each computer they sold, regardless of whether MS-DOS was on that specific computer. Since MS-DOS was already the dominant operating system, the business model of the majority of the IBM clone manufacturers depended on selling it with some of their computers. They were therefore left with no choice but to agree to Microsoft's licensing plan. But as they had agreed to it, they were required to pay for two operating systems when they wanted only to put a non-Microsoft operating system on their computer. This, of course, made it rare to find a computer which did not come with MS-DOS, establishing Microsoft's monopoly in the IBM PC operating system market.

The Windows operating system gave PCs some of the power and ease of use that had been associated with Apple computers. Microsoft continued to dominate the software industry as it built applications for Windows. But, never satisfied, in the mid-1990s the company continued to fight for two markets it did not yet dominate: information services like America Online, CompuServe, and Prodigy, and groupware like Lotus Notes, which is a type of operating system for networks.

Netscape was the brainchild of Jim Clark, a former professor at Stanford University who had made a fortune in business and is considered one of the few technology business visionaries. Together with Marc Andreessen, he founded Mosaic Communications. Andreessen had taught himself BASIC before he'd ever used a computer. In college, he became acquainted with the world-wide web and decided to design a program that performed multiple functions behind an easy-to-understand interface. It would require little or no expertise to operate and let users browse the web and gather information from around the world. Together with a friend, Eric Bina, he wrote a 9,000-line program called Mosaic. They released it on the Internet, and within a few months millions of people downloaded it. Since they used college computer labs to write their program, the University of Illinois owned the rights, and their work didn't earn them any money.

Andreessen took a job as a computer programmer. One day he got an email from Jim Clark, suggesting that they set up a company with the goal of building an even better browser. The University of Illinois complained about the company's name, and Mosaic was renamed Netscape Communication Corporation. Netscape's browser, called Navigator, was far easier and more effective than Mosaic. In one year, Navigator had captured 85% of the market. Netscape helped kick off the Internet age, and catalyzed the 1990s dot-com stock market boom with a public offering that left the fledgling company with a market valuation near $2 billion.

Netscape was the first mass-market and user-friendly software allowing people to surf globally. Released in September 1994, Netscape Navigator turned the Internet from an elite province of academics and scientists into a pervasive medium that fundamentally changed the way people interact within cyberspace. It was fast enough to make surfing fun. It revolutionized communications and business possibilities. Within 18 months, it was used by millions of people. Netscape's software made it safe to conduct electronic commerce by sending credit cards and to exchange confidential information over the Internet. The program could be downloaded for free, but if it was used for business purposes, a license fee had to be paid. The company released new and revised products at breakneck speed in order to maintain its dominance.

Bill Gates originally regarded the Internet as an interesting product with little relevance to Microsoft, letting Netscape capture a huge slice of the emerging market. Once he realized the potential, he organized one of the most dramatic turn-arounds in American corporate history. He purchased the rights to Andreessen's original Mosaic from the University of Illinois and assigned a group of programmers to update the product, to be called Internet Explorer. In a sudden change of course, Microsoft began pursuing Netscape with imitative offerings.

Netscape was free of charge and seemed out to marginal-ize Windows. For a while, Internet Explorer played catch-up to Netscape. Gates then turned to aggressive strong-arm tactics. PC makers were faced with the threat that unless their desktops used the Internet Explorer icon when it was switched on for the first time, their Windows license would not be renewed, which would put them out of business. They all meekly fell into line. Justice Department prosecutors preparing for the Microsoft antitrust trial asked in vain to persuade personal-computer executives to take the stand against Microsoft; they saw no advantage in publicly taking on their chief supplier. Several executives were subpoenaed, and their taped testimony was used at the trial. [11]

In December 1995, Gates announced that Explorer would be included free, with every copy of the Windows operating system. Netscape responded by making its browser download-able for free, and most users agreed that Navigator was a supe-rior product, but it was a hopeless competitive mismatch. In 1999, Netscape was sold to AOL, and by 2002 Navigator's mar-ket share had dropped below four percent. Andreessen, mean-while, left Netscape shortly after AOL bought the company.

In 1996, Netscape and Microsoft released new versions of their browsers. Reviewers ranked the two companies' products about even. It was Microsoft's free bundling of the browser with Windows and its monopoly-based influence over PC mak-ers that chipped away at Netscape's lead. Windows' ownership of desktop software created endless opportunities to marginal-ize Netscape's client software.

In 1997, Internet Explorer became the standard browser in the majority of Internet starter kits. Internet Explorer had overtaken Navigator, and the writing was on the wall. Microsoft's victory was won by default. In 1998, AOL decided to buy Netscape.[12] AOL agreed to use Internet Explorer as its default browser, in return for getting an icon on the Microsoft desktop. AOL became the world's largest Internet service provider.

In 2000, AOL announced its merger with Time Warner. At that time, Microsoft was in the midst of a massive antitrust battle with the US government. By late 2001, after a trial in which Netscape executives testified for the prosecution, a judgment ordering the breakup of Microsoft, an appeal that reversed the breakup order <u>and an anticlimactic settlement</u>, Microsoft was completely dominant in the browser market.

In 2003, Microsoft, the world's largest software company, entered licensing agreements with AOL Time Warner, one of the world's largest entertainment conglomerates. Microsoft will grant AOL a seven-year royalty-free license to its Internet browsing software and vowed to work closely with AOL to "develop a successful digital media environment that is secure from piracy."

In Microsoft's Redmond headquarters, the lives of thousands of highly-skilled and technologically proficient staffers are single-mindedly committed to work and sleep. The company cafeteria never closes. People can come in and get work done 24 hours a day. Wages are not very high; many programmers earn less than they could elsewhere, but stock options are generous and an integral element of compensation for all employees. Stock multiplied in value nearly 100 times over a decade. Microsoft has probably more millionaires working for it than any other firm on earth.

Microsoft actively seeks individuals who demonstrate creativity, mental agility, and a passion towards their craft. The company demands exceptional performances from each of its employees. Capitalizing on this shared trait, the company has formed a community that sets standards and expectations at extremely high levels.

Microsoft employees are motivated by a desire to make lives better, to create high-quality products and to contribute to society. Personality clashes and breakdowns in communication occasionally generate pressures and frustrations, leading to personal checkmates and defeats. The best performers become multimillionaires, wealthy enough to retire if they want to, and young enough to start their own company. Senior managers who don't fit in any more fall on their sword and are replaced. Microsoft people work long hours, and Gates sets the standard. He is chief strategist, oversees extensive product-development efforts, and meets regularly with his top executives, often on weekends. In January 2000, Gates stepped down as chief executive and handed over the reins to long-time friend and company president Steve Ballmer, while remaining chairman.

Microsoft has very creative ways to insinuate itself into legislators' good graces. Political donations and other trappings of traditional lobbying are part of the formula. The company has immense success in Washington by doing things that please the lawmakers.

Microsoft's dominance in PC software is being challenged by other operating systems such as Linux as well as by inexpensive Internet appliances and handheld computers. Microsoft faces a formidable foe in America Online. In August 2002, Microsoft, suffered a blow when Hewlett-Packard chose a rival software package for its consumer PCs, a week after Dell Computer announced it would offer WordPerfect software from Corel of Canada instead of Microsoft's Works.[13] In September, Sun Microsystems let it be known that it was donating its new office software package to schools in Europe and Africa, hoping to attract students before they develop a habit of using Windows.[14]

Microsoft's success has been legendary. Gates' intensely competitive personality and business genius moulded the company into a feared, admired and hugely wealthy organization. Any firm that dominates the market as thoroughly arouses resentment of competitors and suspicion of regulators. Antitrust investigators have actively scrutinized its activities.

They claimed Microsoft was a monopoly, and therefore should be subjected to investigation, and possibly be compelled to restrictions. The logical implication of the antitrust laws is that any company that distinguishes itself by unusual success is a potential target for prosecution.

Microsoft's Windows operating system accounts for about 90 percent of the PC market, and has become the standard for home and business computer applications. In 1990, the Federal Trade Commission launched an investigation into Microsoft's alleged monopolistic practices. When the FTC decided not to pursue the case, the Department of Justice picked it up, together with 18 states and the District of Columbia. In 1995, both sides reached a consent decree, whereby Microsoft agreed to refrain from requiring companies purchasing Windows to also license other Microsoft applications. Two years later, the FTC accused Microsoft of violating that decree by bundling its Internet Explorer browser with Windows 95. Microsoft eventually won the case on appeal. But the Department of Justice filed a broader antitrust case in May 1998.

In April 2000, US District Court Judge Jackson ruled that Microsoft "engaged in a concerted series of actions" to suppress competition in order to protect its monopoly, thus harming customers. Two months later, he ordered the company broken into two separate entities. In June 2001, the US Court of Appeals upheld Jackson's decision; but it overturned his order, removed him from the case, and turned the proceedings over to Judge Kollar-Kotelly of the US District of Columbia.

In November 2001, the Department of Justice, nine of the states and Microsoft agreed to the outline of a final settlement which required Microsoft to give computer manufacturers more freedom in the design of the Windows desktops. The company's competitors accused the Justice Department of selling out to the software giant. The case's final outcome remained uncertain and complex. Unsatisfied by the government settlement, several states wanted stiffer restraints on Microsoft.

After several months of negotiations, the parties reached a settlement from which Microsoft emerged essentially unscathed. The company was however required to disclose application programming interfaces and communications protocols to software developers. On November 1, 2002, a federal judge largely accepted the proposed settlement. Bill Gates described the approval of the settlement as a major milestone, adding that he was personally committed to full compliance. Microsoft appeared to have won the day. The House Majority Leader welcomed the decision: "In a time of economic distress, the court has delivered a homerun for consumers. Businesses should not be afraid that when they create popular products, they'll be saddled with endless litigation. They shouldn't be second-guessed by lawyers and bureaucrats. This is a case that the government should never have brought."

In less than two decades, Bill Gates burst from nowhere to dominate the global IT industry. Whether admired or detested, glorified or vilified, Gates is a household name, the most successful businessman of our time, and the preeminent icon of the Information Age. A hypercompetitor, he combines the skills of a technologist, an entrepreneur and a corporate architect. A tactical genius who created a company in his own image, driven and hard-driving, Gates engenders envy, imitation and accusations of unfairness. To many, he personifies the abuse of market power. Although his career is distinguished by decency, his fabulous success has generated sarcasm. He deserves more credit than he can ever receive for his contribution to enriching the lives of millions of people. Under his leadership, Microsoft has continually advanced and improved software technology, and made it easier, more cost-effective and more enjoyable to use computers.

A few years after his passion for computers led him to drop out of Harvard University, Gates created a little company. He had the right blend of youthful energy, technical acumen, intellectual breadth and business savvy to adjust as his company matured. Microsoft is an accidental monopoly. Gates' success is due to a combination of smart business decisions, lucky breaks, mistakes by competitors, and sharp tactics. In his early years, he was at the right place at the right time, and had the wisdom to take advantage of it.

In an industry where ruthless maneuvering is standard procedure, an error of judgment can be costly, even fatal. Nobody navigates this chaos more deftly than Bill Gates. He has the strength of his convictions and the ability to decide when the market is strategically ready for a new product. His vision has been central to his success.

His genius has consisted in seeing the near-future more clearly, and understanding much better than his competitors how to exploit it. Time and again, Gates recognized the potential in someone else's idea and simply did it better, always in marketing and sometimes in design.

Software is a unique business. A good application can take tens of millions of dollars to create. But once a program is written, the cost of replication is almost nil. In many cases, the total cost of fulfilling an order, even for multi-million dollar systems, is nothing more than reproducing a set of CDs and manuals.

Gates has always been a clever aggregator rather than an innovator. Microsoft's domination of the computer industry has come about through a combination of strategic brilliance, luck and exceptional ruthlessness. Bill Gates' laser-sharp vision, meticulous planning and execution have put Microsoft on top and keep it there. Gates can be abrupt and argumentative. He relies on hard-nosed conversational engagement to make decisions.

Gates is a computer addict with a genius for showing up at the right place at the right time. His overwhelming interest is not the physics or the electronics, the art or mathematics of software: just the plain computer. He represents the embodiment of the American dream. He uses financial power to eliminate competition or to acquire technology in new areas, while investing heavily in R&D to ensure primacy in technology.

Gates has democratized richness: work hard, be smart and get rich. The idea that a successful corporation should enrich not merely its executives and big stockholders but also a fair number of ordinary line employees is actively practiced in Microsoft.

Gates has been able to identify technological bottlenecks for which he designed proprietary standardized software, thereby imposing conformity and compatibility onto the entire PC industry. He then charged computer manufacturers and users royalties for the privilege of the standardization.

He had the ability to foresee the potential of nascent technologies, and to develop unheard-of products the market was ready to absorb. He recognized the significance of the microprocessor chip and its potential for fostering an entirely new industry. Gates was among the first to perceive the importance of industry standards, parlaying the MS-DOS operating system into the key building block for the entire PC industry. Even when he isn't the first to sense the promise of a key technology, he is unbeatable at marshaling resources to exploit and market it.[15]

Bill Gates is feared by his competitors because he competes more efficiently than anyone else. He exploits his near-monopolist position, and keeps leveraging it further. He has been more conspicuously successful than all others in a cut-throat game. The company's strong-arm approach has provoked competitors, would-be allies and prosecutors. Some of those who have become obsessed with toppling him from his pedestal have done unto others more or less as Gates has done unto them. A powerful alliance of competitors keeps lobbying for Microsoft to be declared a monopoly. His opponents paid dozens of lawyers and antitrust experts huge fees to amass the evidence intended to persuade the government to take Microsoft to court.

Microsoft's products cover almost everything that the computer has ever been conceived to do, from movie making to personal finance, operating systems to application development environment and people's private lives. Is Microsoft fated to dominate technology forever? This same question once applied to IBM, then admired and feared nearly as much as Microsoft is today.

Less than twenty years after its foundation, Microsoft was valued higher by Wall Street than any other company. Bill Gates was the most commanding personality in the computer industry, by far the smartest leader in business world and the youngest self-made billionaire in history. He combines a sense for future markets with key hard negotiating power. He is the visionary who built a billion-dollar company that changed the world for the better. He deserves every bit of his success.

Bill Gates has taken other people's ideas and released them as his own product. He took the GUI from Apple, but the case was dismissed because he was smart enough to get permission from Apple to do so. He has intelligently paid for several good ideas and repackaged them: the programming language BASIC for the Altair 8800 was someone else's idea. And so was MS-DOS. Extremely driven, impatient and sometimes highly confrontational, he operates with an insatiable competitive spirit. Better than anyone, he understands how to run a profitable company in a highly competitive environment. This got him into trouble many times, but also helped him learn.

Gates' success story delivers a message: it is sometimes wiser to follow than to lead, to pick up a good idea rather than spend time and energy on exploring new avenues. Gates let the program designers do the development work and picked up their brainchilds. He jumped on an opportunity, plugged one idea into the other, and came up with gigantic hits.

The Windows monopoly is protected by a barrier to entry. An operating system with all the functions of Windows would cost tens of billions of dollars to develop. Microsoft dominates the market, but computer technology is constantly changing, and Gates knows that if he stands still, some other company will come along and try to grab the leadership.

He once said he feared growing old, because when you're beyond thirty, you're not as smart anymore, and good ideas are slower to come. He has constantly surrounded himself with the smartest people he could find. The company is committed to a long-term view, reflected in its huge investments on research and development. He knows what happened to IBM and many other big companies when they became complacent and stodgy. He doesn't want to see it happen to Microsoft.

The Internet's open standards have allowed Linux, a free and open-source operating system to make good progress in the server market, as governments and large firms find it less costly, more flexible and more secure. Linux poses little danger to Windows on PCs, but it has erected big hurdles to Microsoft's extending its monopoly in the markets in which it operates. To keep growing, Microsoft must expand beyond its traditional markets, such as high-end enterprise software. Its moves into handheld computers, interactive television, games consoles and smart mobile phones have failed so far.

Gates acquired his quasi-monopoly by creating a new market in a new technology. For more than two decades, Microsoft has dominated the industry. The company has billions of dollars in cash in the bank. CEO Steve Ballmer intends to remake the company that Bill Gates built into a "great, long-lasting company" that will be "amazing in the positive impact that we have on society. But we have to do some things a little bit differently to be as amazing as we hope we can be." The mission he visualizes for Microsoft is "To enable people and businesses around the world to realize their full potential." He hopes that his code of conduct will make Microsoft a better corporate citizen. He wants to make sure that the company's core values of honesty, integrity, and respect will shine through with customers, partners, and the tech industry. [16]

Philanthropy is important to Bill Gates. He and his wife Melinda have endowed the Bill and Melinda Gates Foundation with billions of dollars to support initiatives in the areas of global health and learning opportunities in low-income communities. In partnership with the Rockefeller Foundation, they are helping to spur a Green Revolution that could move tens of millions of people out of hunger and poverty in Sub-Saharan Africa. Warren Buffett, the world's second richest man is giving away 85 percent of his wealth, most of it to the Bill & Melinda Gates Foundation.

12

SILICON ASIA

To get rich is glorious.
Deng Xiao-ping

In the space of four decades, Japan and several countries of the Pacific Rim embarked on the fastest process of industrialization and economic growth the world has ever seen, thereby lifting millions of people out of poverty and into middle class. For them, these are the glory days of global capitalism. The mix of new technologies and economic integration has created unparalleled prosperity and transformed their world. Having joined the global labor force, hundreds of millions of Asian workers have won a chance to escape from hardscrabble existence and misery. Hundreds of millions more stand to join them.

The Asian countries are one after another achieving their industrial take-off by supplying the world with low-cost, high-quality manufactured goods incorporating proven US technology, thus generating complementary growth on both sides of the Pacific. Nations with radically different cultures, human and natural resources, histories, religions and ideologies emerged from third-world desolation by deploying the right policies and nurturing a climate of creativity. While each of the Asian economies differs in important respects, the sources of their spectacular growth are relevant to a greater or lesser extent to all of them.

They had several ready-made economic models from which to learn. They have flourished on the back of other countries' technology. The recipe they adopted was simple: free enterprise, accelerated industrialization, energetic entrepreneurs, hard work, thrift, order, heavy investment in education, an up-to-date infrastructure, borders open to foreign capital and foreign technology, low-grade production to start with - plastic flowers, cheap garments, toys, and footwear - and constant upgrading to higher value-added industries; massive exports; high savings and investment rates; low levels of taxation, restrained public spending and borrowing to keep inflation low and currencies stable.

They all started from a low base. They developed a technology-based economy at stunning speed by letting market forces do heir work. By intelligently copying American technology, Japan became the standard-bearer of the electronic age. Japanese entrepreneurs excel at picking up a basic idea and converting it into a marketable product. They keep themselves ahead through intense interaction - both competitive and cooperative - with one another, and with the many firms that cluster around them in the Tokyo-Osaka corridor. A manufacturing philosophy that emphasizes highly-trained workers, continuous efforts to eliminate defects and lean production that minimizes waste made Japan a world beater. Ever since Japan's "economic miracle" of the 1960s and 1970s, Tokyo has used investment and technology transfers to coax neighboring countries to follow in its wake. South Korea and Taiwan inherited Japan's sunset industries - initially light manufacturing, and later steel, petrochemicals and shipbuilding. In turn, they handed obsolete technologies and labor-intensive industries to Indonesia, Malaysia and the Philippines.

Taiwan and South Korea welcomed American corporations, with hopes of gaining technological expertise and US dollars, while providing employment for their growing populations. Companies were invited to erect manufacturing plants with the enticement of tax breaks and low wages. American companies in electronics moved production a stage at a time, starting with low-end unskilled labor, and gradually moving to high-skilled operations. Almost every major American semiconductor firm and computer company owns offshore assembly plants in Asia, where they offer the best-paying jobs available.

Most of the political class was a third-world mix of greed and corruption. The rulers had the foresight to put in place policies and strategies that encouraged technology import, absorption, adaptation and innovation; they let their economies take their course. They relied on the business class, free markets and private investment. They understood that their countries would thrive if entrepreneurial spirits were given full rein. Democratic traditions are weak; the political leaders base their legitimacy on economic progress, and leave it to the business community and to the bureaucrats to run the show. Living by their wits on top of an ingrained system of patronage, they have enough common sense and political pragmatism to realize they should not get involved in managing the economy, and that their major responsibility lays in the creation of an infrastructure that attracts foreign investment and generates rapid industrial growth.

Asian values have been a convenient justification for authoritarian governments under which several Asian nations have joined the global economic mainstream. Asia has its business stars, outstanding entrepreneurs, innovators and financiers.

From the beginning, clever administrators often intervened with skill and flexibility to systematically refashion their country's economy. They placed a high value on an educational system that focused on practical and scientific knowledge, in order to maximize the technological absorption, the skills and competence directly usable at the work-place. They also financed the extensive development of education and training institutions.

Work, discipline, order and effort, entrepreneurial drive and organizational ability turned agrarian populations into a highly educated and industrialized society. Entrepreneurs of modest origin reinvented industry; production was constantly upgraded and diversified, workers switching from labor-intensive and low-cost products to sophisticated consumer electronics. Business had to care for the workers; wages were adjusted to the requirements of a balanced national labor market and to the relative competitive position in the export markets.

Asia's work ethic combined with a market economy has largely contributed to extremely rapid growth and booming economies. In most countries, the social contract is based on worker participation. Work being a virtue "lazy" people are reminded that they should return to the right path. Asians work much longer days than Europeans. Diligence, perseverance, moderation, the family, authority and unequal relationships between people are part of the Confucian ethic, which is also very elitist. The mass of the workforce in most Asian countries have not yet reached the level of income that will drive them to make demands for better working conditions, or allow them to make their own free allocation between leisure and work.

The absence of powerful trade unions prevented the workforce from demanding immediately a share of the benefits of industrialization. For years, motivated people were eager to spend most of their waking hours at the factory, for a fraction of the wages demanded by European workers. The educational system produced an increasingly literate and trainable manpower and anthills of engineering graduates. This allowed industry to seize the competitive high ground, capture fast-growing new technologies, while pushing European-made goods out of the world markets.[1]

Initially, American firms established their own affiliates which focused on very simple "screw driver" assembly, making few demands on the mental capacities or skills. Excellent infrastructures, a business-friendly environment and tax holidays attracted footloose capital and, with it, technological know-how. Industries were built around a core of strong manufacturing abilities, without practically any research and development. Asian entrepreneurs successfully managed the assimilation of

American technology, while their technological capabilities accumulated up to levels of globally-competitive innovation. The semiconductor companies of the Pacific Rim have established themselves at the leading edge of technological complexity. American companies usually entered the market with cutting edge products. But they often failed to pursue further innovations and eventually, their products became second rate when Japan borrowed American technologies, enhanced and re-marketed them as products superior to America's stagnant, first-generation output.

There is no single East Asian miracle: foreign investors dominate in Singapore; small local entrepreneurs abound in Taiwan and Hong Kong; whilst in South Korea the chaebol conglomerates take by far the largest share of production. Asian countries' dominance of some consumer-electronics markets is phenomenal. Taiwanese companies make eighty percent of the circuit boards found in the world's personal computers and half of the keyboards plugged into them. Singapore makes some 40 percent of the world's disk drives; a third of PC microprocessors is packaged and tested in Malaysia.[2] Asia now complements the strengths of the US computer industry.

On June 25, 1997, the Asian economic miracle came to an abrupt end. Thailand's new finance minister was horrified when he discovered that, with the blessing of his superiors, the central bank's chief currency trader had locked up practically all of the country's foreign exchange reserves in forward contracts. On top, the central bank had lent massively to struggling financial institutions draining the government's fiscal surpluses. The financial system had become a black hole, sucking out government money with no end in sight. In July, Thailand was forced to free its currency from its long-standing peg to the US dollar, plunging East Asia into financial turmoil.

The currency crisis spread to Malaysia, Indonesia, and the Philippines. In South Korea the impact was dramatic. The won collapsed; several major firms were declared insolvent and smaller firms were failing at the rate of fifty per day. Short-term interest rates soared to 30 percent and above. The IMF, the

World Bank, the Asian Development Bank and governments
of eleven countries committed $57 billion to a rescue package.
The IMF attached strenuous conditions to its South Korean
loan package, including the closure of firms and financial institutions deemed to be insolvent.

The Asian economies were thrown in disarray by the global
financial markets. Asian business cultures and financial systems
are unable to stand up to sudden destabilizing capital move-
ments. Most corporations are steeped in secrecy, dealmaking
and nepotism. Regulators lack the watchdog experience and
the clout to police them; banking supervision is superficial.

Asia's fall from financial grace has triggered much speculation. The post-crisis economies rebounded quickly, Malaysia
and Singapore being the growth leaders. There are strong
fundamentals to support continued growth: huge foreign
exchange reserves, massive direct investment, competitive
export-led industries. Nothing has fundamentally changed
to keep the disaster from occurring again. However flawed
their financial and corporate structures, Japan, and to a lesser
degree Taiwan and South Korea, remain the Asian examples
for the rest of Asia.

Asia seems to have learned from the crisis. Many companies
who once exploited political connections to monopolize business contracts are struggling for survival. New governments
have taken over, prying open closed political establishments.
Thailand's new constitution has stiff anticorruption provisions.
Government oversight of corporate behavior is also having an
impact. The most pressing problem remains the complete
cleanup of the banking sector and the release of new capital.[3]

Asia's hard-working and thrifty peoples produce a dispro-
portionate share of the world's consumer goods. Asian holdings
of US dollars have risen at a prodigious rate and help finance
America's current account deficit. The long-term prospects
of Asia's economies are excellent: they are the world's export
champions and the huge unfilled domestic demand should
allow them to spend their way out of inevitable downturns.
Having shaken off the era of colonialism, growing affluence

has restored self-confidence. They have become conscious and proud of their identity. If ever proof were needed that the benefits of sound economic policies do trickle down, Asia has provided it.

The four tigers, Taiwan, Singapore, Hong Kong and South Korea, copied the Japanese model and improved upon it by avoiding some of the mistakes. While the governments consider electronics as central to their economic development, the level of government involvement varies. The economic fortunes of Asian economies are bound up with electronics. Nearly every country in Asia is involved in some aspect of the industry, making cellular telephones, computers, televisions, pocket calculators or the chips that make them work.

Asia is reaping the benefits from its position as the world's largest electronics producer; but the electronics industry is on a continual surge.[4] In the long run, the electronics industry will provide higher living standards, but there are likely to be short-term adjustment costs. Asian countries are under constant pressure to move up the value-added chain.

The dramatic impact of globalization on economic interdependence is demonstrated by the fact that the world's largest country has also become the world's most popular location for foreign investment. China got a new economic start just by dumping Marx, Lenin and Mao, and by adopting hypercapitalism. Its economic ascension appears to be unstoppable. Indeed, the perception is that every factory closing in America or Europe is destined to reopen in China. The combination of cheap labor, robust domestic growth and market deregulation helped China attract a record $52.7bn in FDI in 2002 - more than any other country. China's arrival as a new manufacturing and economic superpower is reshaping world trade. China has become the benchmark for low-cost manufacturing.

Chinese capitalism is raw and unregulated. When Deng Xiaoping coined the phrase: "to get rich is glorious", scores of Chinese took his words. Thousands of entrepreneurs all over southern China have set up factories churning out goods. China's rapid economic progress has transformed its cities and coastal areas. Never before has so much wealth been created for so many in such a short time.

The Chinese trade union law stipulates that all employees have the right to join the ACFTU, the country's sole trade union organized by the communist party. However, they are not allowed to form independent unions or organize collective bargaining activities outside the ACFTU. Independent trade unions are illegal. This way, the government maintains the absolute competitiveness of the industry.

Life for many millions of Chinese in the country's vast, rural hinterland is in some ways the same as it always was. There are 900 million poor farmers in China's countryside, waiting to move to a factory. The implications for the rest of the world are troubling. China's emergence as factory to the world is putting enormous pressure on every economy in the region. Even for the richer countries like Japan and South Korea, competition from China could push unemployment higher while dragging down prices, exports, and profits.

Doing business in China, however, is not without risks. The Chinese openly turn a blind eye to intellectual property rights. Stories abound of foreign investors finding local companies churning out identical goods to their own, but under a different brand. Having moved a big chunk of their production to China, many companies are reluctant to put any more of their eggs in the same basket.

China's neighbors are trying to adjust to this new reality with a varied array of coping mechanisms. Taiwan's manufacturers have boxed up vast swaths of their machinery and shipped it to the mainland, where cheaper labor enables them to remain competitive in global markets. Those that have opted to stay in Taiwan are importing lower-cost workers from the Philippines. Japanese firms are stepping up efforts to sell to the China market. China and Japan are each other's biggest trading partner. Some 16,000 Japanese firms do business on the Chinese mainland. Japan's technology and China's low-paid workers make a natural and mutually advantageous fit.

East Asia is the world's most dynamic economic region and the scene of a developing economic community. Asian countries cooperate in many ways. The Asian production network is hierarchically structured by Japan. In the late 1980s, the Japanese industry developed a growing tendency to view the Pacific region as a single market from which to pursue a global corporate strategy. For the last 30 years, US companies have led in the invention of new products while Asian firms have played a secondary role, lowering the costs to manufacture US inventions. But Asian firms have begun to challenge that division of labor.

The Asian countries prefer organic integration as opposed to European-style legalistic, political and bureaucratic integration. The APEC secretariat in Singapore is headed by a director-general from the country that currently holds the chair, a deputy from the country that will take over the chair the following year and a few dozen officials, whose salaries are paid by their respective countries. A score or so of secretaries assisted by support personnel are on the APEC payroll. Matters are resolved in the capitals of member countries at ministerial levels. Southeast Asian states are steadily integrating their economies into a large web through trade and investment treaties.

JAPAN has been dominant in the hierarchy of the Asian production network. After World War II, the country emerged from the rubble, with no natural resources, except the energy of its population and a consensus that they must export in order to survive. Its entrepreneurs rebuilt its economy from scratch. Japan adopted strict rules of balanced budgets, low taxes, predominantly non-interventionist economic policies and efficient management techniques. Within less than three decades, the country came back from defeat to become the largest producer of consumer electronics in the world. The government devised a set of policies to achieve rapid industrialization: priority to scientific education, a bureaucracy that stresses achievement and meritocracy; taxes levied on low-tech industries to fund the development of new high-tech industries. Japanese exports shifted dramatically away from industries where labor intensity provided comparative advantage, to industries where sophisticated manufacturing skills and technology are of central importance. Within a few years, it allowed Japan to catch up, and even to surpass the United States in many areas of high technology.

The reconstruction was achieved under ultra-conservative Liberal Democrat governments whose elderly statesmen busied themselves with politics. The real power was in the hands of a business-cum-civil-service machine. Most of the government support consisted of technical assistance from government laboratories and joint R&D efforts among major electronics companies and universities. The government encouraged, but did not intervene. Co-operation in research did not prevent fierce competition.

Japan's economic achievements were not due to industrial policy. They resulted from hard work, private savings and intelligent business leadership. The benefits of this policy were equally distributed: 75 percent of people identified themselves as middle-class. In the post-war years, Japanese companies had no access to an efficient capital market. The post office had a virtual monopoly on private savings deposits controlled by the government. Funds were made available to specific industries through the Ministry of Finance and the Bank of Japan. As domestic credit markets matured and companies had access to eurodollar credits, the government lost control over the flow of capital.

MITI - the Ministry of International Trade and Industry - tried to coordinate research and development; but industry heeded its guidance only if it was useful. Whenever Japan's bureaucrats selected priority industries and intervened with planning and funding, as in shipbuilding and aerospace, the results were disastrous. The automobile and electronics never received much assistance, and occasionally encountered some resistance from MITI. Although MITI did fund consortia on issues such as personal computers, most well known Japanese companies with which Americans are competing are consumer electronic companies whose successes have nothing to do with MITI. Sony, Matsushita, Toyota, Honda, Canon and many other companies have been hugely successful not through government-funded programs, but thanks to the entrepreneurial spirit of a few key personalities within each company.

The Japanese focused on investment in production rather than consumption, creating conditions for rapid export-led growth. Technology acquired from abroad was swiftly adopted by skilled engineers. The market was closed to foreign firms. American technology was implemented and improved in a rapidly growing domestic economy. Innovations in production, industrial organization and technology development were generated and entrenched.

The Japanese economy has benefited from low tax rates, private savings and the absence of a social security system. In two decades, entrepreneurs turned a war-battered nation into an economic juggernaut. They had access to relatively cheap labor until economic growth bid up wages. But the labor force had a strong work ethic, six-day weeks and short vacations. Japanese companies do an excellent job in controlling production costs. They display a remarkable ability to train, motivate and retain their employees, thus stifling the power of labor unions by taking care of worker morale and productivity.

Japanese industry initiated a shop-floor production revolution involving flexibility, speed, quality, just-in-time delivery, automation and lean production. This approach created the capability of producing a variety of products with shorter production runs manned by smaller teams of multi-skilled workers.

The history of the Japanese electronics industry is an object lesson in how a nation can climb the ladder of manufacturing sophistication. The Japanese electronics industry came into existence by "free riding" on the inventions made in the United States. Realizing they were behind, they had the common sense to "pay tuition" for imported technology. In the 1950s, companies began assembling electrical components imported from the United States, simultaneously copying and often improving upon them. The Japanese have a unique flair for sensing the potential of a new device developed elsewhere and whose economic value has been overlooked by the inventor. They are champions of "creative imitation".

The United States has been generous to Japan, and was among the first to grant the "most favored nation" treatment. In the late 1950s, IBM engaged in protracted negotiations with MITI, resulting in substantial technology transfer licensing agreements. In the mid-1960s, the Japanese government extracted from IBM an agreement to license its patents to Japanese companies in exchange of IBM's further presence in the country. The Japanese, on the other hand, have refused to admit foreign capital - apart from a modicum of portfolio investment – until their own industries were strong enough to compete.

Japanese companies were technically inferior, but they caught on very rapidly. Highly skilled in reverse engineering and adaptation, they copied American technology and often improved upon it. Government procurement policies, tax breaks, low-interest loans and high tariffs kept them growing. Japanese industry developed a range of science-based industries able to challenge the Americans on their own ground. Within a few years, Japanese brands dominated the US market for radios, television receivers, videocassette recorders, cameras and other mass-produced electronics.

When Japanese companies turned to electronics, they closed down the obsolete plants, unleashing entrepreneurial energies to build new industries and strengthen the edge in technology and manufacturing, laying the building blocks for sustained growth and development. Sony paid $25,000 in 1953 for a license to manufacture transistors. Japanese companies followed a similar strategy in the semiconductor field, copying a US design and then producing a product of higher quality at a lower price. NEC had technical assistance agreements with Intel and Texas Instruments, Hitachi had a technology licensing agreement with Motorola, and Fujitsu had a pact with AMD. These technology-for-sale deals were made prior to Silicon Valley's awakening to the Japanese threat.

Contrary to most countries, Japan placed a straight ban on the influx of American capital even though it caused a strong resentment in the United States. MITI knew that to be a leader in computers, Japan would have to first reach a dominant position in semiconductors. In the late 1970s, MITI decided that the future lay in the computer industry, particularly the semiconductor industry on which it is based. MITI contributed to a research program which helped Japanese semiconductor companies catch up to and, in certain areas, surpass their Silicon Valley counterparts.

Japanese firms had strong advantages. They benefited from their diverse product portfolios, their profound experience and their intense interaction, both competitive and cooperative, with one another and with the many firms that clustered around them in the Tokyo-Osaka corridor.

From the early 1970s through the late 1980s, integrated Japanese electronics producers were increasingly dominant. In short order, they took over consumer electronics and gained the lead in world market share in semiconductor chips. By 1980, Fujitsu, Hitachi, Nippon Electric Company (NEC), Toshiba and Mitsubishi were ready to export their semiconductors production and to compete with the Americans. They even set up a semiconductor-distributing subsidiary in Silicon Valley. In the early 1980s Japanese manufacturers developed a system of ultra-strict quality-control procedures rather than depending on post-production inspection and testing. This made the Japanese chips more reliable than the American.

Japanese competition reduced prices of semiconductors, of computers and other electronics products in which semiconductors are a component: technological innovations were brought more rapidly to the marketplace, and Japanese competition forced US semiconductor firms to improve their quality of production.

In the early 1990s, despite their dominance of the memory-chip business, Japan's semiconductor firms were being left behind in the race to master the next generation of devices. American chip makers, led by Intel, won more than 90 percent of the burgeoning market for so-called "flash" memories. The irony is that flash memory is a Japanese invention.

Japanese industry has a virtual stranglehold in the technologies for making cameras, television sets, video equipment, fiber optics, robots, quality steels and composite materials. Capitalizing on its genius in manufacturing, Japan makes the video recorder, not the movie; the hi-fi, not the music or the record; the camera, not the film; the computer, not the program.

By 1986, the Japanese had taken 65 percent of the world market for memory products, while the US share was reduced to less than 30 percent. Japanese producers had moved offshore most of their low-end electronics production, including audio systems, low-end cameras, calculators and low-end appliances like microwave ovens. The strategy consists of spreading assembly throughout Asia, while keeping tight control over the underlying component, machinery and materials technologies by regulating their availability to Asian producers and keeping advanced production at home.

Japanese electronics firms affiliate loosely with other firms in a keiretsu, a collection of companies with interlocking boards of directors and cross-ownership of stock. Japan's industry remains dominated by huge, hardware-fixated hierarchical conglomerates best suited to staid businesses. Japan's giant companies employ two-fifths of the workforce; they provide lifetime employment. The *nenko*, or seniority pay system, exacts financial penalties on anyone who moves job. In large firms, people are employed for life, and job-hopping is considered disloyal. Business runs itself and its workers consider themselves corporate warriors going into battle every day to make Japan stronger. The official work week is 44 hours, and the average worker takes one week of holidays per year.

The core of glistening, large-scale modern enterprises survive recurrent economic slowdowns by meting out austerity to the mass of tiny and frequently ramshackle family concerns that cluster around them. The small businesses are extremely flexible about wages and working practices. This gives the impression that the country is blessed with an efficient and fully-employed workforce. The unemployment figure understates the true problem. Because pensions are low, almost a quarter of men over 60 are still working. The family, not the government, is expected to be the primary provider of a safety net for the individual in time of need.

Japan pioneered a set of institutional arrangements between the state, society and industry, designed to optimize the nation's comparative advantage. The *keiretsu* system creates virtual integration on a massive scale and the capability to target key technologies by channeling capital and by stimulating competition between companies and encouraging early forays into export markets.

Japan's electrical and electronics industry provides jobs for over two million workers, or 18 percent of the manufacturing workforce. Japan's success derives not only from production of advanced devices but also from development of new equipment and procedures to manufacture and assemble those devices. The combination of high levels of literacy of the workforce; the lifetime employment practices of the large firms; the recruitment and promotion practices relating to managers; the flexibility provided by the extensive use of subcontractors, the financial linkages of the big firms to private banks and public credit intermediaries, all these idiosyncrasies constitute the pillars on which Japan's commercial primacy is founded.

The ability of Japanese industry to keep its exports globally competitive and to maintain productivity-inducing labor relations has kept unemployment within narrow limits. Youth unemployment is low because school-leavers' wages are a fraction of mature adults' wages. People save for old age because pensions are barely subsidized. Life expectancy exceeds that of the United States or Europe. The large companies provide their workers with regular precautionary check-ups in company-run hospitals geared to preventive medicine, in order to keep them fit.

Matsushita is the largest consumer electronics company in the world. Sony is the most innovative company in Japan, and arguably in the world. Its strength lies not simply in having clever ideas, but in being able to push them ferociously through to commercial fruition. Its criteria for success are attention to detail, clear understanding of customer needs, and flawless execution.

Government and industry are partners in a joint endeavor. Their relationship is an alliance. Interaction between government and industry occurs in an organized way, through formal associations and via informal relationships. Originally, the Japanese government guided and assisted the catch-up exercise in computer hardware and software through tax breaks, low-interest loans and high tariffs; but Japanese manufacturers neither asked for nor received any subsidies. Private industry finances virtually all its R&D.

Japan's business statesman Akio Morita has observed: 'In the US and Europe today, old-fashioned low-level jobs are being protected while the new technologies are being neglected... Modern industry has to be brain-intensive and so does the employee... People in America have been conditioned to a system in which a person sells his labor for a price. In a way, that's good because people cannot coast; they know they have to work to earn their money or be fired... In Japan we do take the risk of promising people job security, and then we have to keep motivating them.... People need money, but they also want to be happy in their work and proud of it... Our plan is to lead the public rather than ask them what kind of products they want. The public does not know what is possible, but we do"[5]

Human resources are the firm's most important strategic asset: individuals identify with the firm, collaborate in teams, and compete across groups; profits are shared as bonuses. Japan's devoted *sararimen* commute every day to work in packed trains. Their hard-work ethic makes them stay late in the office and take even less holidays than what they are entitled to. They enjoy lifetime employment, seniority, extensive welfare benefits and comfortable retirement. Employees are motivated to display craftsmanship, so that each production worker becomes a quality control expert. The government forbids strikes as well as slowdowns by railway workers, power company workers and civil servants.

The Japanese consider economics as a branch of geopolitics, and the key to the nation's strength or vulnerability in dealing with other powers. This has produced a fate-sharing consensus between management and employees to pursue the common goal of surpassing American and European competitors by increasing productivity and quality.

Unemployment insurance is very limited. One third of the Japanese labor force has a social compact for lifetime employment. To lay off workers, even to shift them, is very difficult. People are expected to save for a rainy day, and to provide a safety net in case of trouble.

Japanese technology policy is limited to modest investments in high-risk projects with commercial payoffs; co-operative R&D is encouraged by favorable tax and regulatory treatment or rapid depreciation of equipment; MITI regularly sends signals that certain technology developments fields are a high priority. Japanese industry has operated under the belief that technology developments must be focused on continually upgrading products to meet customer demands for highest possible quality at lowest possible cost.

R&D initiatives by the Japanese government emphasize basic research and broad infrastructural support for high-technology industries in general. Firms such as Hitachi, Fujitsu, NEC, and Toshiba, though co-operating in upstream research, compete fiercely in the domestic market, which enables them to compete more effectively than European firms in international markets.

The 1990s are widely considered a "lost decade" of economic stagnation. The country has been hit by a banking and "bad loan" crisis, dating back to the collapse of the "bubble economy" in 1990-92. Ever since, Japan suffers from falling prices of consumer goods and housing, as well as mounting fiscal deficits. Its private financial system has been paralyzed by an overwhelming amount of non-performing loans. The Japanese government struggled, with limited success, to deal with these financial problems. For years, the interest rate of the central bank has been set at zero. Property prices declined for over a decade. Lack of consumer and business confidence sapped the domestic economy. In 2003, the country finally exited the long slump that began in 1991, and has entered a new phase of growth, driven by a virtuous cycle in which an increase in exports lead to a pickup in production and corporate profits, which in turn raised capital spending.

The country remains mired in a decade-long financial mess of its own making. Banks are loaded with bad loans made during the expansionary years of the mid-1990s. That lending surge also resulted in a build-up of excess industrial capacity that is still sapping corporate profitability. In the 1990s, massive government spending failed to stimulate the economy, which has deterred most Asian governments from large-scale fiscal policies. But many governments have been more than happy to encourage private-sector demand by liberalizing the financial sectors. They have sparked higher consumer expenditure. Falling interest rates, traditionally low levels of personal indebtedness and unemployment, have increased the capacity to spend. Many banks, previously compelled to provide cheap credits to industry, have turned to consumer banking as a new and profitable area for growth.

Japanese companies have been the contractors and financiers in many Asian mega-projects in recent decades. Japan itself suffers economic difficulties, but its industry is doing remarkably well. Japan's GDP per capita is approaching $40,000, whereas several of Asia's poorest countries only reach figures of $200-300. The Japanese economy is considered the world's second-strongest. Measured by technological prowess, per capita income and wealth-creation, Japan has been the most successful industrial nation during the past half-century. After Hiroshima and total defeat, Japan climbed back to pride. While America's companies competed against one another, Japan's, for national honor, competed against the world.

Japan's achievements are unparalleled in the annals of industrial history. From the late 1960s to the late 1970s, the Japanese industry led by Sony and Matsushita conquered world markets. Sony became the world's foremost commercializer of new technologies in consumer electronics including the Walkman, Triton Color TV, the VCR, the CD (and CD-ROM) and the DVD. Matsushita became the industry's most successful firm in product development, production, and marketing worldwide. By the late 1980s, together with Sanyo and Sharp, they had driven the U.S. and European consumer electronics companies out of the world markets.

HONG KONG has a population of 6.3 million. In 1949, when more than one million refugees from Communist China fled into the colony, the British authorities decided to build cheap housing for them. Thousands of little workshops sprung up and within a few years Hong Kong was supplying the world with T-shirts, plastic flowers and sandals. The tiny factories grew into a substantial industry, producing textiles, handbags, toys, watches and shoes for export to America and Europe. By 1960, nearly half the workforce was employed in manufacturing. Hong Kong is a duty-free port; it still benefits from the colonial legacy of common-law institutions, relatively strong judiciaries, and low corruption.

In 1978, Communist China opened up some of its coastal regions to foreign investors. Suddenly, Hong Kong's businessmen had a new supply of cheap labor and new land for factory-building. Most of the light manufacturing that used to take place in Hong Kong crossed the border into China. By 1997, when the territory regained its sovereignty, manufacturing's share of Hong Kong's jobs was down to a mere 15 percent. But across the border, some five million Chinese were employed in factories owned by Hong Kong entrepreneurs. The bulk of their output was imported for re-export. The head offices are responsible for product development, engineering, prototype production, quality control, management, marketing and logistic support. Hong Kong has one of the biggest ports in the world; an entrepôt for the global trading system, the terminals are owned, developed and operated by the private sector.

Hong Kong's electronics industry is the largest export earner. Electronics firms are small in comparison to global competitors. Their range of capabilities is limited and they invest little in research and development. The primary strength of Hong Kong's electronics industry is due to its reliance on China's low-cost labor. In value terms, in 1999, Hong Kong was the world's largest exporter of calculators, radios and telephone sets.

With China's entry into the WTO, Hong Kong companies will be free to market their parts and components to mainland enterprises, as they will be allowed to establish sales offices and agency networks there. This is critical to the parts and components business, which relies heavily on sales engineers and agents to provide on-site technical services, especially the design houses and semi-finished/finished goods manufacturers.

Most of Hong Kong's electronics exports are consumer electronics for domestic and personal use. The largest category is audio-visual equipment, consisting of radios, cassette recorders and players, cassette and CD walkmans, hi-fi equipment, music centers, TV sets, video cassette recorders, video compact disc players, digital disc players, electronic toys, games and related articles, battery-powered toys and TV games, as well as electronic watches and clocks.

Hong Kong also exports a variety of computer products, such as desk-top, notebook and palm-top computers, magnetic and optical disk drives, as well as telecommunications products like telephones and cordless phones. Other items with smaller export value include calculators, digital diaries, digital organizers, electronic dictionaries and translators, batteries and personal security and smoke alarms.

Companies are well known for their adaptability and responsiveness to the rapidly evolving consumer tastes. They have constantly upgraded their capability in aesthetic design and the production of fashion products. China's accession to the World Trade Organization partly reduces Hong Kong's role as the manager and marketer of the mainland's exports. On the other hand, its role as the capital-raising window for China remains strong.

Hong Kong is the most densely populated country in the world. It imports all of its oil and raw materials, and even most of its water. When World War II ended, the prospects for Hong Kong were dismal. But by making cheap products for export, it managed to become the powerhouse of Southeast Asia. Hong Kong's economic miracle did not depend on having money, natural resources, foreign aid, or even formal education, but rather on the industry, enterprise, thrift and ability of highly motivated people. Britain adopted a laissez-faire economic policy, except in the area of subsidized housing and education. Communist China has pursued a largely non-interventionist approach since it took over in 1997. Hong Kong continues to flourish with a stable currency, a free port and low taxes. Its maximum income tax rate is 18 percent, and it imposes no capital-gains tax.

TAIWAN, an island of 23 million inhabitants, is in many ways almost a replica of Silicon Valley. Its economic model is unique: decentralized, it is driven by thousands of entrepreneurial, ambitious and resourceful businessmen. In the 1960s and 1970s, the country developed from an agrarian state to a capital-intensive economy and is now one of the world's leading exporters of high-tech goods.

RCA, Zenith, Admiral, Philips and other large companies started assembling television sets to take advantage of cheap labor. They supplied capital and trained a vast number of assembly-line engineers, generating technology transfer, a pool of subcontractors and a skilled workforce. Many people had a fair chance to become successful and wealthy.

In order to create an environment favorable to industrial development, the government put primary emphasis on the development of manpower and industrial infrastructures. Education focused on science and engineering, with emphasis on experimentation and self-training. The universities graduated mathematicians and scientists who went on to earn advanced degrees in the US. About 60 percent of Taiwan's university population consists of science and engineering students, compared with 44 percent in Korea and 36 percent in Japan.[6]

To stimulate the high-technology sector, the government showered the industry with tax holidays and investment credits. The rationale was that new industries create new jobs and exports; this produces for the government incomes in personal taxes and stock transaction taxes far superior to what the foregone corporate taxes would bring. The semiconductor companies make huge profits and virtually pay no corporate taxes. There is no capital gains tax because it is a bias against saving and investment. The capital market is very broad. New ventures are set up every day and capital flows to them. At the start-up stage capital traditionally comes from the savings of family and friends. Very few countries have so many people willing to put money into high-risk ventures. Taiwan makes it easy for new companies to start, and for older companies to fail. Failure is no sin.

In the 1970s, the government set up Hsinshu industrial park. Located near universities and government research institutions, it attracted an increasing number of companies. Many of the firms clustered in the 60-mile corridor between Hsinshu and Taipei, are run by Taiwan-born engineers and scientists who have returned from the US with skills, experience and contacts. When they came back, they transplanted technology, ideas and the Silicon Valley spirit to Taiwan. By combining American know-how and Taiwanese entrepreneurship, engineering and manufacturing skill, they have created enormous new wealth. By the early 1980s, the island had gone from poverty to prosperity. Lucrative stock bonuses allowed Taiwan's semiconductor engineers to earn $400,000 to $500,000 a year.

Full employment had been reached, wages had increased and the labor-intensive industries were abandoned because no longer competitive.

Many Taiwanese firms embarked on building their own-brands, where they directly controlled the distribution channels, the link to the customers, and a larger share of profits. Building brand recognition and distribution channels proved very difficult. Acer was successful, but most other producers retreated from their expensive marketing campaigns to concentrate on components.

In the early 1980s, industry shifted its emphasis on the production of personal computers. Some companies were founded by people with first-hand experience in information technologies; some were set up by multinationals. Taiwan has often allowed foreign direct investment only on condition of technology transfer. The Taiwanese personal computer industry really took off in 1982-83 when Acer started copying Apple computers. In response to US pressure, the Taiwanese government cracked down on these illegal clones. Several Taiwanese makers decided to make IBM PC clones instead, which they could do legally. With Compaq introducing its IBM compatible computer at the Comdex electronics show in 1982, Acer's Shih saw that this was a major potential market, and Acer joined the IBM-compatible producers about a year later. From then on, the Taiwanese PC industry continued to grow largely on the back of the success of competitively priced, high performance computers.

Acer became the world's third-largest manufacturer of personal computers. Its founder is Stan Shih. His father died when Stan was 3 years old. He started his business life selling ducks' eggs off a street stall. After earning a master's degree in 1972, Shih took a job as a design engineer with a manufacturer of electronic calculators. In 1976, he started Acer, a little company which survived by designing hand-held electronic games. He steadily invested in making original products under Acer's own brand name and took his company public in 1988.

Until 1993, Acer's computer motherboards were assembled in Taiwan. But when local wages approached $600 a month and local labor was so short that workers had to be brought in from other countries, the company opened factories in China's Guangdong province and in the Philippines. Two-thirds of its output of motherboards and nine-tenths of its computers are made outside Taiwan. The Hsinchu plant concentrated on research and product development, plus pilot production of new models. [7]

The decentralized Taiwanese economy is well adapted to the rapid change of computer technology. The typical firm concentrates on one or two components with the purpose of outdoing competition. Product cycles in computer technology are very short. Only the fastest producers survive. When prices drop, they can lower costs faster than anyone else, because they outsource so much of their production to China.

Taiwanese companies make a quarter of Compaq's desktop computers and 60 percent of Dell's. Taiwan is the world's largest producer of monitors, desktop scanners, modems and several other categories of information-technology equipment. As the world's fourth largest producer of semiconductors, it has earned the nickname Silicon Island.[8]

Taiwan has what it takes to succeed: the entrepreneurial spirit, the venture capital, an abundant pool of skilled engineers and a broad technological and industrial base. American industry provides research, creative ideas, and marketing. The Taiwanese have positioned themselves as the production partner. Anything that comes from the United States, they want to do better, cheaper and faster.

Constantly changing technology in production process and intensifying competition narrows profit margins and increases the pressure to reduce costs. Since production line workers are increasingly difficult to find, students take a job during the day and study at night. Wages in Taiwan are five times higher than in the Philippines and at least 15 times higher than in mainland China. They are set by the market and, compared to

Japan, Korea and Hong Kong, salaries are low. Engineers and qualified personnel in high-tech industries earn surprisingly modest wages, but companies attract employees by offering stock options and bonuses.

Taiwan has emerged as the strongest economy in Asia. The cloud that hangs over its relations with China has not prevented Taiwanese companies from investing heavily in factories established on the mainland. The close economic relations are a valuable asset for both. China insists that Taiwan must accept the principle that only one China exists, but they are drifting together. The mainland is catching up, compelling Taiwan to upgrade.

The high-tech industry is the mainstay of the economy and has provided a niche for Taiwan in the world market. Taiwan's PC industry has suffered major shake-outs, forcing many companies to shut their doors. Notebook makers numbered as many as 40 at the end of the 1980s; by 1993, they were about 15. In 2001, the country recorded its worst recession ever.

China has become a haven for the production of notebook computers and semiconductors at which Taiwan excels. Many Taiwanese fear their industry will shrink unless they create innovative design companies such as those that thrive in Silicon Valley. Taiwan ranks second behind the US in revenues of chip-design companies that focus on designing specialty chips or licensing their intellectual property to other semiconductor developers.

Taiwan Semiconductor Manufacturing Co. is the world's premier foundry, or made-to-order chipmaker. TSMC developed world-class semiconductor process technology in just a few years. With rivals in China and Malaysia competing for business at the low end, the foundries will have to stay on top by investing in more advanced technology. Taiwan Semiconductor introduced a new business concept: making chips for companies that don't manufacture their own. Traditionally, major chip companies handed contract work to their own fabs. TSMC produces every type of chip imaginable. TSMC and UMC account for around 70 percent of the world's foundry production, making Taiwan's IT industry crucial to the global economy.

Several companies have copied the idea. They hire highly skilled engineers, helping Taiwan make the transition to an economy driven by knowledge-based industries and services. But China also boasts an army of young microelectronics engineers and is a rising force in low-cost chip manufacturing.

Taiwan had side-stepped the worst of the Asian financial crisis. The export economy remained dynamic, but the domestic market was in recession. An overcrowded financial sector was lending only to risk-free companies. Labor-intensive industries moved to lower-cost China. The island's struggling banks, steelmakers and retailers increased layoffs. Cheaper agricultural imports were expected to put 20,000 farmers out of work. The transition from an export powerhouse to a slower-growing, domestic-led economy required a structural adjustment; but the government was bogged down fighting the opposition, and unable to pursue the necessary reforms. Taiwan's miracle economy had become far less inspiring, but is nevertheless well-positioned to grow. Adjustments will have to be made, mainly a drive into higher value-added products. But the country's entrepreneurs have demonstrated significant capability to adjust to structural change.

Taiwan is well set to face the future and remain competitive: the top corporate tax rate is 25 percent; increased industrial production keeps generating substantial new investment and jobs; wages are stable and inflation remains low; government expenditures as a share of GDP amount to about 23 percent; the central bank holds one of the world's largest foreign exchange reserves.

SINGAPORE, a city-state of 4.2 people, mainly ethnic Chinese, equals the United States in terms of per capita wealth. Its standards of administration, communications, health, education and security are among the highest in the world. Scores of factory buildings are emblazoned with the logos of American computer companies such as Apple, Compaq and Hewlett-Packard. Electronics accounts for half its manufacturing output. Its port is the world's busiest in terms of shipping tonnage and contributes five percent to the country's GDP. Trucks roll away from loading docks carrying computers, monitors, printers and disk drives bound for air cargo terminals and then to markets around the world. Other cargo planes arrive filled with various components and subassemblies. Singapore plays host to more than 1.500 American companies and is home to more than 17,000 Americans. As a trading partner with the United States, it outranks France and Italy.

Singapore has achieved this by turning itself into one of the most hospitable places for multinational corporations to do business. In 1968 Britain shut down the naval base of its former colonial trading post which employed 20 percent of the city's workforce. The government now focused on developing an industrial, export-oriented economic base, and embarked upon a program intended to develop industries geared to exports by inviting foreign companies to set up operations. During the 1970s, multinationals set up manufacturing facilities, and exported their production back to their own countries. This meant the country needed a better-educated and co-operative workforce.

A modern infrastructure was set in place and an educational system developed to meet the needs of the industry. Taxes were low and barriers to trade virtually non-existent. The top corporate tax rate of 25.5 percent and no capital gains tax still remain the major offsetting factors to the high cost of doing business.

Singapore is a unique cocktail of state planning and capitalism. The state tightly controlled economic and social policy and put a tight lid on freedom of expression, while developing the free-trade spirit. Petroleum refining, petrochemicals, electronics assembly as well as trade-related and financial services made Singapore's economy grow by leaps and bounds, virtually impervious to recession.

By the late 1970s, the government decided that the model was not sustainable. One of the obstacles to continued development was the attitude of the communist trade unions. The government decided they would no more be tolerated. Some multinational corporations, like Hewlett-Packard, made it clear that they did not want any unions. The strategy put an end to disturbances on the factory floor, and allowed a rapid increase in the manufacturing capabilities in computers and high- tech in general.

Ruled for decades with an iron hand by the city's founding father, Lee Kuan Yew, Singapore started from almost nothing. In 1980, the Committee on National Computerization was formed with a staff of 25. The government instituted a wide range of programs to support the development of targeted industries such as semiconductors, communications, displays, and data storage businesses. The strategy was intended to create high-value-added activities, develop R&D capabilities, and train skilled workers. The initial plan was to use Singapore as a platform for assembly. Apple was the first major computer manufacturer to invest in Singapore. After a few years, being very pleased with the productivity of the operation, production of Apple II's also moved there.

The open-door policy towards foreign investors, imposing virtually no restrictions on the level of capital participation, management control or sector of activity, proved very effective. In no other Asian country do foreign enterprises play such an important role: they number over 7,000, employ 60 percent of the labor force, produce 70 percent of the value-added and 80 percent of the exports.

During the 1980s, Singapore went from literally nowhere to the dominant producer of hard disk drives. Singapore dominates the world sound card business. One of the original goals of the 1980 Singapore computerization plan was the development of a regional software center, but that has largely not happened, although the government continues to try to build up its software and systems integration capabilities. Creative and

Aztech are local companies with "pioneer status", which gives them tax and other advantages.

In September 1991, the National Science and Technology Board recommended doubling R&D expenditures to two percent of gross domestic product and raising the number of scientists and engineers. It also advocated grants and tax incentives to encourage companies to conduct more R&D, especially in computer hardware.

Singapore is an example of successful government intervention in the economy. An authoritarian ruler helped propel the city from third world into first in one generation. The government created a welcoming environment for foreign investors, the right conditions for balanced growth and then stood back, or intervened whenever necessary. Restrictions on wage increases and union activity, plus a government forced-savings scheme were the main assets. An educated and enlightened bureaucracy pursued sound macroeconomic policies, with limited but effective levels of regulation. The government has a firm grip on power, but the system is formally democratic.

As part of their plan to become the world's first "intelligent island", Singapore officials invested heavily in infrastructure, with some of the most sophisticated freight-forwarding and document-processing systems in the world. Trading firms use a special computer network system called TradeNet to submit import and export permits electronically, cutting approval time from the previous two-day minimum to about 15 minutes. LawNet enables legal firms to access statutes and court notices directly, which sometimes means instant answers for clients. Combined with a telecommunications system which rates the world's best, this kind of information-intensive investment has lured multinational companies to use Singapore as their regional data hub.

Universities produce about 6,000 graduates with relevant degrees every year, and private institutes turn out another 10,000. The educational system is being shaken up to produce more graduates imbued with creativity and dynamism. The status accorded to entrepreneurs has traditionally been low, and there have been few role models to inspire Singaporeans to take financial risks by giving up a salaried job and start a new business. To change the predominant risk-averse mindset the government has decided to emulate the success of Silicon Valley by cultivating the entrepreneurial spirit. To compensate for the absence of a venture-capital industry, the government has put aside $1 billion for high-tech and knowledge-based start-ups. Immigration hurdles will be lowered for talented entrepreneurs. The government organizes networking events, where high-tech starts, potential investors, venture capitalists, service providers, and other interested parties have an opportunity to meet.

The country's economic planners are determined that industry remains a major part of the economy. Singapore has 14 chip fabricators, and the government is intent on seeing more set up shop. With that in mind, the government announced a plan to set aside 60 hectares of land and a new facility for the production of high-grade purified water, an important ingredient in the chipmaking process. A program to train people in the skills required by the semiconductor industry is planned. The island's planners are also struggling to shift away from electronics, chemicals, and other labor-intensive manufacturing activities vulnerable to Chinese competition. [9] Semiconductors drove the economy for much of the 1980s. In the early 1990s, Singapore moved from oil refining into being a leading producer of petrochemicals. Pharmaceuticals and biomedicine have become the industry of the future. Most of the world's leading drug firms make products for global consumption.

An undercurrent of anxiety keeps people striving to improve. In 1997, the World Economic Forum ranked Singapore as the world's most competitive economy for the second year in a row. Rather than celebrate its status, the government appointed a panel of officials and business executives to examine policies apt to sharpen the edge. Singapore's primary-school students score among the world's best in science and math. Nevertheless, the government decided to shake up the education system in order to achieve greater personal creativity.[10]

Singapore continues to attract investment funds on a large scale despite its relatively high-cost operating environment. In order to maintain its competitive position despite rising wages, the government seeks to promote higher value-added activities in the manufacturing and services sectors. It also has opened, or is in the process of opening, the financial services, telecommunications, and power generation and retailing sectors to foreign service providers and greater competition. The government has also pursued cost-cutting measures, including wage and rent reductions to lower the cost of doing business.

The government wanted to provide a sustainable base for financing a competitive and affordable social security system, consistent with its socio-political environment and the need to compete economically. The social security system and the retirement system consist of state-mandated and state-managed individual retirement accounts. This way taxes are not levied on the young to pay for the old. People are required to save for their retirement. Compulsory savings are tax exempt at the time of deposit and at the time of withdrawal. They may be used to purchase homes, invest in stocks and bonds and non-residential property, pay for health care, purchase life and disability insurance or finance a college education. As a result of this system, about 85 percent of the population lives in homes they own - the highest home ownership rate in the world. At age 55, it is permitted to withdraw all the money above a minimum of $40,000. Foreign workers, who constitute about 18 percent of the labor force, casual and part-time workers and certain categories of contract workers, are not covered.[11]

Over the years, Singapore has proven itself remarkably adept at solving whatever problems come its way. In 1995, because of acute labor shortage, 450,000 Malaysians were given a job. The National Trades Union Congress (NTUC), the sole trade union federation, comprises almost 99% of total organized labor. Extensive legislation covers general labor and trade union matters. The <u>Industrial Arbitration Court</u> handles labor-management disputes that cannot be resolved informally through the Ministry of Labor. The government stresses the importance of cooperation between unions, management and government. There has been only one strike in the past 15 years. Singapore has enjoyed virtually full employment for long periods of time. Amid an economic slump, the unemployment rate rose to four percent in 2001. Unemployment has since declined and in 2005, the unemployment rate was 2.5 percent.

The People's Action Party has been in power since 1959. Its pragmatic, business-friendly economic policies have delivered wealth, homes and jobs. Singapore is not a liberal democracy in the Western sense, but that does not seem to worry its citizens. At elections, the vast majority of people who can vote choose the PAP which won all but two seats in Parliament, in the 2001 elections.

SOUTH KOREA has achieved an incredible record of economic growth and integration into the high-tech world economy. In one generation South Korea transformed itself from a very poor agricultural country ruined by war, into one of the world's leading industrial and commercial states. This was achieved through a process of government/business interaction, including selective credit, import restrictions and sponsorship of specific industries.

The Korean War, which lasted from 1950 to 1953 had destroyed most production facilities and killed about one million people. The industrial growth program began in the early 1960s, when the government instituted sweeping economic reforms emphasizing exports and labor-intensive light industries. Massive American aid made it possible to import raw materials and capital goods. The government selected a few companies and granted them all kinds of preferential treatment in exchange of kickbacks to politicians and bureaucrats. Such a system breeds complacency and spawns corruption, two hallmarks of the South Korean economy. It generated family-run conglomerates called *chaebol.*

Originally, manufacturing was limited to light industries such as textiles and wearing apparel. Light manufacturing was followed by shipbuilding, iron and steel, automobiles and petrochemicals. Hyundai and Daewoo became leading producers of oil supertankers and oil-drilling platforms.

Under the guise of guided capitalism, the government financed companies to undertake projects. Bureaucrats decided where and when capital was to be allocated. Money was mobilized through a restrictive banking system that provided loans without regard to underlying economics or financial discipline. The government guaranteed repayment if a company was unable to repay its creditors. In their quest to expand, the *chaebol* became ever more reckless in their disregard for return on investment.

Political leaders and government planners relied on the ideas and cooperation of the *chaebol* leaders. The government provided the blueprints for industrial expansion; the *chaebol* realized the plans. However, the *chaebol*-led industrialization accelerated the monopolistic and oligopolistic concentration of capital and of economically profitable activities in the hands of a limited number of conglomerates. The government encouraged inflows of foreign capital to make up for the insufficiency of domestic savings. The results were remarkable: during the 1962-73 period; the annual growth rate of GNP averaged about nine percent, while the value of total exports increased by 30 percent per annum.

The development of human capital has been one of the major factors of Korea's remarkable economic success. A notable feature of Korea's rise to industrialization is the quality of its educational system. Education was considered a key factor for youngsters to get good jobs that offer economic rewards and social status. Internationally comparable tests of pupils' achievement in cognitive skills such as numeracy, literacy and scientific reasoning show that Korean students come out on top of the list. Thanks to the strong growth of school enrolments, the educational attainments of the labor force have been of outstanding quality and have largely contributed the economic development of the country. Outward-orientation played a key role in the absorption of advanced technology from developed nations. Under the pressure of competition, export-oriented industries are required not only to constantly upgrade their technology but also the levels of education.

Labor had grown accustomed to full employment and acquiesced to working hard for low wages. In the early 1980s, a 60-hour work week at the factory or construction site was the norm. But by the mid-1980s, dissatisfaction with economic and political outcomes was set to explode. Labor relations became especially contentious. Popular discontent arose from the desire for greater political freedom and resentment toward growing inequality in the distribution of wealth.

Korea's economic growth benefited from the education level of its human resources, which played a key role in absorbing advanced technology from abroad. When Japan became a leading manufacturer of semiconductors, the Korean government realized the importance of the technology, and decided that this new industry would be able to foster future growth. In 1971, the Korea Advanced Institute of Science and Technology was set up in order to foster the specialized manpower that would be required. Several science and technology research institutions were organized to provide educational programs for the development of manufacturing and engineering skills.

In the early 1980s, semiconductor fabrication started. Led by conglomerates such as Samsung, Hyundai, and LG Semicon, Korea's memory chip industry boomed. Ever since, Korea's growth was largely based on exports of this single commodity. The electronics industry is dominated by big conglomerates with world-class efficiency of production. Samsung Electronics became the world's largest maker of memory chips.

In the early 1990s, financial markets were deregulated; banks and other financial institutions were allowed to borrow and lend without control. In 1993, the economic situation deteriorated: higher wages and lower efficiency weakened the competitive position of the industry.

In 1994, the government embarked on a policy of prestige and launched the motto of "globalization", inciting industry to invest abroad and allowing easy foreign borrowings. The *chaebol* were the spearhead of South Korea's policy to build international economic clout. They expanded by borrowing. Many went into debt-ridden expansion both at home and abroad. In 1997, South Korea's listed companies invested about $3 billion to build foreign subsidiaries or buy a stake into foreign firms. In order to be closer to their customers, chip makers invested heavily in plants in America and in Britain. Hyundai Electronics set up a £1 billion semiconductor plant in Scotland, creating 1,000 jobs initially, with the prospect of a further £1.4 billion investment in a second chip plant.[12]

In 1995, in exchange for membership in the OECD, the government agreed to loosen controls on financial institutions. This enabled foreign banks to speculate against the won. Companies that had borrowed dollars saw their debt spiral out of control. The government had neglected to monitor the banks as they lent recklessly, taking out loans from international institutions, and financing risky ventures. When many of these businesses went bankrupt, the banks were stuck with heavy losses. This created a crisis for the entire commercial banking system, as businesses and individuals withdrew their money. Because of the panic, many companies went bankrupt.[13]

Although remarkably successful, the Korean economy was not immune to the financial crisis that broke out in East Asia in 1997. The won lost over 50 percent against the dollar and foreign reserves dropped to dangerously low levels. In order to stave off economic collapse, a $58 billion loan was granted by the IMF, the World Bank and the Asian Development Bank.

Many small banks closed, and restructuring was imposed on the *chaebol.* Job losses became a growing problem. Lifetime employment guarantees were abolished. The militant trade union movement, fighting a rearguard action against rising unemployment and a loosening of the labor laws, proved difficult to tame.

When the financial crisis froze economic activity at home, firms put a brake on foreign expansion. Profitability instead of prestige became top priority. The financial crisis and the resulting industrial turmoil led to a big shake-up in the corporate landscape. Dozens of industrial conglomerates collapsed under the weight of huge debts. The government's drive to reduce the *chaebols'* debts and to close ailing factories drew fire from the labor unions which staged regular strikes. In an economy that had been labor-short and had imported workers from other Asian countries, unemployment soared to 6.5 percent, while bankruptcies kept rising.[14]

The financial crisis left a number of insolvent companies at the mercy of foreign competitors. Ford, General Motors, Deutsche Bank and many other companies engaged in long and frustrating negotiations with Daewoo, Hynix and a number of debt-laden companies controlled by creditors. Tension arose between those who were reluctant to sell South Korean assets to foreign investors, fearing job losses and restructuring and young reformers, often educated in the West and keen to throw the country's economy open to market forces.[15]

South Korea's 1997 financial crisis was brief. Economic revival was stunning. The stock market rose, industrial output and exports picked up remarkably well. A new breed of entrepreneurs emerged that changed the industrial structure. Investors, mainly American and Japanese, alarmed by the demise of the *chaebol,* and wary of the banking system, poured money into business start-ups and established firms.

The impressive recovery was led by a jump in business investment in equipment, and by exports. The cash flow improved rapidly, and allowed companies to resume targeted investments in the equipment they need to remain competitive. Samsung strengthened its memory chip production by bolstering its investment in its newest fab in Austin, Texas, and abandoned less profitable and non-strategic products. At a time when Japanese competitors were cutting back and retrenching, Samsung increased production capacity.

The industry added nearly a million jobs. The unemployment rate dipped. The IMF approved a $720 million loan, but the government refused, saying it intended to correct the economy's structural problem: its fragile financial system and the economy's dependence on the *chaebol*. Even with its stellar growth rate, South Korea remains vulnerable to outside shocks and the whims of foreign investors.[16]

The huge investment in new chipmaking capacity suggests that it will be a force to be reckoned with in semiconductors over the next few decades. A new breed of businessmen has brought about fundamental changes to South Korea's corporate culture. They focus on profit margins rather than on revenue growth. They make business more transparent. They try to motivate workers by offering employees stock options, and by setting pay according to merit instead of the accustomed age-based pay scales. They have begun to make the rigid labor market more flexible.

The trade unions have become increasingly militant and strikes are very frequent. The Labor Ministry has proposed legislation that will allow several million workers to work only 40 hours per week, spread over five days, rather than the present 44 hours, including Saturday mornings.

South Korea has restructured much of its financial system since the crash of 1997-98. Korean banks have increased their lending to consumers. Retail sales have grown while house prices have been rising. But Korea's banking system is highly vulnerable. By propping up companies, the government is making things worse. A third of the employees in the financial sector have lost their jobs. The financial system needs fixing, and this will be for some time the biggest economic challenge.[17]

Korea faces the problems of a rapidly rising wage rate that is forcing the country to change its industrial base from manufacturing labor-intensive and low- technology goods to technologically advanced products. Meanwhile, the government is moving away from targeted policies that support further growth of giant Korean industrial conglomerates. Instead, it is providing new incentives to encourage its larger companies to downsize and restructure for greater flexibility. The government believes such efforts will enable Korean computer makers to compete more effectively in the rapidly changing global computer market.

For decades, four *"superchaebols"* employed over half a million people and controlled the jobs of millions more: Hyundai with its massive tanker production; Samsung as world leader in electronics; the Daewoo group and Lucky Goldstar Electronics. They accounted for about 45 percent of GNP.[18]

The Daewoo Group bankruptcy in 1999 and the Hyundai Engineering & Construction liquidity crisis the following year, posed considerable challenges to the government's program of financial reform. The government has begun to break the hold of the *chaebol* over the financial sector and increased regulation to prevent them from arbitrarily channeling money into their subsidiaries.

Amidst all its problems South Korea's GDP continues to increase at a very satisfactory rate. Consumer spending has become a major engine for economic growth. Corruption and cronyism have yet to be eradicated. Rising wages have led to inflation and soaring property prices. Foreign exchange reserves have grown to more than $210 billion, which is about 10 times larger than the bail-out fund borrowed from the IMF in 1998 to tackle the currency crisis.

MALAYSIA is linked to Singapore by a narrow causeway. A former British colony dependent upon exports of rubber and tin, Malaysia has undergone a dramatic transformation over the course of four decades. A nation of 19.5 million people, it has a world-class economy exporting a vast range of high-tech products. Manufacturing concentrates on assembly and testing of semiconductor and electronics components, a labor-intensive process that ranks low on the scale of technology know-how. Because there is a shortage of adequately skilled engineers, the majority of technicians in senior positions are recruited from abroad.

Industrial development grew out of a decision in the 1960s to encourage foreign investment and allow foreign businesses to operate there. American, German and Japanese companies set up operations at Bayan Lepas, the country's first free trade zone where multinational corporations have sited manufacturing facilities. Today, nearly 700 factories employing over 150,000 workers are operating in seven industrial zones.

US subsidiaries helped make Malaysia one of the largest producers of semiconductors in the world. One of the most significant changes in the 1990s has been the development of factories producing hard disk drives. Malaysia is still a relatively cheap manufacturing site compared to Singapore, with only about one third the labor costs. One of the main attractions is its stable and dedicated labor force.

The Malaysian government provides guidance for overall economic growth by accelerating industrialization, technology upgrading, human resource development, and industry linkages. The Malaysian Technology Development Corporation provides seed capital to develop and commercialize indigenous technologies, transfer university and institutional technologies, transfer technologies from abroad and develop venture capital companies. The Malaysian Institute of Microelectronics Systems invests in semiconductor technology, microprocessor engineering, radio frequency engineering, surface mounting technology, and digital signal processors. The Human Resource Development Fund is styled after Singapore's Skill Development Fund to improve engineering and technical skills.

The Penang Economic Council's Strategic Development Plan was devised in 1991 to promote skill-intensive and technology-intensive, value-added industries and shift Malaysia's manufacturing competency from labor-intensive to capital-intensive manufacturing. Penang was able to attract firms like Hewlett-Packard, Intel, Siemens and Seagate Technology.

One of the most ambitious state-run projects ever conceived in Asia is the Multimedia Super Corridor (MSC), the brainchild of former Prime Minister Mahathir Mohamad. Intended to transform the nation into a knowledge-based economy, it was a grandiose project started in 1995 and spanning an area of more than 750 square kilometers. It links the capital, Kuala Lumpur with a new international airport. Intended to propel Malaysia into the Internet Age, it makes available research facilities, generous tax breaks and many other advantages to any multinational setting up shop. It was an ambitious plan intended to upgrade Malaysia's role in the global economy, by having Malaysian companies co-operate closely with multinationals, thus building a high-technology nation of knowledge workers by the year 2020. But the project has failed to attract significant investment from foreign high-tech companies. If ever completed, it will be significantly scaled down.

The Malaysian government has forced firms to consolidate in banking, broking and insurance, partly to strengthen them against foreign competitors; it also announced a series of rules to overhaul stock market practices. The problem is that Malaysia needs to move up the technology chain. With its manufacturing base squeezed by lower-wage countries such as China, Malaysia must become more of a knowledge-based economy.

But Malaysia is short of technology specialists. Shortage of IT professionals is acute. The educational system is redirected toward the development of local research and development. A government-subsidized school has nearly 3,000 students and plans to eventually enroll 15,000. Relative to China or other new investment areas, Malaysia is no longer a low labor cost semiconductor production base. The government expects that foreign investment, an experienced labor force and strong relations between business and government will continue to make the country an attractive site for higher-value semiconductor production. It is expected, however, that production of low-end items will increasingly be shed, and that semiconductor production will become more automated and move upstream. New investment focusing on increasingly sophisticated assembly and test equipment will be required.

Malaysia is moving upward in technological mastery and high-tech production in an effort to develop into the next Asian "tiger". It has attracted large amounts of foreign investment, much of it in the form of high-tech manufacturing facilities. Even if these facilities are mostly assembly operations today, future capacity will be devoted to more complex processing. While it still has a long way to go, the country is developing the resources it will need to compete in world markets.

But Malaysia's economic future is under threat, as rising costs undermine the basis of the economy. Labor is no more cheap and abundant. Land costs have escalated. Industrial growth is expected to continue over the next few years but China, India, the Philippines and Vietnam, where labor and land are much cheaper are becoming increasingly attractive to multinationals. In order to maintain its economic momentum, Malaysia must find ways to increase the value generated by its products and services, so that increased production costs can be offset.

The government has relied on foreign labor. Next to large Chinese and Indian minorities, Indonesians form the bulk of both the legal foreign workers, and also of the million-odd illegal ones. They do the dirty, dangerous and demeaning work the locals turn their back on: washing dishes, laying bricks and tending oil palms. But immigration creates problems. The government has tried to cut back on foreign labor and periodically cracks down on illegal immigrants, in order to reduce crime and preserve jobs for locals. Since Malaysians spurn the sort of work immigrants do, getting rid of them will not generate jobs acceptable to locals. Besides, keeping them lowers the cost of doing business in general.[19]

Malaysia has quickly and successfully changed the structure of its economy. In order to make up for the shortfall in experienced personnel, the government has set up training institutes in high-end manufacturing and biotech. It now has important medium- and high-tech industrial sectors and in practice all that is preventing even faster economic development is a labor shortage. Malaysia has an ambitious economic development program covering the period up to the year 2020, and so far the targets set have been exceeded.

A wide-ranging development plan to spur industrialization while diversifying the economy has been worked out. Certain industries have been targeted for specific zones: high-tech, heavy industry such as aluminum smelting, timber, boat building, palm oil industries, deep-sea fishing.

After the country's financial system was laid low in the crisis of 1997-98, Prime Minister Mahathir Mohamad engaged in a campaign of America-bashing. He lamented that foreign currency traders had killed the Asian tigers. His decision to impose capital controls and fix the ringgit at 3.8 to the US dollar has not prevented the outflow of money, while keeping foreign investors away. Foreign direct investment has dwindled and many companies have shed jobs. Malaysian businessmen are causing a balance-of-payments problem by keeping their money out of the country rather than converting it to ringgit.

The government wants to make headway toward a knowledge-based economy, rather than simply making goods. A utopian technopolis, Cyberjaya, is under construction. It will be the showcase and the infrastructure of the country's commitment to growth in high-technology, and is intended to attract foreign capital and industries producing high-value products. Companies will be able to take advantage of substantial tax breaks, unrestricted use of local and foreign employees, freedom to source funds globally, duty-free importation of capital goods and equipment, discounts on telecommunications and many other advantages.

THE PHILIPPINES is a troubled developing nation that is rapidly industrializing. Extreme disparities of wealth and poverty are obvious, but the urban middle classes are expanding. Ruled by a succession of dictatorial, inept and corrupt governments, it is one of the fastest-growing outposts of the high-tech economy. Even in the face of political turmoil, industrial production is stable and growing relatively rapidly. The country was able to insulate itself from the worst effects of the Asian currency crisis. A revolution is under way where an increasingly sophisticated technology industry is competing for investment dollars with established regional rivals.

Attracted by tax breaks and a skilled and inexpensive workforce, multinationals have set up plants, in some cases shifting production from elsewhere in Asia. Texas Instruments, Intel, Seagate Technology, Hitachi, Philips and many others have established manufacturing and research facilities. Cypress Semiconductor and Analog Devices, two of the world's biggest makers of telecoms-related chips, have set up production. These investments have transformed the economy.

Taiwanese and Japanese companies have moved disk-drive and other production lines from their home countries. A law enacted in 1995 allows private firms to set up duty- and tax-free industrial zones such as Gateway Business Park, 90 minutes by car south of Manila. Gateway has become a center for the assembly and testing of some of the world's most sophisticated computer components. Workers in spacesuit-like uniforms pore over microscopes, assembling the latest computer chips. In five years, gleaming new buildings with dust-free "clean rooms" sprouted where once there were only rice fields and a few local firms. Privately owned zones are scattered across the country.

In recent years, the relative political and economic stability has contributed to the industry's growth. The population enjoys a literacy rate of 95 percent. A large and growing pool of English speaking engineers who absorb technological training very rapidly, makes it easy to communicate. In any year, some 370,000 Filipinos study technical subjects at tertiary level.

Universities and colleges offer degrees in computer science and related programs. Close to 400 vocational-technical schools offer short-term courses. Thanks to its well-educated workforce and good endowment of natural resources, the Philippines should continue to prosper. Colleges and universities churn out an average of 20,000 IT graduates annually, but a lack of industry-driven IT curricula and outdated methodologies are being blamed for a mismatch of skills and demand. Because many graduates do not have the required skills, companies have to retrain them.

Another attraction for investors has been the cost of labor. Wages for high-tech shop workers are at least 30 percent lower than those in some neighboring countries. The industry pays shop-floor wages of $200-250 a month, compared with $800-1,000 in Malaysia. A production manager might earn $1,000-2,000 a month, compared with around $3.600 in Malaysia.

Filipino industry is dominated by a few powerful family companies. Started in the 1970s with the simplest type of chip packaging, the Philippines have climbed the technology ladder, moving to chip assembly, testing, microprocessor assembly and even design. The industry has shifted toward more complex products. Included among these are the latest Pentium chips, laptop computers and digital-signal processors used in cell-phones.

By the mid-1990s, the Philippines were home to some 350 firms engaged primarily in the manufacture of consumer electronics, equipment for telecommunications, computers and their peripherals, as well as components and devices such as semiconductors. About 30 percent of the firms were locally owned. Chips had replaced garments as the country's major export earner and played a major role in sustaining economic growth. Many of the world's leading chip and computer makers have substantial and growing investments in the country. Philips Semiconductors chose it over China and Indonesia for a chip plant. Several Taiwanese and Japanese companies have moved disk-drive and other production lines from their home countries: Taiwan's Acer is assembling laptops in Subic Bay while Japan's Toshiba, Hitachi and Fujitsu are producing hard disks or CD-ROMS.

Electronics has brought jobs: some 30,000 jobs were added in 1998 to an industry whose workforce had grown to 250,000. Electronics accounts for a quarter of all jobs in firms employing ten or more workers. Wages are around 40 percent higher on average than in other sectors.

One-third of the people lives in abject poverty, yet Philippine labor cannot match Chinese production costs, mainly because of the poor infrastructure and rampant corruption. Exports are a cornerstone of the economy. Many companies were caught up in the chaos that prevailed during the administration of President Estrada.

The government recognizes that the long-term growth of the semiconductor industry can only be sustained if it moves on to the next level of higher value-added and higher design content products. Several industrial parks are planned to this end. Exports have weathered the adverse effects of the financial crisis, but the Philippine industry is handicapped by the low level of value-added activity. To maintain the electronics industry well-positioned to sustain its growth, will require private sector initiatives and public sector policies. If the initiatives and policies are effectively carried out, the Philippine electronics industry can expect robust growth.

Between the 1970s to the mid-1990s, the economy boomed, generating pockets of wealth in major cities. But grinding poverty, especially among the Muslim majority, fostered violence in parts of the country. Communist and Muslim separatist guerrillas spread lawlessness and resorted to organized kidnappings of wealthy businessmen. Then came the Asian financial crisis, which caused substantial currency devaluation. The instability caused investment to plummet.

The business community, concerned about the deterioration of the economy, was very unhappy with the corrupt administration of President Estrada and joined in street demonstrations to oust him. His successor, Gloria Arroyo, has managed to restore stability. She took a firm hand to the economy and has consistently held the fiscal deficit below target. In order to convince foreign investors to return, she intends to speed the long-promised plans to finish roads, ports, railways and other projects.

The Philippines' economic fundamentals are sound. But the electronics industry faces many challenges: electricity is expensive, roads are ropy and political stability is by no means assured. Future economic prospects depend on the government's ability to maintain political, social and economic stability. Many companies continue to invest, while others have pulled out. Highly publicized kidnapping and crime have damaged the reputation. Foreign investors are wary of putting money into a country fraught with violent crime and plagued by separatist and communist insurgencies.

INDIA'S unique hybrid of highly-skilled English-speaking, inexpensive software engineers and well-educated youth has placed the country in the space of ten years at the top rank for software development outsourcing, making it an essential part of the global economy. India is extremely poor and its economy is undeveloped. Post-colonial India was ruled by socialist governments imbued with the high-minded ideas of self-sufficiency and economic planning proclaimed by Prime Minister Jawaharlal Nehru.

After Nehru, successive revolving-door governments put the country on the road to economic reform. Under the socialist governments, the economy was autarchic and highly regulated. Progress was slow, particularly in the areas of reining in the budget deficits, privatization, and the pricing of public goods and services. Potential entrepreneurs were isolated from the global economy and there was little room for private enterprise. The reforms of 1991 entailed deregulating business and gradually opening India up to foreign trade and investment.

Bangalore is the epicenter of India's software industry. The home of the Indian Institute of Science and the base for defense companies and research institutes, it teemed a vast reservoir of engineering talent. When the government set up tax-exempt zones, allowed duty-free imports of equipment and guaranteed access to high-speed satellite links and reliable electric power, a growing number of foreign companies began locating offshore development centers. Between 1990 an 1999, software and computer services soared from $150 million to more than $4 billion.

The government came to recognize the potential of the software industry in a market economy. Indian entrepreneurs saw an opportunity to exploit domestic human resources in global markets. The initial boost came when American companies discovered the advantages of outsourcing software. IBM, Intel, Compaq and many other American companies looking for talent, discovered Bangalore. They started out by entrusting sophisticated software development to programmers who soon became experts at writing concise, elegant code for architecture conceived elsewhere.

The Infosys campus on the outskirts of Bangalore looks like a chunk of the rich world that has been reassembled amidst the dust and debris of India. The echoes of Silicon Valley are everywhere.

India's greatest asset is a large, English-educated workforce that is willing to work at relatively low wages; and they do it better and cheaper than anybody in the world. Every year India produces around 2.5 million university graduates, including 400,000 engineers and 200,000 IT professionals. The technical colleges supply the raw talent that must be molded through elaborate training schemes in order to update their computer technology and keep up with innovation. The availability of experienced people remains the permanent concern and challenge.

Throughout the 1990s, such Indian software powers as Infosys, Wipro, Satyam, and Tata Consultancy Systems grew by providing smart engineers to do work outsourced from Western multinationals. The Indians rapidly built up a high level of trustworthiness. World-class software companies aspire to become powers in their own right. They wall themselves up in gated campuses. Infosys and Wipro are private oases in a declining metropolis with their own power and communications, security, water, gyms, and wading pools. Infosys even sports a nine-hole golf course. In Bangalore, wages and real-estate prices are soaring to record levels, though still generally at a fraction of US costs. Software companies create their own worlds. Sheltered inside sparkling new office campuses surrounded by manicured lawns in the huge industrial zones and crowded with smartly dressed men and sari-clad women, they can only be reached by driving over potholed roads bordered by dismal slums and overcrowded with people, cows and bullock carts.

India has undergone huge changes in recent years. A nouveau-rich urban-educated class is very noticeable, giving the country a glittering face to the outside world. But nearly 30 percent of the population still live below the poverty line and the same number are only marginally better off. The contrast exposes the chasm between wealth and grinding poverty.

Major suppliers of highly technical brainpower, most Indian software companies do not develop and sell their own products. They have won recognition as low-cost providers of software services to multinationals from all over the world, mainly from the United States. They produce lines of software code as sub-contractors, conduct testing, verification and maintenance according to specifications set up by their customers. This includes being able to design and manage entire projects and to move into software development in niche areas.

Export-oriented companies can set up operations zones that are exempt from the national burden of regulations. They are entitled to a ten-year tax holiday and are exempt from import duties and licenses on capital goods. The bureaucracy, however, remains very punctilious.

Many of America's largest companies are there, developing software next to Indian companies. They hire eager graduates from the top technical universities, and pay a software engineer about one-fifth what he would earn in California.[20]

The software industry employs about 340,000 people. Indian universities graduate about 80,000 software engineers annually; private institutes add another 40 to 50,000. Yet, the labor market is tight, and wages increase fast. Starting salaries for software engineers range between $3,000 and $5,000 a year. An MBA with three years experience in India will make about $12,000 a year, compared with $100,000 in the United States; a programmer will make $5,000, compared with $60,000. Many start out at an Indian company, gain a few years experience and get off to America. Indian immigrants are top executives in many of Silicon Valley start-ups.

While the mass of the population remains mired in poverty and hopelessness, high tech has given thousands a chance to move into the middle-class, and has minted hundreds of millionaires and even a few billionaires living in air-conditioned splendor. India has its star entrepreneurs. Sabeer Bhatia, a young software engineer became a legend in 1997 when he invented Hotmail and sold it to Microsoft for $400 million. Azim H. Premji, a Stanford University grad, owns 84 percent of Wipro Ltd., India's second-biggest software exporter. He inherited his father's edible-oils business, but decided to set up a software company and became the wealthiest man in the country. When the Indian stock market crashed in February 2000, his net worth plummeted from $40 billion to $6.5 billion. He claims he does not care for personal wealth, drives an ordinary Ford sedan and stays in mid-priced hotels.[21]

Other locations in India are also beginning to grow. As costs rise in Bangalore, they could benefit from the outsourcing of certain activities by Bangalore firms. Microsoft has a software development center in Hyderabad where out-of-college software engineers are plentiful and work for $3.500 a year.

Keeping valued employees is a problem. Aware of the global demand for their skills and the substantially higher compensation available in more developed economies, many aspire to work for foreign companies. American employment agencies exacerbate the brain drain by offering high-paying contracts for software jobs in the United States.

Bangalore, along with emerging tech centers in Hyderabad and Pune, are India's star business attractions. The software talent and the best schools are there, and foreign money managers keep exploring for promising start-ups.

There are 350,000 software developers in India. There is a massive shortage of experienced engineering and technology staff and of senior and mid-level management. University graduates with a computer science degree move massively to the United States after they have been trained. Many, however, return to set up their own firms.

Because of the lack of managerial talent, the high degree of state intervention in the economy and the lack of a venture capital industry, Indian industry will not move up the IT value chain very soon. Originally, venture capital was a family-and-friends affair. The venture capital industry is still hamstrung by draconian regulations. The supply of venture capital is restricted by a multiplicity of conflicting and cumbersome regulations and discriminated against in a variety of ways. The rules have gradually been relaxed, but the industry remains small.

India has valuable natural resources: forests, fish, oil, iron ore, coal and agricultural products. It has achieved self-sufficiency in food since independence in 1947, yet deep poverty persists. The economic policy adopted by Nehru and other Indian leaders in the decade after independence is largely responsible for this situation. They practiced central planning along Soviet lines: five-year plans, nationalization of heavy industries. They perpetuated the British tradition of foreign exchange controls and licenses to start businesses. In 1991, facing default on its foreign debt, India abandoned four decades of economic isolation and planning, and gave more freedom to entrepreneurs. The government sold off many of its state companies; cut tariffs and taxes and eliminated most price and exchange controls. As a result, India became one of the world's fastest-growing economies in the 1990s, averaging nearly 10 percent growth per year. While the rich have gotten richer, a vast number of people live in abject poverty. Even today, India is a bureaucratic nightmare. Corruption is widespread in public service at every level.

A growing number of American and European companies rely on an offshore organization, linked by satellites, for complex application development projects, which allows them to obtain results much faster and at substantial cost savings over using home-based consultants.[22] World-wide demand for information technology and software services is growing steadily, and the Indian software industry should continue to grow at the same pace. India has a future in the new economy. India could resolve not to invent another thing, and still prosper mightily.

CHINA, the world's most populous nation, is in the throes of history's most gigantic experiment in capitalism, with far-reaching implications for future global competition and power. In 1978, when Deng Xiaoping announced his market reforms with the slogan: "To get rich is glorious", he launched the most dramatic surge of wealth creation in human history. He radically changed the direction of China's economy with his introduction of an "open door" policy encouraging foreign investment and trade. Chinese entrepreneurs were quick to learn about the market economy. The result was two decades of fabulous growth.

The Chinese people, led by freewheeling entrepreneurs and speculators, rushed into fulfilling Deng's dictum. Commerce became the symbol of freedom. In 1979 the Chinese government opened up some of its coastal regions, including the area on Hong Kong's border. Foreign investors were invited to participate in the industrial development.

The Chinese are well aware of the fact that before the 15th century their country outstripped Europe in its understanding of hydraulics, iron smelting and shipbuilding. Twice in history, its economic development had been stalled. Mao's Cultural Revolution had crushed the economy and executed thousands of businessmen. Centuries ago, Chinese scientists and entrepreneurs had created the technologies necessary to launch an industrial revolution that could have given them world dominance: the blast furnace and piston bellows, gunpowder and the cannon; the compass and the rudder; paper and movable type, the plough, the horse collar. Chinese armadas explored Africa's east coast while Portugal and Spain were sending much smaller expeditions down the west coast. In the 16th century an inventor had built and tested a rocket-propelled chair in which he planned to ascend to heaven. On launch, the chair, 47 rockets, two kites and the inventor evaporated in flame and smoke.[23]

The imperial court perceived new technologies as threats. Imperial edicts prohibited building ocean-going ships and sailing away from the Chinese coastline. Confucian scorn for commercialism ruined the merchant class. Power and prestige was turned over to the mandarins, assisted by an army of lesser office holders whose ability was evaluated by their capacity to pass examinations in Chinese classics. China lost its edge by suppressing entrepreneurs; the price of atrophy was defeat in the face of European imperialism.

After decades of communism, the 1982 constitution caused an explosion of entrepreneurial activity by legitimizing the "individual economy" alongside the socialist public one. Amendments in 1988 referred to the "private economy", and a year later private activity was dubbed as an important part of the "socialist market economy". In 2004, yet another amendment declared private property "inviolable". Even so, public ownership retains a preferred status and is considered "sacred". China's leaders still call themselves communists, but they are pragmatic and have become capitalists in practice. The nine members of the Politburo Standing Committee are university trained engineers. Their decisions are made in secret.

The silicon revolution has delivered a major reversal to the erratic pattern of the country's technological and economic ups and downs. Two decades after its rulers allowed private enterprise to develop the business instinct of its people, thousands of entrepreneurs swept away the crushing legacy of the socialist economy. China is now restless with technological ambition and is on the way to become the factory floor of global information technology and a high-tech manufacturing colossus. With its 1.3 billion people, it has the potential to be the second-largest economy in the world. Foreign investment has helped make China a formidable export machine. China makes the entire value chain, simple and sophisticated, at prices nobody can compete with. The near-limitless pool of cheap labor added to the growing supply of educated graduates should allow China to out-export its Asian competitors.

In the early 1990s, the capabilities of the electronics industry were extremely weak, offering little else than low-cost manufacturing and a disciplined workforce. Within a few years the entrepreneurs mastered a range of technologies, creating an efficient high-tech manufacturing area around Shanghai and a budding R&D industry in Beijing. Year after year, China astounded the world with double-digit annual growth rates while attracting over $300 billion in foreign investment capital.

Until the mid-1990s, Chinese factories screwed together radios, telephone handsets, and electronic toys from components shuttled in from Hong Kong, Taiwan, and Japan. They manufactured for export simple and cheap products, and reinvested the profits to start high-tech production of computers and components. Now, foreign manufacturers are relocating semiconductor, high-end circuit-board and other sophisticated electronics plants to China. Intel has not only production facilities, but also operates several research labs.[24]

China has re-emerged as an economic powerhouse and the world-beating exporter of an unprecedented assortment of products. A flood of foreign investment allowed Chinese entrepreneurs to master a broad range of technologies: sweatshops in Shenzhen, efficient high-tech manufacturing around Shanghai and a budding R&D industry in Beijing, all coexist at once. The work force ranges from unskilled to tech-savvy.

Liberalization swept across all the sectors of the industrial economy, but electronics and information technology have been targeted for growth through export. Well-funded development zones are functioning as national centers of excellence at the forefront of the electronics technology revolution. Some companies establish themselves in China to address the Chinese market; some use the talented and low-cost labor pool as a venue for manufacturing goods for export. While still producing labor-intensive subassemblies, plants in China are now assembling a growing number of final products. Legend is China's top PC and parts manufacturer and one of the world's top motherboard producers.

China has an abundant pool of young, high-school-educated workers, with millions more entering the workforce each year. A vast number of universities and institutes are turning out well-trained, yet relatively low-paid engineers, making the country a formidable manufacturing center. Phone service, ports, electrical power, and other infrastructure in key coastal cities are excellent; approvals for the building of new factories are often granted within a few days.

Factories run round the clock, on two 12-hour shifts. Most employees in Guangdong come from outside the province. Recruited from vocational high schools, the young women working in the electronics factories in Shenzhen for $65 per month stand in line for the jobs, not only because the salary is, by their standards high, but because they receive three meals daily and live in modern dormitories provided by the company, with heat in the winter and in some cases air conditioning in the summer. Dressed in bunny suits, they lay down integrated circuits on ultrapure silicon with utmost meticulousslesness. They are mostly single and work five days per week plus Saturday morning, 8 hours regular time plus 4 hours overtime per day. They were destined to help their peasant fathers harvest the rice or palm oil; now they have a bank account; they are independent and proud. Most accumulate sufficient money for a dowry when the time comes to go home and look for a husband.

China is sucking up almost all of the new manufacturing investment in Asia, and is emerging as an export juggernaut in low-wage garment and shoe production, as well as in high-end electronics. In less than one generation, Shanghai metamorphosed from a dilapidated city into a futuristic metropolis. The skyline of Shanghai's is dominated by shiny skyscrapers with space-age flourishes at the top.

Internet start-ups are proliferating. Even though a PC can cost half a year's pay, after people have a TV, a washing machine and a refrigerator, the PC is the next thing they want. Some of the fastest machines come from tiny local shops that sell only a few hundred PCs a year. Such assemblers account for some 35 percent of the market. China is Intel's largest market and is far ahead of local microprocessor manufacturing. But Microsoft has a huge piracy problem. [25]

The private sector contributes about one-third of GDP. It is unclear whether gains in economic efficiency are enough to offset the chronic misdirection of resources by state-controlled enterprises. Innumerable state factories have been closed. While the process was painful for those involved, exports are the main drivers of growth, creating a huge trade surplus.

By 1992, 850 electronics firms had moved manufacturing facilities to the Pearl River Delta area. By 1996, over 8,000 foreign firms had labor-intensive facilities in that area. Intel, Dell Computer and a vast number of American companies have moved production from Taiwan and Malaysia to China. Matsushita, Sony and Samsung transferred production facilities. Microsoft operates research-and-service centers in Beijing and Shanghai. China is Microsoft's biggest market, providing the company with ten percent of its revenues.[26] International Information Products, IBM's joint venture with Great Wall Computer, is the leading foreign vendor in China with seven percent of the market.[27]

In 1995, Hewlett-Packard was the lone building in an empty field called the Pudong Area Economic Free Zone. It was a new area offering incentives to attract foreign high-tech investment. Within three years Intel, IBM, AT&T, Texas Instruments, Ricoh, Philips joined in. Multinationals move in almost every month. A similar boom is taking place at the China-Singapore Suzhou Industrial Park, near Shanghai. Opened in 1995, the park's advanced infrastructure and one-stop approval office has pulled in dozens of electronics multinationals and attracted $2.5 billion in investment so far. These two areas, located in China's Jiangsu Province, are only second in electronics production after Guangdong Province in the South, near Hong Kong.

Direct foreign investment increased by 20 percent in 2000. That is more than the rest of Asia combined. Matsushita, Sony, and Samsung are preparing a wholesale transfer of production facilities. By 2006, Motorola's total investment in China amounts to $10 billion. China attracts more foreign investment than the rest of non-Japan Asia combined. About half of the "Taiwanese" computers, digital cameras and motherboards are made on the mainland; in scanners, the figure is almost 90 percent.

China has the largest mobile telephone market in the world. Foreign telecom operators are able to own parts of Chinese networks. Multinationals have the right to set up their own distribution networks rather than working through Chinese corporate middlemen. China has already passed the US as the world's biggest user of mobile phones.

The Chinese government envisions the construction of at least 40 major chip-production lines within the next 10 years. Occupying both the high and low ends of the market with unique advantages, Chinese industry can underbid almost everyone in the world on wages and prices. It has the capacity to profoundly disturb the balance of commercial power and to eventually become a nightmare for the global economy. Across Asia, China's emergence as a world-beating exporter of an unprecedented range of products has generated a mix of alarm and despair. Japan, South Korea and Taiwan fear a "hollowing out" of their industries, as investment, production and trade move to the low-cost mainland.

China's arrival as a manufacturing superpower is reshaping world trade. Its advantages are formidable: cheap labor, millions of talented engineers and good infrastructure. While many Chinese have joined the middle class, millions are slipping into a new underclass of displaced peasants, unemployed factory workers, and low-level laborers whose working conditions are horrendous and whose wages barely sustain them. The majority of those who live in the country cannot afford electricity; they still burn coal. The threat of social instability is real. Even after shedding 50 million workers over the past three years, Chinese state-run companies are still likely to fire 20 million more. Over 100 million peasants have flocked to the cities in search of work, adding to China's angry underclass.[28]

China intends to develop a world-class semiconductor industry. In 2002, 14 fabs were in development or in the planning stages. This will require a very large amount of capital and access to intellectual property from the United States, Europe, Japan and Taiwan. China is fast becoming one of the world's biggest microchip consumers, and its central planners believe that development of a world-class semiconductor industry is critical to the development of a strong information technology industry. It has been estimated by US experts that by 2010 China's information technology market will exceed the US. [29]

China gets mightier all the time, and increasingly emerges not only as a huge market and a low cost production platform, but also as a significant potential source of skills. Currently 200,000 IT are involved in the software export industry, with an additional 50,000 entering the workforce each year. Many IT professionals have some experience working abroad. While most service employees have strong technical skills, they are short in knowledge of the English language.[30] Labor shortage is one of the problems of the semiconductor industry. The universities churn out talented engineers, but many of the best designers go to America. Many will set up their own company, hoping to strike it rich. Wealth has become a yardstick of achievement and respect.

The nation's education system puts tremendous emphasis on technical skills. Each year, Shanghai's universities produce a bumper crop of capable, inexpensive engineers. The government has educational policies for building a high-tech talent pool. Building human resources will also take time, but the Chinese government is implementing policies that are intended to mature over the next 20 or 30 years.[31]

Chipmakers can count on plenty of inexpensive land and an abundant supply of cheap electricity and water. Chipmaking ventures with assets of more than $100 million are eligible for a five-year tax holiday followed by five years of 50 percent tax discounts. Equipment and components imported for chip production are exempt. Chinese banks have been ordered to grant generous loans to chip-related ventures.

China's political system is unstable and plagued by corruption. Communist bureaucrats and capitalist entrepreneurs are intimately entwined. The people in charge show little respect for human rights or copyrights. In spite of these drawbacks, however, China is proving irresistibly attractive to the world's most advanced technology companies.

Hong Kong is China's most important trading partner. Labor costs represent about ten percent of those in Hong Kong. Asia's most advanced economies, Japan's included, will continue to shift manufacturing to the mainland while offering technological expertise, developing brands and conducting research outside. Japanese companies keep increasing their investment in China, while closing down operations elsewhere.

Beijing regards Taiwan as a breakaway province and bans any investment worth more than $50 million. Despite these restrictions, an estimated 50,000 Taiwanese businesses have invested in China since it opened its economy in the 1980s. They have pumped more than $45 billion into production facilities on the mainland.[32]

China's accession to the World Trade Organization came at a time of political change, when reform-minded leaders were about to take charge. The immediate impact on the economy will not be considerable, but provides the incentive needed for economic liberalization. In the long-term, consequences will be transformational. The new leaders, many educated in the West, understand the potential of economic liberalization and the limits of political intervention in the economy.

The Asian financial crisis sparked a debate over "Asian" versus "Western" capitalism, and more precisely, about whether the root cause of the crisis was a failure of Asian capitalism or a failure of Western capitalism. While triggering financial turmoil among the "tigers", China was shielded from the disciplines of global trade and finance. Admission to the World Trade Organization has stripped that shield away. China's economic transition has reached a critical stage, forcing the government to more aggressive reforms of the state-owned enterprise system. China's leadership is acutely aware of this, but has no plan for a leap toward Western capitalism since this might trigger a profound economic, social and political crisis.

The most palpably unsustainable aspects of Chinese capitalism, notably the financing of loss-making state-owned enterprises must be corrected. The Chinese Communist party plans to achieve this through a "socialist market economy": an oxymoron that is part of official rhetoric.

The Chinese government faces the formidable challenge of keeping gross domestic product growing fast enough to provide a cushion against the shocks and dislocations resulting from accession into the World Trade Organization. Millions of jobs must be created in order to alleviate a rural economic crisis, to whittle down a mountain of bad loans in the banking system and to prevent a bubble in domestic stock market values from deflating. All this needs to be done at a time when external drivers of growth - trade and inflows of foreign direct investment - may be hobbled by sluggish economies elsewhere. It is a daunting balancing act, but one to which Beijing is determined to prove equal.

Corruption and fraud are rampant. Entrepreneurs receive business licenses in exchange of kickbacks. This should not be surprising, given that China emerged from the Cultural Revolution of the 1960s without even the remnants of the institutions that market economies elsewhere take for granted. It had factories that were run by ministries as welfare organizations, but no incorporated companies; it had no "property", no "assets and liabilities". It lacked concepts such as bankruptcy and contract. In fact, China had no legal system in any conventional sense.

The government is trying to build these institutions with a remarkable sense of urgency. The country's leaders realize that their reforms are causing social dislocation. After massive layoffs, most state-owned enterprises are still overstaffed. The private sector is growing fast, but still far too small to absorb these workers.

Despite China's WTO membership, an international agreement still bars US, European, and Japanese companies from selling China the most sophisticated manufacturing equipment out of concern that the machines will be used for military purposes.[34]

Rapid industrialization has created vast inequalities between the rural poor and people making a living in the major cities. It remains to be seen how 900 million peasants, a 250 to 300 million industrialized population and a minority of new-rich will interact. The Chinese are increasingly reclaiming their rightful place as an international powerhouse. Interference in their affairs by Western visitors under the pretext of democratic principles or humanitarianism is strongly resented. China has a love-hate relationship with the United States and the United Kingdom. The memories of the humiliations inflicted by the Opium Wars are deeply engraved in their minds. The country is becoming a major economic force; it has the largest army in the world, nuclear capability, modern aircraft and missiles. With increased prosperity, it will have to push its way to get access to resources like oil. Sooner or later, its geopolitical weight will have to be considered.

For every gleaming factory on the China coast that's producing world-class goods, there's a rusting hulk of a state-owned enterprise that's barely holding on. While many Chinese are now joining the middle class, millions are slipping into a new underclass of displaced peasants, unemployed factory workers, and low-level laborers whose working conditions are horrendous and whose wages barely sustain them.

The Communist party attempts to balance expanding economic freedoms with its firm hold on political power. The government's uncanny ability to balance capitalism and autocracy is turning the country into the tech titan of the 21st century. American and European companies continue to make huge investments.

Shortly before his retirement, Chairman Jiang Zemin expressed his intention to contribute to an equitable political and economic world order: "We do not want any single power to be the world's policeman." As for his domestic concerns: "We want to see part of the population prosper more rapidly than some other groups, provided they do it legally and through honest work... We are building a socialist nation with a Chinese character... Our country is poor. We must stand together for a better future... As a young man I fought actively for the revolution, but my concept of Communism was superficial and simplistic. It took 78 generations to build Confucianism. For the construction of Socialism, we need at least two... The whole world benefits from China's political stability... The fact that discussions are taking place within the Communist party shows how democratic it is." [35]

In November 2002, Hu Jintao replaced Jiang Zemin at the head of the Communist Party's Politburo. The Standing Committee was expanded to nine members. Eight of them were trained engineers. The party formally abandoned the worker-peasant class base and asserted itself as the 'vanguard' of the entire Chinese people, including private entrepreneurs. But China's paramount ambitions - stability, prosperity, modernity - require more reform, global integration and comity with the democratic world.

Increasing civil unrest poses a challenge to the Communist Party. Despite historic economic growth that has lifted millions out of poverty, protests and riots are occurring with increasing frequency, growing in size and often ending in violence. Such incidents erupt between ethnic and religious majorities and minorities, as protests against the widening wealth gap and government corruption; the seizure of farmland for development and layoffs associated with the transition from socialism to capitalism. Most protesters are among the poor unable to adapt to the market economy and to protect their traditional rights through government channels. The government has adopted a carrot-and-stick approach, giving in to some demands while arresting activists. The government restricts or bars news reporting of unrest. But with the growing use the Internet and e-mail, widening access to overseas news media and the prevalence of cell phones and text messaging, censorship is becoming difficult. The Communist Party is worried that these outbursts of discontent, including attacks on party and state officials, might coalesce into large-scale, organized opposition to its rule.

These problems ought to be seen as growing pains - transitional and, with luck, surmountable. As prosperity spreads, and more and more Chinese people are able to afford life's little luxuries, China's domestic economy is starting to become a powerful engine of growth in its own right. China's amazing economy has been built on the export market. The economic dynamo that is Shanghai is spreading growth inland, allowing hundreds of millions - deprived of material comforts by the insanities of Maoism – to catch up and create in the long run a healthy home market.

In December 2004, IBM sold its PC hardware division to China's number one computer maker Lenovo, formerly known as Legend. It was the first major inroad of Chinese industry on the way to globalization. The merged firm became the third largest PC vendor with sales of about $12bn a year. But the new management announced that it would not be satisfied with its number three position. A huge Chinese company with headquarters in upstate New York came to symbolize the dawn of a new era.

EPILOGUE

The year 2004 marked the 50th anniversary of the Silicon Revolution. On May 10, 1954, Texas Instruments announced the commercial availability of silicon transistors. These transistors were constructed by cutting a rectangular bar from a silicon crystal that was grown from a melt containing impurities. The man responsible for the achievement was Gordon Teal, who had worked 20 years at Bell Labs before joining Texas Instruments. Shortly after Bell Labs announced the invention of the transistor, Bardeen and Brattain had been sidetracked. Shockley pursued his P-N junction ideas, while Teal experimented with germanium and gradually developed crystal-growing experience. At Texas Instruments, it took him several years to produce the ultra-pure silicon required for semiconductors.

The silicon transistor was a marvel of modern science. Germanium transistors were much easier to manufacture, but their amplification ability varied greatly as temperature rose above room level. Scientists knew that silicon possessed superior temperature stability and power handling characteristics; but the semiconductor material had to be "grown" to the purest substance, with less than one part impurity in one billion.

The silicon transistor was a turning point in Texas Instruments' history. The first silicon transistors were used in military applications, radio and television sets, telephony, mainframe and minicomputers, programmable calculators, teletype machines and much more. Sales rose almost vertically, lifting the company suddenly into the big leagues.

In 1959, the world of electronics was revolutionized by the development of the integrated circuit, which was to become the basic building block of the computer. The combination of both active and passive electronic parts on a single piece of semiconductor material was a major breakthrough. No invention has done more to usher in the Information Age than the integrated circuit. The rapid advance in the number of transistors per chip led to integrated circuits with continuously increasing capability and performance.

At Fairchild Semiconductor, Bob Noyce pursued the idea of integrating a number of transistors and the other required elements on a single chip of silicon. The problem was how to connect the transistors. Jean Hoerni developed the "Planar process", which became the only practical way to build reliable silicon-based integrated circuits. Independently, Jack Kilby, an engineer at Texas Instruments, had developed the same concept of integrating several transistors on a single chip a few months before. However, he could not solve the problem of interconnections in a practical way. Noyce received the patent as the inventor, which launched a longstanding lawsuit by Texas Instruments. Noyce and Kilby were finally conceded the title of co-inventors.

The integrated circuit brought along a tremendous miniaturization in the field of electronics and inaugurated a decline in the cost of computers, while increasing their capacity to perform ever greater and more complex operations. Soon many companies entered the semiconductor market. With few exceptions, like Texas Instruments and Motorola, they were located in Silicon Valley.

In January 1971, a company called Intel introduced the world's first single chip microprocessor, the Intel 4004, invented by Federico Faggin, Ted Hoff, and Stan Mazor. The Intel 4004 chip took the integrated circuit down one step further by placing all the parts that made a computer think (i.e. central processing unit, memory, input and output controls) on one small chip. Programming intelligence into inanimate objects had now become possible.

In April 1972, the release of the 8008 microprocessor inaugurated a new era in integrated electronics. Eight months later, a company located near Paris delivered the world's first microcomputer to the French Ministry of Agriculture. Called Micral, it provided a performance close to that of the minicomputer.

Over the next two years about 2,000 units were sold to public and private institutions. In May 1974, the Micral was demonstrated without success at the National Computer Conference in Chicago. Leslie Solomon, the technical director of Popular Electronics picked up the data sheets and the leaflets detailing the characteristics and performance of the computer. He passed all this information on to his friend Ed. Roberts and told him to put together a microcomputer kit, the Altair. Paul Allen and Bill Gates wrote the software for the Altair, while Steve Wozniak and Steve Jobs used components to build the first Apple. By demonstrating the feasibility of building a commercial computer around a microprocessor and developing a market for it, the Micral sparked the computer revolution.

Thousands of computer fans bought the Altair kit. They saw what no one in the industry had seen, and were amazed. The Homebrew Computer Club, where an informal group of engineers, programmers, hobbyists, experimenters and entrepreneurs met regularly, spun off dozens of companies that formed the core of the nascent personal computer industry. They assembled their machines with off-the-shelf parts, making an improvement here and there, and taking advantage of the exponential increase in computing power and in demand for computers.

Some emerged as computer or component manufacturers in their own right. The successful ones found niche market. When Steve Jobs brought out Apple computers, he made it affordable to put powerful computing devices on the desktop. When IBM reluctantly and belatedly decided to enter the PC market using Intel microprocessors and Bill Gates' software, it set the de facto standard for the industry.

In 1982, Compaq announced the production of an IBM clone, leading an entire sub-industry that would imitate and improve on the IBM standard. IBM had underestimated the popularity of clones, and suffered immensely for its overconfidence. A new battlefield emerged in which Compaq and a bunch of start-ups took on IBM.

The Silicon Revolution is the outgrowth of the creativity displayed by exceptional individuals, computer fanatics, innovators, entrepreneurs. In two decades, they reshaped the world at unimaginable speed. The computer occupies the central battleground of the Information Age and launched humanity into a new era of scientific development, economic evolution and interdependence. It has broadened perception and knowledge in a way comparable to the information explosion produced by the printing press. The electronics industry is the benchmark and the barometer of innovation and industrial capability. Brutally competitive and disruptive, it has sparked a profound economic and social transformation.

A global marketplace has arisen, where surviving competitors from around the world fight it out for a share of the market by bringing out new products, more choices and higher quality at lower costs. The marketplace is a laboratory and learning environment where innovative and clever business ideas and models are tested. Some succeed; most fail. Competition to meet the expectations of consumers accelerates the rate of technological progress.

The secret behind America's economic success lies in the spirit of entrepreneurship. Occasionally a gifted youngster makes history when he visualizes the potential of new processes and technologies, and puts together a globe-spanning business with the crumbs of scientific discoveries. Steve Jobs, Bill Gates, Michael Dell, Marc Andreessen and a few others were young entrepreneurs with maverick ideas, operating sometimes at the edge of disaster. As their business grew, most of them had to hire a manager who knew how to run a company.

The ascendance of the personal computer replaced the vertically-integrated structure of the mainframe industry into a horizontal industry structure. The mainframe industry was nationally oriented, while the PC industry soon became organized around a global production network. The industry is highly globalized, with common technology standards used around the world. Silicon Valley is the dream factory where new ideas germinate. Asia is the factory floor.

The Silicon Revolution is a textbook example of Schumpeter's celebrated description of "creative destruction" as the heart of vibrant capitalism, incessantly revolutionizing the economic structure from within, incessantly destroying the old one while creating a new one. The strategic nature of the electronics industry and of its critical importance for enhancing productivity, competitiveness and long-term growth are obvious. Hardly anybody could have foreseen that with the transistor something new had arisen on the planet that would not fit the assumptions, models and paradigms left over from the industrial age. It affects all nations, with profound consequences for the global distribution of wealth, albeit in different ways.

The information technology industry has been an early and enthusiastic adopter of global marketing, manufacturing, engineering, and development. The personal computer revolution of the 1980s has generated a new American model of manufacturing. While US companies remain the leaders in most segments of the industry, the actual production of computer equipment has shifted away from the US, mostly to Asia. The United States and Asia combined have taken the leadership in the world economy.

The increasingly demanding requirements of global competition have reshaped the entry barriers and the structure of the industry. The scope of international production covers all stages of the value chain. To the extent that proximity advantages can be replicated abroad, outsourcing has become the rule. Once manufacturing moves abroad, it has tendency to stay there.

A typical computer contains components manufactured and assembled in many parts of the world: semiconductor chips made in Taiwan or Malaysia, a disk drive made in Singapore or Thailand, a cathode ray tube monitor made in Japan, circuit boards made in China and assembled in Mexico or Costa Rica.

It might also be assembled in Ireland, using components from all the above-named countries, plus a few others.

Globalization is decentralization at the planetary level. Information technology permits enterprises to operate world-wide systems of production, distribution and finance in an integrated world economy. Globalization offers many rewards but also imposes many challenges. The old hierarchical world is giving way to the web world. Information technology has already created new divisions in the global economy, both within nations and between nations. Individuals and nations slow to master the new technology, drop behind in the distribution of new wealth. The revolution cannot be stopped, and for better or worse, it is leading to a future that will produce winners and losers. The Silicon Revolution has produced global technologies controlled by large companies who are writing the rules of the game.

The global computer industry is a very complex network of R&D and manufacturing, with a high degree of interpenetration, defying state intervention. Capital flows to areas where it is used most effectively by promoting increased investment, faster economic growth and better standards of living in recipient countries. For investors in capital exporting nations it offers higher returns and diversification of risks. The free flow of capital in the past decades proved it as an engine for unprecedented world growth. Although labor costs comprise only a fraction of the cost, they are significant. Companies seek out the least expensive areas, particularly for the most labor-intensive processes.

Globalization has advanced faster than anyone was able to predict. It allows many electronic systems to be sold worldwide with only minor modifications. It embraces capital flows, production and investment, in common with science, technology and innovation. The onward march of globalization deprives governments of tasks to perform. Politics no longer has the traditional instruments of power to wield.

The world economy is shaped by market forces rather than by government policies. State power is undercut by market power and bypassed by multinational enterprises. When technology is in the hands of individuals, the only viable regulatory structure is the one endorsed by those individuals themselves. The obstacles to controlling such decentralized decision-making are insuperable. Globalization has bolstered the fortunes of the American economy and of the Pacific Rim. The rise of a globally integrated knowledge economy is a blessing for developing nations. For companies adept at managing a global workforce, the benefits can be highly rewarding.

Information technology is creating global politics for the next generation. Globalization of industry, markets and technologies has significantly affected the capacity to act in technology policy. The global economy follows its own logic and develops its own web of interests. Europe may well fail to face up to the challenge of the Global Age. Container ships, jumbo jets and instant telecommunications shrank the world. Information technology has created a global and fundamentally unmanaged economic system. Firms are global players or niche players. Globalization is creating a single-market world. It is increasingly hard to determine the nationality of a product. The proprietary technology in these machines is buried in the components and the manufacturing processes used to produce them.

The early years of the Silicon Revolution were a showcase for America's specific capabilities. New companies were suddenly catapulted in front rank, while others faded away. Laggards succumbed, freeing up energy, opportunities and capital for newcomers. The American high-tech sector illustrates how fast economic expansion occurs in a relatively unregulated market with a flexible and mobile labor force and efficient capital markets. In Silicon Valley entrepreneurs can decide to form a company and have it operational within a few days.

Silicon Valley is a hierarchy of imagination and venture capital rather than a hierarchy of academic doctorates. At its core there are three interconnected markets: a market for ideas, a market for capital and a market for entrepreneurial talent. Money is cheap in Silicon Valley for anyone with a good idea. It is the presence of venture capital and venture-backed enterprises that makes the difference between the US and any other industrialized economy in the world.

Nowhere else have venture capitalists such a close connection with the industry. They supply funds to budding entrepreneurs who want to start their own companies but cannot raise capital on the stock market. The Valley represents the distilled essence of entrepreneurial energy. Venture capital starts with an idea for a new product. Newcomers create most of the new wealth. Exciting new ideas immediately attract investors. Never has so much wealth been created in so little time by so few people. Many Silicon Valley entrepreneurs are corporate exiles who couldn't get a hearing in the company that employed them.

The US government takes a laissez-faire attitude toward the private sector. The helping hand is supposed to be the "invisible hand" proposed by Adam Smith. In reality, the invisible hand is close to a non-existent hand. This allows market forces to develop on their own and breeds a successful venture capital industry, putting money, people and technology together with few administrative or bureaucratic impediments. Successful ventures become competitive in the system while failures are allowed to die.

Compared to the eurozone, the United States is a tax haven. In 1998, the Silicon Valley venture capital industry succeeded in quietly pushing through Congress a capital gains tax break. The bill allows anyone who invests via a venture capital partnership, to roll over tax free again from the sale of a "qualified small business stock" when the proceeds are reinvested in another small business stock. The rationale for the bill was to encourage individuals to invest in emerging growth companies, and to encourage them to reinvest their profits once the original investments mature. The bill reflected the recognition by the government of the crucial role venture capital played in the success of Silicon Valley and other segments of the economy.

Venture capitalists make it possible for entrepreneurs to build businesses without having to borrow and pay high interest rates. Venture capitalists not only finance risky ventures;

they are equally important because they are experienced business managers who provide mentoring and monitoring to new and undeveloped companies. During a boom, venture capitalists tend to become careless and to invest in companies that are not worthy. When the stock market bubble bursts, many just disappear.

Innovation requires a state of mind: the willingness to think differently. By outsourcing production to Asia, American companies were able to concentrate on product design, architectural standards, global marketing, and the control of distribution channels. These activities generate high profit margins, enabling them to remain market leaders through product development and more sophisticated entry barriers. Relocation back home is no longer an option. The products are so small that shipping them around the world is not an issue. If the best trained people are in Shanghai, Taiwan or South Carolina, new facilities will be built there.

With 1.7 million jobs, the high-tech industry is the largest manufacturing employer in the United States, and also the largest exporter. No other industry provides stock options to its rank and file employees like the high-tech industry does. Concentration of a vast number of technology-based firms enables people to change employers without altering their environment or life style.

American entrepreneurs are well equipped to deal with economic stress. Leadership in key information technologies, deregulation of communications, corporate restructuring, improved international competitiveness, low unemployment and moderate inflation, and military superiority are the basis of its strength and resilience.

The United States holds a commanding lead in most industries that are crucial to the information society. American start-ups had the skills to create proprietary standards that allowed them to capture monopoly or semi-monopoly profits. Their comparative advantage rests on the ability to create new products that generate new industries. Control of product design, definition, and marketing then allows American firms to force component and sub-system technology to be sold as commodity products.

Market capitalism is the engine that runs the world economy. American capitalism emphasizes competition and a limited role of the state. Private enterprise is about maximizing short-term profits and long-term staying power. Its focus is not a harmony of interests, but competition. Americans are much more willing to accept trade-offs involving benefits for some against losses for others.

Technological innovation was the engine that powered the rapid expansion of both the technology business and the US economy. No other industry in the world has produced as many innovations over the past decade as America's high-tech sector. Technological revolutions have two consecutive lives. The installation period is one of exploration and exuberance. Entrepreneurs compete ferociously to capture a share of the market. Spectacular financial successes by initial investors attract more and more capital, leading to a bubble. During the second period the leading firms of the new economy concentrate on making technology easier to use, more reliable and secure. Technological innovations become less important than the efficiency of the supply chain. The industry keeps consolidating. The merger of Compaq and HP was the largest in history. There will be more corporate marriages on a smaller scale, and many more companies will go bankrupt. But there are still innumerable things to try out and plenty of opportunities in IT that will melt into the mainstream and enrich our lives, society and the world.

THE EUROPEAN HIGH-TECH FIASCO. One of the great mishaps in the history of electronics has been the debacle of the European computer and microelectronics industries. Not only were they outclassed by American start-ups, they were outdone by Japan and by Asian developing countries.

The American and Japanese computer manufacturers have been the driving force behind economic growth and productivity. They have succeeded fabulously well, without government oversight. The undoing of the European computer industry after years of subsidies and bailouts brings up a vast number of questions that have not been addressed. In information technology, Europe has become a wasteland, almost entirely dependent on imports.

Europe is the birthplace of the semiconductor revolution. But within two decades, the combination of American technological prowess and Asian productivity has transformed the global industrial landscape. The synergy between the technological revolution and global capitalism has reshaped the foundations of the world economy. Europe has been compelled to cede the IT market - and the jobs - to foreign competitors and with it the manufacturing expertise and technical competence. The dream of national or European champions has evaporated. So has the view that governments can rescue high-tech companies against the harsh logic of the global marketplace.

The theoretical foundations of the technology were laid mainly in Germany, Britain and France. The electromechanical computer, the programmable computer, the commercial computer, the personal computer, the transistor, the transistor radio, the www, all originated in Europe. The integrated circuit and the microprocessor are products of the brain drain: they germinated in the minds of European scientists working for Intel.

In the 1960s, IBM and several American companies started selling mainframes in Europe. IBM had risen to worldwide leadership through superior technology, management and marketing. The company was able to maintain its dominance by constant innovation. A number of European companies set up production of computers, but they were unable to respond to IBM's price-performance, software availability and service and support levels.

The computer industry called in the aid of the political class in order to ward off the strains of competition. The "national champions" were protected and subsidized by their governments in order to retain domestic market dominance. When it became evident that the national-champion policy failed, the governments turned to the European commission.

Europe had acquired a new definition when six countries founded the European Economic Community. The EEC was set on dynamizing the continent's industrial economy, making it able to compete in the world markets. An EEC-wide free trade zone had been set up, out of which, it was hoped, European-based companies of sufficient size and strength would emerge to "rise to the competitive challenge posed by the USA and Japan". It was intended to fashion a distinctly European standard that would achieve enough scale and momentum to allow the European industry to compete with American and Japanese rivals.

Harmonizing became a top priority, and the European commission was in charge of technology policy. The decision was made to take IBM head on by coordinating Europe-wide precompetitive research. Technology policy became a catch-up game tending to imitate the existing product mix. It pushed European firms into market segments dominated by the Americans. The commission launched a partnership with the leading EU electronics and information companies. The decision-making process was highly bureaucratic, unaware of the realities of the business world and short of know-how about the economics of the market, thereby affecting the viability and competitiveness of research proposals. Time spent on an invention that is not commercialized is wasted, and so is the money. A fundamental weakness of the European economy is the inability to create an environment that integrates research, innovation and managerial talent in an overall strategy. Great ideas can easily fall apart on paper or, worse still, in the marketplace. The soundness and the energy of the people who peddle them are as important as the ideas themselves.

European governments and the commission regularly draw attention to the fact that Europe is not spending enough on research and development, and that more public subsidies are needed to support industrial innovation. In fact, US and

Japanese companies finance most of their R&D. In the United States, the research and development of the Department of Defense has made some important technological contributions, notably the genesis of the internet, but most of these contributions became useful to the commercial sector only by accident. American science and technology policy is largely disconnected from economic policy-making. The tremendous sums of money the US government pours into R&D are devoted primarily to national defense. It has few potential applications outside of the military establishment.

A small part of the knowledge developed for the military may have civilian usefulness. The overwhelming quantity of military research and production has only military importance since it has been designed for tasks totally different from civilian needs. Europe has simply been unable to develop the entrepreneurial scientific culture that is found in the United States with its many start-up and spin-off firms.

The Silicon Revolution took the European computer industry and the commission by surprise. When an unheard-of company such as Apple started selling personal computers, this seemed of little relevance. When the 'Compaq shock' served notice that there were new players in the game, it took quite some time to realize that these start-ups were creating a new global industry. The European computer industry was undone by the onslaught of these start-ups and by the misdirected guidance and support of the commission. Convinced that integration in terms of traditional economies of scale would deliver economic results, resources were channeled into traditional industries. When the personal computer industry started generating jobs in the United States and Asia, while unemployment mounted in traditional industries, the awakening was rude.

The failure to comprehend the potential of the new technology radically different than the one they knew, led to irreversible mistakes. The 1990s became a decade of lost opportunities for Europe. The ballyhooed economic integration fizzled, as did most of Europe's major economies. Slow growth, high unemployment and declining international competitiveness became the sad watchwords. In IT, things were even worse. European hardware vendors all but disappeared. With rare exceptions, such as SAP, most of Europe's software and service providers failed to keep pace with bigger and stronger US companies.

Initially the research was purely pre-competitive, but when the computer industry became extinct, the emphasis shifted to diffusion and use rather than the creation of technologies. European research is part of the global research effort and is in competition with global research efforts. The Framework Programme policy of supporting science and technology is aimed essentially at encouraging co-operation between European researchers. While valuable, the approach falls short of today's needs.

European technology policy was misdirected and mismanaged because neither the industry nor the commission understood what was going on in faraway California and in Asia. Unacquainted with the technology and unaware of the market, they did not see through the nature and the scope of the challenge. The inherent inertia of big administrations, the slowness of the decision-making process rendered the program ineffective. The major computer companies and a lot of research institutions received huge amounts of public money without leaving anything of value behind. In the United States, the personal computer resulted from the combination of the scientist with his invention, the entrepreneur to market it and the investor putting up his money.

The programs aimed at the reinforcement of scientific and technological bases of European industry especially in the field of IT. When the European computer industry disappeared from the scene, the priorities turned towards the satisfaction of social demand: the environment, medicine, socio-economic concerns. The programs have become encyclopedic for fear of forgetting essential elements. The industrial base having largely disappeared, R&D pursues its activities in a no-man's-land. Money sustains infrastructures and research teams. Everybody is content and talks about how useful these programs are. Most research serves to finance the hobbies of laboratories or individuals, without the potential of adding much to science, and still less to the European economy. The programs are accessible primarily to those capable of writing the right proposals. The institutions themselves have become more important that the research itself or the quality of the research teams.

Within two decades, the European habitat and the world around it underwent a fundamental permutation. Europe is gently sliding into second-class without even noticing the declension. The causes are diverse and must be reviewed separately. The Silicon Revolution has its origin in the development of a new technology. Competing in such an environment requires scientific excellence, marketing expertise and a constant upgrading of human resources. In an industry where everything is changing very rapidly, not only in the field of technology but also in people's perceptions, tastes and interests, any society that is slow in grasping the sense of direction will regress.

The failure of the European computer industry is the result of mistaken policies and of corporate structure and political cultures. After the Second World War, several governments developed an activist welfare state economy committed to full employment. For years, the problem was to find workers; now the problem is to find jobs Europeans have the highest minimum wages, the most elaborate employment laws, the most rigid wage structures, the longest vacations, the shortest working week, the youngest pensioners, the most secure and generous welfare system and safety net and the most egalitarian society, but also the highest unemployment rates. Material welfare has not generated a sense of security, or even a sense of social justice.

The welfare state has destroyed the link between effort and reward and stripped away individual independence and dignity. Too many people are out of work and too few are seeking it. Young people while away their days in idleness. Their unemployment compensation is such that they have no

interest in taking a low-paying job. The price paid for generous unemployment benefits is a high tax on labor, which in
turn discourages hiring. In several countries of the European
Union unemployment rates are exceedingly high; yet there is
a scarcity of labor in some areas, both skilled and unskilled.
The social-insurance trap is such that many people don't work
because they would lose their subsidies. People who know
how to milk the system take the money from those who still
prefer to work for it.

In today's world, people are living longer and therefore
drawing benefits longer; those benefits are scheduled to rise
dramatically over the next decades. The ageing of the population and the fundamental economic and social consequences
of future demographic developments will make the "pension
time bomb" go on ticking louder as time goes on, with the prospect of passing a bankrupt system on to the next generation.

Europe's ambiguous relationship with capitalism did not
deliver the technology, the entrepreneurial drive, quality of
management, and salesmanship required to upgrade its competitiveness, productivity, and economic efficiency. Inevitably,
the invisible hand delivered its blows. Europe faces a complex
web of interlocking challenges - economic, technological and
cultural. The "social dimension" of the commission's policies,
combined with centrally imposed economic regulations, have
burdened the competitiveness of the European economy with
production costs incompatible with the pattern of the global
economy.

Within a few years, Ireland has been transformed from
a poor agricultural country to Europe's largest high-tech
producer, thanks to investments by American and Asian companies. The main attraction for foreign investment was an
educated workforce and a tax rate of 12.5 percent, a fraction
of most other European tax rates. The commission has advocated that tax rates be made uniform throughout Europe. This
would be disastrous for the Irish electronics industry which is
97 percent foreign-owned.

The harmonization process leads to regulatory edicts that
undermine Europe's competitive advantage and threaten

industry and prosperity. In Europe nothing is simple. Over-politicized and over-bureaucratized, the European Union brought to power a multi-level system of government where democracy and oligarchy shade into each other, generating problems of a new type, hidden agendas, disagreements and dissension. The euro was to be a symbol of solidarity and a mechanism for centralizing economic power. The economic costs and benefits could not be understood nor evaluated.

The plain certainties of bureaucratic socialism and entrepreneurial capitalism have been amalgamated in a dichotomy called the "third way." There is a persistent belief that governments can produce better results if they control, direct and regulate. In fact, the recasting and redistribution of wealth-creating work takes place on a global scale. European policies were bound to fail as they did not take account of the global economics of the IT industry. Globalization has allowed several countries to make the transition from underdevelopment to middle-class prosperity. Europe is the only industrial center that has taken a beating. As economic globalization runs its seemingly relentless course, the demands on the European economy and on the social consensus are set to increase further in the years to come.

Globalization of industry, markets and technologies has significantly affected the capacity to act in technology policy. The global economy follows its own logic and develops its own web of interests. Europe may well fail to face up to the challenge of the Global Age. Container ships, jumbo jets and instant telecommunications have shrunk the world. Information technology has created a global and fundamentally unmanaged economic system.

The future of European society depends on the contribution its industry can make to addressing global challenges, not on second-hand policies of political spin-doctors. The socialist and green parties are business-unfriendly. The collapse of socialist regimes should teach them something about the future of the "third way".

Future living standards will depend largely on today's productive capabilities. Europe is very wealthy, but its industrial and technological ability has fallen behind, and its competitive potential keeps shrinking. The high cost of social policies is reflected in wages and taxes. This obstructs the development of an entrepreneurial society and a balanced economy. The paucity of successful new enterprises raises troublesome questions.

Europe has developed a unique corpus of core values and norms: social cohesion through solidarity and redistribution, and security provided by an active state whose role it is to reduce inequality and promote equal opportunity. The orthodoxies of socialism and capitalism have been amalgamated in the complexities of the heavily regulated government-led European economic and social model. By patching together elements from two antagonistic systems, the political establishments have introduced a dichotomy that casts doubts about the long-term potential and viability of the model.

Europe is an inhospitable place for entrepreneurs. Red tape makes it very difficult to create a new enterprise and jobs. An important but overlooked challenge to Europe's competitiveness comes from regulatory burdens the national governments and the commission impose on industry, in addition to excessive taxation and bureaucratic red tape. Europe is headed toward a critical collision with globalization. The conventional wisdom no longer adequately reflects global economic realities. The global economy is increasingly interlinked: labor costs, manufacturing technology and productivity determine where and how products are manufactured. Money moves freely around the world; jobs do not. The people who decide about new investments adapt to the realities of global capitalism and cannot be primarily preoccupied with social responsibilities.

The European industry has been the main loser in the globalization process because, unlike America, it has been unable to adapt to new challenges and invent new products and new industries. The employment contrast between the two economies is staggering. In the early 1970s, unemployment in the

United States was twice as high as in the EEC; the position has since been reversed. In the United States, millions of high-paying and low-paying jobs have been created. In Europe, globalization has destroyed millions of jobs.

During the past two decades microelectronics has become the largest and fastest growing manufacturing industry in the world and the largest employer in the United States and Asia. Its reliance on international markets and production is unrivaled by any other industry.

The competitiveness of the electronics industry is important not only intrinsically, but also because of interactions with other parts of the economy. Nothing scientific, social or technical exists in isolation. It is a new order of which the new economy is only one facet. Throughout history, new technologies have generated momentous social and economic consequences, and dislodged established regions or nations from the top ranks of wealth and power. The "digital divide" has narrowed the income gap between the IT-haves and have-nots.

The high-tech industry is brutally competitive. The European ethos leans more toward sentimentalism, concern for the underprivileged, generous jobless benefits, equality of opportunity, leisure time, early retirement, long vacations, solidarity and bringing the less developed countries up to par.

Technology generates and eliminates jobs. New technologies require a differently skilled labor force, thus creating more challenging, higher paying jobs. They lead to new products and services, and expanded markets. Technological innovation is the major determining factor for long-term economic growth. Nations unable to develop or attract and nurture new industries risk being left behind.

In order to be able to compete in this new economy, companies and nations must adapt to an ever-more-competitive market. They must build a "wealth pyramid" using building blocks such as a solid social organization, entrepreneurial skills and an educational system encouraging creativity and innovative behavior.

Ever since the desktop computer took over the menial office tasks, European companies have experienced a severe shortage of trained and skilled high-tech workers: engineers, systems analysts and programmers. For two decades, designing, developing, procuring, installing, managing, maintaining and supporting information systems has been the fastest growing workforce. Qualified high-tech specialists are able to command very high salaries, putting themselves out of the range of small and medium businesses. But even so the profession is perceived as too arduous, with few opportunities to reconvert if demand should dry up.

The jobs dilemma is partly grounded in the education system. The demand for high-tech skills is far greater than the number of students coming out of the universities. School leavers lack the basic skills they need for employment in a modern economy, whereas a major concern of the educational system should be employability. Science and technology subjects should be an integral part of the curriculum at all levels from primary through to third level.

Information technology requires considerably higher than average intelligence, as well as training in chemistry, mathematics and science. These disciplines are short of students in European schools and universities. Students increasingly shun mathematics and the hard sciences for non-engineering subjects like management, law, economics, behavioral and political sciences and humanities.

Ensuring that more young people have the education and training they will need for work in an information age presupposes the availability of teachers with up-to-date skills in technology. The problem is that good math and physics graduates prefer to work for large firms rather than spend their lives as low-pay teachers. Schools must be given the tools they need and teachers must be trained to impart to students the skills they need.

European universities are funded by governments. There is a large divide between higher education intelligentsia and the business world. Academics generally cultivate the ethos of pure science for its own sake, and do not wish to be tainted by commercialism. The educational institutions should move to a system that is much more demand-led. Universities need to forge new partnerships with industry to ensure that courses deliver the skills needed in industry. Inviting computer specialists from India or Eastern Europe does not recognize the need for long-term IT skills. When they leave, the situation will be worse than before.

The economic well-being of the advanced industrial nations relies on a continual evolution toward value-added, high-productivity, innovation- and knowledge-rich activities. It is in the start-ups that the jobs of the future will be created. But Europe is not ready for an environment where new firms can easily be started, enter the market, grow and create jobs.

The number of entrepreneurs is an indicator of the dynamism the economy. More entrepreneurs will lead to more business activity and more economic growth. The quality of these entrepreneurs will impact the rate of growth. The major responsibility of the government is to understand the mechanism of growth and make it work.

The European ethos is wary of capitalism and ruthless competition in business. The permanent tension and occasional conflict in industrial relations and the anti-business regulations imposed to industry have developed a widespread reluctance to start a new enterprise. Business leaders are hardly visible in Europe, except when their misdeeds hit the newspapers. And there have been quite a few in recent years. The successful self-made businessman does not capture popular imagination, but rather meets with suspicion. Successful entrepreneurs do not turn into folk heroes. Hence, Europe has few of them.

Capital accumulation, technical innovation and the advance of knowledge are the major sources of economic growth. For entrepreneurial business formation in high-tech, low tax rates on capital gains are particularly important. When governments raise taxes on wealthy individuals, proven moneymakers and job creators lose control over the investment of their funds.

In Europe, an entrepreneur who needs financing will face a risk-averse bank or a larger corporation interested in buying his idea. Huge amounts of "mattress money" are hidden in foreign bank accounts and other liquidities. This is money that people do not want the tax man to see. Therefore they do not invest it in start-ups.

Governments are necessary to the functioning of society. They provide public services through government expenditures and contribute positively to private economic activity. But there is an optimal size of government and an optimal rate of taxes. Beyond a certain level, government becomes a net drain on the private sector and results in reduced growth. Resources allocated privately tend to be allocated to the highest-valued use as entrepreneurs and capitalists seek the highest economic rate of return on their assets. Politicians are mainly concerned with themselves and with the next elections.

The support of voters is marshaled through advertising campaigns, not direct participation in reasoned debate. For the overwhelming majority, the understanding of economic dynamics is very tenuous. When they allocate resources, they seek to please the electorates that will put them into power.

There is a bizarre belief that things can go on as usual. Any attempt to tamper with social security or pensions touches off public anger and massive demonstrations. The problems of the European economies are largely due to the embedded adversarialism between entrepreneurial employers and anti-business trade unions. Wage bargaining is conducted through nationwide horse-trading with the trade unions. In some countries, the trade unions almost constitute a shadow government.

Trade unions are confrontational organizations. They impose their logic, and have been very successful in pushing up the price of brawn to the highest levels in the world.. They thrive on militancy but the conflicts they generate are disrupting. In most European countries, they have been too successful, pushing wages up to uncompetitive levels. Whether the adversarial relationships between management and organized labor still serve the best interests of both and of the economy is open to question.

A nation's standard of living is the touchstone of its past economic performance. Economic growth is driven by the coalescence of human capital, the corpus of knowledge or innovative ideas held by people in business, education, and politics. Without such capabilities, an economy has no enduring potential to operate at the technological frontier, with all that this implies for maintaining national well-being. The rise of the global knowledge industry is so recent that it is impossible to fathom the implications. European competitiveness, the educational and training system, the research and development complex have eroded much faster than is commonly acknowledged. But alarm bells rang far too late.

The European economy is forced to rely almost totally on technology and equipment from the US and Asia. Once at the vanguard of the Industrial Revolution, the European economic model has been unable to adapt and reconstruct in time to meet the challenges of the Silicon Revolution. Europe is increasingly looking less like a land of opportunity and more like a danger zone. Every day brings it usual smattering of gloomy news: massive layoffs, bankruptcies, delocalizations, endangered public finances. The short-lived European computer industry has suffered a number of indignities from which it will not recover. There is no indication that history will give the European economy a second chance.

NOTES

PROLOGUE

1 Mahoney, M. S. *Issues in the History of Computing.* Forum on History of Computing, ACM/SIGPLAN. Cambridge, MA. 20-23 April, 1993.

2 Chandler, A. D. *Gaps in the Historical Record: Development of the Electronics Industry.* Harvard Business School, Working Knowledge. Oct. 20, 2003.

CHAPTER 1

1 Jolley, N. (ed.) T*he Cambridge Companion to Leibniz.* New York: Cambridge University Press, 1995.

2 Rutherford, D. *Leibnitz and the Rational Order of Nature.* Cambridge: Cambridge University Press, 1995.

3 MacHale, D. *George Boole: His Life and Work.* Dublin: Boole Press Ltd., 1985.

4 Hyman A. *Charles Babbage: Pioneer of the Computer.* Princeton, N.J. Princeton University Press, 1985.

5 Austrian, Geoffrey D. *Herman Hollerith: Forgotten Giant of Information Processing.* New York: Columbia University Press, 1984.

6. Maney, K. *The Maverick and his Machine: Thomas Watson Senior and the Making of IBM.* New York: John:Wiley & Sons, 2004.

7 Pierce, J. R. *An Introduction to Information Theory.* Mineola, NY: Dover Publications, 1980.

8 Copeland, Jack. *Colossus: The First Electronic Computer* New York: Oxford University Press, 2006.

9 McCartney, Scott. *The Triumphs and Tragedies of the World's First Computer.* New York: Walker and Company, 1999.

10 Ifrah, Georges. *The Universal History of Computing: From the Abacus to the Quantum Computer.* New York: John Wiley & Sons, 2000.

11 Wilkes, M. *Memoirs of a Computer Pioneer.* Cambridge: MIT Press, 1985.

12 Ferry, <u>Georgina</u>. *A Computer Called LEO: Lyons Tea Shops and the World's First Office Computer.* London: HarperCollins Publishers, 2003.

13 Riordan, M. and Hoddeson, L. *Crystal Fire. The Invention of the Transistor and the Birth of the Information Age.* New York and London: W. W. Norton & Company, 1997, pp. 115 -142.

14 Reid, T.R. *The Chip: How Two Americans Invented the Microchip and Launched a Revolution.* New York: N.Y. Random House, 2001.

CHAPTER 2

1 Sueur, R. *Le transistron triode type P.T.T. 601.* L'Onde Electrique, No. 272, pp.389-397.

2 Aisberg, E. *Transistor = Transistron? La Technique française n'abandonne pas.* Toute la Radio, juillet-août, 1949.

3 Bosch, B. *Der Werdegang des Transistors 1929-1994: Bekanntes und weniger Bekanntes.* 1994.

4 Bosch, B. *Happy Birthday, Transistor!* Deutsches Amateur-Funk Magazin, Dec. 1997.

5 Hillmer, H. *Der Transistor – die Entwicklung von den Anfängen bis zu den frühen integrierten Schaltungen.* Erlangen: Georg Heidecker GmbH, 2000.

6 Keen, R. *The **Life and Work** of **Friedrich Wöhler** (1800-1882)* Nordhausen: Traugott **Bautz,** 2005.

7 Hars, F. *Ferdinand Braun (1850 1918) Ein wilhelminischer Physiker.* Berlin: GNT-Verlag, 1999.

8 Haustein M. *Clemens Winkler. Chemie war sein Leben.* Frankfurt/M: Harry Deutsch, 2004.

9 Seitz, F. and Einspruch N. G. *Electronic Genie. The Tangled History of Silicon.* pp. 52-53. Urbana and Chicago: University of Illinois Press, 1998.

10 Johnson, J.B. *More about the solid-state amplifier and Dr.Lilienfeld.* Physics Today. May, 1964, pp. 60-62.

11 Walz, Rüdiger. *Die Entwicklung der Liebenröhre.* Funkgeschichte Nr. 52, Jan/Feb 1987, pp. 7-28.

12 Johnson, J.B. *Electronic noise, the first two Decades. IEEE Spectrum,* February, 1971.

13 Döring, H. *Oskar Heil zum Gedenken.* Funkgeschichte Nr. 100, 1995.

14 Teichmann, Jürgen. *Robert Wichard Pohl* in *Die großen Physiker.* Munich: Beck Verlag, 1997, volume II, pp.170-177.

15 Deutsches Museum. *H. Welker Nachlass, box 006.*

16 Feldtkeller, E. and Goetzeler, H. *Pioniere der Wissenschaft bei Siemens.* Erlangen: MCD Verlag, 1994.

17 *Herbert Mataré*, Leaders of the Information Age. D. Weil (Editor), New York: H. W. Wilson, 2004, pp. 363-366.

18 Mataré, H. F. *The lesser known History of the Crystal Amplifier,* unpublished paper.

19 Mataré, H. F. *The Transistor in Gestation,* IEEE Spectrum, Oct.1998, pp. 8-9.

20 Mataré, H. F. *Das Rauschen von Dioden und Detektoren im statistischen und im dynamischen Zustand.* Elektrische Nachrichten-Technik, 1942, Bd 19 H. 7.

21 Mataré, H. F. *Erlebnisse eines Deutschen Physikers und Ingenieurs von 1912 bis zum Ende des Jahrhunderts.* Erlangen: Georg Heidecker GmbH, 2001, pp. 19-32.

22 Mataré, H.F. *Breakthroughs recalled on Transistor Precursors in Germany.* Physics Today, May, 1998, pp. 94-98.

23 Mataré letters to A. Van Dormael, June 6, 2002, July; 20, 2002, Sept. 28, 2003.

24 Hillmer, H. *Der Transistor – die Entwicklung von den Anfängen bis zu den frühen Integrierten Schaltungen.* Erlangen: Georg Heidecker GmbH. 2000.

25 Mataré, H. F. *Erlebnisse eines Deutschen Physikers und Ingenieurs von 1912 bis zum Ende des Jahrhunderts,* Erlangen: G. Heidecker GmbH, 2001.

26 Mataré, H. F. *Empfangsprobleme im UHF-Gebiet unter besonderer Berücksichtigung des Halbleiters.* Munich: R. Oldenbourg GmbH, 1951.

27 Mataré, H.F. *Remarques concernant l'Amplification observée sur des Semi-conducteurs.* L'Onde Electrique, Nov. 1950.

28 Mataré, H. F. *Defect Electronics in Semiconductors.* New York: Wiley Interscience, 1971.

29 Handel, K. *Anfänge der Halbleiterforschung und – Entwicklung.* Doctoral Dissertation, Aachen University, 1999.

30 Botelho, A. *The Industrial Policy that never was: French Semiconductor Policy, 1945-1966.* History and Technology, 1994, Vol. 11, pp. 60-61.

31 C. Möller, *Deutsche Transistoren.* Funk-Technik, Nr. 21, 1953.

32 Mataré, H. F. *Erlebnisse eines deutschen Physikers und Ingenieurs von 1912 bis zum Ende de Jahrhunderts.* Erlangen: Georg Heidecker GmbH. 2001, pp. 51-57.

33 Ibid., pp. 58-64.

34 Ibid., pp. 65-69.

35 Ibid., pp. 70-72.

36 Ibid., pp. 73-77.

CHAPTER 3

1 *Nobel Lectures, Physics 1942-1962*, Elsevier Publishing Company, Amsterdam, 1964.

2 Gartenhaus S.; Tubis A.; Cassidy D.; Bray R. *A History of Physics at Purdue. The War Period, 1941-1945.* Purdue Physics, Vol.5, Nr.1 Fall, 1997.

3 Bardeen, J. *The Early Days of the Transistor, 1946 to 1951.* p. 5. Southwest Museum of Electricity and Communication.

4 Bray, Ralph. *A Glance at the Past by One of the Early Participants.* Lafayette Journal and Courier, Nov. 2, 1948.

5 Gartenhaus S.; Tubis A.; Cassidy D.; Bray R. *A History of Physics at Purdue. The War Period, 1941-1945.*

6 Brinkman W. F.; Haggan, D. E.; Troutman, W. W. *A History of the Invention of.* IEEE Journal of Solid-State Circuits.Dec. 12, 1997. p. 1858. 7 *The New York Times,* Feb. 4, 2003.

8 Riordan, M. and Hoddeson, L. *Crystal Fire.* New York: W. W. Norton & Company, 1997. p. 128.

9 Hoddeson, L. and Daitch, V. pp. 130-131.

10 Riordan, M and Hoddeson, L. pp. 137-138.

11 Riordan, M. and Hoddeson, L. p. 164.

12 Mataré, H. F. *Erlebnisse eines Deutschen Physikers und Ingenieurs von 1912 bis zum Ende des Jahrhunderts* Erlangen: Georg Heidecker GMBH, 2001 p.44.

13 Morita, Akio. *Made in Japan.* London: HarperCollins Publishers, 1994, p. 67.

14 Morita, A. p.71.

15 Morita, A. p.72.

16 Rosenberg, N. *America's University/Industry Interfaces, 1945-2000.* Unpublished manuscript. Stanford University. July 2000, pp. 13-14.

17 Rosenberg, N. *Science and Technology. Which Way does the Causation Run?* Stanford University, Center for Interdisciplinary Studies of Science and Technology, November 1, 2004.

18 Bray, R.; Gartenhaus, S.; Tubis, A.; Cassidy, D. *The Post-war Years, 1945-1958.* Purdue University. Purdue Physics, Vol. 5, No. 1, Fall, 1997.

19 Neil Armstrong's 1999 Space Flight Award Acceptance Speech at the AAS 46th Annual Meeting in Pasadena, on November 17, 1999. The Journal of Astronautical Sciences. Vol.39, Nr.1.

20 Kelly, M. J. *The First Five Years of the Transistor.* Bell Telephone Magazine. summer 1953.

CHAPTER 4

1 Rojas, R. *Konrad Zuse's Legacy: The Architecture of the Z1 and Z3.* IEEE Annals of the History of Computing. Apr.-June 1997. Vol. 19, pp. 17-24.

2 *Über Computer wurde nur im kleinen Kreis geredet.* Computerwoche, June 22,1990.

3 Zuse, Konrad. *Der Computer - Mein Lebenswerk.* Berlin: Springer-Verlag, 1984. Rojas, R. *Die Rechenmaschinen von Konrad Zuse.* Berlin: Springer Verlag, 1998.

4 Caminer, D.; Aris, J.; Hermon, P.; Land, Fr. *The World's First Business Computer: User-Driven Innovation.* London: McGraw-Hill, 1996.

5 Williams, M. R. *History of Computing Technology.* Los Alamitos: IEEE Computer Society, 1977. pp. 321-36.

6 Gannon, P. *Trojan Horses & National Champions.* London: Apt-Amatic. 1997.

7 Kemper, Kl., *Heinz Nixdorf, Eine deutsche Geschichte.* Bonn: Verlag Moderne Industrie AG, 1986.

8 Brulé, J.-P. *L'informatique, malade de l'Etat.* Paris: Les Belles Lettres, 1993.

CHAPTER 5

1 Narjes, K. H. Europe's Technological Challenge: A View from the European Commission, *Science and Public Policy.* Dec. 1985. pp. 395-402.

2 *Computerwoche,* Mar. 23, 1984.

3 Japanese Technology. *The Economist,* Dec. 2, 1989.

4 Morita, A. *Made in Japan*, HarperCollinsPublishers, 1987, p. 222.

5 Molina, A. H. *Transputers and transputer-based parallel computers.* Research Policy, volume 19, issue 4, August 1990, pp. 309-333.

6 *01 Informatique*, Feb. 23, 1990.

7 *The Economist*, Oct. 6, 1990.

8 *The Economist*, Oct. 6, 1990.

9 Commission of the European Communities (1998). *Second European Report On S and T Indicators. Key Figures*, p.46.

10 *Financial Times*, Oct. 22, 1990.

11 ERCIM: *Views on information technology in Europe.* July 1996, p. 6.

12 Esprit III Review Board Report. *Report of the Esprit Review Board, 1996.* Chaired by Umberto Colombo, Nov. 1996.

13 *The Economist*, Sept. 8, 1990.

14 Commission of the European Communities (2000). *Towards a European Research Area.* COM 18 Jan. 2000.

15 *Le Point*, June. 17, 1985.

16 *Computerwoche*, July. 26, 1985.

17 *The Economist*, July. 5, 1986.

18 *Computerwoche*, Sept. 21, 1990.

19 *Computerwoche*, July. 29, 1988.

20 *Computerwoche*, Sept. 29, 1988.

21 *Computerwoche*, Aug. 17, 1990.

22 *The Economist*, Sept. 1, 1993.

23 Science *News*, Nov. 19, 2004.

24 European Council 23 and 24 March 2000 Lisbon.

25 Council of the European Union Brussels 2 May 2007.

CHAPTER 6

1 Commission (1994) *The European Report on Science and Technology* Indicators 1994, Report EUR 15897 EN, Luxemburg, DG XII, European Commission.

2 Europe's Technology Policy. *The Economist*, September 1, 1993.

3 Esprit III Review Board Report (Colombo Report).*Making Progress Happen through Development. Application and Diffusion of Information Technologies.* November 1996.

4 *EE Times*, December 1, 1999.

5 Cordis Focus, March 26, 2001. Issue Nr. 169.

6 *Computer Weekly,* May 4, 2000.

7 World Economic Forum, Press release, January 21, 2002.

8 IP/02/852. Researchers send in thousands of new ideas for European research. Brussels, 12 June, 2002.

9 *Dataquest,* June 8, 1999.

10 AAAS Report XXVI Research and Development FY 2002.

11 Rodgers, T. J. *"Silicon Valley versus Corporate Welfare."* Cato Institute Briefing Paper, nr. 37 April 27, 1998.

CHAPTER 7

1 *Computergram International,* November 5, 1998.

2 Siemens, G.: *History of the House of Siemens,* New York: Arno Press, 1977.

3 Halbleiter-Debakel, *Computerwoche,* July 25, 1975.

4 Siemens will die angeschlagene SNI in den Konzern eingliedern. *Computerwoche,* Oct. 25, 1991.

5 *Wall Street Journal,* Feb. 7, 1996.

6 *Business Week,* Feb. 2002.

7 *Spiegel Online International,* Nov. 28, 2006 and June 26, 2008.

8 *Time Europe.* May 31, 1993.

9 *Computerworld,* March 9, 1999.

10 *Business Week,* Feb. 3, 1997.

11 *Computer Weekly,* Jan. 3, 1974.

12 *Computer Weekly,* Sept. 19, 1974.

13 Europa's Computerindustrie kurz vor dem Ausverkauf. *Computerwoche,* August 10, 1990.

14 Brulé, J.-P. *L'informatique malade de l'Etat,* Paris: Les Belles Lettres, 1993.

15 *The Economist,* Dec.5, 1981.

16 Bull: Schlussverkauf oder Comeback? *Computerwoche,* August 31, 2001.

17 Bellec, J. *Histoire des Grands Systèmes Bull, General Electric, Honeywell,* In Actes du 5e colloque de l'Histoire de l'Informatique. Toulouse, 1998.

18 *The Economist,* Nov. 27, 1982.

19 *Computerworld,* Aug. 4, 1997.

20 *Financial Times*, March 14, 2002.

CHAPTER 8

1 America's High-Tech Crisis. *Business Week*, March 11, 1985.

2 *The Economist*, March 29, 1997.

3 Kenney, Martin. *Understanding Silicon Valley: The Anatomy of an* Palo Alto, Cal.: Stanford University Press, 2000.

4 That Something Special. *New Scientist*, 22 March 2000.

5 Malone, Michael. *The Valley of Heart's Delight: A Silicon Valley Notebook 1963-2001*. New York: Wiley, John & Sons, 2002.

6 Who will feed the start-ups? *Fortune*, June 26, 1995.

7 Sigismund, Charles. *Champions of Silicon Valley; Visionary Thinking from Today's Technology Pioneers*, New York: John Wiley & Sons, Inc. 2000.

8 Silicon Valley's Dirty Side, *TheDaily News*, April 18, 2000.

9 The High-Tech Homeless in Silicon Valley, a Dark Side to Booming Economy. *Washington Post*, February 12, 2000.

10 The Digital Divide. *The Economist*, April 17, 1999, p. 63.

11 *Los Angeles Times*, October 18, 1999.

CHAPTER 9

1 Schein, E.H. *DEC Is Dead, Long Live DEC*. Berrett-Koehler Publishers, 2003.

2 Bardini, Th. *Bootstrapping: Douglas Engelbart, Coevolution, and the Origins of the Personal Computer*. Palo Alto, CA: Stanford University Press, 2000.

3 Noyce, R. N., Hoff, M. E. *A History of Microprocessor Development at Intel*. IEEE Micro. Feb. 1981, pp. 8-21.

4 Interview with Federico Faggin. Interviewer: John Verdalas. 27 May, 2004. IEEE Global History Network.

5 Interview with Bill Gates. Interviewer: David Allison. National Museum of American History, Smithsonian Institution. Bellevue, Washington.

6 Gernelle, Fr. *La Naissance du Premier Micro-ordinateur: Le Micral N. Histoire de la micro-informatique en France et en Europe »*, Colloque, Calenda, 9 décembre 2003.

7 Gernelle Fr. *Communication sur les choix architecturaux et technologiques qui ont présidé à la conception du « Micral » Premier micro-ordinateur au monde. Actes du 5ᵉ Colloque Histoire de l'Informatique. Toulouse, 28-30 avril, 1998. Editions Cépaduès. pp. 81-94.*

8 Beckmann, J. C. memo to the author.

9 Ackermann J. C. memo to the author.

10 Bellec Jean. *Histoire de la micro-informatique en France et en Europe.* Calenda, December 2003.

11 *Qui êtes-vous François Gernelle ? (Who are you François Gernelle?)* 01 Informatique, March 1979.

12 Veit, S. *Stan Veit's History of the Personal Computer.* Asheville, N.C.: Computer Shopper, 1993.

13 Kenney M. *Understanding Silicon Valley: The Anatomy of an Entrepreneurial Region.* Stanford, CA: Stanford Business Books, 2000.

14 Ceruzzi, P. E. *A History of Modern Computing* Cambridge, MA.: The MIT Press, 1998. pp.243-280.

15 Rheingold, H. *Tools for Thought: The History and Future of Mind-Expanding Technology.* Cambridge, MA: The MIT Press, 2000.

16 Carroll, P, *Big Blues: The Unmaking of IBM.* New York, NY: Three Rivers Press, 1994.

CHAPTER 10

1 *Industry Week,* March 15, 1999.

2 *Business Week,* April 24, 2002.

3 *Business Week,* April 24, 2002.

4 *Business Week,* January 18, 2002.

5 Dell, M., *Direct from Dell: Strategies That Revolutionized an Industry.* New York: Harperbusiness. 1999.

6 *Wired,* November 2, 1998.

7 *Fortune,* February 5, 2001.

8 *Business Week,* April 29, 2002.

9 D. Kirkpatrick, Can Netscape compete? *Fortune,* June 9, 1997.

10 *Business Week,* May 28, 2001.

11 *Business Week.* May 24, 2004.

CHAPTER 11

1 Jackson, Tim. *Inside Intel: Andrew Grove and the Rise of the World's Most Powerful Chip Company.* New York: Harper Collins, 1997.

2 The War of Tomorrow's Worlds. *The Economist,* August 24, 1985.

3 Grove, A. S. *Only the Paranoid Survive.* New York: Doubleday, 1996.

4 Yu, Albert. *Creating the Digital Future: The Secrets of Consistent Innovation at Intel.* New York: Simon & Schuster, 1992.

5 Malone, M. S. *The Microprocessor: A Biography.* New York: Springer, 1995.

6 Intel's amazing Profit Machine, *Fortune,* 17 Feb. 1997.

7 Jackson, Tim.*nside Intel: Andy Grove and the Rise of the World's Most Powerful Chip Company.* New York: Viking Penguin, 1997. Freiberger, P & Swaine, M. *Fire in the Valley. The Making of the Personal Computer.* New York: McGraw-Hill, 1999. p.40.

8 *Business Week,* May 7, 1998.

9 Wallace, J. and Erickson J. *Hard Drive: Bill Gates and the Making of the Microsoft Empire.* New York: HarperCollinsPublishers, 1993.

10 The Billion-dollar Whiz Kid. *Business Week,* April 13, 1987.

11 *Business Week,* Feb. 19, 1998.

12 Cusumano M. and Yoffie, D. *Computing on Internet Time: Lessons from Netscape and its Battle with Microsoft.* New York: Touchstone Books, 1999.

13 *Financial Times,* Aug. 27, 2002.

14 *Financial Times.* Sept. 17, 2002.

15 Damn the Torpedoes! Full Speed Ahead. *Fortune,* July 10, 2000.

16 Ballmer's Microsoft. *Business Week,* June 17, 2002.

CHAPTER 12

1 Wade, R. *Governing the Market: Economic Theory and the Role of Government inthe East Asian Industrialization.* Princeton: Princeton University Press, 1990.

2 *The Economist,* Nov. 9, 1996.

3 *Business Week,* July 1, 2002.

4 *Business Week,* June 24, 2002.

5 Morita, Akio. *Made in Japan.* London: HarperCollinsPublishers 1994, pp. 196,197 and 182.

6 *Time,* Sep. 25, 1995. p. 41.

7 Meet the Global Factory, *The Economist.* June 20, 1998.

8 *Industry Week:* Made in Taiwan. Feb. 15, 1999.

9 *Business Week,* Nov. 5, 2001.

10   National Center for Policy Analysis. National University of Singapore. Report No. 198, Sept. 1995.

11 A Blunt Talk with Singapore's Lee Kuan Yew. *Fortune Magazine,* Aug. 4. 1997.

12 *The Economist,* Oct. 12, 1996.

13 *New York Times,* Nov. 27, 1997.

14 *The Taipei Times,* Aug. 2, 2001.

15 *Financial Times,* March 19, 2002.

16 *Business Week,* Sept. 11, 2000.

17 *The Economist,* Jan. 11, 2001.

18 *Financial Times,* September 23, 1998.

19 *The Economist,* February 14, 2002.

20 *Business Week,* March 30 2001.

21 *Business Week,* July 2, 2001.

22 *Computerworld,* Jan. 21 2002.

23 *The Economist,* April 13, 2002.

24 *Business Week,* Oct. 22, 2002.

25 *Fortune,* Aug. 17, 1998.

26 *Computer Weekly;* 10 Jul. 2000.

27 *Electronics Times,* 26 April 1999.

28 *Business Week,* Oct. 22, 2001.

29 *Computerworld,* July 2, 1997.

30 *Computerworld,* Feb. 19, 2002.

31 *Electronic News,* Jan. 7, 2002.

32 *Washington Post,* Feb. 20, 2001.

33 *The Economist,* Jan. 15, 2005.

34 *Business Week,* Jan. 21, 2002.

35 Harmonie ist das oberste Gebot. *Der Spiegel,* April 8, 2002, pp. 158-161.

www.ingramcontent.com/pod-product-compliance
Lightning Source LLC
Chambersburg PA
CBHW071354050326
40689CB00010B/1638